JAPAN

PROFILE

OF

A

NATION

JAPAN

PROFILE

OF

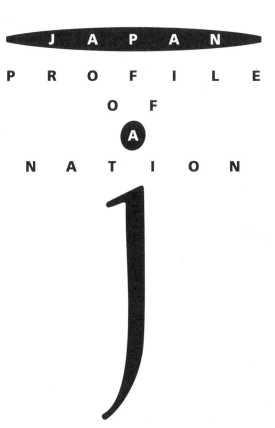

A

NATION

Kodansha International
Tokyo·New York·London

Kodansha International Ltd.,
1-17-14 Otowa, Bunkyo-ku, Tokyo 112, JAPAN
Kodansha America, Inc.,
114 Fifth Avenue, New York, NY 10011, U.S.A.

Copyright © 1994 by Kodansha International Ltd.
All rights reserved.
Printed in Japan

First edition 1994
94 95 96 10 9 8 7 6 5 4 3 2 1

JAPAN: PROFILE OF A NATION. -- 1st ed.
p. cm.
ISBN 4-7700-1892-4 (hd)   ISBN 4-7700-1918-1 (pbk)
1. Japan. I. Kôdansha Intânashonaru Kabushiki Kaisha.
DS806 . J228 1995
952--dc20 94-9908
CIP

Color photos by TOYOTAKA, Ryuzo
Photos for chapter title pages:
"History" by HIBI, Sadao
"Geography" by TATEISHI, Akira, Marine Photo Library
"Government and Diplomacy" by PANA
"Economy" and "Life" by Steve Gardner
"Society" by Kodansha Photo Library
"Culture" by YAMAMOTO, Ikuo

Book design by Katsui Mitsuo Office

During the closing years of the twentieth century, we have
seen worldwide interest in Japan grow as the nation takes
on more prominent and active role on the international
stage. Many have felt the need for an accurate and reliable
reference source that is both comprehensive and accessible
by the general reader. With this in mind, JAPAN: PROFILE
OF A NATION was compiled from the valuable and detailed
resource, *Japan: An Illustrated Encyclopedia* published by our
parent company Kodansha Ltd. A generous selection of
entries from this treasure trove of information have been
reorganized into thematic sections such as "geography",

EDITOR'S PREFACE "history", "government and diplomacy", "economy", "society", "culture", and "life". Furthermore we have
supplied a full index of all entries at the back of the book for
quick and easy reference. Consistent romanization of
Japanese words are used throughout this volume and for
further clarity all Japanese words are itallicized when they
first appear in the article. Those readers requiring more specialist information about Japan are advised to consult *Japan:
An Illustrated Encyclopedia.*

We sincerely hope that the publication of JAPAN: PROFILE
OF A NATION will promote better international understanding through an authentic and fascinating portrayal of
all that is Japan.

Kodansha International
May 1994

CONTENTS

Shinjuku, Tokyo

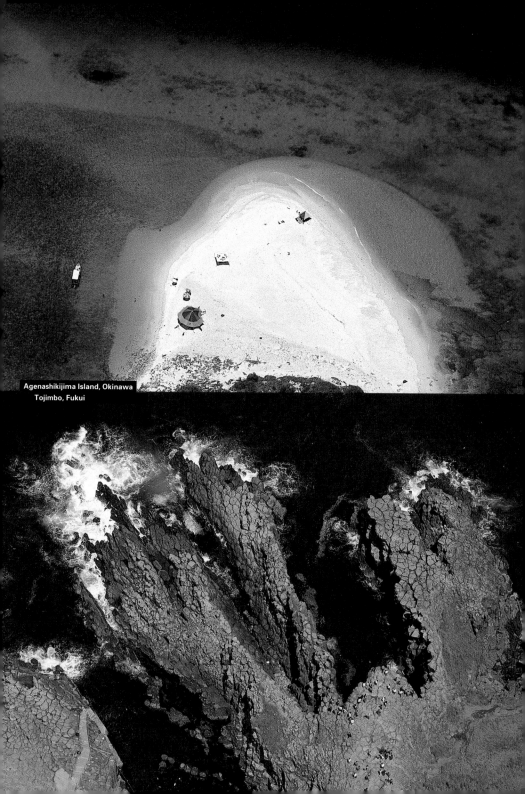

Agenashikijima Island, Okinawa
Tojimbo, Fukui

Mt. Fuji

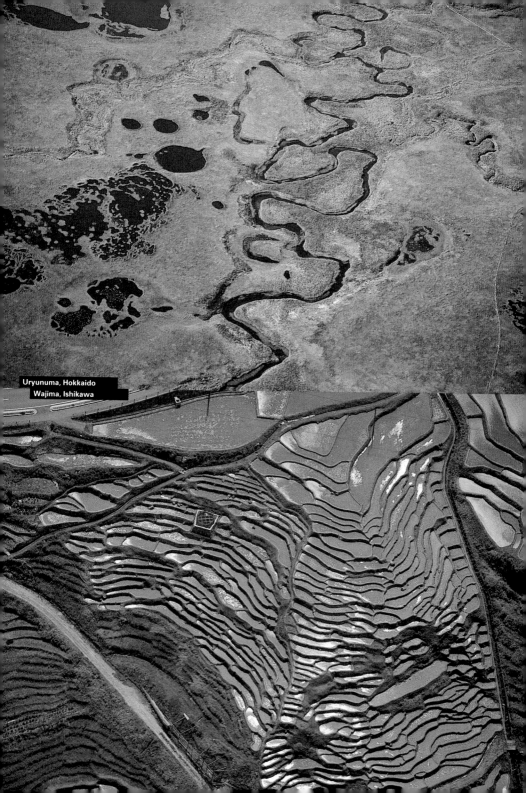

Uryunuma, Hokkaido

Wajima, Ishikawa

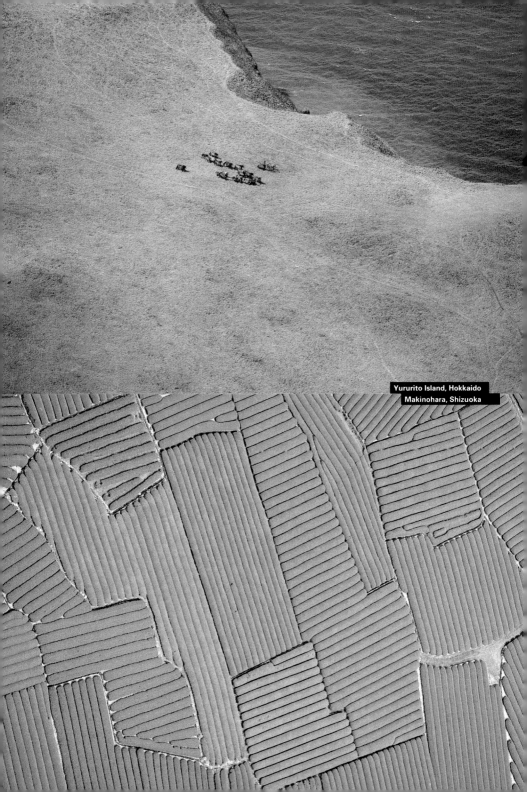

Yururito Island, Hokkaido
Makinohara, Shizuoka

Toshimaen, Tokyo
Shinobazunoike, Tokyo

Seibu Stadium, Saitama
Yoyogi Park, Tokyo

Regions and Cities

RUSSIA

CHINA

Yuzhno-Sakhalinsk

Wakkanai

Abashiri

Asahikawa

Daisetuzan

Sapporo

Kushiro

Hakodate

Aomori

Hokkaido

NORTH KOREA

Akita

Morioka

Pyongyang

Honshu

Sendai

Chugoku

Niigata

Tohoku

Seoul

Toyama

Mito

SOUTH KOREA

Kanazawa

JAPAN

Tokyo

Kyoto

Fujisan

Yokohama

Oakayama

Kobe

Nagoya

Hiroshima

Osaka

Kanto

Kitakyushu

Takamatsu

Fukuoka

Kochi

Asosan

Chubu

Kumamoto

Kagoshima

Kinki

Shikoku

Kyushu

Naha

Nansei(ryukyu) Islands

Vladivostok

Okinotorishima

The sea around the Ryukyu Islands, Okinawa Prefecture. These small islands surrounded by coral reefs are typical of the more than 160 islands that make up the Ryukyu chain.

Japan
(Nippon or Nihon).

TERRITORY AND ADMINISTRATIVE DIVISIONS

Japan consists of an archipelago extending approximately from northeast to southwest. It lies off the east coast of the Asian continent. The total land area as of October 1989 was 377,688 square kilometers (145,825 sq mi), only slightly larger than that of Finland or Italy and about the same size as the US state of Montana. The four major islands of Japan are Hokkaido, Honshu, Shikoku, and Kyushu. Claimed by the Japanese, the northernmost islands of Kunashiri (Kunashir), Etorofu (Iturup), the Habomai Islands, and Shikotan were occupied by the Soviet Union at the end of World War II and were still occupied by the Russian Federation. The Ogasawara Islands and Okinawa Islands, under American rule after World War II, were returned to Japan in 1968 and 1972, respectively. The areas of the main geographical divisions of Japan (including offshore islands under their administrative control) are as follows: Hokkaido 83,520 sq km (32,247 sq mi), Honshu 230,940 sq km (89,166 sq mi), Shikoku 18,808 sq km (7,262 sq mi), Kyushu 42,164 sq km (16,279 sq mi), Okinawa Prefecture 2,256 sq km (871 sq mi), Total 377,688 sq km (145,825 sq mi). Following the recent tendency among countries to enlarge territorial waters, Japan set its territorial limit at 12 nautical miles from the coast in 1977.

Population

At the time of the Meiji Restoration (1868) Japan's population was about 33 million. In 1990 it was 123,612,000, seventh largest in the world. The density per square kilometer (0.386 sq mi) was 332 persons in 1990. Although this figure is comparable to 359 persons in the Netherlands and 325 in Belgium, the density of the Japanese population per unit area under cultivation is the highest in the world, because over two-thirds of Japan is occupied by mountainous terrain, and alluvial plains occupy only 13 percent.

The population was distributed comparatively equally all over the country about a century ago, when Japan was still predominantly agricultural. With industrialization, however, there was a strong tendency toward regional concentration. As a result, 43.1 percent of Japanese live in the three major urban areas of Tokyo, Osaka, and Nagoya. The Tokyo Metropolitan Area in particular, although less than 2.0 percent in terms of area, has a concentration of 23.4 percent of the national population.

Formation of the Country

Among the various theories on the formation of Japan as a nation-state, one school holds that, because of its proximity to the Asian continent, northern Kyushu was the site of the first political center. By the 4th century a sovereign court had emerged, which by conquest and alliance eventually unified the country. The Yamato court (ca 4th century — ca mid-7th century) repeatedly dispatched expeditionary forces to northeastern Honshu and succeeded in subduing it in the 7th century, thus establishing the prototype of a unified Japan consisting of Honshu, Shikoku, and Kyushu. Under the Taika Reform of 645, the *kokugun* system of administration was instituted, and the country was divided into 58 (later 66) provinces (*kuni* or *koku*) with subunits called *gun*. This division remained in effect nominally until the Meiji Restoration (1868). However, during the Edo period (1600 — 1868), the *bakuhan* (shogunate and domain) system was superimposed on the *kokugun* system.

Changes in Territory

The territory of Japan has remained essentially the same from the 7th century, but its history is nonetheless one of numerous modifications. In 1609 the *daimyo* of the Satsuma domain (now Kagoshima Prefecture) established control over the Ryukyu Kingdom of the Okinawa Islands. The Ogasawara Islands (also known as the Bonin Islands) were discovered by the Japanese in 1593 and were officially incorporated into Japan in 1876. Hokkaido, once called Ezo, was settled by the Japanese in the Edo period. As trade developed with the Ainu people in the interior, the Japanese gradually made their way into the southern part of Sakhalin (J: Karafuto) and the Kuril Islands, where they came into conflict with the Russians. In 1875 Japan concluded the Treaty of St. Petersburg with Russia and gave up the southern part of Sakhalin in exchange for the Kuril Islands. After the Sino-Japanese War of 1894 — 1895 Japan acquired Taiwan, and after the Russo-Japanese War of 1905 it acquired the southern half of Sakhalin and leased the southern part of the Liaodong Peninsula. It annexed Korea in 1910 and secured a mandate over former German territories in the South Sea Islands after World War I. Thus at the time of the outbreak of World War II, the total land area was 680,729 square kilometers (262,830 sq mi). However, after its defeat Japan was stripped of all territories acquired during its period of colonialism and, until the restoration of Okinawa in 1972, was left with essentially the four main islands.

Modern Administrative System

After the Meiji Restoration the country was administratively reorganized into the prefectural system. Tokyo, Osaka, and Kyoto were made *fu* (urban prefectures) in 1871, and the rest of the country was divided into

302 *ken* (prefectures). By 1888 this system had been integrated into a system of 3 *fu* and 43 *ken*. Hokkaido was initially administered directly by the central government but later came to be treated equally with other prefectures, although it was called a *do* (circuit) rather than a *ken*. In 1943 Tokyo Fu was designated as a special administrative area and named Tokyo To (officially translated as Tokyo Metropolis). At present Japan is administratively divided into 1 *to* (Tokyo To), 1 *do* (Hokkaido), 2 *fu* (Osaka Fu and Kyoto Fu), and 43 *ken*.

NATURAL FEATURES OF JAPAN
Topography

The chief feature of the Japanese archipelago is its geological instability, including frequent volcanic activity and many earthquakes. Another distinctive characteristic of the topography is the fact that the Japanese archipelago is made up almost entirely of steep mountain districts with very few plains.

High, precipitous mountains of about 1,500−3,000 meters (5,000−10,000 ft) run along the Pacific Ocean side of southwestern Japan. Deep, V-shaped valleys are cut into these mountain districts. In contrast, on the Sea of Japan side of southwestern Japan are groupings of plateaus and low mountain districts with a height of about 500−1,500 meters (1,600−5,000 ft), such as the Hida, Tamba, and Chugoku mountain districts; the Kibi Highland; and the Tsukushi Mountains.

The large number and variety of volcanoes found throughout the Japanese archipelago constitute another remarkable feature. There have been 188 volcanoes active at some time or another since the Quaternary geological period, and more than 40 of these remain active today. Among these are volcanoes that have had numerous violent eruptions, such as Asamayama and Bandaisan. Further, a special characteristic of Japan's volcano zone is the development of large craters or calderas such as those at Akan, Daisetsu, Hakone, Aso, and Aira. The caldera at Aso is on a scale unrivaled anywhere in the world.

A small number of large rivers, such as the Ishikarigawa, Shinanogawa, Tonegawa, Kisogawa, Yodogawa, and Chikugogawa, have fair-sized delta plains at their mouths. Diluvial uplands and river and marine terraces have developed in many coastal areas of Japan, and these are utilized along with the plains for both agriculture and habitation.

Climate

Located in the monsoon zone of the eastern coast of the Asian continent, the most notable features of the climate of the Japanese archipelago are the wide range of yearly temperatures and the large amount of rainfall. However, because of the complexity of the land configuration, there are numerous regional differences throughout the seasons.

Spring When low-pressure areas pass over the Pacific coast of Japan in March, the temperature rises with each rainfall. When low-pressure areas start to develop over the Sea of Japan, the strong wind from the south called *haru ichiban* (the first tidings of spring) blows over Japan. This wind causes flooding due to suddenly melting mountain snow and the foehn phenomenon, which sometimes results in great fires on the Sea of Japan side.

Summer The onset of the rainy season (*baiu* or *tsuyu*) takes place around 7 June. It starts in the southern part of Japan and moves northward. With the end of the rain around 20 July, the Ogasawara air masses blanket Japan, and the weather takes on a summer pattern. The peak of summer is late July, and the summer heat lingers on into mid-August.

Fall September is the typhoon season. Weather resembling that of the rainy season also occurs because of the autumnal rain fronts. The weather clears in mid-October, and the winter winds start to blow.

Winter In December, when the atmospheric pressure configuration has completely changed to the winter pattern, northwest winds bring snow to the mountains and to the plains on the Sea of Japan side, and a dry wind blows on the Pacific Ocean side. The peak of winter comes around 25 January.

Life and Nature

Japan's land area is small but its configuration is complex, so that the climate and the flora and fauna vary regionally, extending from the subarctic zone in the north to the subtropical zone in the south; there is also much seasonal change. An abundance of hot springs, which are popular as health resorts, accompany the many volcanoes.

Japan's seasonal changes and geological structure bring many natural disasters. Heavy rains due to the *baiu* front and the autumn typhoons bring about landslides, floods, and wind damage. Heavy winter precipitation causes snow damage as well as flooding and cold damage. In addition, earthquakes on the scale of the Tokyo Earthquake of 1923, which was assigned a magnitude of 7.9, strike somewhere in Japan every several decades. Typhoons and the tidal waves accompanying earthquakes also inflict damage on heavily populated, low-lying coastal areas. Flooding and land subsidence have also occurred as the result of land reclamation and excessive pumping of groundwater.

GEOLOGICAL STRUCTURE
Topography

Topographically, the Kuril Arc; the Sakhalin-Hokkaido Arc; the Honshu Arc, connecting Kyushu, Shikoku, Honshu, and the western part of Hokkaido; and the Ryukyu and Izu-Ogasawara arcs make up the Japanese islands. The Kuril, Japan, and Izu-Ogasawara trenches constitute one continuous trench. This trench is a narrow, submarine channel with a depth of about 9,000 meters (30,000 ft) in some areas. The Japan Trench, however, is not connected to the shallower Nankai Trough in the offing of Shikoku and Kyushu, nor is the Nankai Trough connected to the Ryukyu Trench. The Philippine Basin is separated from the Pacific Ocean by the Izu-Ogasawara Arc, and the Nankai Trough and the Ryukyu Trench together correspond to the northern edge of the Philippine Basin.

The Sea of Okhotsk, the Sea of Japan, and the East China Sea separate Japan topographically from the Asian continent. They are generally shallow, although some basins in the Sea of Okhotsk and the Sea of Japan are 3,000–4,000 meters (9,800–13,000 ft) deep.

The border of northeastern Japan and southwestern Japan is a great fault called the Itoigawa-Shizuoka Tectonic Line. The beltlike area east of this fault and running from the western part of Niigata Prefecture to the central part of Nagano Prefecture and from Yamanashi Prefecture to the eastern part of Shizuoka Prefecture forms a single valley crossing Honshu that is called the Fossa Magna. The mountain ranges and volcanic zones that form northeastern Japan turn south-southeast at the Fossa Magna and are connected to the Izu Islands. Southwestern Japan is divided into an inner belt (the side facing the Sea of Japan) and an outer belt (the side facing the Pacific Ocean) by the great fault called the Median Tectonic Line, which runs lengthwise along the axis of southwestern Japan from the Ina Mountains to Oita Prefecture. These belts can be traced as far as the Ryukyu Islands. In southwestern Japan there are fewer volcanoes than in northeastern Japan, and they are concentrated in the area facing the Sea of Japan and Kyushu. Volcanic activity is vigorous in northeastern Japan.

Crustal Movement

The Japanese islands have severe crustal movements, which are still progressing. Crustal movements include movements of short duration, such as seismic activity, and also slow movements of long duration. Volcanic activity, gravity anomaly, and crustal heat flow are also directly caused by the crustal deformation. Volcanoes have been particularly active in northeastern Japan since the Quaternary period. There is a narrow nonvolcanic zone along the Pacific coast, the rest of the region being volcanic.

Sea of Japan

(Nihonkai). One of the three marginal seas around Japan. It is situated between the Asian continent and the Japanese archipelago and is connected to adjacent seas by the straits of Mamiya, Soya, Tsugaru, Kammon, and Tsushima. It is the smallest of the three seas (1,008,000 sq km; 389,000 sq mi) and the deepest (maximum depth: 3,712 m; 12,178 ft; average depth: 1,350 m; 4,430 ft). The Sea of Japan provides good fishing grounds and is an important factor in the heavy winter snowfalls on parts of Honshu.

Volcanoes

(*kazan*). The many active volcanoes in Japan form a part of the so-called circum-Pacific volcanic zone, which surrounds the Pacific Ocean. While volcanic eruptions have significantly influenced the life of the Japanese people since earliest times, causing heavy loss of life, they have also produced beautiful natural views and features and provided fertile soil.

Distribution of Volcanoes

The volcanoes are located in a line that generally runs parallel to the Japanese archipelago. The eastern edge of volcano distribution in Hokkaido and northern Honshu forms a line running almost parallel to the central mountain range that forms the backbone of the archipelago; to the west of this edge line, called the volcanic front, volcanoes are distributed as far as the Sea of Japan. The volcanic front turns abruptly southward in the northwest corner of the Kanto region of Honshu near Mt. Asama (Asamayama) and, by way of the Yatsugatake volcano group, Fuji-Hakone-Izu National Park, and the eastern side of the Izu Peninsula, goes through the Izu Islands to the volcanic islands of the Marianas. In southwestern Japan the distribution is not so dense, but a volcanic front runs across western Honshu, extends southward to central Kyushu, and is connected to the volcanoes of Taiwan by way of the Ryukyu Islands.

Structure and Activity of Japanese Volcanoes

Many Japanese volcanoes have a conical shape similar to that of Mt. Fuji (Fujisan), which has become a symbol of Japan. These volcanoes, called stratovolcanoes, were formed by the alternate accumulation of lava flows and of volcanic blocks and bombs emitted from the summit crater. One characteristic of this type of volcano is its profile, which consists of a beautiful exponential curve with wide, gentle skirts.

Mt. Fuji in winter.

Many of the smallest volcanoes were formed by a single eruption and have never resumed activity. One such type, the pyroclastic cone, is usually formed over a period ranging from several days to several years

Geography and Nature

by an effusion of pumice, scoria, and volcanic ash. Another type is the lava dome, in which highly viscous lava is gradually pushed up as a huge mass. Most pyroclastic cones and lava domes are no more than 200 meters (650 ft) in height, and they often occur in groups.

Two rarer kinds of eruption activity are known for their destructive power. One is a large steam explosion, which is a characteristic feature of the stratovolcano toward the end of its life. In the 1888 eruption of Mt. Bandai (Bandaisan), a series of violent explosions lasting several minutes each was followed by a huge landslide. The other type of destructive eruption is caused by the effusion of an enormous amount of magma onto the ground within a brief period. The magmas contain large quantities of gaseous components (mostly water vapor) that, during volcanic eruptions, separate themselves from the magma in the form of foam, much like the foam of beer that rises when a bottle is opened. The foamy magma splits into pieces and is violently ejected as a mixture of rocks, pumice, volcanic ash, and gas known as a pyroclastic flow.

Disasters Due to Eruptions and Their Prevention

In a vulcanian eruption, which is the most common type of eruption in Japan, it is only rarely that volcanic rocks and bombs are ejected from the crater over a horizontal distance of several kilometers. It has become possible to foretell explosive eruptions, and when warning signals occur, entry into the danger area around the crater is prohibited. At a greater distance from the volcano than the range of volcanic bombs, damage to buildings from other factors, such as the shock wave of the eruption, is a major concern. Even more dangerous, however, is the fall of pumiceous rocks that have been blown high into the sky and drift with the wind to land in areas far from the crater. Damage to crops from accumulation of volcanic ash is a serious economic hardship, and several famines are attributed to destruction of rice paddies by volcanic eruptions.

Microearthquakes and any change in the earth's crust are observed regularly and continuously at 19 active volcanoes throughout Japan, including Asamayama, Miharayama, Asosan, and the Unzendake group. At these volcanoes instruments such as seismometers, tiltmeters, extensometers, and laser beams are used to make precise measurements of any changes. The Global Positioning System (GPS), which uses artificial satellites, is also utilized to monitor conditions. Thus, it is unlikely that a major eruption could occur without some forewarning. However, means of preventing disasters stemming from volcanic eruptions remain inadequate, as volcanic eruptions are natural phenomena involving the release of huge amounts of energy.

The eruption at Unzendake, May 1991.

In November 1990 there was an eruption at Fugendake, the highest peak of Unzendake, which last erupted in 1792. During the 1991 eruption pyroclastic flows claimed 44 lives including missings.

Earthquakes

(*jishin*). Earthquakes are a frequent phenomenon in Japan; nearly 10 percent of the energy released worldwide by earthquakes each year is concentrated in and around the Japanese islands. In the last century Japan has experienced 23 destructive earthquakes with magnitudes of 6 or higher on the scale used by the Meteorological Agency of Japan. This scale roughly approximates the better-known Richter scale used in the West. Both scales measure the magnitude of an earthquake by the energy released from its epicenter.

The most famous earthquake was the great Tokyo Earthquake of 1923, which was later given a magnitude of 7.9 on the scale. Centered near metropolitan Tokyo and Yokohama, the quake resulted in more than 100,000 deaths and billions of dollars in property loss. In Tokyo alone it took the lives of more than 60,000 people, of whom more than 50,000 died in quake-related fires.

Causes and Distribution of Earthquakes in Japan

The Tokyo earthquake was caused by movement along a fault, that is, a fracture in the earth's crust. The upper layer of the fault zone shifted about 6 meters (20 ft) east and about 3 meters (10 ft) south with respect to the lower layer. The surface of the earth moved upward and toward the Pacific Ocean. This same type of movement is seen in virtually every earthquake that occurs along the Pacific coast of Japan.

Earthquakes tend to recur periodically, the interval between occurrences varying with locale. Seismologist Kawasumi Hiroshi (1907–1972) estimated that the mean time between major earthquakes in the southern Kanto region is 69 years. There are also "swarms," sustained periods of numerous small quakes. The longest recorded swarm took place in the mid-1960s at Matsushiro in Nagano Prefecture.

Earthquake activity in Japan is accompanied by various forms of crustal distortion and fault displacement depending on the geographic and geologic area involved. For example, the tips of such peninsulas as the Boso, Miura, and Kii, all of which jut out into the Pacific Ocean, slowly sink into the ocean at the rate of 1 centimeter (0.4 in) a year. But a major earthquake would then lift the tip to compensate instantly for the accumulated depression. On the other hand, earthquakes occurring in southwestern Japan, west of the Fossa Magna, are created by sudden movements of the earth along an existing fault zone, and unlike earthquakes on

The 1984 western Nagano earthquake.

the Pacific coast, these quakes are not preceded by crustal movement.

The crustal distortion accompanying Pacific coast quakes is caused by mantle convection within the earth. In the southeastern Pacific Ocean there is a ridge, toward which mantle convection surges from the earth's core and then moves horizontally toward Japan before creeping downward again to the core. When mantle flow gets into the core, the movement causes one plate on the mantle to subduct, or dive under the other, and become absorbed in the underlying mantle. The involvement of peninsula tips in this movement causes their slow depression between earthquakes, the rate of depression being equal to the speed of mantle convection. The sudden upheaval of a peninsula's tip in an earthquake is due to "elastic rebound."

Pacific coastal areas are gradually compressed by mantle convection in the intervals between earthquakes, and in a large earthquake they rebound toward the Pacific. Accordingly, the greater the accumulation of pressure from the Pacific Ocean, the greater the probability that an earthquake will occur in the region.

Earthquake Prediction

Since 1965, funds have been allocated for research on earthquake prediction, most of it centering on characteristic crustal distortions. In 1969 the Meteorological Agency, the Geographic Survey Institute, and several national universities formed the Coordinating Committee for Earthquake Prediction to pool the results of their research. It was decided to conduct surveys over the entire area of Japan and to repeat measurements of geologic changes at short intervals by means of leveling and triangulation in comparatively small areas of the country deemed important, such as the southern Kanto area and the Tokai region (Shizuoka and Aichi prefectures). Distortion and faulting also have been monitored continuously, using sensitive instruments such as the tiltmeter and extensometer. It is known that microelastic impact waves are generated in considerable numbers before rock fractures under the accumulation of strain, which is thought to resemble foreshock activity preceding large earthquakes. The flow of heat that is transmitted from the core of the earth to the surface is closely related to crustal phenomena; further, terrestrial magnetism and earth current are said to change in relation to a large earthquake. Therefore, these phenomena are being measured to determine if there is some connection that will contribute to earthquake prediction.

Three factors: when, where, and how severe are essential to earthquake prediction. Although quakes do occur periodically and are accompanied by characteristic crustal movements, the difficulties of predicting precisely when a quake will strike are not likely to be solved soon, and the likelihood of a quake's occurrence will continue to be based on statistical probability.

Most of the enormous damage accompanying large earthquakes comes from fire following building collapse, and also from the effects of *tsunami*, a large sea wave. Earthquakes are particularly destructive in Japan because closely packed structures, usually of wood, make for inadequate firebreaks, while the popularity of small space heaters fueled by gas or kerosene increases the chance of fire.

Areas and Cities

Hokkaido

The northernmost and second largest of Japan's four main islands. It is separated from Honshu to the south by the Tsugaru Strait and bounded by the Sea of Japan on the west, the Sea of Okhotsk on the northeast, and the Pacific Ocean on the south and east. Several mountain ranges cross Hokkaido, and those belonging to the Ezo Mountains run from north to south across the center of the island, separated into two strands by a series of basin areas. To the west of these mountains lies the broad Ishikari Plain. To the southwest of the plain is a long peninsula, which is the area closest to Honshu. The climate is unlike that of the rest of Japan, being notably colder and drier.

Lake Mashu, a caldera lake in eastern Hokkaido.

The prehistoric culture of Hokkaido seems to have shared many of the characteristics of the early culture of Honshu, except that it lacked the culture of the Yayoi period (ca 300 BC — ca AD 300). Hokkaido, or Ezo, as it was known, was inhabited by the Ainu and not included in Japan proper. In the Edo period (1600 — 1868) the Matsumae domain was established in the extreme southwestern corner of the island. After the Meiji Restoration of 1868, the new government placed great emphasis on Hokkaido's economic development, setting up a colonial office (kaitakushi) and encouraging settlers to come from other parts of Japan. The name of the island was changed to Hokkaido (literally, "Northern Sea Circuit") in 1869. The present prefectural form of administration was established in 1886. (Within Japan's prefectural system, Hokkaido alone is called a *do* [circuit] rather than a *ken* [prefecture]; however, it is the equivalent of a prefecture.)

The main agricultural crop is rice; grain and vegetable farming as well as dairy farming are active. Fishing and forestry have long been an important part of Hokkaido's economy. They also form the basis for much of Hokkaido's industrial activity, including food-processing, woodworking, pulp, and paper industries.

Hokkaido is noted for its dramatic and unspoiled scenery, which includes active volcanoes, large lakes, and vast virgin forests. Major tourist attractions are Shikotsu-Toya, Akan, Daisetsuzan, Shiretoko, and Rishiri-Rebun-Sarobetsu national parks. Area: 83,520 sq km (32,247 sq mi); pop: 5,643,647; capital: Sapporo. Other major cities include Hakodate, Asahikawa, Otaru, Muroran, Tomakomai, Obihiro, and Kushiro.

Tohoku region

(Tohoku *chiho*). Region encompassing the entire northeastern part of Honshu and consisting of Aomori, Iwate, Akita, Yamagata, Miyagi, and Fukushima prefectures. The region is largely mountainous, and most towns and cities are concentrated along the Pacific and Sea of Japan coasts and in the centers of several basins. The climate is highly seasonal, with short summers and long winters.

The area is primarily an agricultural area and forestry and fishing are also important. There is some petroleum and natural-gas production, and the iron, steel, cement, chemical, pulp, and petroleum-refining industries have been developing. The principal city is Sendai. Area: 66,912 sq km (25,835 sq mi); pop: 9,738,285.

The Hakkodasan volcano group in the Nasu Volcanic Zone, Aomori Prefecture.

Kanto region

(Kanto *chiho*). Located in east central Honshu, consisting of Tokyo, Chiba, Saitama, Kanagawa, Gumma, Ibaraki, and Tochigi prefectures. This is Japan's most heavily populated region and is the political, economic, and cultural center of the nation. The regional center is the metropolitan area that includes Tokyo, Yokohama, Kawasaki, and Chiba. The region is dominated by the Kanto Plain.

The term Kanto (literally, "east of the barrier") originally referred to the area east of the barrier station (*sekisho*) at Osakayama in what is now Otsu, Shiga Prefecture; the term was used in contradistinction to the Kansai region west of the station. The border was later moved twice, finally being set much farther east at the barrier station at Hakone (in what is now Kanagawa Prefecture).

The Tokyo-Yokohama district in the center of the region is Japan's leading commercial and industrial area. Agriculture plays a declining but still important role in the region's economy. Coastal fishing in the Pacific Ocean and Tokyo Bay has declined because of increased pollution and land reclamation in Tokyo Bay. Area: 32,385 sq km (12,504 sq mi); pop: 38,543,517.

Tokyo

Capital of Japan. Located on the Kanto Plain, on the Pacific side of central Honshu. Bordered by the prefectures of Chiba on the east, Saitama on the north, Yamanashi on the west, and Kanagawa on the southwest, and by Tokyo Bay on the southeast. Under its administration are islands scattered in the western Pacific, among them the Izu Islands and the Ogasawara Islands.

Tokyo Prefecture comprises the 23 wards (*ku*) of urban Tokyo, 27 cities (*shi*), 1 county (*gun*), and 4 island administrative units (*shicho*). The county and the island units contain 14 towns and villages (*cho, son*). Area: 2,183 sq km (843 sq mi); pop: 11,833,962 in 1994.

The residents of Tokyo live in a total of 4,914,146 dwellings, with an average floor space of 60 square meters (645 sq ft). The average household has 2.4 members.

Geography and Climate

Tokyo was known by the name Edo (literally, "Rivergate") before the Meiji Restoration (1868), and the principal rivers of the Kanto region—the Edogawa, Arakawa, and Sumidagawa—still flow to the sea through eastern Tokyo. Along the alluvial plains of the old river Tamagawa, volcanic ash emitted from the Fuji-Hakone Volcanic Range accumulated to form the Musashino Plateau, where the western wards (commonly known as the Yamanote district) and outlying districts are located. Some areas in the eastern wards (the *shitamachi* district) lie 2−3 meters (6.5−10 ft) below sea level.

Downtown Tokyo.

The four seasons are sharply delineated, and the climate is generally mild, with the highest average monthly temperature in August (26.7°C; 80.1°F) and the lowest in January (4.7°C; 40.5°F). The annual precipitation is 1,460 millimeters (57.5 in).

Fauna and Flora

Pollution and unchecked land development ravaged the animal and plant population in Tokyo Prefecture during the 1960s, but, with stricter pollution controls, 370 out of the approximately 570 bird species found throughout Japan have been sighted within Tokyo. Other wildlife found in the mountainous areas include the Japanese antelope, raccoon dog, fox, flying squirrel and rabbit.

The official tree of Tokyo is the ginkgo, which is utilized as a shade tree throughout the city. Other common trees in Tokyo include the cherry, zelkova and Japanese oak.

History

Where Tokyo now stands relics have been found dating from the Jomon (ca 10,000 BC−ca 300 BC), the Yayoi (ca 300 BC−ca AD 300), and the Kofun (ca 300−710) periods. During the 7th century Japan was divided into some 50 provinces, and Musashi Province was established in what is today Tokyo, Saitama, and eastern Kanagawa prefectures. Its administrative center was located in what is now the city of Fuchu, which served as the political center of the province for nearly 900 years. During the civil wars of the 15th century, the warrior Ota Dokan (1432−1486) constructed the predecessor of Edo castle at the present site of the Imperial Palace.

After nearly a century of warfare, Toyotomi Hideyoshi (1537−1598) partially united the country and dispatched Tokugawa Ieyasu (1543−1616) to Kanto in 1590 as lord of Edo Castle. After Hideyoshi's death Ieyasu completed the unification of Japan and established the Tokugawa shogunate in Edo in 1603. He constructed a castle town there with a *samurai* residential district on the castle's western side. To the east marshland was reclaimed, and a commercial and industrial area came into being. As the city flourished merchants and artisans flocked to Edo; the population reached one million by 1720, making Edo the largest city in the world at that time.

In 1867 the Tokugawa shogunate came to an end, and, with the Meiji Restoration the following year, Edo, renamed Tokyo ("eastern capital"), became the national capital. The imperial family took up residence at Edo Castle in 1869. In the following years Tokyo grew steadily in importance as the political, commercial, and financial center of Japan. Almost completely destroyed in the Tokyo Earthquake of 1923, the city was soon rebuilt and administratively enlarged in 1943, merging surrounding districts and suburbs into Tokyo To (Tokyo Prefecture; officially, Tokyo Metropolis).

A portrait of Tokugawa Ieyasu, the warrior chieftain who survived Japan's late-16th-cebtury wars to set up the Tokugawa shogunate.

Much of Tokyo was destroyed during World War II by American bombing. After Japan's defeat Tokyo remained the seat of government, with the General Headquarters of the Supreme Commander for the Allied Powers (SCAP) located there until the end of the Occupation in 1952. During the period of economic recovery starting in the 1950s, large enterprises increasingly concentrated their managerial operations in Tokyo. This resulted in an increase in population from 6.3 million in 1950 to 9.7 million in 1960.

The city undertook a feverish building program in preparation for the 1964 Tokyo Olympic Games, and by 1965 the population had reached 10.9 million, resulting in serious housing problems and skyrocketing land prices. A program of building urban subcenters has since been carried out to alleviate the concentration of company head offices in the central Tokyo area, and the pollution problems that were severe in the late 1960s and early 1970s have now been alleviated to a degree; the waters of the river Sumidagawa in eastern Tokyo are relatively clean once more. The four-lane intracity expressway system that was begun in the 1960s is still often severely congested, however, and a further period of rapidly spiraling land prices since the mid-1980s has put home ownership beyond the reach of most Tokyoites.

Local and Traditional Industry

Local industries were long centered in the three *shitamachi* wards of Taito, Sumida, and Arakawa, but in recent years are expanding to the surrounding wards, particularly Adachi and Katsushika. Products include clothing, knitted goods, precious metals, toys, and leather goods. Among traditional industries, fabric making has been prominent. Cities within Tokyo Prefecture such as Hachioji, Ome, and Musashi Murayama have been noted for the production of fabrics since the Edo period (1600 – 1868), and the island of Hachijojima is noted for its *kihachijo* dyed fabric. Many of the craftsmen making traditional products face the problems of weak consumer demand and the difficulty of financing successors.

Modern Industry and Finance

Tokyo developed into a center of manufacturing and heavy industry from the Meiji period (1868 – 1912) until the end of World War II. After 1965, however, tertiary industries—commerce, finance, transportation, communication, wholesale and retail stores, and service industries—began to surpass secondary industries. As of 1991 primary industries constituted only 0.2 percent of the total industries in Tokyo; secondary industries, 24.4 percent (compared to 50 percent in the 1960s); and tertiary industries, 75.4 percent. Tokyo boasts a total of approximately 799,500 enterprises employing nearly 9.5 million workers. Most of these enterprises are small and medium-sized concerns. The total output of Tokyo Prefecture in 1991 was ¥86.1 trillion.

As new office buildings take over the central part of the city, small shops and permanent residents have been forced out to suburban areas, creating the so-called doughnut phenomenon. The pollution of the 1970s also forced large manufacturing plants and related factories from the *shitamachi* lowlands to the outlying districts or to reclaimed land in Tokyo Bay and adjacent prefectures. With the soaring urban and suburban land prices in recent years, more companies have been relocating their research and development centers and some of their head office departments to buildings equipped with the latest communications technology in outlying areas of Tokyo. However, most large Japanese corporations, foreign companies, and the national press and mass media still have their head offices in Tokyo; these are particularly concentrated in Chiyoda, Chuo, and Minato wards.

Another recent development has been the growth of the Shinjuku, Shibuya, and Ikebukuro districts. Now known as satellite city

Tokyo Metropolitan Government Offices, Shinjuku, Tokyo. Completed in March 1991.

centers or urban subcenters, they have become flourishing business and recreation districts. The doughnut phenomenon, originally confined to the old city center, has spread to these satellite centers, and between 1985 and 1990 the population of the 23 urban wards of Tokyo Prefecture fell by 190,000.

Tokyo is also a major financial center. The Tokyo Stock Exchange is one of the largest in the world in terms of aggregate market value and total sales, and deposits in Tokyo banks constitute 34 percent of the nation's total deposits.

Transportation

Tokyo is served by two airports: Tokyo International Airport (commonly called Haneda Airport), the main terminal for domestic flights in the southern end of the city, and New Tokyo International Airport (commonly called Narita Airport), located 66 kilometers (41 mi) east of Tokyo.

The nation's main railway lines are concentrated in Tokyo, with terminals at Tokyo, Ueno, and Shinjuku stations. Trains for the west (Nagoya, Osaka, Kyoto) leave from Tokyo Station (Tokaido and Shinkansen "bullet train" lines); trains for Tohoku, Hokkaido, and Niigata originate from Ueno Station (Tohoku, Joban, Takasaki, and Joetsu lines; the Tohoku and Joetsu Shinkansen lines originate from Tokyo Station). From Shinjuku Station trains connect the city with the mountainous regions of central Japan (Chuo trunk line).

The principal commuter railway lines in Tokyo are the Yamanote line, a loop around the heart of the city; the Keihin Tohoku line, running through Tokyo and Saitama and Kanagawa prefectures; the Chuo line, running through western Tokyo; and the Sobu line, connecting Tokyo and Chiba. A network of private railway lines radiates outward from the principal stations on the Yamanote line, and 12 private and metropolitan subway lines have replaced the old network of streetcars. Tokyo is also well served by bus lines, and expressways connect the city to various regions.

Education

In recent years a number of colleges and universities have moved away from the crowded city, but Tokyo is still a major educational center, with 79 junior colleges and 106 universities as of 1989. The city is also the location of numerous academic societies, including the Japan Academy and the Japan Art Academy.

Cultural and Recreational Facilities

The arts Western culture was introduced into Japan through the gateways of Yokohama and Tokyo after the Meiji Restoration, and Tokyo today offers a variety of modern arts as well as traditional arts such as *kabuki* (drama), *nagauta* (singing), *buyo* (dance), and *rakugo* (a form of comic storytelling). There are eight large-scale theaters in Tokyo, including the Kabukiza and the National Theater. There are also numerous concert halls, museums, and art galleries.

The media   Tokyo is also a major information center. Eight general newspapers are published in Tokyo (including four in English), as well as three economic and industrial newspapers and seven sports newspapers; an average of more than 6,685,000 newspaper copies were printed each day in 1989. In addition, it is estimated that roughly 2,400 monthly and weekly magazines were being published in Tokyo in the early 1990s.

Parks and sports facilities   Although most parks are small by Western standards, a considerable number are scattered throughout Tokyo. Major parks in central Tokyo include the Imperial Palace grounds, Hibiya Park, Ueno Park, and the Meiji Shrine Outer Garden. There are also some 10 zoological and botanical gardens in the metropolitan area. Major national parks in Tokyo Prefecture include Chichibu-Tama National Park, Ogasawara National Park, and part of Fuji-Hakone-Izu National Park.

Points of Interest

Situated in the center of Tokyo and surrounded by a moat and high stone walls is the Imperial Palace, still retaining vestiges of its former glory as the residence of the Tokugawa family. To the east lies the Ginza, an area known for its fine shops, department stores, and numerous restaurants, bars, and cabarets.

North of the Ginza is Nihombashi, the commercial hub of the city, from which all distances from Tokyo to places throughout Japan are measured. Nearby are the districts of Kanda, renowned for its bookshops and universities, and Akihabara, famous for its discount stores selling all kinds of electrical appliances. Further to the north lie Ueno and Ueno Park that houses the Tokyo National Museum, the National Science Museum, the National Museum of Western Art, the Ueno Zoological Gardens, and the temple Kan'eiji. To the east of Ueno is the oldest temple in Tokyo, Asakusa Kannon, in the heart of the *shitamachi* district, with its many shops still selling traditional handicrafts.

Sensoji temple, Asakusa, Tokyo.

Another point of interest in the capital is the Diet Building in Nagatacho. Nearby Roppongi and Azabu, situated close to Tokyo Tower, house many foreign embassies. Neighboring Akasaka is known for its luxurious nightlife. Near Shibuya Station lie Meiji Shrine, Yoyogi Park, the National Stadium, and Harajuku, a fashionable district popular with young people.

The area around Shinjuku Station—which has the highest rate of passenger turnover in the country—is rapidly being developed, with restaurants and theaters in the Kabukicho area on the eastern side of the station and numerous skyscrapers on the western side, including the new Tokyo Metropolitan Government Offices in the striking 48-story twin-tower building (243 m; 797 ft) designed by the world-famous architect Tange Kenzo (1913—). Another fast-growing commercial center is Ikebukuro, where the 60-story Sunshine City complex was completed in 1980.

A major project under way in the Tokyo Bay area is the Tokyo Frontier Project. This is a huge development on landfill sites that are planned for completion in the early 21st century on the Ariake and Daiba sites (448 hectares; 107 acres), and will include blocks of high-technology "intelligent" buildings, sports and leisure facilities, and international conference centers. Complementing this colossal undertaking is the equally ambitious Tokyo Bay Bridge and Tunnel project, construction on which began in 1989 and is due for completion in 1996. Connecting the city of Kawasaki in Kanagawa Prefecture with Kisarazu in Chiba Prefecture, this project will serve as a key link in the Tokyo Bay ring road, which, it is hoped, will reduce traffic congestion in central Tokyo.

Chubu region

(Chubu *chiho*). Encompassing Niigata, Toyama, Ishikawa, Fukui, Yamanashi, Nagano, Gifu, Shizuoka, and Aichi prefectures in central Honshu. Geographically divided into three districts: the Hokuriku region on the Sea of Japan side, the Central Highlands (or Tosan), and the Tokai region on the Pacific seaboard. The principal city of the region is Nagoya. The region, largely mountainous, is dominated by the Japanese Alps and contains numerous volcanoes including Mt. Fuji (Fujisan). Some of Japan's longest rivers, the Shinanogawa, Kisogawa, and Tenryugawa, flow through the region. The Niigata Plain along the Sea of Japan is one of the largest rice-producing areas in Japan, and the Nobi Plain on the Pacific coast is the most densely populated and highly industrialized area in this region. Numerous inland basins have very cold winters. The Pacific side is generally mild, and the Sea of Japan side has long snowy winters.

The Chubu region includes three industrial areas (the Chukyo Industrial Zone and the Tokai and Hokuriku industrial regions). Among traditional products of the district are lacquer ware and ceramics. Agricultural products include rice, tea, mandarin oranges, strawberries, grapes, peaches, and apples. Fishing is important all along its coast. Area: 66,777 sq km (25,783 sq mi); pop: 21,020,562.

Kinki region

(Kinki *chiho*). Located in west central Honshu and consisting of Osaka, Hyogo, Kyoto, Shiga, Mie, Wakayama, and Nara prefectures. It is the nation's second most important industrial region. The terrain is mountainous with many small basins in between and numerous coastal plains on the Inland Sea, Osaka Bay, and the Kii Channel. The Kii Peninsula is warm even in winter. The northern part of the region faces the Sea of Japan and is noted for its heavy snowfall.

The Kyoto-Nara area was the cultural and political center of Japan in ancient days, but it lost its political significance after the capital was moved to Tokyo in 1868. The Osaka-Kobe district is the center of commerce and industry for western Japan. This area is called the Hanshin Industrial Zone. Rice and citrus fruit production, lumbering, and fishing are important activities. Principal cities include Osaka, Kyoto, and Kobe, one of the country's most important ports. Area: 33,075 sq km (12,767 sq mi); pop: 22,206,747.

Kyoto

City in southern Kyoto Prefecture, in the Kyoto fault basin. The ancient capital of Japan and from 794 to 1868, Kyoto, rich in historical sites, is today the seat of the prefectural government and one of Japan's largest cities. Kyoto is renowned for its fine textiles and traditional products and is also a thriving center for industry.

Daibutsu, the Great Buddha at Nara, was completed in 752. Todaiji, Nara Prefecture.

Natural Features

The low Tamba Mountains surround the city to the north, east, and west. Two peaks, Hieizan and Atagoyama, dominate the northeast and northwest of the city. The rivers Kamogawa and Katsuragawa flow through the central and western districts of the city. Kyoto's landlocked location accounts for its cold winters and hot summers. The annual average temperature is 15.2 °C (59.4 °F) and annual precipitation is 1,600 mm (63 in).

History

The Kyoto fault basin was first settled in the 7th century by the Hata family, immigrants from Korea. In 603 Koryuji, the family temple of the Hata, was constructed at Uzumasa in the western part of the basin. In 794 Kyoto, then called Heiankyo, became the capital of Japan. The plan of the new city was patterned after China's Tang dynasty (618–907) capital of Chang'an (modern Xi'an). Its rectangular shape measured 4.5 kilometers (2.8 mi) east to west and 5.2 kilometers (3.2 mi) north to south.

Nijojo, a residential castle located in the city of Kyoto, erected by Tokugawa Ieyasu.

Kyoto was temporarily eclipsed as the center of national power by Kamakura during the Kamakura period (1185 – 1333), but during the Muromachi period (1333 – 1568) a shogunate was established in Kyoto, and the city regained its status as the nation's political center. During the Onin War (1467 – 1477), which signaled the end of the Muromachi shogunate, a large part of the city was destroyed.

During the Edo period (1600 – 1868) the Tokugawa shogunate was firmly established in Edo (now Tokyo) and the political focus of the country again shifted away from Kyoto. However, the city still prospered as an artistic, economic, and religious center. Particularly notable were fabrics such as *nishijin-ori* (brocade) and *yuzen-zome* (printed-silk), pottery, lacquer ware, doll making, and fan making. The city received a great blow when the capital was transferred to Tokyo after the Meiji Restoration (1868), but responded with a rapid program of modernization.

Kyoto Today

Lacking a harbor and surrounding open land, Kyoto was slow in developing modern industries, but today, as part of the Hanshin Industrial Zone, Kyoto has numerous electrical, machinery, and chemical plants. The city is also an educational and cultural center. There are some 37 universities and private institutes of higher learning, including Kyoto and Doshisha universities. Kyoto has 24 museums, including the Kyoto National Museum, and it possesses a total of 202 National Treasures (20 percent of the country's total) and 1,684 Important Cultural Properties (15 percent). In addition the city itself is a veritable historical storehouse. The Kyoto Imperial Palace and the Nijo Castle are both remarkable examples of Japanese architecture. The Katsura Detached Palace with its lovely pond and teahouses, and the Shugakuin Detached Palace, famed for its fine garden, draw visitors from afar. Located close to Kyoto Station are two temples of the Jodo Shin sect, Nishi Honganji and Higashi Honganji, both imposing examples of Buddhist architecture, as well as Toji, noted for its five-tiered pagoda.

East of the Kamogawa are the temple Kiyomizudera, with its wooden platform built out over a deep gorge; the Yasaka Shrine, where the annual Gion Festival is held in July; and the Heian Shrine, where the annual Jidai Festival is held in October. Other noted temples include Chion'in; Ginkakuji, built in 1482 and famed for its garden; and Nanzenji, situated in a pine grove east of the Heian Shrine. In the northern part of the city are the Kamo Shrines, where the Aoi Festival is held in May each year. To the northwest are the Zen temple Daitokuji, with its priceless art objects; Kinkakuji, with its three-story golden pavilion; Ninnaji, renowned for its cherry blossoms; and Koryuji. The natural beauty of the Hozukyo gorge, the Sagano district, and the hills of Takao also attracts visitors. Kyoto is the national center for the tea ceremony and flower arrangement and is the birthplace of No, *kyogen*, *kabuki*, and other traditional performing arts. Area: 610.6 sq km (235.7 sq mi); pop: 1,461,140.

O_{saka}

Capital of Osaka Prefecture. The third largest city in Japan after Tokyo and Yokohama, it is the financial center of western Japan. In the 7th and 8th centuries Osaka was a port for trade with China and the site of several imperial residences. The national unifier Toyotomi Hideyoshi (1537 — 1598) built Osaka Castle as his headquarters in 1583. In the Edo period (1600 — 1868) Osaka served as the entrepôt for goods, especially tax rice, for the entire nation and was called Japan's "kitchen."

Osaka is the center of the Hanshin Industrial Zone. Its principal industries are textiles, chemicals, steel, machinery, and metal. Besides Osaka Castle, attractions include the Osaka Municipal Museum of Fine Arts, the remains of the ancient capital of Naniwakyo, the temple Shitennoji, and the Sumiyoshi Shrine. Cultural attractions include the *bunraku* puppet theater as well as *kabuki*. Area: 220 sq km (85 sq mi); pop: 2,623,801.

C_{hugoku region}

(Chugoku *chiho*). Encompasses the entire western tip of Honshu, comprising Hiroshima, Okayama, Shimane, Tottori, and Yamaguchi prefectures. With the Chugoku Mountains as the dividing line, the Inland Sea side is called the San'yo region and the Sea of Japan side, the San'in region. It is a mountainous region with many small basins and coastal plains. The most heavily populated areas are along the Inland Sea coast, around the cities of Hiroshima, Kurashiki, and Okayama. The Inland Sea coast is a major area of industry and commerce. The Okayama Plain and the coastal plains along the Sea of Japan are important rice-producing areas. The warm, dry climate of the Inland Sea coast is also ideal for citrus fruit and grapes. The waters off the coast were once among Japan's richest fishing grounds, but catches have declined because of industrial pollution. Area: 31,790 sq km (12,274 sq mi); pop: 7,745,085.

S_{hikoku region}

(Shikoku *chiho*). Region consisting of Shikoku, the smallest of Japan's four main islands, and numerous surrounding islands. Shikoku lies across the Inland Sea from western Honshu and across the Bungo Channel from northeastern Kyushu. It consists of Kagawa, Tokushima, Ehime, and Kochi prefectures. Shikoku's high mountains and steep slopes severely limit agriculture, habitation, and communication. The climate is subtropical and on the Pacific Ocean side of the island there is heavy rainfall in summer.

Much of the island is a thinly populated agricultural region, with little large-scale industry. Two recently completed chains of bridges linking Shikoku with Honshu are expected to bring in many new industries. Extensive land reclamation in Kagawa and Tokushima prefectures should provide more room for this industrial expansion. Takamatsu and Matsuyama are the largest cities. Area: 18,808 sq km (7,262 sq mi); pop: 4,195,069.

Kyushu region

(Kyushu *chiho*). Region consisting of Kyushu, the third largest and southernmost of the four major islands of Japan, and surrounding islands. Kyushu comprises Fukuoka, Nagasaki, Oita, Kumamoto, Miyazaki, Saga, and Kagoshima prefectures. Okinawa Prefecture is sometimes included in the term Kyushu. Geographically divided into north, central, and south Kyushu, the region has a mountainous interior with numerous coastal plains, volcanoes, and hot springs. The climate is subtropical with heavy precipitation.

Rice, tea, tobacco, sweet potatoes, and citrus fruit are the major crops, and stock farming, hog raising, and fishery also flourish. Heavy and chemical industries are concentrated in northern Kyushu. The major cities are Kita Kyushu and Fukuoka. Area (including Okinawa Prefecture): 44,420 sq km (17,150 sq mi); pop: 14,518,257.

National parks and quasi-national parks

(*kokuritsu koen to kokutei koen*). These terms denote scenic land declared public property by the Japanese government with a view to preservation and development for purposes of recreation and culture. National parks (*kokuritsu koen*) are administered by the Environment Agency of the Prime Minister's Office, and quasi-national parks (*kokutei koen*) are administered by the prefectural governments under the supervision of the Environment Agency. These parks represent a concerted effort to protect Japan's environment, which began in the 1930s and gained momentum in the 1950s. The first national parks were the Inland Sea and the Unzen (now Unzen-Amakusa) national parks, established in

1934. In 1994 there were 28 national parks and 55 quasi-national parks.

Nihon Sankei

(The Three Views of Japan). This refers to the three most famous scenic spots in Japan: Matsushima, a group of islands in Miyagi Prefecture; Amanohashidate, a pine-tree-covered sandbar in Kyoto Prefecture; and Itsukushima, an island in Hiroshima Prefecture.

Plants and Animals

Animals

(*dobutsu*). The Japanese islands are inhabited by Southeast Asiatic tropical animals, Korean and Chinese temperate-zone animals, and Siberian subarctic animals. Japan's fauna includes many species and relics not found in neighboring areas. Some of these relics are found on Honshu, but a larger number inhabit the Ogasawara Islands and the islands south of Kyushu.

Overall Characteristics

In zoogeographic terms, the sea south of central Honshu belongs to the Indo-Western Pacific region, which is part of the tropical kingdom; it abounds in bright coral fish, sea snakes, and turtles and is inhabited by the dugong and the black finless porpoise. The sea north of central Honshu belongs to the Northern Pacific region, part of the northern kingdom, which extends along the southern coast of the Aleutian Islands and the west coast of the United States down to California and is inhabited by the fur seal, Steller's sea lion, and Baird's beaked whale. Finally, Hokkaido, which largely faces the Sea of Okhotsk in the Arctic region, is visited occasionally by animals indigenous to the Arctic region, such as the walrus.

In the zoogeographical division of the Japanese islands by land animals, the Ryukyu Islands south of Amami Oshima are sometimes regarded as part of the Oriental region extending from the Malayan Peninsula to India and sometimes as a transition zone from this region to the Palaearctic region; the area north of Yakushima off southern Kyushu is considered part of the Palaearctic region. The Ryukyu Islands are inhabited mostly by tropical animals, such as the flying fox, crested serpent eagle, variable lizard, and butterflies of the family Danaidae. In mainland Japan (Honshu, Shikoku, and Kyushu) and Hokkaido, which belong to the Palaearctic region, two groups of animals are predominant: those of deciduous forests of Korea and central and northern China, such as the raccoon dog, sika deer, Japanese crested ibis, mandarin duck, and hairstreak; and those of coniferous forests of Siberia, such as the brown bear, pika, hazel grouse, common lizard, and nine-spined stickle-back.

Of these animals, those of the Korean and Chinese group are confined mostly to the Japanese mainland and those of the Siberian group to Hokkaido. Consequently, it is common to include the mainland in the Manchurian subregion of the Palaearctic region and Hokkaido in the Siberian subregion. However, the geological history of the Japanese islands, marked by repeated separation from and reunion with the Asian continent, is exceedingly complex, giving rise to a corresponding complexity of animal migration and, as a result, noncontinuous distribution. The fauna of Japan differs slightly from those found in corresponding areas of the continent and not a few species are endemic to Japan.

For the protection of endangered species, countermeasures such as the conservation of habitats, artificial breeding, and feeding have been reviewed by the Environment Agency, and some proposals already have been implemented. In order to protect animals and insects, in 1979 the agency started a quinquennial survey of the status of animal populations.

Animals in Japanese Culture

Many of the beliefs and views held in Japan about various animals stem from native traditions, Buddhist sources, and the classic works of Chinese literature. Such traditional animal symbols as cranes and turtles (for felicity and long life) and swallows (for faithful return) were adopted from the Chinese by the Japanese ruling class in the proto-historic and ancient periods. It was not until the late medieval period (mid-12th—16th centuries) that a set of animal symbols that were truly Japanese evolved.

Until the late 19th century, the vast majority of Japanese refrained from slaughtering four-legged animals and relied chiefly on fish for animal protein. This practice derived mainly from Buddhist teachings. The Japanese view of animals includes the role played by *jikkan junishi*, or the sexagenary cycle of the ancient Chinese calendrical system. The cycle is broken down into subcycles of 12 years, each of which is represented by an animal. Even today, it is common practice to associate a person's character and fortune—based on his or her birth date—with those of the corresponding animal in the sexagenary cycle (e.g., "the year of the dragon"). In addition, animals and flowers are often used in artistic and poetic descriptions to elicit a sense of time and season.

Plants

(*shokubutsu*). Extending north to south for some 3,500 kilometers (2,175

mi), the Japanese archipelago has a great diversity of climate and vegeta-
tion. Botanists estimate that there are 5,000 to 6,000 native species of
plants. This article deals chiefly with certain seed plants (spermato-
phytes) that are of particular importance to the Japanese people.

Types of Plants in Japan

In terms of plant distribution, Japan is included in the East Asian
temperate zone and may be roughly subdivided into the following five
zones:

1. The subtropical zone, which includes the Ryukyu and
Ogasawara island groups. Characteristic plants are the *gajumaru* (Ficus
microcarpa) of the Ryukyus and the *himetsubaki* (Schima wallichii) of the
Ogasawaras.

2. The warm-temperate zone of broad-leaved evergreen forests,
which covers the greater part of southern Honshu, Shikoku, and Kyushu.
The *yabutsubaki* (Camellia japonica), the *shiinoki* (Castanopsis sieboldii),
and the *kusu* (Cinnamomum camphora) are among its characteristic
plants.

3. The cool-temperate zone of broad-leaved deciduous forests,
which covers central and northern Honshu and the southwestern part of
Hokkaido. Characteristic plants include the *konara* (Quercus serrata) and
the *buna* (Fagus crenata).

4. The subalpine zone, which includes central and northern
Hokkaido. Characteristic plants include the *kokemomo* (Vaccinium vitis-
idaea) and the *tohi* (Picea jezoensis).

5. The alpine zone, which covers the highlands of central Honshu
and the central part of Hokkaido, with the *haimatsu* (Pinus pumila) and
komakusa (Dicentra peregrina) among the characteristic plants.

Although some plants came to Japan very early in the nation's history, most of the naturalized plants were introduced in rapid succession
after the beginning of the Meiji period (1868−1912). The number of naturalized plants is said to be between 200 and 500. Although most came
from Europe, the United States has in recent years become a major source.

Uses of Plants in Japan

Throughout their recorded history, the Japanese have utilized
plants for food and for countless other purposes, including clothing,
medicines, dyes, oils, tools, roofing, sculpture, paper, matting, hats,
ropes, baskets, and fuel. Most plants now being put to such uses are
indigenous to Japan, but the majority of edible plants are thought to
have been introduced from the Asian continent.

Plants in Literature

The beauty of nature, embodied in the term *kacho fugetsu* ("flowers, birds, wind, and moon"), has been a principal theme in Japanese

literature, especially *waka* (31-syllable poetry) and *haiku*. The fact that flowers have been given first place in this phrase does not seem to be coincidental. *The Tale of Genji*, written about the year 1000 and noted for its superb descriptions of nature, makes reference to 101 kinds of plants. Frequent use of trees and plants in similes is often considered one of the characteristics of Japanese literature.

For the Japanese, nature has not only been an object of aesthetic appreciation but also an agent evoking intense poetic sentiments. They have loved flowers not so much for their fragrance and color as for their form and emotional import. The special significance Japanese have attached to the seasons in their poetry is an expression of their close observation of and affection for plants as signs of the ever-vanishing, ever-perpetuating pattern of nature. An understanding of this attitude is essential to the appreciation of traditional Japanese literature.

Plants in the Visual Arts

Pictorial and other arts in Japan have also traditionally relied heavily on the artist's sensitivity to nature and have generally tended toward the simple, compact, and sparely graceful. Traditional Japanese renditions of landscapes do not display the wide range of color seen in Western-style oil paintings. In sculpture, too, works are in general delicately carved and small in scale. Plants, flowers, and birds or their patterns are frequently reproduced in lifelike colors on fabric, lacquer ware, and ceramic ware. A love of natural form and an eagerness to express it ideally have been primary motives in the development of traditional Japanese arts, such as flower arrangement, the tea ceremony, tray landscapes (*bonkei*), *bonsai*, and landscape gardening.

Plants and Folklore

In the hope of avoiding natural disasters, early people formulated sacred rites of exorcism, ablution, and divination. These mystico-religious activities and an awe of nature in general led people to see symbols of the divine in trees and flowers. An excellent example is the once widely practiced worship of primeval evergreen trees—pines (*matsu*), cedars (*sugi*), cypresses (*hinoki*), and camphor trees (*kusunoki*)—which the early Japanese believed offered habitation (*yorishiro*) to deities who descended from heaven. The practice of decorating the gates of houses with pine branches (*kadomatsu*) on New Year's Day derives from the belief that this was a means of welcoming deities.

Another folk custom involving flowers, the flower-viewing party (*hanami*), also dates back to antiquity. Originally an event closely related to agricultural rites, it later became a purely recreational activity. The most popular flower for viewing has been the *sakura* (flowering cherry). An annual cherry-viewing party sponsored by the imperial court became an established custom in the Heian period (794–1185). During the Edo period (1600–1868) the practice of holding annual flower-viewing parties spread among the common people. Besides the sakura, the *ume* (Japanese plum), *fuji* (wisteria), *kiku* (chrysanthemum), and *hasu* (lotus) are common objects of viewing.

Plants and Religion

The early Japanese worshiped nature as divine. They believed that natural features such as mountains, rivers, stones, and plants all had spirits and offered prayers to and sought salvation from them. For religious festivals, evergreen trees such as pines and *sakaki* (Cleyera japonica) were used because they were thought to be dwellings of gods, and marine products (seaweed, fish, and shellfish) and fresh farm vegetables were offered to the deities instead of animal flesh. These traditions survive in present-day Shinto. Buddhism, which was introduced to Japan in about the 6th century, banned the destruction of living creatures, so flowers and plants were used for its rituals, a practice that is still followed.

Plants in Modern Japan

During the Meiji period, the Japanese became preoccupied with modern and Western values and much less concerned with nature. At one time this change was generally regarded as a sign of progress, but a major consequence of Japan's rapid industrialization (especially since World War II) has been the indiscriminate exploitation of nature, including reckless deforestation. This in turn has led to widespread pollution that has affected every element of Japanese society. People have recently come to realize that the "progress" they once believed to be entirely beneficial is not necessarily so and that conservation and rehabilitation of the natural environment should be a major priority. Many Japanese now feel strongly that their country's great wealth of plant life should be protected and reconsidered in light of old values.

Birds

(*chorui*). There is no endemic genus among the 490 bird species found in Hokkaido and Honshu. The only genera endemic to Japan are those represented by the *meguro* (Bonin honeyeater; *Apalopteron familiare*) and the extinct Ogasawara *mashiko* (Bonin grosbeak; *Chaunoproctus ferreorostris*) of the Ogasawara Islands and the *noguchigera* (Pryer's woodpecker) of Okinawa, all of which are native to islands far from the Asian continent.

Mainland Species

The four truly endemic mainland species are the *yamadori* (copper pheasant), the black *karasubato* (Japanese wood pigeon; *Columba janthina*), the red-cheeked *aogera* (Japanese green woodpecker), and the black-backed *seguro sekirei* (Japanese wagtail). The *komadori* ("horse bird"; Japanese robin) and the *nojiko* (Japanese yellow bunting; *Emberiza sulphurata*) breed only in Japan and can be classified endemic, but they migrate to warmer climes in winter.

Seabirds

Among seabirds seldom seen outside Japan are the very rare *ahodori* (short-tailed albatross; *Diomedea albatrus*) found in Torishima and the Senkaku Islands; the *umineko* (black-tailed gull), which breeds in Hokkaido and Honshu; and the *kammuri umisuzume* (Japanese auk; *Synthliboramphus wumisuzume*), which breeds in the mainland and the Izu Islands.

Nonendemic Species

Japan's common, nonendemic birds include the *tancho* (Japanese crane), which breeds in Hokkaido; the *oshidori* (mandarin duck); the *karugamo* (spotbill duck), found year round throughout Japan; the *sashiba* (gray-faced buzzard eagle), which breeds in the mainland; the mountain-dwelling *kumataka* (Hodgson's hawk eagle), a mainland inhabitant used for hawking; the giant *shimafukuro* (fish owl; *Ketupa blakistoni*) in Hokkaido; the *kijibato* (eastern turtledove; *Streptopelia orientalis*) and the *hiyodori* (brown-eared bulbul; *Hypsipetes amaurotis*), found all over Japan; the sweet-voiced *uguisu* (bush warbler); the lemon-breasted *kibitaki* (narcissus flycatcher; *Ficedula narcissina*); the long-tailed *sankocho* (black paradise flycatcher; Terpsiphone atrocaudata); the trainable *yamagara* (varied tit; *Parus varius*); and the nectar-sucking *mejiro* (Japanese white-eye; *Zosterops japonica*).

Japanese cranes at Kushiro Marsh in Hokkaido.

Other birds worthy of mention are the rare *toki* (Japanese crested ibis; *Nipponia nippon*), the *onaga* (azure-winged magpie; *Cyanopica cyana*), the giant *owashi* (Steller's sea eagle; *Haliaeetus pelagicus*), the *umiu* (Temminck's cormorant; *Phalacrocorax filamentosus*), several species of *hototogisu*, the *akashobin* (ruddy kingfisher; *Halcyon coromanda*), the *raicho* (ptarmigan), the high-mountain-dwelling *iwahibari* (alpine accentor; *Prunella collaris*), and the *kiji* (common pheasant).

Fishes

(gyorui). There are about 3,000 species of freshwater and seawater fishes in and around the Japanese islands. Important freshwater fish include the river-dwelling *ayu* (sweetfish); the *iwana* (charr; *Salvelinus pluvius*), of mountain streams; the *moroko* (*Gnathopogon elongatus*), of rivers on plains; the *wakasagi* (*Hypomesus olidus*), of lakes and swamps; the *koi* (carp), distributed intermittently in Europe and East Asia; the *funa* (crucian carp), found throughout the world; the *medaka* (Japanese killifish;

Oryzias latipes); and the *dojo* (loach; *Misgurnus anguillicaudatus*). More than 10 species of the beautiful *tanago* (bitterling; *Acheilognathus moriokae*) inhabit rivers and swamps in northern Japan and lay eggs in the gills of such shellfish as the *karasugai* (*Cristaria plicata*); many of these are endangered endemic species, such as the *miyako tanago* (*Tanakia tanago*) in rivers on the Kanto Plain. The *mahaze* (goby) is found along the coast from Hokkaido down to Kyushu, and the *tobihaze* (mudskipper; *Periophthalmus cantonensis*) is found in the western part of Tokyo Bay and along the coasts of South Asia, Australia, and Africa.

Natural monuments and protected species

(*tennen kinembutsu*). The Japanese term *tennen kinembutsu*, usually translated as "natural monument," has a wider range of meaning than any one English equivalent. In the strict sense it refers to natural objects and phenomena (including species of animals and plants) characteristic of or peculiar to Japan that have been designated for preservation under the Cultural Properties Law of 1950 or similar local laws. These include certain geologic or mineral formations and areas (other than national parks) of special historic, scenic, or scientific interest, as well as certain species of animals and plants found only in specific areas of Japan. Natural monuments and protected species are classified into two categories: those designated for preservation by the national government under the Cultural Properties Law (953 in 1992, including 75 classified as "special natural monuments") and those set aside for protection by the laws of local public bodies such as prefectures, cities, towns, and villages.

Protected Areas

Areas of specific interest that have been set aside as *tennen kinembutsu* are classified under a number of official designations such as Nature Protection District, Primeval Forest, and Shrine Forest. Nature Protection Districts include Lake Towada; the river Oirasegawa; the Kurobe gorge; the Oze, Torishima, and Kushiro bogs; and the island of Minami Iojima. Primeval Forests include the Daisetsuzan area in Hokkaido, the Sarugawa Headwaters Primeval Forest, the Maruyama Primeval Forest, the Kasugayama Primeval Forest in Nara, and the Aso Kitamukidani Primeval Forest. One Shrine Forest is the Miyazaki Kashima Forest in Toyama Prefecture.

Animals

Indigenous species of Japanese wildlife designated as *tennen kinembutsu* include the Amami *no kurousagi*, the *meguro* (Bonin honeyeater), and the giant salamander (*o sanshouo*). Other *tennen kinenbutsu* include cranes and their migration grounds in Kagoshima Prefecture, the natural habitat of sea bream in the waters of Tainoura in Chiba Prefecture, and the breeding grounds of the horseshoe crab in the waters near Kasaoka, Okayama Prefecture. Naturalized species include the magpie, the turtledove and domestic birds and animals (such as certain varieties of fowl), the *misaki* horse (*misaki uma*), Mishima cattle (Mishima *ushi*), and the long-tailed cock (*onagadori*).

Plants

Certain rock-zone flora found in specific locations and the boundary zones of distribution of certain plants found only in limited areas are also classified as *tennen kinenbutsu*. A great number of very old or very large individual trees have also been designated as natural monuments.

Geologic formations that have been designated as natural monuments include the group of cirques (deep, steep-walled basins) at Yakushidake, the limestone cave known as Akiyoshido in Yamaguchi Prefecture, and the upthrust coasts of Kisakata in Akita Prefecture. A number of unique mineral formations and fossil sites have also been designated.

The *o sanshouo* salamander is the world's largest amphibian.

Ise Shrine in Mie Prefecture. One of two treasure repositories of the Outer Shrine. The shrine is razed and rebuilt every 20 years in a rite called *shikinen sengu*.

History of Japan

(*nihonshi*). Observers in Europe and the United States are naturally tempted to view Japanese history in terms of its encounters with the West. From this perspective, the "Christian Century" from ca 1540 to ca 1640, and the century and a half from the arrival of Commodore Matthew Perry's fleet and the "Opening of Japan" in the mid-19th century to the present, tend to be viewed as the major phases of Japanese history. The Japanese themselves, of course, see these periods of contact with the West, especially in modern times, as vital phases of their historical development, but they also look to their relations with the Asian continent. They prize the formative contacts with China and Korea in the premodern era and recall with regret Japan's imperialist aggression in Korea, China, and Manchuria in the period leading to World War II, a tragic episode that has shaped their modern history in numerous ways and with which they are still coming to terms.

Despite the importance of these contacts with other societies, however, it is the unfolding history of the Japanese people within the islands of the Japanese archipelago itself that must take center stage in any discussion of the Japanese past. That past can be divided into seven major phases: prehistoric (*senshi*), protohistoric (*genshi*), ancient (*kodai*), medieval (*chusei*), early modern (*kinsei*), modern (*kindai*), and contemporary (*gendai*).

The Prehistoric Period

Archaeologists who specialize in the earliest phase of Japanese social development usually divide the prehistoric phase into four major periods: a long paleolithic preceramic period prior to ca 10,000 BC; the Jomon period (ca 10,000 BC – ca 300 BC), which saw the introduction of ceramics; the Yayoi period (ca 300 BC – ca AD 300), when metals and sedentary agriculture became widespread; and the Kofun period (ca 300 – 710), age of the great burial mounds and the beginnings of political centralization. However, this latter period, which was one of transition to the era of written records, is also known as the protohistoric period.

The first inhabitants of the Japanese islands were paleolithic hunter-gatherers from the continent who used sophisticated stone blades but had no ceramics or settled agriculture. This paleolithic culture persisted until the close of the Pleistocene epoch, about 13,000 years ago, when the Japanese climate ameliorated and sea levels began to rise. In these changing climatic circumstances a new culture began to overlay the older paleolithic culture. This new culture is known as Jomon (literally, "cord marked") from the magnificent pottery that characterized it. Although it has been commonly thought that the Jomon people

Jomon pottery from Fukushima Prefecture.

were hunter-gatherers who did not practice cultivation, recent research suggests that by about 1000 BC in Kyushu they were cultivating a green-leaf condiment known as *shiso* and had begun to cultivate rice, which was not native to Japan.

From about 300 BC Jomon culture was overlaid by a distinctly different culture, the Yayoi, characterized by less flamboyant ceramics, a knowledge of bronze and iron technologies, including fine weaponry, and the systematic development of wet-field rice agriculture. These developments laid the basis for the strong martial current found in Japan's early history and for the agricultural way of life that profoundly shaped Japanese society into the modern era. They also contributed to greater social stratification and the emergence of a hierarchy of local clans (*uji*), ruling service groups (*be*), and slaves. Yayoi culture had spread through Kyushu, Shikoku, and Honshu by the mid-3rd century AD.

The Protohistoric Period

Before the close of the Yayoi period, from about the mid-3rd century, clans in the Yamato region and other areas of central and western Japan were building impressive mounded stone tombs, *kofun* for the burial of their chieftains. The largest of these kofun, built in the Yamato region are said to be the mausoleums of the first powerful political dynasty in Japan, the Yamato, which eventually asserted political control over the entire country.

Tumuli continued to be built in Japan until the end of the 7th century. By then, however, the old clan society was being restructured and Japan was already well on the way to the articulation of a Chinese-inspired centralized imperial administration. The Asuka period (593–710) marks the final phase of this transition between protohistory and history proper. The Asuka period dates from the establishment of the court of Empress Suiko (r 593–628) in the Asuka region of Yamato, south of the present-day city of Nara. That same year (593) Prince Shotoku (574–622) began to serve as her regent. For more than a century the area was the site for the palaces of the rulers of the Yamato lineage and the powerful uji supporting it. Buddhism had been introduced to this region in the mid-6th century and it was here that Prince Shotoku labored to elevate the power and prestige of the imperial line and set the country on the course of centralized reform heralded in his Seventeen-Article Constitution. The Japanese court sponsored Buddhism; built temples, palaces, and capitals after Korean and later Chinese models; began to write histories using Chinese characters; and laid out a blueprint for a Chinese-style imperial state structure later known as the *ritsuryo* (legal codes) system.

One of the many representations of Prince Shotoku, the great Asuka Period statesman.

The Ancient Period

In 710 a magnificent new capital, called Heijokyo and modeled on the Chinese Tang dynasty (618–907) capital at Chang'an, was established at Nara. During the course of the Nara period (710–794) Japan received even more direct cultural and technological influences from China. Japan's first chronicles, the *Kojiki* (712, Records of Ancient Matters) and *Nihon shoki* (720, Chronicle of Japan), were compiled at this time. Buddhism and Confucianism were harnessed to support political authority, and temples were constructed in the capital and in each of the provinces. Centralized systems for the administration of taxation, census, and landholding were instituted. By the closing years of the 8th century, however, the centralized imperial administration and public land system were showing signs of strain. Politics in Nara were upset by rivalries among nobles and clerics. In 784 Emperor Kammu (r 781–806) decided to make a new start and tried to revive the *ritsuryo* system by moving the capital to a new site. In 794 a new capital, called Heiankyo (literally, "Capital of Peace and Tranquillity"), was established where the modern city of Kyoto now stands. This was to serve as the home of the imperial court and the capital of Japan until the 19th century, when the capital was moved to Edo, which was renamed Tokyo.

Kojiki (Record of Ancient Matters).

The period from 794 to 1185, which was the heyday of the imperial government's rule of Japan from Heiankyo, is known as the Heian period. It saw the full assimilation of Chinese culture and the flowering of an elegant courtly culture. Politically, however, the imperial court and the imperial office itself came to be dominated by nobles of the Fujiwara family, and the court had difficulty in maintaining its control over the administration of the provinces. In the absence of an effective centralized military system, warrior bands began to assume more power, first in the provinces and then over the court itself when the Taira family seized power in the capital in the mid-12th century.

The Medieval Period

The Taira were overthrown in 1185 by warriors led by Minamoto no Yoritomo (1147–1199), who was granted in 1192 the title of shogun and established a military government, called the Kamakura shogunate, in the small town of Kamakura in eastern Japan. The first four centuries of warrior domination, covering the Kamakura period (1185–1333) and the Muromachi period (1333–1568), are usually described as Japan's feudal era. The court was not displaced by the creation of a military government in Kamakura but its influence steadily weakened. The shogunate assumed control of the administration of justice, the imperial succession, and the defense of the country against the attempted Mongol invasions of Japan in the late 13th century. Headed first by

Yoritomo, the Kamakura shogunate was overthrown in 1333 by a coalition led by Emperor Go-Daigo (r 1318–1339), who was seeking to restore direct imperial rule .

Go-Daigo himself was ousted in 1336 by Ashikaga Takauji (1305–1358), who had helped bring him to power. Takauji, using a rival emperor as a puppet sovereign, established a new shogunate in the Muromachi district of Kyoto. After several decades of civil war between the rival Northern and Southern courts the shogunate was put on a firm footing by Ashikaga Yoshimitsu (1358–1408), the third Ashikaga shogun. Later Ashikaga shoguns were less successful in controlling the feudal coalition. Beginning with the Onin War (1467–1477), the country slipped into the century of sporadic civil war known as the Warring States period (Sengoku period; 1467–1568), in which local feudal lords (*daimyo*) ignored the shogunate and the imperial court and struggled with each other for local hegemony.

The Early Modern Period

From the mid-16th century, a movement toward national reunification gradually emerged out of the violence of the warring feudal domains and was carried through by three powerful hegemons, Oda Nobunaga (1534–1582), Toyotomi Hideyoshi (1537–1598), and Tokugawa Ieyasu (1543–1616). The short but spectacular epoch during which Nobunaga and Hideyoshi established their military control over the country and began to reshape its feudal institutions is known as the Azuchi-Momoyama period (1568–1600). This was an age of gold, grandeur, and openness to the outside world. Hideyoshi had visions of conquering Korea and establishing an enduring dynasty, though he lived to see his Korean invasions end in brutal failure. His death in 1598 left his heir vulnerable to rival daimyo. One of these, Tokugawa Ieyasu, after a striking victory over pro-Toyotomi warriors at the Battle of Sekigahara in 1600, assumed the title of shogun and established a powerful and enduring shogunate in the city of Edo, ushering in the Edo period (1600–1868) in Japanese history.

Ieyasu's victory gave him preponderant power and allowed him to rearrange the political map of Japan. He established a carefully balanced political structure known as the *bakuhan* (shogunate and domain) system in which the Tokugawa shogunate directly controlled Edo and the heartland of the country while the daimyo (classified on the basis of their loyalty to the Tokugawa) governed the 250 or so domains (*han*). Ieyasu and his shogunal successors were able to maintain a strong centralized feudal structure by balancing the daimyo domains; enforcing status distinctions between samurai, merchants, artisans, and peasants; instituting a hostage system of alternate-year attendance by daimyo in

An Edo-period illustration of Nihombashi, starting point of the Tokaido and the symbolic center of Japan during the Edo period.

Edo (*sankin kotai*); eradicating Christianity; controlling contacts with the outside world, especially the West; and enforcing regulations for samurai, nobles, and temples. This structure was dominated by samurai and relied heavily on the tax yield of the peasants, but it also gave scope to the merchants of Edo, Osaka, Kyoto, and the castle towns to develop commerce and a lively urban culture.

The Modern Period

The Tokugawa system, oppressive as it was in many respects, gave the country more than two centuries of peace and relative seclusion from the outside world. This was threatened in the 19th century as Russian, British, and American vessels began to probe Asian waters and press for trade with China and Japan. The shogunate's failure to "expel the barbarians," the concession of unequal treaties, and the opening of ports after Perry's visit in 1853 set in motion a chain of events that led the powerful domains of Satsuma, Choshu, and Tosa to use the imperial court to challenge the shogunate, which was overthrown in the Meiji Restoration of 1868. The young samurai who carried through the restoration wanted to preserve, revitalize, and strengthen the country. This process moved ahead rapidly during the course of the Meiji period (1868 — 1912). The slogan of the new leadership of Japan was *fukoku kyohei* (Enrich the Country, Strengthen the Military). This meant reforming most social, political, and economic institutions along Western lines. Japan adopted a constitution in 1889, opening the way to parliamentary government. It achieved industrial progress and built up sufficient military power to defeat China in 1895 and Russia in 1905, and to annex Korea in 1910, emerging as the major imperialist power in East Asia.

The Taisho period (1912 — 1926) was marked by Japan's acceptance as a major power, a period of party government sometimes known as Taisho Democracy. The Showa period (1926 — 1989) began on a note of optimism but quickly descended into military aggression in Manchuria and China and Japan's departure from the League of Nations. Ultranationalism and political oppression at home eventually led to war with the United States and the Allied powers in Asia and the Pacific .

One of Perry's "Black Ships."

The Contemporary Era

The defeat of Japan in 1945 under atomic clouds brought the Allied Occupation, demilitarization, dismantling of the old industrial combines (*zaibatsu*), renunciation of divinity by the emperor, a new constitution, democratization, and a new educational system. After a painful period of postwar rehabilitation, the Japanese economy began to surge ahead in the 1960s and 1970s. The Tokyo Olympics in 1964 brought Japan renewed international recognition. The nation's continued prosperity has been based on a security treaty with the United States, a consistent stress on economic growth and business-oriented policy making, an emphasis on education, and the frugality, energy, and sustained efforts of the Japanese people. In recent years the Japanese, under international pressure to liberalize trade, have been moving from an export-oriented economy to one that is more accessible to foreign imports. This is part of a larger effort by the Japanese to overcome a strong historical tendency to view themselves as somehow unique and aloof from other nations. They are now attempting to truly internationalize their society and bring it into fuller cooperation with an increasingly interdependent world.

Japanese people, origin of

(*nihonjin no kigen*).Thousands of artifacts and caches of broken animal bones have been recovered from rock shelters, limestone fissures, and glacial loam sites, some dating from as early as the end of the second glacial period a half a million years or more ago. The oldest identified human (*Homo sapiens*) remains, although incomplete, date from about 30,000 BC. The oldest remains satisfactory for comparative analysis are from the early part of the Jomon period (ca 10,000 BC—ca 300 BC), but Jomon skeletal assemblages satisfactory for statistical analysis date from about 5000 BC.

The Jomon population was generally short-statured with heavy skeletal structure; skulls were longheaded, and faces were short and broad with markedly concave nasal profiles. Multivariate discriminant analyses place Jomon skulls between those of the native Ainu and modern Japanese but closer to the Ainu and more variable.

The historical Japanese known as the Yamato (Yamatobito) are probably mainly descendants of the cultivators of the Yayoi period (ca 300 BC—ca AD 300) with regionally varying admixtures of the earlier Jomon population and a continually increasing immigrant population from the insular south and, more especially, Korea and China.

GOVERNMENT AND DIPLOMACY

Members meet in the main
chamber of the House of
Representatives.
The speaker of the house
sits on the raised dais
behind the central podium.

Constitution of Japan

(Nihonkoku Kempo). The Constitution of Japan, successor to the Constitution of the Empire of Japan (1889; also known as the Meiji Constitution), became effective on 3 May 1947. It is notable for its declaration that sovereignty resides with the people, its assertion of fundamental human rights, and its renunciation of war and arms. A thoroughly democratic document, it revolutionized the political system, which under the Meiji Constitution had been based on the principle that sovereignty resided with the emperor.

Enactment

The Japanese surrender in World War II took the form of acceptance of the terms of the Potsdam Declaration, which called for the removal of obstacles to democratic tendencies and the establishment of a peace-loving government in accordance with the freely expressed will of the Japanese people. In October 1945 Prime Minister Shidehara Kijuro appointed Matsumoto Joji to head a committee to investigate the question of constitutional revision. The following February the staff of US General Douglas MacArthur, the supreme commander for the Allied powers (SCAP), became convinced that the Matsumoto committee was incapable of adequately democratizing the constitution and that the Far Eastern Commission (representing the Allied powers) might soon intervene in the matter. MacArthur directed his Government Section to formulate a model constitution for Japan. The Government Section's hastily drafted constitution was based in part on a policy paper of the American State-War-Navy Coordinating Committee (SWNCC). On 13 February 1946 Government Section officials delivered their draft to the Japanese cabinet.

After difficult negotiations the SCAP and Japanese officials agreed on a draft constitution based on the SCAP model. On 6 March 1946 the Shidehara cabinet published the text as its own handiwork.

To ensure legal continuity with the imperial constitution, the proposed new constitution was passed in the form of a constitutional amendment almost unanimously by both houses of the Imperial Diet, and on 3 November 1946 it was promulgated by the emperor, to become effective 3 May 1947.

Provisions

The new Constitution of Japan declares that the emperor shall be "the symbol of the State and of the unity of the people, deriving his position from the will of the people with whom resides sovereign power." All acts of the emperor in matters of state now require the advice and approval of the cabinet, and the emperor has no "powers related to government." The emperor appoints as prime minister the person selected by the Diet and appoints as chief judge of the Supreme Court the appointee of the cabinet.

The new constitution enumerates the rights and duties of the people, such as freedom of speech. Discrimination "in political, economic or social relations because of race, creed, sex, social status or family origin" is forbidden. The people have the right to maintain "minimum standards of wholesome and cultured living," and the state is expected to promote social welfare and public health. The right to own property is declared inviolable. The most famous provision of the constitution is article 9, which states that the Japanese people "forever renounce war" and that "land, sea, and air forces ... will never be maintained."

If the lower house passes a resolution of no confidence in the cabinet, the cabinet must resign or the lower house must be dissolved within 10 days. Thus the new constitution established the parliamentary-cabinet system of democracy, similar to that of Great Britain. The two houses of the Diet designate the prime minister, but if the two houses are unable to agree, the choice of the House of Representatives (lower house) prevails. The defeat of a bill by the House of Councillors (upper house) may be overridden by a two-thirds majority vote of the lower house, except that a lower-house simple majority may prevail where the budget, a treaty, or the designation of the prime minister is involved.

The Japanese Supreme Court has explicit authority to determine the constitutionality of legislation and government acts.

The New Constitution in Practice

Shortly before and after the new constitution became effective, the Diet passed 45 laws to implement its provisions. This legislation included the new Imperial Household Law, the Cabinet Law, the Diet Law, the Local Autonomy Law, electoral laws, and amendments to the Civil Code and the Code of Civil Procedure.

Since the Occupation ended in 1952, the government has interpreted the constitution to mean that it may dissolve the House of Representatives without having to wait for a vote of no confidence. The government, which had been dominated by the conservatives, had dissolved the lower house at times advantageous to the conservatives. Since the governing conservatives had usually held majorities in both houses, they had been able to dominate the system.

Over the years, the constitutionality of the Self Defense Forces has been frequently challenged in the courts, but the Supreme Court has avoided ruling definitively on this issue. Although conservatives have

Government and Diplomacy

advocated amendments that would clarify the right to maintain military forces, the Japanese people have thus far not altered a word of their democratic constitution.

Democracy

(*minshu shugi*). Japan has a functioning democratic system, that is, a system in which sovereignty resides in the people, who exercise it through elected representatives and who are guaranteed the civil liberties essential to its exercise.

History

Japan's democratic tradition stretches back to the early Meiji period (1868−1912). In the 1870s dissatisfied former *samurai* and landowners who were not represented in the new government launched a movement for representative institutions, or "popular rights". Led by such people as Itagaki Taisuke (1837−1919), they formed several political parties. Ideologically, Itagaki and his followers were influenced by the ideals of French radicalism, while Okuma Shigenobu (1839−1922), based his platform on the ideas of English liberalism and parliamentary goverment.

Itagaki Taisuke, leader of the Freedom and People's Rights Movement during the Meiji period.

In 1889 the Japanese government adopted a constitution that permitted a weak House of Representatives and a limited franchise. Political parties gradually became accepted in government after the first party cabinet was formed in 1898, reaching a peak of power during the Taisho period (1912−26).

The end of World War I, with the apparent victory of democracy in the West and of Marxism in Russia, coupled with a postwar recession in Japan, stimulated a movement for social, economic, and political reform in Japan among many students, writers, intellectuals, journalists, politicians, and labor leaders. They called for reforms ranging from the introduction of socialism and Marxism and the formation of labor unions to the development of true liberal democracy. The Sodomei (Japan Federation of Labor) was formed in 1919 and a communist and several socialist parties were formed in the 1920s.

Okuma Shigenobu, an important politician of the Meiji and Taisho periods and founder of Waseda University.

The Japanese government responded to demands for reform with a series of both conciliatory and repressive acts. Some progressive factory and labor laws were adopted and the Universal Manhood Suffrage Law was passed in May 1925, but these acts were coupled with the repressive Peace Preservation Law of 1925 and a series of police raids that destroyed many left-wing groups or drove them underground by the early 1930s.

From 1930 on army and navy officers involved themselves in a series of incidents that indicated their ability to intervene in civilian affairs. Key events included the Manchurian Incident in 1931 and the assassination of Prime Minister Inukai Tsuyoshi (1855—1932) in 1932, and a full-fledged military insurrection in 1936. Political parties lost their power and prestige and the military held sway over Japan politically, economically, and socially until the end of World War II.

Postwar Development

Japan's present democratic system centers on the primary authority of a bicameral Diet (parliament) of representatives elected by the people. Executive power is exercised by a prime minister (chosen by the Diet) and by a cabinet he appoints. Judicial power resides in the Supreme Court and lower courts. Popular control over local government is exercised through a system of local and prefectural assemblies and executives elected by the people. A system of checks and balances distributes power among the executive, legislative, and judicial branches and assures the people of a voice in government.

However, public confidence in democracy has been severely tested in postwar Japan. A series of scandals from 1970s to 1990s, including the Lockheed Scandal, the Recruit Scandal, and other corrupt practices have occasioned a certain amount of disillusionment and discontent with the actual workings of Japan's political system.

The infrequency with which elected legislative bodies initiate legislation has also been a problem. Representation rarely means the introduction of bills, since at all levels of government most bills are introduced by the executive branch after limited consultation with parties and interest groups. The subsequent process of negotiating a consensus occurs behind closed doors, and even the legislative committee "hearings" are not really open either to the public or to interest groups. A predictable consequence of this situation has been a general loss of public confidence in government and increasing feelings of apathy and detachment from the political process. That politicians have sensed this trend and begun to respond to public demands for more thoroughly democratic practices was evidenced in the early 1990s, as plans began to take shape for the first significant reform in the system of election districting since 1945.

Renunciation of war

(*senso no hoki*). Doctrine arising out of article 9, the most famous and most controversial article, of the Constitution of Japan (1947). Article 9 reads as follows:

"Aspiring sincerely to an international peace based on justice and order, the Japanese people forever renounce war as a sovereign right of the nation and the threat or use of force as a means of settling international disputes."

"In order to accomplish the aim of the preceding paragraph, land, sea, and air forces, as well as other war potential, will never be maintained. The right of belligerency of the state will not be recognized."

The San Francisco Peace Treaty of 1951 specifically stated that the Allied powers "recognize that Japan as a sovereign nation possesses the inherent right of individual or collective self-defense." With that provision as the basis, the Diet in 1954 passed a law creating the Self Defense Forces (SDF). The twin questions of the development of the SDF and the possible violation of article 9 have been highly controversial issues in Japanese politics.

The Supreme Court of Japan has not dealt directly with the constitutionality of the SDF, only on the constitutionality of the United States-Japan security treaties that permit US bases in Japan. However, the court has refused to declare such bases unconstitutional, arguing that matters relating to national security are by their nature political and must therefore be decided by the sovereign people, who can express political judgments on security matters by exercising their suffrage in free elections.

Emperor

Emperor

(*tenno*; literally, "heavenly sovereign"). The title *tenno* was first assumed by Japanese rulers in the 6th or 7th century and has been used by all subsequent Japanese sovereigns.

Japan's imperial institution, the oldest hereditary monarchy in the world, was already in existence when Japan emerged into recorded history and has since been perpetuated in a predominantly male line of descent. Although the emperor has almost always been regarded as the titular head of the national government, the most striking feature of the office through most of Japanese history has been the tendency to emphasize instead the emperor's role as chief priest in the indigenous Japanese religion, Shinto, and to delegate most of the effective powers of government to others.

From Early Historical Times to the Mid-12th Century

The emperor figures centrally in a mythology preserved in the historical chronicles *Kojiki* (712, Record of Ancient Matters) and *Nihon shoki* (720, Chronicle of Japan). According to these, the sun goddess Amaterasu Omikami, chief divinity of the Shinto pantheon, bequeathed to her grandson Ninigi no Mikoto a mirror, jewels, and a sword, which he in turn passed on to his descendants, the emperors of Japan, the first of whom was the emperor Jimmu.

The emperor was thought to possess magical powers to propitiate or intercede with divinities. But because of the awe surrounding his person, it was also considered inappropriate for the emperor to concern himself with the secular business of government. That business, including both the making and execution of policies, belonged to ministers serving the emperor, and there was a tendency from very early historical times for those ministers to form political dynasties of their own.

The only extended period of Japanese history in which the emperor combined the roles of both high priest and functioning head of government was from the reign of Tenji (r 661 — 672), in the latter half of the 7th century, through the reign of Kammu (r 781 — 806) at the end of the 8th century and the beginning of the 9th. It was Tenji who, in the Taika Reform of 645, made the first major attempt to bring the powerful provincial clans (*uji*) under the control of a strong central regime.

This period of direct imperial rule was characterized by the effort to establish a centralized bureaucratic state in Japan patterned on the example offered by Tang dynasty China. The key instrument in this process was the adoption of law codes, known collectively as the *ritsuryo* (legal codes) system, that established an elaborate hierarchy of offices headed by the emperor and prescribed the procedures of governmental administration at both national and provincial levels.

According to the ancient chronicles of the Kojiki and Nihonshoki, the emperor Jimmu was the legendary first sovereign (*tonno*) of Japan.

However, the 9th century saw several efforts to personalize imperial rule by freeing it from the entrenched bureaucracy backfired, beginning a process in which the emperor was increasingly isolated from the machinery of government. This tendency was exacerbated by the creation or revival of two other extrabureaucratic posts to which the emperor delegated the authority he had formerly wielded personally: *sessho* (regent for an emperor still in his minority) and *kampaku* (regent for an adult emperor). From the late 9th century onward, both posts were dominated by members of the powerful Fujiwara family, who, while making no claim to the emperor's title or ritual role, ruled in his name.

The last century of the Heian period (794 — 1185) saw a waning of the power of the Fujiwara regents and a brief return of power to the imperial house. The leading figures through most of this period, however, were not reigning emperors but retired sovereigns who retained headship of the imperial house after abdication.

Medieval Period (mid-12th — 16th centuries)

Three more families, again nonimperial, held sway over the national government and the imperial institution from the closing years of the Heian period to the end of the Kamakura period (1185—1333), ushering in the age of warrior rule that was to last until the Meiji Restoration of 1868.

The first of these, the Taira family, ruled from Kyoto and legitimated themselves by occupying high offices within the imperial court. The second, the Minamoto family, destroyed the Taira in 1185 in a bloody war they waged from their base at Kamakura in eastern Japan. Remaining there after their victory, they established a wholly new pattern of national government, the Kamakura shogunate. The emperor remained in Kyoto and continued to preside over the imperial government, but these institutions were now reduced to almost complete impotence, real power devolving on the shogunate. Imperial legitimization for this situation took the form of a commission from the emperor naming the head of the Minamoto family to the office of *seii tai shogun*, or "barbarian-subduing generalissimo", and thus by implication granting him absolute authority over territories and population beyond the reach of the much reduced imperial power.

Minamoto no Yoritomo, founder of the Kamakura shogunate, as portrayed in a late-12th-century hanging scroll.

The third family to dominate the national government in this period was the Hojo family, whose members ruled from 1203 as shogunal regents (*shikken*). This initiated a complex and many-tiered delegation of power that has few parallels in world history. The emperor in Kyoto reigned, but the imperial government was controlled by a Fujiwara regent. The effective national government was in Kamakura, nominally headed by a shogun, but also in fact controlled by the Hojo regent. To complicate matters further, from the mid-13th century the shogunate began to interfere actively in the imperial succession, creating schisms within the imperial house that further decreased its power.

A clean sweep of this meaningless institutional complexity was undertaken by Emperor Go-Daigo (r 1318—1339) in 1333, who made war on the Hojo, destroying the Kamakura shogunate and became head of a reinvigorated imperial government. This revival of imperial authority was, however, pathetically brief. In 1336 Ashikaga Takauji (1305—1358), Go-Daigo's chief military commander, turned against the emperor, deposed him, and set up in his place a puppet from a different branch of the imperial house, the Northern Court. The latter then appointed Takauji shogun, initiating the 240-year Muromachi shogunate.

Go-Daigo established a rival court, the Southern Court, that maintained a precarious existence until 1392, when the rivalry between the two Courts was finally resolved by the third Muromachi shogun, Ashikaga Yoshimitsu (1358—1408). The material circumstances of the imperial house reached their nadir in the course of the Muromachi period (1336–1573) and the Imperial Palace was destroyed in the disastrous Onin War (1467 -77).

Early Modern Period (mid-16th – mid-19th centuries)

The restoration of the court's fortunes awaited the reunification of Japan, accomplished between 1568 and 1603 by three men, Oda Nobunaga (1534–1582), Toyotomi Hideyoshi (1537–1598), and Tokugawa Ieyasu (1543–1616)—each of whom derived sanction for his rule from the imperial institution. After the collapse of rule by the senior two men, Ieyasu followed long precedent in having himself named shogun in 1603, commencing more than 250 years of rule by the Tokugawa shogunate.

The shogunate devoted great attention to the maintenance and control of the imperial institution. The Imperial Palace was restored to its former grandeur, and residences were provided for the entire court nobility (*kuge*). Income from designated lands was earmarked for the imperial treasury. Yet at the same time rigorous restraints were imposed on the freedom of the imperial family and court nobility.

The imperial court in Kyoto had little if any influence on practical state affairs, but the emperor continued to perform certain functions important to the shogunate. The public acts of the court consisted wholly of the performance of rituals associated variously with Shinto, with Buddhism, or with Confucianism.

Oda Nobunaga, the leading figure in Japan's 16th-century reunification.

Quite apart from this, however, the imperial institution came to play a new symbolic role in Japanese political thought, constructed in the course of the Edo period (1600–1868) by writers and thinkers known as *kinnoka*, or "imperial loyalists," who drew their ideas chiefly from various modifications of Confucian theory or from the indigenous intellectual tradition of Kokugaku (National Learning). Their stress on the centrality of the imperial house within the Japanese polity proved to be an explosive concept in the mid-19th century, when it combined with the crisis touched off by Western pressure to "open" Japan to foreign trade and diplomacy. The result was a political movement aimed at fending off the foreign threat, abolishing the shogunate, and replacing it with a new national government under direct imperial rule. Within 15 years of Commodore Matthew C. Perry's arrival in Japan in 1853, this upsurge of imperial loyalism proved a key factor in the toppling of the Tokugawa regime and the initiation of the Meiji Restoration of 1868.

Modern Period (1868–1945)

The leaders of Meiji Japan engaged in 20 years of pragmatic political experimentation to redefine the imperial institution. With the proclamation of the Constitution of the Empire of Japan on 11 February

Toyotomi Hideyoshi, warlord of humble origins, who in 1590 completed the work of national reunification begun by Oda Nobunaga.

Government and Diplomacy

1889, the emperor became a constitutional monarch in a centralized and unitary state that was to exercise greater political power than any previous form of government in Japan's history.

According to the constitution, the emperor was "sacred and inviolable," and sovereignty rested with him as the head of the Japanese empire. He commanded the armed forces, declared war, made peace, and concluded treaties; he had emergency powers to maintain public order and declare a state of siege. All laws required the emperor's sanction and enforcement.

Paradoxically, however, the supreme authority accorded the emperor in the constitution, and the other efforts made to bolster his centrality to the Japanese polity, were not accompanied by real political power. In fact, the system was designed instead to preserve the emperor's political immunity while he served as the sacrosanct basis for rule by others, namely, the ministers of state and the chiefs of the armed forces. The emperor's primary political role from 1889 to 1947 was to ratify the policies and personnel decisions reached by his government leaders and to put the seal of the imperial will on political decisions they had forged, not to actually make decisions or dictate policy himself.

Contemporary Monarchy (1945—)

Japan's defeat in World War II and the subsequent Allied Occupation wrought momentous changes in the imperial institution and its place in Japanese politics and society. In the early years after the surrender the issue of imperial responsibility for the war was of heated debate, leading to calling for outright abolition of the "emperor system." A more moderate approach prevailed, however, and the 1947 Constitution of Japan retained the emperor, though in a drastically altered relation to the state and made the emperor "the symbol of the State and of the unity of the people, deriving his position from the will of the people with whom resides sovereign power." He was to have no political powers. All acts by the emperor in matters of state were reduced to merely formal and ceremonial functions, requiring the advice and approval of the cabinet. The autonomous Imperial Household Ministry was demoted to the status of an agency of the Prime Minister's Office, the peerage was eliminated, and Emperor Showa (Hirohito, r 1926—1989) himself declared on New Year's Day 1946 that he was "not divine". Thus the prewar Japanese state with its theory of imperial prerogative was thoroughly dismantled.

Along with these fundamental changes in the legal and institutional relationship of the emperor to the political system, efforts were made to "popularize" the imperial family as the nation's first family, united with the people in warmth and affection. No longer was the

Succeeding to the throne in 1867, Emperor Meiji became the symbolic focus of the movement to overthrow the Tokugawa shogunate.

The reign of the Emperor Showa (1926—1989) was the longest in recorded Japanese history.

emperor to be surrounded by an aura of sanctity, elevated in transcendence above his people who were now no longer subjects, but citizens. As a symbol the "new" emperor was to mirror a modern, democratic, and middle-class Japan.

Doubts about the imperial institution have remained. A small but vocal minority of Japanese believe that the emperor, by his very nature as a hereditary monarch, contradicts democracy, while others believe that a resurgence of Japanese fascism or absolutism is possible so long as the imperial institution is permitted to exist. But the vast majority of Japanese citizens favor the status quo. This was confirmed when, in January 1989, Emperor Akihito (r 1989—)became the first emperor to succeed to the throne under the present constitution. Despite dissenting voices, it seems clear that the consensus in Japan continues to support the retention of the imperial house, within a carefully defined legal framework.

Emperor Akihito is the 125th sovereign (tenno) in the traditional count.

Akihito, Emperor

(1933— ; Akihito Tenno). The present emperor and the 125th sovereign (*tenno*) in the traditional count (which includes several legendary emperors). Eldest son of Emperor Showa (1901—1989) and Empress Nagako (1903—), the present empress dowager. From 1946 to 1950 he was privately tutored in the English language and Western culture by Elizabeth Gray Vining, an American teacher known for her authorship of children's books. In 1952 he entered the Department of Politics at Gakushuin University, and in November of that year his coming-of-age ceremony and his investiture as crown prince were conducted. While still a college student, he left Japan in the spring of 1953 for a state visit to the United Kingdom to act as his father's representative at the coronation of Queen Elizabeth II. On his tour, he visited 13 countries in Europe and North America before returning to Japan in October. He completed his course of studies at Gakushuin University in March 1956.

In April 1959 Crown Prince Akihito married Shoda Michiko, eldest daughter of Shoda Hidesaburo, then president of the Nisshin Flour Milling Co, Ltd, breaking with the long-established tradition that the wife of the crown prince should be chosen from among the ranks of the imperial family or the former peerage. In their family life they have achieved a relative freedom from the restrictive precedents of court tradition.

While still crown prince, Akihito represented Emperor Showa on a number of state visits overseas, visiting 37 countries in the course of 22 separate trips. He also served as the honorary president of Universiade

1967 in Tokyo and of Expo '70 in Osaka. During Emperor Showa's tour of Europe in September 1971 and his tour of the United States in 1975, Crown Prince Akihito conducted affairs of state in his absence. In 1975 he was the first member of the imperial family to officially visit Okinawa after its reversion to Japan in 1972.

On 7 January 1989 he became Emperor Akihito, succeding to the throne after his father's death. The following day he adopted the formal reign title Heisei ("Establishing Peace").

Like his father, Emperor Akihito is known as a scholar of marine biology and ichthyology and for his research into the fishes of the family Gobiidae. He also enjoys sports and is a lover of music, playing cello in impromptu performances with other members of the royal family. He and Empress Michiko have three children: Crown Prince Naruhito, Prince Akishino, and Princess Sayako.

Empress Michiko.

Michiko, Empress

(1934— ; Michiko Kogo). Wife of Emperor Akihito. Eldest daughter of Shoda Hidesaburo, founder of the Nisshin Flour Milling Co, Ltd, and his wife Fumiko. She is a graduate of the University of the Sacred Heart in Tokyo. In April 1959 she married then crown prince Akihito. As the first imperial bride to be selected from outside the circle of the imperial family and the former peerage, her marriage to Crown Prince Akihito was broadly welcomed by the Japanese people as a symbol of the democratization of the imperial house. On 7 January 1989 she became empress upon her husband's ascension to the throne as Emperor Akihito. Empress Michiko maintains a lively interest in literature, arts , and music and serves as honorary president of the Japan Red Cross Society.

Naruhito, Crown Prince.
Princely title Hiro no
Miya.

Naruhito, Crown Prince

(1960— ; Naruhito Kotaishi). Princely title Hiro no Miya. Eldest son of Emperor Akihito and Empress Michiko. The crown prince graduated from Gakushuin University in 1982 and completed his initial coursework for the doctorate in history there in 1988. From 1983 to 1985 he studied at Merton College, Oxford University, where he conducted research into the sea trade routes and port cities of medieval Europe. On 7 January 1989 he became crown prince when his father ascended to the throne as Emperor Akihito. In June 1993 Crown Prince Naruhito married Owada Masako (b 1963).

Imperial Palace

(Kokyo). Official residence of the emperor. Situated in Chiyoda Ward, Tokyo, occupying 1.15 square kilometers (0.44 sq mi). Japanese emperors and their families have resided here since after the Meiji Restoration of 1868, when Edo Castle was designated the official imperial residence (before the Meiji Restoration, emperors resided in Kyoto). A new palace was completed in 1888, but this was destroyed in air raids in 1945. The present palace complex, the Kyuden, was completed in 1968. Its individual buildings include the Omote Gozasho, the emperor's office for affairs of state; the Seiden, for official ceremonies; the Homeiden, for banquets entertaining guests of state; and the Chowaden, for evening receptions. These buildings are connected by corridors surrounding a large central courtyard. To the northwest is the Fukiage Gosho, formerly the private residence of Emperor Showa, now occupied by his widow. A new palace residence for Emperor Akihito was completed in May 1993. Part of the palace grounds is open to the public.

National anthem

(*kokka*). The de facto Japanese national anthem is "Kimigayo" (His Majesty's Reign). Basil H. Chamberlain (1850−1935), author of *Things Japanese* (1890), translated the anthem as follows: *Kimi ga yo wa Chiyo ni yachiyo ni Sazare ishi no Iwao to nari te Koke no musu made* :

> Thousands of years of happy reign be thine
> Rule on, my lord, till what are pebbles now
> By age united to mighty rocks shall grow
> Whose venerable sides the moss doth line

The words of the song are from the 10th-century anthology *Kokinshu*. The author is unknown. The tune was composed by Hayashi Hiromori (1831−96) in 1880. In 1893 the Ministry of Education made it the ceremonial song to be sung in elementary schools on national holidays. Soon it was sung at state ceremonies and sports events. Although popularly identified as the national anthem for many years, "Kimigayo" has never been officially adopted as such.

National flag

(*kokki*). The national flag of Japan has a crimson disc, symbolizing the sun, in the center of a white field. It is popularly known as the Hinomaru (literally, "sun disc"). The Tokugawa shogunate (1603−1867) adopted the flag for its ships in the early 1600s. In the mid-19th century the

Government and Diplomacy

shogunate decreed that all Japanese ships fly flags with the sun on a
white field. In 1870 the Meiji government officially designated it for use
on Japanese merchant and naval ships. It has never been officially designated as the national flag; however, it has become so by customary use.

Major Components of the Government

Diet

(Kokkai). The legislative branch of the Japanese government. According
to the Constitution of Japan, the Diet is "the highest organ of state power"
and the "sole law-making organ of the State." The Diet consists of two
chambers: the House of Representatives (Shugiin), or lower house, and
the House of Councillors (Sangiin), or upper house. All Diet members are
selected in popular elections. The Imperial Diet (Teikoku Gikai), the direct
predecessor of the present Diet, was established in 1890 through provisions in the Constitution of the Empire of Japan (1889) and consisted of a
House of Peers (Kizokuin) and a House of Representatives. Constitutionally, the Imperial Diet was weak, primarily because the power of legislation was vested in the emperor and because the cabinet was responsible
to the emperor rather than to the Diet. Initially, the House of
Representatives reflected the opinions of a highly restricted segment of
the public, representing only the 1.5 percent of the population who paid
an annual tax of ¥15 or more. Not until the passage of the Universal
Manhood Suffrage Law in 1925 did all male citizens over the age of 25
obtain the right to vote and thus the possibility of influencing their legislative representatives.

The Diet Building,
completed in 1936.

During the Taisho period (1912—1926), substantial changes
occurred in Japan's body politic, including its national assembly:
Sovereignty might be constitutionally vested in the emperor, but legislative power was exercised by him and his advisers with the consent of
the Diet. Diet Members formally organized themselves into
parliamentary parties and articulated alternative policies that were
covered by the newspapers and thus helped shape public attitudes.

Possibly the best indication of the Diet's growing powers in the
1920s was the energy that its opponents devoted to circumscribing
them. Members were accused of being the corrupt tools of vested corporate interests, incapable of protecting the "national polity" (*kokutai*).
Terrorist groups plotted assassinations, some of which were successful.
By the end of the 1930s, parliamentarianism was a flame that flickered
uncertainly. Parliamentary parties were forced to exist but in name in
order to better serve the interests of the nation's predominantly military
rulers. The Diet became a rubber stamp, but those in power did not take

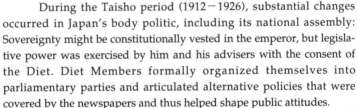

the final step of abolishing it altogether.

The transformation of the Imperial Diet into the present Diet was set forth initially in the postwar constitution (effective in May 1947). Unlike the previous constitution, the new constitution gave supreme legislative power to the Diet and made it the most important organ of the government.

Organization

Bicameralism was retained at the insistence of Japanese authorities, but the hereditary and appointive House of Peers was replaced by the elected House of Councillors, which consists of 252 members who serve six-year terms. The prime minister and a majority of his cabinet ministers were required to be members of the Diet and, "in the exercise of executive power, shall be collectively responsible to the Diet"; this is in direct contrast to the relationship that had prevailed under the Meiji Constitution. A revolution in constitutional doctrine had taken place: the entire membership of the Diet would be publicly elected, and the cabinet, in which executive authority was vested, would be responsible to the Diet. The doctrine of parliamentary supremacy had supplanted that of imperial prerogative.

At the same time, the new constitution altered the relationship between the two chambers. The House of Representatives and the House of Councillors share legislative power: "A bill becomes a law on passage by both Houses..." However, the 511 representatives of the lower house, whose term of office is four years unless the house is dissolved, have authority in three important areas. First, in the designation of the prime minister, if there is disagreement between the two chambers, "the decision of the House of Representatives shall be the decision of the Diet." Second, the national budget must first be submitted to the House of Representatives. Furthermore, if the two houses fail to reach agreement on the budget, and if joint committees fail to resolve the matter or no decision is made by the House of Councillors within 30 days, the will of the lower house prevails. Third, while international treaties may first be introduced for approval in either chamber, the decision of the lower house prevails over a contrary judgment by the upper house if joint committees fail to resolve the matter or no decision is made by the House of Councillors within 30 days. Also, in all fields of legislation, the House of Representatives can override the House of Councillors by a two-thirds vote. Thus the Diet is bicameral, but the House of Representatives is predominant in certain crucial spheres.

Members meet in the main chamber of the House of Councillors.

The Workings of the Diet

If an item of legislative business is not controversial, the system usually works smoothly. Legislation is drafted by government bureaucrats in the various ministries. Then it follows a process leading to final approval that is carefully programmed by the majority party, with the tacit concurrence of the opposition parties. In contrast, parliamentary procedures have been subjected to almost unbearable strain whenever the Diet has become the battleground for the resolution of conflict. For the governing majority party, highest priority must be accorded to maintenance of intraparty consensus on the substance of the proposed legislation as well as on the parliamentary tactics to be employed. For the opposition-party representatives and councillors, the harsh reality of their minority status involves serious tactical problems. They recognize that, barring a split in the majority party, their chances of prevailing against the governing party's overwhelming power are virtually nil.

The Diet is a legislative institution, but it is also a representative assembly. To be sure, the electoral system has been criticized as not being entirely fair. First, rural voters, a declining percentage of the public, are overrepresented. Second, campaigning is becoming increasingly expensive, giving an advantage to the wealthy and those with close ties to corporate interests. Third, because members must spend an inordinate amount of time performing "errand-boy" functions for their constituents, they have too little energy to devote themselves to being their nation's supreme legislators.

It is important to note, however, that a lengthy career in the Diet has become an absolute prerequisite to high political office.

Elections

(*senkyo seido*). Japan has had a national election system since the promulgation of the Constitution of the Empire of Japan on 11 February 1889. The extension of the franchise, limited at first to a small proportion of the adult male population, took place gradually, culminating in the adoption of universal suffrage shortly after the end of World War II.

The Prewar System

The first national election for the House of Representatives took place in 1890, but the right to vote was restricted to males who paid annual taxes of ¥15 or more. Over the next three and a half decades the number of enfranchised voters grew from fewer than 500,000 to about 3 million. The Universal Manhood Suffrage Law of 1925 expanded the electorate to about 12 million by granting the vote to all male citizens 25 years of age or older, though women were not enfranchised until December 1945.

Before 1945 there were fewer opportunities for popular participation in Japanese government. Members of the House of

Representatives were elected, but seats in the House of Peers were either appointive or hereditary. Local government was directly subordinate to the central government. Local assemblies were popularly elected, but prefectural governors were appointed by the national government. City mayors were appointed by prefectural governors from a list of names submitted by city assemblies. Headmen and mayors of villages and towns were elected by their respective local assemblies.

Current Practices

The election system was given its present form by the Public Office Election Law of April 1950. All Japanese citizens are eligible to vote if they have reached the age of 20 and have met a three-month residency requirement (for voting in local elections). Candidates for political office must meet the stated age requirement for each office. Members of the House of Representatives and of prefectural and local assemblies must be at least 25 years old. Members of the House of Councillors and prefectural governors must be at least 30.

Japan has had a comprehensive election system incorporating all levels of government since the end of World War II. Under current election laws, members of all legislative bodies, including both houses of the Diet and prefectural, city, town, and village assemblies, are selected by popular vote. Political executives, including prefectural governors and mayors or other chief officials of local governments, are also chosen in popular elections. The prime minister, who is elected by the Diet, is the only political executive not chosen by direct popular vote.Today elections for half of the 252 members of the House of Councillors are held every three years in a combination of nationwide and prefectural districts. In the House of Representatives, 511 members are elected for four-year terms, typically in elections held irregularly after the dissolution of the House by the emperor at the request of the prime minister. Elections are held every four years for most prefectural and local executive offices and assemblies.

The two national legislative bodies have traditionally been elected in multimember districts, but the size of these districts has varied over time. At present, the 511 members of the House of Representatives and about a quarter of the 252 members of the House of Councillors are elected in multimember constituencies. Unlike European practice, in elections to the House of Representatives there is no proportional formula for allocating seats in multimember districts according to the party's share of the vote. Rather, winners are selected from among the top vote-getters in each constituency, with each enfranchised citizen having one vote. In 1983, however, a proportional representation system was introduced in elections for the 100 seats in the House of Councillors that are elected on a nationwide basis.

In an effort to achieve representational parity among districts for the House of Representatives, the number of Diet seats allocated to each constituency is decided on the basis of population. In the wake of the rapid population growth in Japan's cities and suburbs after 1950, the number of seats allocated to certain urban and suburban constituencies was split and new constituencies were formed. This resulted in an overall growth of the House from 466 seats in 1946 to 511 seats in 1993. Still, considerable underrepresentation of urban districts has continued. In 1991 the number of people represented by a single Diet member in the most heavily populated (urban) district was still more than three times as great as the number represented by a single Diet member in the least populous (rural) district.

The medium-sized constituency system (*chu senkyoku sei*), in which each district sends between three and five representatives to the lower house, has been frequently criticized since the 1970s as the breeding ground for political corruption. In response to public outcry over the continued existence of "money politics", serious deliberation over reform measures that would introduce proportional representation and smaller election districts into elections for the House of Representatives began in the early 1990s.

Political Reforms

The Liberal Democratic Party (LDP) failed twice in its efforts to carry out political reforms—under Prime Ministers Kaifu Toshiki (1931—) and Miyazawa Kiichi (1919—). This resulted in the LDP's ouster in 1993 after four decades as the governing party. In 1993, a coalition of opposition parties formed a government under Prime Minister Hosokawa Morihiro, and the LDP became an opposition party. In early 1994, the Hosokawa cabinet finally succeeded in passing a political reform package through the Diet, but only after negotiating a major compromise with the LDP. The legislation calls for a fundamental change in the electoral system of the House of Representatives, an inevitable result of which will be a radical realignment of Japan's political map. The major parts of the political reform bills are as follows:

The Electoral System The number of seats in the House of Representatives will be reduced from the present 511 seats to 500. These will consist of:

(1) Single-Seat Constituencies: The nation will be divided into 300 electoral districts, each of which will elect and be represented in the House of Representatives by a single seat.

(2) Proportional Representation: Separately, the entire nation will be divided into 11 regional blocs, and the remaining 200 members

of the House will be elected from these multi-seat blocs on a proportional representation basis. A party must win at least 2 percent of the proportional representation votes to win a seat.

Fund Raising After a 5-year period all fund raising by individual candidates will by prohibited. During this transituional period each candidate will be permitted to set up one fund raising body. This body can then accept annual contributions of up to ¥500,000 from any single company or organization.

State Subsidies for Political Parties The Government will subsidize recognized political parties to the limit of 40 percent of the party's total income from political contributions during the preceding year. The purpose of this subsidy is to offset the tighter limits imposed on campaign contributions from the private sector.

Administration

Japan's electoral system is overseen by election administration committees within each administrative division of the country, i.e., prefectures, cities, towns, and villages. Administrators in local-government election sections assist the election committees in carrying out the day-to-day tasks of managing the system.

Laws specifying acceptable campaign practices are extremely detailed and strict in Japan. The period within which campaigns can be conducted, campaign funding and expenditures, and such matters as the number of posters permitted are precisely spelled out. Such practices as sponsorship of parties for constituents, door-to-door visits to solicit voter support, and gift-giving by candidates and their supporters are prohibited. It is the first overhall of the electoral system of the House of Representatives since 1947.

House of Councillors

(Sangiin). One of the two elective bodies that make up the Diet. Under Japan's post-World War II constitution, the House of Councillors replaced the hereditary, appointive House of Peers, which had been established under the Meiji Constitution. Although the House of Councillors and the House of Representatives share power, the latter predominates in decisions on legislation, designation of the prime minister, budgetary matters, and international treaties. Every three years, half of the 252 representatives in the House of Councillors are elected by popular vote to a six-year term of office that is not terminated in the event of dissolution of the House of Representatives. One hundred of the seats are filled on a proportional representation system; the remaining 152 seats are filled on a system of prefectural districts.

House of Representatives

(Shugiin). The lower house of the Diet. According to the provisions of the Constitution of Japan, the House of Representatives and its collective decisions take precedence over the upper house (the House of Councillors) in the areas of legislation, the budget, treaty ratification, and the selection of the prime minister. The representatives, who have numbered 511 since July 1993, are elected by popular vote. Their term of office is four years, unless the House has been dissolved before their term has elapsed.

After detailed measures to implement the political reform bills of 1994 have been worked out, Representatives will be elected to the 500 seats in the Lower House under this new electoral system.

Political parties

(seito). Political parties emerged in Japan after the Meiji Restoration (1868), gained increasing influence with the opening of the Imperial Diet (1890), and attained temporary political ascendancy following World War I. Outmaneuvered by the military, they declined in the 1930s and were dissolved and absorbed by the Imperial Rule Assistance Association in 1940. Political parties were revived under the Allied Occupation in the wake of World War II, and since 1952, when Japan regained its independence, they have been the primary force in national and local politics.

Parties in the Making

"Political associations" (seisha), which arose in the 1870s and were usually groups of disgruntled former samurai, rural landowners, and urban intellectuals, were the precursors of political parties. Their demands for a popularly elected national assembly brought them into confrontation with the Meiji oligarchs or genro, who reacted by promulgating repressive laws to control publications, political libel, and public assemblies.

The two major party builders of the early Meiji period (1868–1912) were Itagaki Taisuke (1837–1919) and Okuma Shigenobu (1838–1922). Itagaki had joined the government in 1871 but resigned in 1873 and in the following year to found the first protoparty, the Aikoku Koto (Public Party of Patriots), which memorialized the government on the need to institute an elected assembly. Itagaki and his compatriots also established a regional group in Osaka called the Aikokusha (Society of Patriots), which was the basis for the founding in 1881 of Japan's first national party, the Jiyuto (Liberal Party). Many emulators among disaffected former samurai set up similar parties and between 1882 and

1886 mounted armed revolts against the government, whose reaction was the enactment of the Peace Preservation Law of 1887, which tightened restrictions on political activity.

Okuma resigned from the government in 1881 and in 1882 formed the Rikken Kaishinto (Constitutional Reform Party), which drew its membership mainly from the fledgling urban intelligentsia. It remained active until 1896. More conservative parties, such as the Rikken Teiseito (Constitutional Imperial Rule Party; 1882), represented themselves as defenders of the oligarchic government.

Parties in the Diet

Parliamentary politics in the Diet, which opened in November 1890, was marked by an intense rivalry between the oligarchic government, which reserved the right to appoint cabinets, and the Liberal and Constitutional Reform parties. The Constitutional Reform Party, which was initially overshadowed even by some of the pro-oligarchy groups, such as the Kokumin Kyokai (Nationalist Association; 1892), was reconstituted as the Shimpoto (Progressive Party) in 1896 and consolidated its position as the second party. In common parlance the Liberal and Progressive parties were termed *minto* (popular parties), while groups of supporters of the oligarchic bureaucracy were referred to as *rito* (bureaucrats' parties). Neither of the popular parties had representation in the hereditary and appointive House of Peers, nor did they control local politics, for key local officials were appointed by the central government. Yet despite the popular parties' intransigent opposition to the antiparty policies of the oligarchs, the *minto* platforms reflected the interests of the rural elite and were no less conservative and nationalistic than the pronouncements of the oligarchs.

The Politics of Compromise

Rapprochement between parties and oligarchs was spurred in 1898 when Prime Minister Ito Hirobumi (1841—1909), who was a *genro*, dissolved the Diet due to opposition by the popular parties to his proposal for extra land taxes. The Liberal and Progressive parties merged to form the Kenseito (Constitutional Party), which won a majority in the Diet in the succeeding election. Ito resigned and invited Okuma and Itagaki to form a cabinet, Japan's first party cabinet, which was led by Okuma as prime minister and Itagaki as home minister. The alliance collapsed within months and the Progressive Party faction reorganized as the Kensei Honto (True Constitutional Party; 1898) and later as the Rikken Kokuminto (Constitutional Nationalist Party; 1910). However, in 1900 Ito formed the Rikken Seiyukai (Friends of Constitutional Government Party; commonly called Seiyukai), a coalition of former Jiyuto members and bureaucrats that won a majority in the Diet, marking the forthright entrance of oligarchs and bureaucrats into party politics on a basis of compromise with conservative factions of the popular parties. In 1913 General Katsura Taro (1847—1913), protege of the authoritarian oligarch Yamagata Aritomo (1838—1922), formed the Rikken Doshikai (Constitutional Association of Friends), absorbing the wealthier half of the Rikken Kokuminto; in 1916 it was reconstituted as the Kenseikai (Constitutional Association). From 1922 onward, rivalry between the Kenseikai and the Seiyukai, rather than between parties and oligarchs, became the dominant pattern.

With the increasing incidence of cabinets formed by parties during the first quarter of the 20th century, control of local assemblies by parties was achieved even more swiftly than in the Diet, and by 1910 some 90 percent of prefectural assemblymen were affiliated with one of the two major parties.

In the late 19th and early 20th centuries a number of proletarian parties appeared, but they evoked hostile reactions from the leaders of the major parties as well as the oligarchs, and many were banned soon after their formation by the invocation of such repressive laws as the Public Order and Police Law of 1900. Following the Bolshevik Revolution of 1917 and the emergence of labor unions, the Nihon Shakai Shugi Domei (Japan Socialist League) was established in 1920 and the Japan Communist Party (JCP; Nihon Kyosanto) in 1922. The chief threat to the major parties was not the proletarian parties, popular support of which was limited, but the military. The political power of the military was made clear in 1912 when the army minister Uehara Yusaku (1856—1933) resigned to protest the government's decision not to provide funds for two new army divisions. The army's refusal to name a successor to Uehara brought down the cabinet.

Ascendancy of Parties and the Military Takeover

The cabinet formed in 1918 by Hara Takashi (1856—1921), largely made up of members of the Seiyukai, was the first viable party cabinet, and from then until 1932, the premiership was almost always held by the leaders of major parties. Nevertheless, the selection of prime ministers and cabinets was not a democratic process; candidates for the premiership were nominated by the *genro* and their protégés and appointed by the emperor, while ministers, except for those of the army and navy, were chosen by prime ministers in consultation with imperial advisers and confirmed by the emperor.

The two major parties, the Kenseikai (reorganized in 1927 as the Rikken Minseito) and the Seiyukai, alternated in power until the assassination in 1932 of Inukai Tsuyoshi (1855—1932), Seiyukai president and prime minister. Although prime ministers throughout the period were nominally designated by Saionji Kimmochi (1849–1940), protégé of Ito Hirobumi, it was the influence of parties upon the formation of cabinets that distinguished this brief era of Taisho Democracy of early-20th century.

By the early 1930s there had emerged two legal noncommunist proletarian parties, which united in 1932 to form the Shakai Taishuto (Socialist Masses Party), a party that soon began to compromise step by step with the emergent forces of militarist authoritarianism. The JCP, which had been dissolved under government pressure in 1924, was reestablished underground in 1926 and remained active until about 1935, by which time arrests had decimated its membership.

The number of voters quadrupled with passage of the Universal Manhood Suffrage Law in 1925 and political campaigns became vastly more expensive. The industrial and financial combines Mitsui and Mitsubishi, the two largest *zaibatsu*, funded the Seiyukai and the Rikken Minseito, respectively, but both parties tapped additional sources, legal and illegal, and well-publicized malfeasance and corruption among politicians made it easier for the military to denounce party politicians. It was Inukai's death in 1932 at the hands of young naval officers that signaled the end of party cabinets. From that point until the end of World War II, there was a succession of "national unity" cabinets led by military men or their collaborators. In 1940 all political parties were absorbed by the Imperial Rule Assistance Association.

The Postwar Period

With the conclusion of hostilities in August 1945 efforts were made to resuscitate the major prewar parties, and by November all had reappeared, most under new names. The abolition of the military and the replacement of the House of Peers with an elected House of Councillors left the civil bureaucracy as the only major institutional rival of the parties, while the new Constitution of Japan made the National Diet the "highest organ of government" and provided for control of the cabinet by the Diet.

The Occupation Purge, which began in 1946, had a debilitating effect on the postwar conservative parties and also removed many local leaders from positions of influence, requiring all of the parties to rebuild their bases of local power. Revision of the election laws lowered the voting age, granted suffrage to women, and increased the number of members elected from constituencies. This encouraged the participation of independents and minor parties and provoked fierce competition among the major parties, leading to unstable cabinets and frequent stalemates until February 1949, when Yoshida Shigeru (1878–1967) of the Minshu Jiyuto (reorganized in 1950 as the Liberal Party) formed a stable cabinet that endured until October 1952. The land reforms of 1946 eliminated large landed estates and vested title in former tenants, removing an important stimulus to radicalism in rural areas and creating an electorate that became a dependable source of support for the conservatives. However, political corruption, particularly "money politics," was as common as before the war. Moreover, all parties remained ridden with the factionalism that had afflicted their forebears.

The most striking change in party membership was a dramatic increase from 1949, especially in the Minshu Jiyuto, of conservative members who were retired government bureaucrats. The entry of former senior bureaucrats into party politics became a permanent pattern, and while it testified to the new influence and prestige of the Diet, it also brought about an increasingly cozy relationship between the conservative parties and the upper levels of the administrative bureaucracy.

The 1955 Status Quo

Following the restoration of Japan's independence in 1952, division among the conservatives made it impossible for either the Liberal Party or the Nihon Minshuto (Japan Democratic Party; successor of the prewar Rikken Minseito) to form a stable majority in the Diet, while the Japan Socialist Party (JSP) had split in 1951 into parties of the Left and the Right. In 1955, however, the JSP reunited and a month later the conservatives merged to form the Liberal Democratic Party (LDP), thus giving birth to the "1955 status quo" (*gojugonen taisei*), with the LDP controlling both Houses, the JSP holding roughly half the number of LDP seats in each, and the LDP mounting a series of one-party cabinets. From then on, antagonism between the two parties became a dominant pattern in the Diet over almost all major political programs.

During the late 1950s the LDP took controversial stands in favor of the revision of the new constitution, the augmentation of police powers and the revision of the United States-Japan Security Treaty. When the last of these was settled in 1960 after considerable turmoil, the government turned to the problems of economic growth and foreign trade, and in these areas its policies were in general popular.

By the late 1960s, however, the 1955 status quo was showing strain. LDP popularity waned due to a series of political scandals and the party's failure to deal satisfactorily with social and economic issues, such as a housing shortage, environmental pollution, and rising land prices. With the JSP racked by factionalism, the power vacuum was filled by splinter groups, such as the Democratic Socialist Party (DSP; Minshu Shakaito), founded in 1960 by right-wing members of the JSP, and newcomers such as the Komeito (Clean Government Party), which, with the support of members of the religious organization Soka Gakkai, gained an increasing number of seats in the Diet in the 1960s. In 1967 the LDP failed for the first time since 1955 to receive a majority of the popular vote, and its share continued to decline, as did that of the JSP, until the late 1970s.

From the late 1960s the Komeito, the DSP, and the JCP gained increasing support among residents of cities, and they consistently controlled a third of all votes cast. The formation of a multiparty system was further spurred by the establishment of splinter parties: in 1976 critics of the LDP's "money politics" broke away to found the Shin Jiyu Kurabu (New Liberal Club), while in 1977 a group of right-wing members of the JSP founded the Shakai Shimin Rengo (now United Social Democratic Party). Continuing corruption and factionalism contributed to diminishing popular support of the LDP, and in the periods 1976-80 and 1983-86 the party failed to win a majority of seats in the House of Representatives, while the JSP found its share reduced to 20 percent in the 1970s and 1980s.

However, in the 1986 elections for the House of Representatives the LDP won 300 of the 511 seats, and in the wake of the election the dissident Shin Jiyu Kurabu returned to the fold. The LDP lost its majority in the House of Councillors in 1989, but in the 1990 elections it did well, retaining a solid majority in the House of Representatives. The JSP also gained a sizable number of new seats in this election; the losers were the other opposition parties such as the Komeito, JCP, and DSP.

The Downfall of the 1955 Status Quo

The LDP's repeated failures to carry out political reforms led to the breakaway of dissidents who formed the Shinseito (The New Life Party) and the Shinto Sakigake (The Harbinger Party) in 1993. This, in turn, paved the way for breaking the LDP's grip on the government. The LDP Cabinet under Prime Minister Miyazawa Kiichi (1919—) made an outright promise to institute reforms. Its failure to do so opened the way for a overwhelming defeat on a non-confidence vote in the Diet and dissolution, followed by a call for national elections in July 1993. The election resulted in a unprecedented defeat for the LDP and an equally unexpected setback for the JSP which found its seats reduced almost by half. The electoral defeats suffered by the two political parties marked the end of the 1955 status quo. After political maneuvering among the opposition parties, a coalition government was formed in August 1993 under Prime Minister Hosokawa Morihiro (1938—), the head of the Nihon Shinto (Japan New Party, established in 1992), with the Shinseito holding the key posts and the remaining posts going to the other seven coalition parties, including the JSP.

Prime minister and cabinet

(*shusho to naikaku*). The chief executive officer of the Japanese government and his cabinet. The cabinet system was adopted in Japan in 1885 and has continued without interruption until the present. There have, however, been a number of fundamental changes in the powers, functions, and composition of the cabinet, particularly when the prewar cabinet system under the Meiji Constitution is compared with the postwar cabinet system under the 1947 constitution. In the postwar system the constitution vests supreme executive authority in the cabinet, which is responsible to the legislature. In the prewar system the cabinet was not responsible to the legislature and the legislature had no power either to select a prime minister or dissolve a cabinet.

The Prewar Cabinet System

Following the Meiji Restoration (1868), a Grand Council of State (Dajokan) was established in 1868 as the supreme political authority which evolved into a central deliberative body consisting of three state ministers who had direct access to the emperor and seven councillors, or *sangi*. Heads of the various government ministries often served as *sangi* as well, so that by the end of 1881 real power was in the hands of a virtual oligarchy.

The change to the cabinet system in 1885 appears to have been motivated by the effort to strengthen the executive branch in the face of the projected establishment of an independent legislative branch. The prime minister and the various cabinet ministers were made responsible only to the emperor, not to the Diet. Moreover, upon the promulgation of the constitution in 1889, the oligarchs announced their intention to remain aloof from party politics by adhering to the principle of nonparty or "Transcendental" cabinets (*chozen naikaku*).

For the seven cabinets between 1885 and 1898 the prime ministership was rotated among the oligarchs. As the oligarchs retired from the day-to-day administration of cabinet affairs they assumed the role of elder statesmen (*genro*).

The prewar prime minister enjoyed extensive appointment powers, including the appointment of cabinet ministers and vice-ministers, judges, prosecutors, and prefectural governors. Nevertheless, the prime minister was not a strong chief executive but rather had to share the right to advise the throne with the *genro*, the officers of the imperial household, the privy councillors, and the military chiefs of staff.

Until the Taisho Political Crisis of 1912−1913, the oligarchs coordinated the decision-making process behind the scenes through the vehicle of the informal, extraconstitutional *genro* council and through their position on the Privy Council. Following World War I, this single

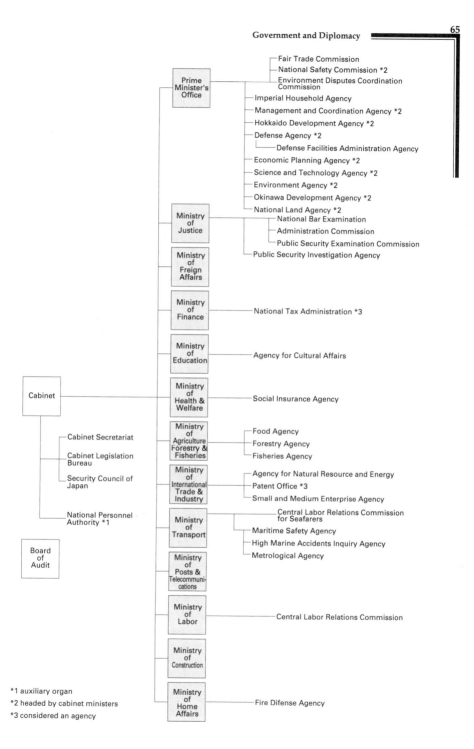

- Fair Trade Commission
- National Safety Commission *2
- Environment Disputes Coordination Commission
- Imperial Household Agency
- Management and Coordination Agency *2
- Hokkaido Development Agency *2
- Defense Agency *2
  - Defense Facilities Administration Agency
- Economic Planning Agency *2
- Science and Technology Agency *2
- Environment Agency *2
- Okinawa Development Agency *2
- National Land Agency *2

Prime Minister's Office

Ministry of Justice
- National Bar Examination
- Administration Commission
- Public Security Examination Commission
- Public Security Investigation Agency

Ministry of Freign Affairs

Ministry of Finance
- National Tax Administration *3

Ministry of Education
- Agency for Cultural Affairs

Ministry of Health & Welfare
- Social Insurance Agency

Ministry of Agriculture Forestry & Fisheries
- Food Agency
- Forestry Agency
- Fisheries Agency

Ministry of International Trade & Industry
- Agency for Natural Resource and Energy
- Patent Office *3
- Small and Medium Enterprise Agency

Ministry of Transport
- Central Labor Relations Commission for Seafarers
- Maritime Safety Agency
- High Marine Accidents Inquiry Agency
- Metrological Agency

Ministry of Posts & Telecommunications

Ministry of Labor
- Central Labor Relations Commission

Ministry of Construction

Ministry of Home Affairs
- Fire Difense Agency

Cabinet
- Cabinet Secretariat
- Cabinet Legislation Bureau
- Security Council of Japan
- National Personnel Authority *1

Board of Audit

*1 auxiliary organ
*2 headed by cabinet ministers
*3 considered an agency

dominant coordinating oligarchy was gradually replaced by a much larger and more diverse set of institutional elites, composed of the parties, the military, the bureaucracy, the peerage, and the court. Much of the political history of the 1918−1945 period can be viewed as a competition among these institutional elites for control of the government. From the mid-1930s the military dominated the cabinet until Japan's defeat in World War II.

Postwar Changes in the Cabinet System

The postwar constitution introduced two major kinds of change in the cabinet system. First, executive power was vested solely in the prime minister and his cabinet. All real executive authority was removed from the emperor, and the throne became a purely symbolic and ceremonial institution. The prime minister is now empowered to appoint and remove all cabinet members at his own discretion. Moreover, to ensure civilian control of the military, the Defense Agency has formally been made a subordinate part of the Prime Minister's Office.

The second major change was the clear establishment of cabinet responsibility to the elected representatives of the people. The prime minister is elected by the Diet, and either house of the Diet may adopt a resolution of impeachment against any individual cabinet member. Moreover, if the lower house passes a nonconfidence resolution, rejects a confidence resolution, or, in effect, fails to support any major cabinet bill, the cabinet must resign en masse within 10 days or dissolve the lower house, call an election, and resign following the opening of the new Diet. Finally, the constitution requires that the prime minister and the majority of all cabinet members be elected members of the Diet.

The Making of the Prime Minister and His Cabinet

The prime minister is selected by a majority vote in each House of the Diet and is formally appointed by the emperor. If the two Houses disagree on their selection or the upper house fails to act within 10 days after the lower house has voted, the choice of the lower house stands as the decision of the Diet. Since the Liberal Democratic Party (LDP) had maintained majority control of both houses of the Diet from its inception in 1955, the president of the LDP had routinely been installed as prime minister until the downfall of the 1955 Status Quo in 1993. New official cabinets come into being following the selection of a new prime minister and after each election of the House of Representatives. In practice, cabinet posts are reshuffled much more frequently, with virtually annual major reconstructions of the cabinet in which over half its personnel are changed. The reasons for this frequent turnover are based on factional politics. Continuity is maintained by the Conference of

Administrative Vice-Ministers, composed of the highest civil-service career officers in each ministry.

Cabinet Powers and Organizations

The prime minister and his cabinet have important judicial and legislative powers as well as executive responsibilities. In the judicial area they are empowered to select the chief justice and the other judges of the Supreme Court and to appoint lower-court judges from a list nominated by the Supreme Court. In the legislative area the cabinet determines the convocation of extraordinary sessions of the Diet, enacts cabinet orders to execute the provisions of the constitution and Diet laws, and, most important, prepares and submits bills to the Diet. The various cabinet staff offices and government ministries and agencies assist the cabinet in the exercise of this extensive concentration of powers.

As of 1994 the cabinet was composed of the prime minister and the heads of the 12 ministries: Justice; Foreign Affairs; Finance; Education; Health and Welfare; Agriculture, Forestry, and Fisheries; International Trade and Industry; Transport; Posts and Tele-communications; Labor; Construction; and Home Affairs (Jichisho). Another 8 ministers of state without portfolios head other important executive offices and agencies such as the Cabinet Secretariat, the Defense Agency, the Economic Planning Agency.

Local autonomy

(*chiho jichi*). The concept of local autonomy in government involves the right of local entities, such as prefectures, cities, towns, and villages, to decide and administer a range of public policies on their own initiative, with relative freedom from supervision ("corporate autonomy"), and the right of local citizens to participate in the formation of such policies ("civic autonomy"). Although the term *chiho jichi* had been widely used ever since the Meiji period (1868–1912), little local autonomy in either sense existed before 1945. The 1947 constitution contains a chapter on "local autonomy," implemented by the Local Autonomy Law (Chiho Jichi Ho) of the same year. In 1949 a successor to the Home Ministry, which had supported the prewar centralization, the Local Autonomy Agency (Chiho Jichi Cho), was created and became the Ministry of Home Affairs (Jichisho) in 1960. Education and police, decentralized under the Occupation, were recentralized to some extent thereafter. Many functions that could be considered local are governed by national laws. The administration of these laws is often delegated to governors and mayors as agents of the national government.

The types and standard rates of local taxes are determined by the Local Tax Law (Chihozei Ho). Local taxes account for about one third of total revenues, the rest being transfers of funds from the national government. The transfers often fall short of local requirements, and financial dependence and financial stringency limit local autonomy.

Local government

(*chiho seiji*). The general trend in local government since the Meiji Restoration (1868) has been for the expansion of local decision-making authority in areas of local concern and the fuller participation of citizens in the local process except for an interlude during the World War II years.

Establishment of the Prefectural System

Following the Meiji Restoration, the government began replacing the approximately 260 domains (*han*) and local administrative organs of the *bakuhan* (shogunate and domain) system with a centralized administrative structure consisting primarily of prefectures (*ken*) and urban prefectures (*fu*). In 1871 the government instituted a nationwide administrative system consisting of 72 prefectures with prefectural governors appointed by the central government. Local administration within prefectures was provided by large and small census districts. The Home Ministry, created in 1873, had the authority to sanction or disapprove of the actions of prefectural governors and became the central administrative element in state control of local government.

In 1878, legislation known as the Three New Laws was promulgated to unify local administrative organization and governance. The first law called for the institution of districts (*gun*) in rural areas and wards (*ku*) in populous urban areas as units of local administration. Prefectural governors appointed and supervised the chief officers of *gun* and *ku*, while citizens selected ruling chiefs on a more local level, such as town or village. The second law established representative assemblies in all prefectures, but reserved for the governors the power to originate bills. Less than 5 percent of the population was enfranchised to vote in these elections. Nevertheless, prefectural assemblies marked the establishment of elective representative institutions in Japanese government. The third law established rules for the collection of taxes at the prefectural and subprefectural levels. Amalgamations reduced the number of prefectures to 47 (3 *fu*, 43 *ken*, and 1 administrative province or *do*) by 1888, further promoting uniformity in subnational governance.

In 1888 the Local Autonomy System superseded the first of the Three New Laws and established a Municipal Code and Town and

Village Code declaring that these units of local government should administer their own affairs "subject to the supreme control of the central government." The codes provided for the establishment of a mayorship and elected assemblies and specified that male citizens who met certain criteria of age, family, and taxpaying status could vote or hold elective office. In 1890 the Prefectural Code and District Code made further revisions to the structure of local government. Prefectural councils were created to handle business delegated to them by the prefectural assemblies. The District Code made the district (*gun*) a unit of local government with a chief, an elected district assembly, and a district council.

Districts were abolished as local government entities in 1923 and as state administrative units in 1926. Universal male suffrage, adopted in 1925, expanded citizen participation in local government. In 1929 local self-government powers were strengthened when the home minister lost the authority to make peremptory cuts in prefectural budgets and local and prefectural assemblies were given more legislative authority.

Wartime Centralization of Government Authority

Following the outbreak of conflict with China in 1937, the Home Ministry ordered in 1940 that community councils (*chonaikai*) be organized in cities, towns, and villages. Neighborhood associations (*tonarigumi*) were made responsible for the policing and welfare of their areas. The last modification in the local government system before the end of World War II came in July 1943 when the government created nine Regional Administrative Councils to coordinate the action of local bodies and further strengthen central authority.

Postwar Local Government System

Decentralization of governmental authority and the strengthening of local government emerged early in the Allied Occupation. The new system of local government was intended to break up concentrated bureaucratic power revolving around Home Ministry-appointed governors, increase citizen participation and control, assure fairness in the conduct of local affairs, and expand the scope of autonomous local jurisdiction. The Home Ministry was eliminated and in December 1947 educational and police affairs were placed largely in local hands. The new Constitution of Japan (1947) in essence guaranteed the decentralization of political authority by confirming the "principle of local autonomy" and by establishing such basic features of the new system as the separation of local from national administration and the direct popular election of prefectural governors and of mayors, as well as local assemblies. The latter provision gave voters the potential for controlling the executive authority, thereby providing incentives for governors and mayors to address the concerns of the local electorate. Further steps were sought to deconcentrate authority at the local level by creating prefectural and municipal commissions in charge of public safety, election management, and inspection of local administration. However, there was a strong bureaucratic resistance to administrative and financial decentralization and skepticism on the part of conservative governments concerning the administrative capacity of local authorities.

Post-Occupation Evolution

The legacy of local governmental reforms under the Allied Occupation was a mixed system combining aspects of prewar centralized administration with postwar local autonomy, an institutional separation between levels of government, and an intensified need for local governmental responsiveness to popular constituencies. During the first postwar decade, controversy centered on the relative merits of the Occupation reforms and on the efforts of central government bureaucracies and conservative parties to recentralize administrative authority. Recentralization of the police and educational systems, completed by 1956, stirred strong opposition from socialists, unionists, and intellectuals fearful of a reversion to prewar authoritarianism. On the other hand, central government elites encouraged amalgamations of municipalities, upgraded the overall quality of public administration, and facilitated the implementation of economic plans and national functions delegated to local authorities.

Beginning in the mid-1950s, local governments became participants in the national drive for economic growth. National authorities created a variety of national and regional development banks to promote public financing and investment in new industrial sites, water resources, and industrial infrastructure. Local authorities joined this effort by trying to attract industry with ordinances that provided for corporate tax breaks and other incentives for industrial development. Furthermore, new national laws for regional development were established in the early 1960s. In response, local authorities competed with each other to receive national government designation as target areas for development, thereby furthering the nationwide spread of the petrochemical, steel, machinery, and other heavy and chemical industries.

By the late 1960s and early 1970s, many local governments began reordering their priorities. Economic growth encouraged a rapid urbanization of the population and urban land prices spiraled, making the provision of an adequate social infrastructure difficult. At the same time, new urban problems such as pollution-related diseases, traffic congestion, and uncontrolled urban sprawl proliferated.

The intensity of such problems resulted in substantial grass-roots protests and efforts by citizens to seek ameliorative policies from local government. Opposition representation in assemblies increased and coalitions of opposition parties formed around new urban issues succeeded in electing reformist local heads in major areas. Under these circumstances, local authorities began to pioneer new forms of communication with residents, pollution-control measures, and social welfare programs. As a result, local priorities diverged significantly from national ones and contributed to the eventual shift in national priorities from unrestricted economic growth to establishing a higher quality of life.

Moreover, government reform efforts of the late 1970s and early 1980s led to an increased reliance on local authorities for the implementation of national social and environmental programs. There emerged, in effect, a broad recognition that local governments had matured in their administrative competence, had a unique role in setting local priorities and coordinating public programs, and were necessary partners of the national government in creating livable communities .

Judicial system

(*shiho seido*). The unified national structure of courts for the administration of justice. The 1947 constitution (art. 76) provides that "the whole judicial power is vested in a Supreme Court and in such inferior courts as are established by law." All courts on all levels are parts of a single system under the sole and complete administration of the Supreme Court. A jury system does not exist.

The structure of the judicial system is as follows: the Supreme Court (Saiko Saibansho); 8 high courts (*koto saibansho*) in the eight principal geographical subdivisions of the country; 50 district courts (*chiho saibansho*) in the principal administrative units; 50 family courts (*katei saibansho*); and 452 summary courts (*kan'i saibansho*) located throughout the country. The Diet as the sole law-making organ can change the organization of the courts by passing the necessary legislation, but the administration of the court system remains constitutionally vested in the Supreme Court.

The Supreme Court is headed by the chief justice, who is appointed by the emperor after designation by the cabinet. The other 14 justices are appointed by the cabinet. The court is organized into a grand bench consisting of all 15 justices and three petty benches of 5 justices each. All cases before the Supreme Court are appeals; it possesses origi-

The Supreme Court Building, Chiyoda Ward, Tokyo.

nal jurisdiction over no cases. The constitution (art. 81) also provides that the Supreme Court is the court of last resort "with power to determine the constitutionality of any law, order, regulation or official act."

The high courts are essentially appellate courts. They are courts of first instance for the crimes of insurrection, preparation for or plotting of insurrection, and of assistance in the acts enumerated.

District courts have original jurisdiction over most cases with the exception of offenses carrying minor punishment and a few others reserved for other courts. In addition, they are courts of appeal for actions taken by the summary courts. Family courts came into existence in 1949. They have jurisdiction over such matters as juvenile crime (the age of majority being 20), problems of minors, divorce, and disputes over family property. Summary courts have jurisdiction over minor cases involving less than ¥900,000 in claims or fines or offenses carrying lighter punishments.

International Relations

International relations, history of

(*kokusai kankei shi*). Japan's relations with foreign nations, following abandonment of the shogunal policy of national seclusion in 1854, can be divided into the period before and the period after the close of World War II. The earlier period includes the entrance of Japan into the community of nations, its participation as an equal in international affairs, and the creation and collapse of the Greater East Asia Coprosperity Sphere. The later period embraces the Allied Occupation (1945−1952), the San Francisco Peace Treaty (1951), admission to the United Nations (1956), and the gradual reestablishment of an independent diplomatic policy.

The Opening of Japan and the "Unequal Treaties"

The arrival in Japan of Commodore Matthew Perry and his "black ships" (*kurofune*) in 1853 led to the signing by representatives of the United States and the Tokugawa shogunate of the Kanagawa Treaty of 1854, which effected the opening of Japan. Formal diplomatic relations were soon established with the United Kingdom, Russia, the Netherlands, and other Western countries. The various friendship and commercial treaties that Japan concluded with these countries provided for broad grants of extraterritoriality and restrictions on Japan's right to levy customs duties and were the means by which Japan was forcibly incorporated into a system of international relations developed by the Western powers. Following the formation of the Meiji government in 1868, Japan embarked on a program of forthright Westernization, with the goal of establishing Japan as a great power. Revision of the Unequal Treaties became a crucial concern, and the issue was raised by a succession of foreign ministers, but the nations of the West were disinclined to relinquish their vested privileges. It was not until the signing of the Anglo-Japanese Commercial Treaty of 1894 that the extraterritorial rights of a foreign power were first abolished. Japan did not fully recover autonomous customs rights or attain equal status with Western nations until 1911.

Expansion on the Asian Mainland

In 1876 Japan compelled Korea to sign the Treaty of Kanagawa, gaining for itself access to three Korean ports, extraterritorial rights, and full exemption from customs duties. Japan thus succeeded in concluding an unequal treaty with Korea ahead of the Western powers. China, however, held considerable influence over Korean diplomatic and domestic affairs, and rivalry with Japan was inevitable. After a series of political coups inside Korea in 1884, Japan and China agreed to withdraw their troops from Korea; however, in the spring of 1894 the Tonghak Rebellion broke out, and the Korean government called on the Chinese for military assistance. Japan too sent an expeditionary force, which clashed with the Chinese in July 1894, leading to the Sino-Japanese War of 1894—1895. The Treaty of Shimonoseki (1895), which ended hostilities, provided for the cession by China of Taiwan and the Pescadores. Reparation money received from China played a significant role in the industrialization of Japan, while the opening of numerous Chinese ports and cities to Japanese commerce and industry enabled entrance into the Chinese domestic market. The Tripartite Intervention by Russia, Germany, and France, however, forced Japan to relinquish the Liaodong Peninsula, which it had also obtained from China.

Following the severance of China's interest in Korea, a new rivalry developed between Russia and Japan. After 1900, Russia now stationed troops in Manchuria, which Japan considered a grave threat to its position on the Korean peninsula. It was under these circumstances that Japan signed with Britain the Anglo-Japanese Alliance (1902), the first military treaty concluded by Japan with a foreign country. Renewed in 1905 and 1911, for 20 years it remained the pillar of Japanese foreign policy.

On 6 February 1904 Japan broke off diplomatic relations with Russia over the issues of China and Korea and on 10 February declared war (Russo-Japanese War of 1904—1905). The terms of the Treaty of Portsmouth (1905), which ended hostilities, gave to Japan the southern half of Sakhalin and the Russian lease concessions in China, including the Liaodong Peninsula; the latter provided a foothold for eventual

Japanese political domination of southern Manchuria. Russia also agreed not to intervene in Korean affairs, and in 1910 Korea became a Japanese colony.

In a series of agreements with Russia in 1907, 1910, and 1912, Japan established a sphere of influence in southern Manchuria and the eastern part of Inner Mongolia. By means of South Manchuria Railway, Japan strengthened its position in the area. This activity, however, was in conflict with the Open Door Policy of the United States, which was based on the principle of equal access to Chinese markets, and led to a dispute between Japan and the United States over the issues of railway rights and interests in Manchuria. Friction was exacerbated by restrictions placed by the United States on immigration from Japan, as well as by rivalry between the US and Japanese navies in the Pacific Ocean.

World War I and Its Aftermath

With the attention of the Western powers turned to Europe, Japan moved to strengthen its position in Asia. In the Twenty-one Demands presented to China in 1915, Japan sought formal recognition of its occupation of German holdings on the Shandong Peninsula, extension of tenure for its leaseholds in China, and appointment by the Chinese government of Japanese as political, financial, and military advisers.

Following World War I, Japan was one of the five victorious nations at the Paris Peace Conference in 1919; it received confirmation of its occupation of the Shandong Peninsula and the mandate for the Pacific Islands formerly held by Germany. However, because of Japan's strong pressure on China, confrontation between Japan and China increased. Following the Bolshevik Revolution in Russia in November 1917, Japan joined the Allied Siberian Intervention (1918—1922). By November 1918 more than 70,000 Japanese troops were entrenched in northern Manchuria and the Maritime Province. The forces of the United States, the United Kingdom, and France completed their withdrawal by April of 1920, but Japan, which had hoped to establish a sphere of influence in eastern Siberia, did not follow suit until October 1922.

At the Washington Conference of 1921—1922 a plan for international cooperation in East Asia, the so-called Washington System, was formulated.Japan agreed to remove its military forces from the Shandong Peninsula, and during the 1920s, while also working to develop its established interests, Japan made an effort not to disturb the political equilibrium in Asia. However, when the Chinese Nationalist Party (Guomindang) extended its sphere of activity to Manchuria and Inner Mongolia, Japan replied with extreme measures such as the assassination of Zhang Zuolin.

Growing Japanese Military Activity in China

The Manchurian Incident of September 1931 and the establishment of the Japanese-controlled puppet state Manchukuo in 1932 brought the Japan-United States confrontation in Asia close to the flash point. Japan ignored the Nine-Power Treaty, which it had signed at the Washington Conference in 1922. The United States, which opposed all of Japan's activities in Manchuria, responded with the Stimson Doctrine.

The Japanese challenge to the Washington System was denounced by a large majority of the member countries of the League of Nations. Japan responded by leaving the League of Nations in March 1933. Japan's economy suffered due to its estrangement from Britain and the United States, and to compensate for its losses Japan extended its influence from Manchuria into northern China. The military dominance of Japan over the entire area of Manchuria created tension with the Soviet Union and led to the signing of the Anti-Comintern Pact in 1936 by Germany and Japan. Triggered by the Marco Polo Bridge Incident of July 1937, Japan's expansion into northern China escalated into general armed conflict. As the scope of military activity in China increased, the United States reacted by declaring an embargo against Japan.

World War II

The 1938 declaration of the Toa Shinchitsujo (New Order in East Asia), which encompassed China, Manchukuo, and Japan, and the announcement in August 1940 of the Greater East Asia Coprosperity Sphere, which included Southeast Asia as well, gave notice of Japan's intention to create a new non-Western political order throughout Asia. It was in the context of the "New Order" that the Japanese-backed Reorganized National Government of the Republic of China was established in 1940.

The sweeping victories of Germany, following the outbreak of World War II in September 1939, convinced Japan of the value of an alliance, and in September 1940 it negotiated the Tripartite Pact with Germany and Italy. In the same month, Japan invaded the northern part of French Indochina.

The collapse of Japan-United States relations appeared imminent; negotiations in Washington proved fruitless. The Soviet-Japanese Neutrality Pact, concluded in April 1941, provided assurance against an attack from the north, and Japan advanced into the southern part of French Indochina. In retaliation the United States froze Japanese assets and banned oil exports to Japan. On 26 November the US secretary of state, Cordell Hull, replied with the Hull Note, which called for radical changes in Japan's Asia policy. This was construed by Japan as an unacceptable ultimatum that left it with no alternative but war.

Overwhelming victories in the Pacific theater in the initial stages of World War II opened the way for Japanese occupation and military administration of French Indochina, the Philippines, the Dutch East Indies, Malaya, and Burma. However, defeat in the naval battle at Midway in June 1942 put Japan on the defensive, and imperial Japan was on the verge of collapse.

Allied Occupation and Dependence on US Military Strength

Japan conceded defeat on 15 August 1945 and formally surrendered to the Allied powers on 2 September. The right of Japanese to rule their nation was made subject to the authority of the supreme commander for the Allied powers (SCAP). As supreme commander, Douglas MacArthur presided over General Headquarters (GHQ) and set about implementing plans for the demilitarization and democratization of Japan.

Following the victory of the communists in China in 1949 and the establishment of the People's Republic of China (PRC), and the outbreak of the Korean War in 1950, the United States moved to restore Japan's independence. In September 1951 Japan and the Allied powers (excluding the Soviet Union, China, India, and Burma) signed the San Francisco Peace Treaty, which became effective in April 1952, enabling Japan to reenter the community of independent nations. Prohibited by the new Constitution of Japan from possessing land, sea, or air military forces, Japan was faced with the problem of national security. The issue was partially resolved when, at the signing of the peace treaty, it concluded the first of the United States-Japan security treaties, bringing Japan under the protective umbrella of the US military. Bases used by the army of occupation remained in the hands of US forces, and during the Korean War the Japanese economy was stimulated by massive US military procurements. With US backing, Japan was accepted in 1955 as a member of the General Agreement on Tariff and Trade (GATT) and in 1956 as a member of the United Nations. At the end of the 1950s, Japan announced its intention to adhere to "three principles" in the determination of its foreign policy: membership in the Asian community, diplomacy centered on the United Nations, and maintenance of Japan's position in the free world. Throughout the 1960s, however, Japan's foreign policy was strongly influenced by that of the United States. Opponents of this relationship were particularly vocal in 1960, when the United States-Japan Security Treaty was revised, and again following the outbreak of the Vietnam War.

Emergence of Japan as an Economic Power

In the postwar era Japan's expanding foreign trade has played an increasingly influential role in the formation of its diplomacy. In the latter part of the 1960s Japan's economy reached a level competitive with those of the United States and the European Community (EC). Friction over trade issues caused Japan-United States relations to enter a new phase. In the midst of a textile dispute between the two countries in 1969 — 1971, President Richard Nixon announced in July 1971, without prior consultation with Japan, that he would visit Beijing to negotiate the establishment of diplomatic relations with China. Out of deference to US anticommunist policy and despite domestic agitation for the normalization of relations with the People's Republic of China, Japan had maintained close ties with the Republic of China on Taiwan, and this radical shift in policy was construed as a shock. On the heels of this "shock" came the announcement by President Nixon, again without consultation, of his New Economic Policy, which resulted in a major appreciation of the yen and the unsettling of Japan's foreign trade.

In the late 1970s friction with the United States, which continued to be Japan's chief trade partner, again grew heated due to several factors: the trade balance was overwhelmingly in favor of Japan; increasing imports of Japanese steel and electronic products had grave consequences for corresponding US industries; and the United States criticized Japan for not opening domestic markets to US goods. Economic friction with the United States persisted through the 1980s, and the criticism was voiced in the US Congress that Japanese trade practices were "unfair".

A similar trade dispute developed between Japan and the nations of Western Europe. Trade imbalances arising from the enormous export volumes of Japanese steel, electronic products, ships, and automobiles caused friction, which intensified in the 1980s and was stimulating the formation of a new protectionism and of new economic blocs in the early 1990s.

Relation with the Soviet Union and China

The conclusion of the first United States-Japan Security Treaty in 1952 inevitably brought Japan into confrontation with the Soviet Union and China. In 1955, during the post-Stalin-era thaw in the cold war, the Soviet Union initiated negotiations on the restoration of normal relations with Japan. However, the talks were suspended in mid-1956 due to a dispute over a number of islands off the coast of Hokkaido that had come under Soviet dominion at the close of World War II and that Japan demanded be returned. Afterward it was decided that an interim agreement terminating the state of war between the two nations would be put into effect, while negotiations continued on a peace treaty. The Soviet-Japanese Joint Declaration to this effect was signed in October

1956, and diplomatic relations were resumed.

In the 1980s, following the emergence in the Soviet Union of Mikhail Gorbachev, international tensions were reduced, bringing an end to the cold war that had dominated world politics for more than 40 years. The state visit to Japan by President Gorbachev in April of 1991—the first ever by a Soviet leader—contributed to the amelioration of Soviet-Japanese relations. However, after many twists and turns such as the dissolution of the Soviet Union and Boris Yeltsin's succession to the Presidency, the issue of the Northern Territories has still to be resolved and there is no prospect for the early conclusion of a peace treaty with Russia.

When the San Francisco Peace Treaty was implemented in April 1952, Japan established diplomatic relations with the Nationalist government on Taiwan, which it recognized as the official government of China. Until 1972 contact with the People's Republic of China was maintained on a largely nongovernmental basis, and only limited and intermittent trade was conducted.

In the 1970s dissension within the communist bloc began to grow and the eruption of armed conflict between China and the Soviet Union in 1969 was a factor in the decision of the United States to negotiate with China for the establishment of diplomatic relations. The China-United States rapprochement paved the way for the issuance of a joint communiqué in September 1972 establishing formal diplomatic relations between Japan and the People's Republic of China (of which Japan recognized Taiwan to be a territory) and the signing in 1978 of the China-Japan Peace and Friendship Treaty.

Relations with Korea

In 1948 the Korean peninsula was divided at the 38th parallel between the Democratic People's Republic of Korea (North Korea) and the Republic of Korea (South Korea), with which Japan established diplomatic relations. This effort, however, was fraught with difficulties due to the deep resentment felt by Koreans toward the nation that had colonized it. The sentiment culminated in the anti-Japanese policies of the first President Syngman Rhee. Following the assumption of power by the government of Pak Chŏng-hŭi, negotiations were resumed and resulted in the signing of the Korea-Japan Treaty of 1965, in which Japan recognized South Korea as the only lawful government on the Korean peninsula. Contacts with North Korea have been largely unofficial, but in 1990 negotiations were initiated to normalize relations.

Relations with Southeast Asia and the Pacific Basin

Japan's postwar relations with Southeast Asia began with negotiations concerning war reparations. The first country with which

Japan reached an agreement was Burma, followed by the Philippines, Indonesia, and the Republic of Vietnam, all between 1954 and 1959. In the 1960s Japan established close economic relations with many countries in the region, and since then, attaching importance to a special relationship with these nations, Japan has placed particular emphasis on foreign aid. In 1967 Thailand, Malaysia, Singapore, Indonesia, and the Philippines organized the Association of Southeast Asian Nations (ASEAN) to increase economic cooperation and their industrial development was accelerated by Japanese capital funding and technology.

With the ASEAN countries, Japan, and a number of other nations in the East Asia-western Pacific area, the NIEs (newly industrializing economies) have become the most dynamic regional influence upon the world's economy. As providers of raw materials, Australia, Canada, New Zealand, and Mexico have become increasingly important to Japan and the other industrialized nations of the region, and growing economic interdependence has lent itself to the idea of a "Pacific Basin Economic Sphere". In November 1989 government representatives of Canada, the United States, New Zealand, Australia, South Korea, Japan, and the six ASEAN nations (Brunei joined in 1984) met for their first conference, at which they established principles for economic cooperation. Japan considers the advancement of regional economic stability and expansion of the international system of free trade to be essential to its well-being.

Japan and the Middle East

Japan is almost totally dependent on the import of oil to meet its needs. In the years since the oil crisis of 1973, Japan has established strong economic relations with the countries of the Middle East, not only in regard to the import of oil but also the export of refining plants and other industrial goods. During this period Japan chose to support the Arab nations vis-a-vis Israel, but in the wake of the Persian Gulf War of 1990−1991 it is likely that Japan's foreign policy will assume a broader view.

Economic Assistance to Developing Nations

Total direct government economic assistance to developing nations provided by Japan had steadily increased to US $9.2 billion by 1990, exceeding that of all other economically advanced nations. Nevertheless, because in that year less than 50 percent of Japanese aid— as opposed to 98.1 percent of British foreign aid and 92.6 percent of US aid—was in the form of outright grants, critics have argued that its effectiveness was severely circumscribed. In step with government aid, private investment by Japanese in developing countries is also increasing, and the scope of Japanese technological cooperation with the developing nations is also expanding.

International cultural exchange

(*kokusai bunka koryu*). Between the opening of Japan to foreign contact in the late 19th century and World War I, Japan stressed the importation of Western culture rather than the introduction abroad of its own culture. Behind this effort was the intention of creating a modern state based on the Western model. Following World War I, the importance of promoting international understanding of Japan through cultural exchange was recognized, and in 1934 the Kokusai Bunka Shinkokai (KBS; the Society for International Cultural Relations) was established.

Following World War II, rapid economic growth and increased visibility of Japan in the international community, however, prompted greater interest in Japanese culture and society among countries overseas. With the aim of conducting Japan's international cultural relations on a more systematic basis, the Japanese government created a new cultural exchange organization, the Kokusai Koryu Kikin (Japan Foundation), in 1972.

Japan's international cultural exchange activities are handled mainly by the Cultural Affairs Department of the Ministry of Foreign Affairs, the Science and International Affairs Bureau of the Ministry of Education, and two public corporations attached to these ministries: the Japan Foundation and the Japan Society for the Promotion of Science. Among the programs administered by these governmental and semi-governmental agencies are (1) educational exchange, including the exchange of students, teachers, and trainees; (2) academic exchange, including the exchange of scholars and researchers, support of Japanese studies, and promotion of Japanese language teaching abroad; (3) artistic exchange, including the exchange of artists and artworks and the sponsorship of visual- and performing-arts programs; (4) cultural materials exchange, including the exchange of books, films, and radio and television programs; and (5) multilateral cultural exchange, including cooperation with UNESCO, the Southeast Asian Ministers of Education Organization, and other international cultural exchange organizations.

There are also some 500 private organizations and foundations in Japan today that are engaged in the promotion of international cultural exchange. They include such organizations as the International House of Japan, the Japan Association of International Education, the Japan Center for International Exchange, the Commemorative Association for the Japan World Exposition, the Hoso Bunka

Foundation, the Toyota Foundation, and the Yoshida International Education Foundation.

Japan Foundation, the

(Kokusai Koryu Kikin). In 1972, the Japan Foundation was established as a special corporation under the jurisdiction of the Ministry of Foreign Affairs, and since that time it has served as the pivot point for Japan's international cultural exchange. Throughout its history, it has continued to work toward truly global international cultural exchange through everything from the development of all types of bilateral exchange between Japan and other nations to the promotion of exchange between third nations. Headquaters are in Tokyo.

Japanese-Language Teaching

Cooperation in overseas Japanese-language education has been one of the major pillars of the activities of the Japan Foundation since its founding. A broad-ranging response has been made to the requests from local overseas educational institutions including the dispatch of specialists to Japanese-language education institutions in numerous foreign countries; the granting of aid for the salaries for local overseas instructors; and the conducting of proficiency tests for people whose native language is not Japanese. Also in areas such as Bangkok, Jakarta, and Sydney, where demand is high, overseas Japanese-language centers have been established to promote the creation of a comprehensive overseas Japanese-language education network and to provide daily-life support to on-site instructors.

The Japan Foundation Japanese Language Institute

The Japan Foundation Japanese Language Institute was opened at Urawa in Saitama Prefecture in 1989 as a subsidiary organ of the Japan Foundation responsible for providing comprehensive support and cooperation for overseas Japanese-language training. At this Institute, training programs are given for overseas Japanese-language instructors and diplomats from Asia and the Pacific area. The Institute also donates Japanese-language teaching materials appropriate to the conditions of the country of their destination; develops language teaching materials and teaching methods; carries out surveys on the present conditions in overseas Japanese-language education; and promotes information exchange.

Introducing Japanese Culture and Arts

One of the most important activities is the broad-scale introduction overseas of all fields of art, from classical and traditional to contemporary. This includes such Japanese formative arts as painting, sculpture, and video art; stage arts such as dance, music, and drama; such visual arts as feature films; and life-culture arts including flower arranging, tea ceremony, *origami*, kites and fireworks. Also, in recent years, there has been an increase in the number of large-scale events held in order to provide comprehensive introductions to Japanese culture.

The Center for Global Partnership

The Center for Global Partnership (CGP) was established in April 1991 in order to administer a ¥50 billion fund for the purpose of deepening and broadening dialogue between the Japanese and American people in various fields.

The major work of CGP will be promote intellectual exchange for global partnership through joint research projects and dialogues on such issues as the environment, the north-south problems and other problems held in common, and to develop better understanding through regional and grass-roots level activities.

Emigration and immigration control

(*shutsunyukoku kanri*). Immigration into and emigration from Japan are both regulated by the Immigration Control Order (Shutsunyukoku Kanri Rei) of 1951 (originally a government order, but a law after 1952). In regard to foreigners' entry into Japan, it states that no alien shall enter Japan without a valid passport or crewman's pocket ledger (art. 3). The Ministry of Justice grants visas, often renewable, of no more than three years' duration; only those in special categories such as diplomats and government officials may receive longer visas. Permanent residence is rarely granted. Entry is denied to aliens judged unsuitable by the authorities, and certain undesirable aliens may be deported. All Japanese nationals may emigrate from Japan to any other country except North Korea. Japanese nationals with a known police record have difficulty obtaining a passport.

United Nations and Japan

(Kokusai Rengo *to* Nihon). Japan was admitted to the United Nations on 18 December 1956, and its foreign policy has since then included "the centrality of the United Nations" as one of its basic guidelines. Japan has established a UN bureau at the Ministry of Foreign Affairs and a permanent mission to the UN headquarters, as well as a permanent delegation to the United Nations' European subheadquarters in Geneva, Switzerland. Since 1958 Japan has been elected to the UN Security

Council as a nonpermanent (two-year-term) member six times and since 1960 has been a regular member of the Economic and Social Council. Tokyo has been the base of the network of research facilities known as the UN University since its founding in 1974, and in 1991 there were 11 other UN organizations operating in Japan, including the United Nations Information Center, the United Nations Children's Fund (UNICEF) Office in Japan, the Japan branch office of the United Nations High Commissioner for Refugees (UNHCR), and the United Nations Development Program (UNDP) Tokyo Liaison Office. The nongovernmental organizations registered with the United Nations in Japan include the Japan Red Cross Society, the United Nations Association of Japan, and the National Federation of UNESCO Associations in Japan. In 1992 Japan was the second largest payer of UN operating expenses, contributing over 12 percent of total expenses.

Despite the increasing importance of Japan's role as a member of the United Nations, until 1992 it had not sent troops to participate in UN peacekeeping activities because of its renunciation of arms as embodied in Article 9 of the Japanese Constitution. That Japan's contribution was limited to an economic one met with criticism from countries overseas during the Persian Gulf War of 1990−1991. In 1990 and again in 1991 the ruling Liberal Democratic Party proposed legislation in the Diet that would enable Self Defense Forces troops to participate in UN peacekeeping activities. But China and South Korea expressed concern, and the Japan Socialist Party argued that the legislation was unconstitutional. Nevertheless, in June 1992 the Diet passed the Law on Cooperation in United Nations Peacekeeping Operations, and, after a formal request from the United Nations, Japanese troops were sent to Cambodia in October of that year.

Territorial waters

(*ryokai*). Japan's first official declaration concerning territorial waters came in 1870, when the Franco-Prussian War broke out in Europe and the Japanese government issued a proclamation of neutrality stipulating that "the contending parties are not permitted to engage in hostilities in Japanese harbors or inland waters, or within a distance of 3 nautical miles (1 nautical mile 1.85 km or 1.15 mi) from land at any place, such being the distance to which a cannonball can be fired." After that, Japan continued to adhere to the 3-mile limit not only for its own territorial waters but also as a rule of international law that should be applied throughout the world.

However the Law on Territorial Waters (Ryokai Ho) enacted in

1977 provides for a limit of 12 nautical miles, except for the Soya Strait, the Tsugaru Strait, the eastern channel of the Tsushima Strait, the western channel of the Tsushima Strait, and the Osumi Strait, for which the 3-mile limit remains in effect pending the outcome of the Third United Nations Conference on the Law of the Sea.

Territory of Japan

(*ryodo*). The territory of a state in international law comprises the land, the territorial waters, and the territorial airspace to which the sovereignty of the state extends.

In the land area of Japan bordering Russia there have been territorial disputes concerning the Kuril Islands and Sakhalin. These have been the subject of several treaties, most notably the Sakhalin-Kuril Islands Exchange Treaty of 1875, the 1905 Treaty of Portsmouth, and the San Francisco Peace Treaty of 1951, by which Japan renounced claim to the Kuril Islands and Sakhalin. By the San Francisco Peace Treaty Japan also renounced claim to Korea, which it had attached in 1910, and to Formosa (Taiwan) and the Pescadores, acquired from China in 1895.

Japan acquired the Ryukyu Islands when the lord of the Satsuma domain forced the ruler of the Ryukyus to swear allegiance in 1609. The Ryukyus became Okinawa Prefecture in 1879. The Ogasawara Islands (Bonin Islands) were put formally under the administration of Japan in 1875. Other islands were annexed to the territory of Japan in the late 19th and early 20th centuries, including Minami Torishima (Marcus Island), the Volcano Islands (Kazan Retto), the Senkaku Islands, the Daito Islands, and Takeshima.

There is ongoing dispute over the Northern Territories, which comprise the islands of Kunashiri, Etorofu, Shikotan, and the Habomai Islands, occupied by the Soviet Union at the end of World War II and, as of 1994, still occupied by the Russian Federation; Takeshima, occupied by the Republic of Korea; and the Senkaku Islands, claimed by the People's Republic of China and Taiwan.

Northern Territories issue

(Hoppo Ryodo *mondai*). Dispute concerning Japan's Northern Territories, which consist of Kunashiri, Etorofu, Shikotan, and the Habomai islands, occupied by the Soviet Union since 1945 and still occupied by the Russian Federation in 1994. The Japanese government maintains that the Russian occupation is illegal and demands the return of these islands.

After Japan's defeat in World War II, it signed the San Francisco Peace Treaty with 48 Allied nations (but not the Soviet Union) in September 1951. In the treaty Japan renounced all rights and title to the Kuril Islands, but the text did not stipulate which islands made up the Kuril chain nor which government was to exercise sovereignty over them.

Asserting that Kunashiri, Etorofu, Shikotan, and the Habomai Islands are not included in the term "Kuril Islands" as used in the San Francisco treaty and that they have historically constituted an integral part of the territory of Japan, the Japanese government sought their return. The Soviet Union refused, contending that the territorial issue had already been resolved. Then during Soviet president Mikhail Gorbachev's visit to Tokyo in 1991, both sides confirmed in a joint communique that final resolution of the issue would be carried out as a part of a future peace treaty between the two countries. However, the Soviet Union was dissolved at the end of that year.

In October 1993, President Boris Yeltsin, the successor to Mikhail Gorbachev, visited Tokyo for two days and met Prime Minister Hosokawa Morihiro, but no pregress was seen on the Northern Territories issue.

Japan International Cooperation Agency

(JICA; J: Kokusai Kyoryoku Jigyodan). Special public corporation established to promote international cooperation through the provision of overseas development assistance. It was founded in 1974 in accordance with the International Cooperation Agency Law.

JICA's main activities include (1) the strengthening of technical assistance programs to developing countries provided by the Japanese government by bringing technical trainees to Japan and by dispatching specialists and providing needed equipment and materials for projects overseas, (2) the facilitation and promotion of grant assistance programs, (3) the extension of loans and equity investment related to development projects, (4) the training and dispatching of Japan Overseas Cooperation Volunteers (JOVC).

JICA's activities are administered by the Ministry of Foreign Affairs; the Ministry of Agriculture, Forestry, and Fisheries; and the Ministry of International Trade and Industry (MITI). Its head office is in Tokyo, with subsidiary agencies, such as the International Training Center, spread throughout the country. JICA maintains 49 offices overseas. In 1990, its staff numbered 1,030, of whom about 200 worked abroad.

Japan Overseas Cooperation Volunteers

(JOCV; J: Seinen Kaigai Kyoryoku Tai). Often called the Japanese Peace Corps. Program founded by the Japanese government in 1965 to provide technical services and instruction to developing countries. Financed exclusively by the Japanese government, the JOCV sent out 10,255 volunteers between 1965 and 1990.

The volunteers, all young people, serve a term of two years and receive a monthly living allowance; their housing is provided by the host country, and they work as members of that country's government. The JOCV places strong emphasis on technical qualifications and experience, and nearly half of its volunteers have been in agriculture, fishing, and other areas of primary industry.

National Defense

National defense

(*kokubo*). The Japanese term *kokubo* encompasses the maintenance of military forces as well as such nonmilitary aspects of a nation's security as economic strength, political stability, and the international environment.

The international environment has changed profoundly since the end of World War II, bringing Japan to realize that the increasing complexity and diversity of threats to world and regional peace call for keener attention to questions of national defense. Instead of relying solely on its own forces to maintain peace, Japan has emphasized the United States-Japan security treaties, peaceful diplomacy, economic relations of mutual interdependence, and cultural exchange with other nations.

Evolving Attitudes

It is said that General Douglas MacArthur, the supreme commander of the Allied forces occupying Japan after World War II, intended to dismantle completely the old military forces and military industries and to transform Japan into "the Switzerland of the Far East". But in 1950, after the outbreak of war in Korea and hardening of the cold war, a National Police Reserve of 75,000 men was formed. In the early days of the cold war, as the United States requested a considerable degree of Japanese rearmament, Prime Minister Yoshida Shigeru resisted on grounds that such action would "suppress the economy and make for domestic instability." In 1952, with Japan's independence restored, the National Police Reserve, adding maritime and air branches, became the National Safety Forces, later reorganized as the Self Defense Forces (SDF).

This combination of the relatively small Self Defense Forces with a bilateral security treaty with the United States remains the core of

Japan's national defense. Japan has pursued Yoshida's policy of "inexpensive defense" and achieved economic development by favoring peaceful coexistence and promoting an international environment favorable to free trade.

National Defense Policy

The Japanese government's basic policy for national defense, enunciated by its National Defense Council (now Security Council) in 1957, sets forth the objectives of preserving Japan's peace and independence, deterring direct or indirect aggression, and repelling any assaults. International cooperation, stabilization of public welfare, a gradual increase in defense capabilities, and reliance on the security treaties were among the original means to achieving those objectives. Since then, a few new principles have been added. These include the Hikaku Sangensoku (the three nonnuclear principles of not manufacturing, possessing, or introducing into Japanese territory nuclear weapons, as approved by the Diet in 1971), a prohibition on the dispatch of troops overseas, a prohibition against conscription, the three principles regarding the export of arms, and the maintenance of a "strictly defensive posture" (*senshu boei*), signifying a passive defense strategy. The strategy centered on the concept of keeping military capabilities to a minimum level necessary for self-defense. The National Defense Program Outline adopted in 1976 called for a limited attack into Japanese territory to be repelled by Japan's own defensive forces, with assistance from the United States should these prove to be inadequate. When this outline was adopted, the Miki Takeo cabinet also enunciated a policy of limiting defense spending to 1 percent or less of Japan's gross national product, a precedent followed almost by succeeding governments.

National Defense Policies of the Major Political Parties

Japan has seen relatively little difference among its political parties on domestic policy, but sharp disagreements over diplomacy and defense. Thus opposition parties such as the Japan Socialist Party and the Japan Communist Party considered the SDF unconstitutional.

By the early 1980s, however, most opposition parties supported the constitutionality of the SDF and accepted the security treaties. According to public opinion surveys conducted in the 1980s, the Self Defense Forces were accepted by over 80 percent of the Japanese people. A somewhat smaller figure supported the security treaties with the United States, but a large majority believed that defense expenditures should remain within the limit of 1 percent of GNP.

Security Council

(Anzen Hosho Kaigi). Cabinet body in charge of matters related to national defense. Established in 1956 as the National Defense Council (Kokubo Kaigi), it assumed its present name in 1986. Its members are the prime minister (chairman), the ministers of foreign affairs and finance, the directors-general of the Defense and Economic Planning agencies, and others appointed by the prime minister. The prime minister is obliged to consult the council on all matters relating to defense, including decisions on emergency military action.

National Defense Program Outline

(Boei Keikaku no Taiko). A policy guideline stipulating minimal defense levels required in peacetime and how to build, maintain, and organize them. Established by the Miki Takeo cabinet in 1976, it has been the fundamental policy for the buildup of defense strength since 1977. It states that the objective of the buildup program is to achieve and maintain the capacity to deal with a limited attack without external aid. Strength levels deemed necessary are specified in an appendix to the outline.

Taxes

Taxes

(*sozei seido*). The present Japanese tax system is largely a result of reform measures based on the recommendation by the Shoup Mission, an American advisory group that visited Japan in 1949. The mission's basic recommendations had a lasting impact on Japanese tax policy and administration. Since that time a dominant characteristic of the Japanese tax system has been its heavy reliance on direct taxes (mainly taxes on personal and corporate income) relative to indirect taxes (sales and excise taxes). In the 1980s well over 70 percent of tax revenues in Japan came from direct taxes.

In 1988 the Japanese government undertook a major tax reform effort, with the objective of a fundamental revision of the Shoup tax system, and tried to reduce the excessive reliance on direct taxes by increasing the importance of indirect taxes. As a result, the government imposed a 3-percent consumption tax and a decrease in income and corporate tax rates. However, since the consumption tax rate is low, and many minor enterprises are exempt from the tax, it provides less than 10 percent of all national tax revenues. The system continues to depend primarily on direct taxes.

One notable difference between the Japanese tax system and that of other advanced nations is that in Japan there tends to be less of a disparity between the percentage of revenues derived from corporate taxes and the percentage of revenues from individual taxes. For example, in 1991 39.5 percent of total tax revenues came from individual income taxes, compared to 29.5 percent from corporate taxes. One explanation for the high level of corporate tax revenues in Japan is that most small businesses are incorporated, providing a large pool of corporate taxpayers.

Tax rates on individual income in Japan were previously divided into 15 progressive brackets. However, a second tax reform in 1989 simplified this system. Today individual income is taxed in 5 brackets of 10, 20, 30, 40, and 50 percent.

Tax law

(*zeiho*). The most significant tax by far is the national income tax, producing some 75.4 percent of the ¥51 trillion in total national tax revenue received for fiscal year 1989. This tax can be classified into two categories. The first is the individual income tax defined in the Income Tax Law (Shotokuzei Ho) and its supporting enforcement orders and regulations. This tax produced 35.6 percent of fiscal 1989 national tax revenue. The second category of national income tax is the corporate income tax imposed on all legal entities (known as *hojin* or juristic persons). This tax is defined in the Corporation Tax Law (Hojinzei Ho) and its supporting enforcement orders and regulations; it provided some 36 percent of fiscal 1989 national income tax revenue.

Although historically the major emphasis of the Japanese tax system had been on direct rather than indirect taxation, six tax reform bills were enacted in December 1988 that, among other things, introduced a new major indirect tax, the national consumption tax. The consumption tax provided 7.1 percent of national tax revenue in 1989.

Income taxation in Japan is based on self-assessment, and therefore, all corporate taxpayers must file a final corporate tax return with the tax office within two months of the end of their business year. However, most individual taxpayers need not file a tax return provided that they have received only remuneration income and all or almost all of that income is from one employer. Their employer calculates their tax amount, which is withheld at source, and makes a year-end adjustment, either collecting additional tax or refunding tax to the taxpayer. Individual taxpayers who have significant renumeration income from two or more sources or who have other types of income are required to file a final income tax return by 15 March of the year following the calendar year for which they are being taxed.

The national Japanese domestic tax system is administered by the National Tax Administration, a semi-independent agency of the Ministry of Finance. This body oversees 12 regional taxation bureaus and 517 local tax offices. Tax policy and international tax negotiations are handled by an internal bureau of the Ministry of Finance called the Tax Bureau. Customs matters come under the Customs and Tariff Bureau of the Ministry of Finance.

For local tax matters, a general framework is established by the Local Tax Law, which is overseen by the Local Tax Bureau of the Ministry of Home Affairs. As the type of local taxes that can be imposed and their rates are regulated by the national government.

A formal procedure exists for settling tax disputes with the government. Protests must first be filed with the chief of the tax office or the director of the regional taxation bureau. If this proves unsatisfactory, the taxpayer may claim review by the tax court called the National Tax Tribunal. A ruling by the tax court may then be appealed to the regular judicial courts.

ECONOMY

Corporations

Trade

Industries

Science

The Tokyo Stock Exchange in the Kabutocho district of central Tokyo.

Economic history
(Nihon *keizaishi*).

PREMODERN ECONOMY (to 1868)
Economic History before 1600

Jomon culture, which flourished from around 10,000 BC to around 300 BC, provides the first evidence of economic activity. Early Jomon people formed a hunting and gathering society that left behind shell mounds containing pottery, tools, and other artifacts. Agriculture entered Japan in the 3rd century BC, and a new culture emerged, Yayoi culture, marking a transition to a settled agricultural society.

Around AD 250 a powerful elite group, known for its great tomb mounds (*kofun*) and an advanced material culture, appeared within Yayoi society. Social differentiation was first visible during the Kofun period (ca 300−710). The ruling clans (*uji*) controlled support groups (*be* or *tomo*) composed of craftsmen, warriors, ceremonial personnel, or cultivators. By the mid-5th century the Yamato uji, forerunner of the imperial house, which claimed descent from the sun goddess, was dominant in western Japan. The emergent Yamato Court, centered in the Yamato Basin, showed evidence of barter and foreign trade.

The 6th and 7th centuries saw new tensions in Yamato society as the Soga family attempted to usurp political leadership. The coup in 645 against the Soga family, which resulted in the Taika Reform, however, reasserted the authority of the sovereign. A new *ritsuryo* (legal codes) system of government, modeled after that of Tang China (618−907), was eventually developed. The state took title to all agricultural land. An elaborate system of land management (the *handen shuju* system) rationalized field boundaries and assigned rights to income and cultivation.

In 723 the government offered tenure for three generations to those who reclaimed lands. Later this was extended to perpetual tenure rights as an incentive for reclamation. These policies undermined state control over agricultural land and contributed to the eventual breakdown of the *handen shuju* system. Economic expansion in the 8th century is indicated by the issuance of coins by the central government in 708. Japan was not yet a monetary society, and coins circulated largely in the Kinai or capital region. Official missions to and from China encouraged the growth of foreign trade.

Private control of land spread in response to government efforts to develop new farmland. Many elite houses and major shrines and temples exceeded their allotments and reclaimed vast tracts of land for private use. While these lands were subject to taxes, permanent tenure was the first step toward the creation of private landed estates (*shoen*), in which the proprietor assumed the duties of governance. By the 12th century 5,000 shoen existed, comprising most of the agricultural land in Japan.

Foreign trade increased in the Heian period (794—1185), and, until it was restricted after 1254 at the request of the Chinese authorities, Song dynasty (960—1279) copper coins (*sosen*) circulated widely in Japan and brought great profits to their importers. The use of coins for transactions became more common during the 13th century. *Shoen* tax goods were increasingly sold at local markets for cash. Members of the *samurai* (warrior) class were increasingly dependent on cash in the Kamakura period (1185—1333), obtaining cash loans from money-lenders. Market towns appeared in the period. Retail shops emerged, and wholesalers (*toimaru*), who began as merchant-officials charged with marketing and storing *shoen* tax goods, appeared to supply them with goods.

The 14th century saw the diffusion of intensive cultivation methods in agriculture, resulting in more monetary transactions in the economically advanced Kinai region. As commerce and the monetary economy grew, the *sake* brewers and pawnbrokers (*doso*) became tax collectors for the shogunate and provincial warlords (*shugo daimyo*). They loaned funds to both daimyo and the urban nobility and amassed great economic power. By the time of the Onin War (1467—1477), wealthy urban residents (*machishu*) administered much of Kyoto, and their authority increased as the power of the Muromachi shogunate declined.

The Onin War destroyed the *shoen* system and the authority of the Muromachi shogunate. Shugo daimyo were replaced by local military leaders (Sengoku daimyo). Sengoku daimyo domains were autonomous and independent of central authority. They instituted a new tax system that replaced *shoen* revenues. All taxing authority was in their hands, and local and absentee power holders were eliminated.

The 16th century was a period of major urbanization. Trade and handicraft production were concentrated in the castle towns (*joka machi*) of the daimyo. Samurai were assembled in the castle towns, leaving village administration in the hands of the farmers. The castle towns became political, economic, and transportation centers of the domains. Daimyo eliminated trade barriers and broke up the monopolistic powers of the guilds , which encouraged trade expansion and accelerated commercial activity. In the 1540s European traders entered Japanese waters bringing new commodities such as European luxury goods and firearms.

By the late16th century, Oda Nobunaga (1534—1582) and his successor, Toyotomi Hideyoshi (1537—1598) surveyed all land under their control and replaced the *kandaka* system of taxes computed in cash with the *kokudaka* system, in which productivity was measured in rice as the tax base. After Nobunaga's death in 1582 and unification of the country by Hideyoshi in 1590, the *kokudaka* system was extended to the entire country. A four-class system (*shi-no-ko-sho*; warrior-farmer-artisan-merchant) was implemented, with warriors, farmers, artisans, and merchants as the major divisions of society.

Edo-Period (1600—1868) Economy

Following the death of Hideyoshi in 1598, Tokugawa Ieyasu (1543—1616) emerged as the most powerful warlord in the country. In 1603 his shogunate was headquartered in Edo (now Tokyo), which soon developed into the largest city in Japan. In order to secure allegiance of the other daimyo, the Tokugawa instituted the *sankin kotai* system, whereby daimyo were required to spend alternate years in Edo to attend on the shogun. This political measure was to have profound economic effects. Edo became the center of a new economic network as all kinds of commodities were shipped to the city for consumption by the daimyo, their samurai retainers, other service personnel. By the mid-18th century, Edo had a population of over 1 million. Osaka, with its easy access to waterborne transport, became the primary commodity market in the central Kinai region. Daimyo from western Japan shipped tax rice to Osaka for sale to obtain the cash necessary to support their Edo residences and their travels to and from the capital. In time Osaka merchants hired by the daimyo as warehouse managers (*kuramoto*) or account agents (*kakeya*) also provided the daimyo with long-term credit as well.

Due to urbanization during the Edo period, population growth continued from the early 17th through the mid-18th century. Demands for food, textiles, utensils, housing, and other essentials led to a rapid expansion in commercial activity. This in turn required increases in the volume of currency and banking facilities. The Osaka money changers (*ryogaesho*) organized an official association, and, by 1670, 10 moneylenders supervised financial activity in the city. Bills of exchange and certificates of deposit circulated like paper money within and between cities, and daimyo domains issued paper currency (*hansatsu*) for circulation within domain boundaries.

Foreign trade during the Edo period was subject to new controls imposed by the shogunate. The shogunate in the early 17th century prohibited foreign voyages by Japanese, and confined foreign trade to the one with Holland through the island of Dejima in Nagasaki. There was trade with Korea through the daimyo of Tsushima, and the Satsuma domain (*han*) also traded with the Ryukyu Islands, but all other trade was monopolized by the shogunate at Nagasaki.

Enterprise size ranged from large merchant houses such as the Mitsui and the Sumitomo, with hundreds of employees and family members, to small retail or craft shops. A wide range of artisans and entertainers made urban life possible and attractive, and many village residents derived their incomes exclusively from wage labor or nonagricultural employment. Trade and craft production were clearly separated from farming. This separation of economic roles, which was the foundation of the Edo-period class system, increasingly became a legal fiction.

Until the late 16th century, there had been few large towns outside the Kyoto-Osaka region, but by the mid-18th century the urbanized population had increased to over 10 percent. Urban life, however, proved difficult for the daimyo and samurai as revenues and incomes failed to keep pace with the costs of city existence. Daimyo were forced to borrow from their retainers, further reducing samurai disposable income. The incomes of both the daimyo and the samurai were based on land taxes paid in kind, while their expenditures were in cash. As tax receipts proved inadequate, the best sources of credit were the merchants who managed their rice warehouses. Merchants thus became major creditors to daimyo and samurai.

By the mid-19th century Japan, which had entered the Edo period as an agrarian society, had become highly monetized and commercialized economy. The economic policies of the shogunate, however, were out of step with economic realities. Land taxes no longer supported the needs of the shogunate or the domain governments. Currency debasement, forced loans, debt abrogations, and temporary levies helped defray immediate crises, but no long-term solutions existed. The stage was set for dramatic changes; the demand of foreigners for trade would totally transform the social and economic order of Tokugawa Japan, forcibly thrusting it into a growing world economy.

EARLY MODERN ECONOMY (1868 – 1945)

At the time of the Meiji Restoration (1868), a number of conditions that had coalesced over time during the Edo period provided a favorable base for industrialization. Among these were the growth of a large educated population; a surplus of labor in the agricultural sector; a highly monetized economy controlled by a wealthy and capable merchant class; and the large samurai class, capable of filling leadership and administrative positions.

The opening of Japanese ports to foreign trade in 1859 exposed the still-underdeveloped economy to the threat of colonial domination by the West. In an effort to avoid the fate of other Asian nations colonialized by Western powers, the Meiji-period (1868−1912) government imposed a number of controls on the economic activities of foreigners in Japan, including travel restrictions and bans on land ownership.

Industrialization and Economic Modernization

In preparation for the rapid development of Japanese industry, much of the socioeconomic system of the Edo period, including the complex *shi-no-ko-sho* class system was dismantled. The *sekisho* (barrier stations) were abolished, and other restrictions on transportation and communication were lifted. Land ownership rights for farmers were established; and restrictions on the planting of crops other than rice were abolished. These reforms led to the modernization of agricultural management. The government also implemented the Land Tax Reform, under which land taxes, which had been paid chiefly in rice since the early Edo period, were made payable in currency. In 1876 the stipends of former samurai (*shizoku*) were converted into government bonds and hereditary pensions were paid off on a sliding scale.

In addition, the Meiji government first abolished the old, complex currency system and established a new, unified national currency system with decimal denominations and standardized units. It also introduced new systems of banking and company organization. The banking system was modeled on the US system of national banks, and in 1882 a central bank, the Bank of Japan, was founded.

Private Sector Development Efforts

The private sector leadership played a key role in the modernization of the economy. Among these entrepreneurs were a number of members of such wealthy merchant families from the Edo period as the Mitsui and the Sumitomo. Most of them, however, came from the ranks of the former samurai, peasant, or merchant classes and became modern businessmen amid the turmoil of the early Meiji period.

The Development of the Factors of Production

Large amounts of capital accumulated in the hands of merchants and landowners in the late Edo and early Meiji periods. This capital was invested in new companies and business ventures, primarily in factories, machinery, and other fixed assets. A large surplus of workers developed during the depression that accompanied the unification of the currency system from 1881 to 1885. These poor people, chiefly former farmers provided a portion of the industrial labor force; low-ranking former samurai and small businessmen also experienced a high rate of bankruptcy, and many then became workers.

Growth Industries

The centerpiece of Japan's expanding industrial development

was the textile industry. The Meiji government strongly promoted the modernization of this industry in order to reduce dependence on imports, employing foreign technicians to supply technical know-how and assistance. In 1897 cotton yarn exports exceeded imports for the first time. By 1918 six giant spinning firms had been formed.

The first major production facility in the iron and steel industry in Kamaishi, Iwate Prefecture, began operations around 1890. The government-run Yawata Iron and Steel Works began operation in 1901 and became Japan's leading ironworks after the Russo-Japanese War of 1904–1905. The shipbuilding industry grew rapidly at the turn of the century, fostered by supportive government policies and the efforts of such firms as Mitsubishi Shipbuilding (now Mitsubishi Heavy Industries, Ltd), Kawasaki Shipyard Co (now Kawasaki Heavy Industries, Ltd), and Osaka Iron.

A number of special banks were established after 1897, including the Nippon Kangyo Bank (now Dai-Ichi Kangyo Bank, Ltd); the Industrial Bank of Japan, Ltd; the Bank of Taiwan; and the Bank of Korea. Bank deposits increased, and, with the cancellation of excess loans, five giant banking concerns had come to dominate by 1917: the Dai-Ichi Bank; the Mitsui Bank (now Sakura Bank, Ltd); the Mitsubishi Bank, Ltd; the Sumitomo Bank, Ltd; and the Yasuda Bank (now Fuji Bank, Ltd).

The Problems of Growth

Behind the rapid growth in the industrial sector, agriculture, which continued to be characterized by a premodern tenancy system, based on small farms averaging less than 1 hectare (2.47 acres), followed a sluggish development. In commerce and industry, alongside the emerging large modern enterprises, numerous small enterprises and cottage industries continued to exist. (This dual structure has continued to be a central feature of the Japanese economy.) Despite the modernization of important industries, the income level of the common people remained low.

In the West, as industrialization spread, so too did the socialist and labor movements. In Japan this was not the case, as the government took active steps to suppress them at home. The Public Order and Police Law of 1900 (Chian Keisatsu Ho) was largely effective in suppressing organized union activity by government surveillance before World War I. Its replacement, the Peace Preservation Law of 1925 (Chian Iji Ho), which was directed against communists and anarchists, suppressed the more radical elements within the labor movement.

Economic growth came to a halt in 1920, when the Japanese economy fell into a severe depression following its rapid expansion during World War I. A tolerable recovery had been achieved when, on 1

September 1923, a massive earthquake struck the greater Tokyo region. In 1927 an unprecedented financial crisis occurred when a number of important banks failed. Then in 1930–1931 the Japanese economy was engulfed by the worldwide depression that followed the 1929 crash of the US stock market.

Throughout this period of crisis, bankruptcies of small and medium-sized enterprises were common in almost all economic activities. There was also a push for the concentration of capital, resulting in a striking growth in the power of the industrial and financial combines known as *zaibatsu*. The Mitsui, Mitsubishi, Sumitomo, and Yasuda zaibatsu developed into conglomerates between 1909 and 1920, and in the following decade they expanded their affiliated enterprises and established positions of firm dominance over the Japanese economy.

The farm economy also suffered. The depression gave independent farmers, as well as tenant farmers a severe blow of debt. Tenant farmer disputes increased in number, and there was an overall growth in social unrest. Against this background the Manchurian Incident occurred in September 1931, and the government soon embarked on a program of increasing military expenditures. Military demand contributed to the recovery of strategic industries, employment, and the farm economy.

On the other hand, the Manchurian Incident was the first in a series of Sino-Japanese conflicts leading to the outbreak of the Sino-Japanese War of 1937–1945 and then Japan's entry into World War II in 1941. Throughout the war the government strengthened its control over the economy and promoted the development of strategic industries, but production in important manufacturing industries dropped, especially after 1943, until it collapsed under aerial bombardment in 1944 and 1945. The wartime economy itself collapsed with Japan's surrender on 15 August 1945. Overall production at the end of 1945 was only one-sixth of prewar (1935–1937 average) levels. At the war's end more than 25 percent of Japan's physical capital stock and 45 percent of the prewar empire had been lost.

OCCUPATION AND RECOVERY (1945–1960s)

The Allied Occupation of Japan lasted 80 months, from 15 August 1945, when Japan accepted the Potsdam Declaration, to 29 April 1952. It is often divided into four periods: reform (August 1945–February 1947), reverse course (February 1947–December 1948), Dodge Line (December 1948–June 1950), and Korean War (June 1950–April 1952). It was a time of economic and political reform, as well as recovery from the physical destruction and economic exhaustion of World War II.

The Reform Period

While economic recovery was left largely in Japanese hands, the activities of SCAP (the Occupation authorities) during 1945—1947 were concentrated upon a series of reforms. The most important of these reforms concerned agriculture (the land reforms of 1946, encouragement of agricultural cooperative associations, and rice price controls), labor (legalization of trade unions and collective bargaining, and enforcement of labor standards), and industry (passage of an Antimonopoly Law, zaibatsu dissolution, and deconcentration of economic power).

As a simple matter of avoiding famine, massive aid was essential to Japan, with the United States the almost exclusive source. The aid program included a wide range of industrial raw materials and paid for more than half of Japan's total imports through 1949.

Although the occupation purge was directed primarily at political and military leaders of the Japanese war effort, an "economic purge" was extended to cover industrial, commercial, and financial leaders judged to have cooperated actively with the Japanese military. The effect of the purge on economic recovery was questionable, and over 200,000 of those purged were later officially depurged by appeals boards and administrative action.

Because Japan financed its political and economic reforms largely by printing new money, the country experienced accelerating inflation in 1945—1949. An initial Occupation effort to check this inflation in February 1946 took the form of an abortive "new yen" currency reform. All pre-1946 currency was invalidated, with new notes issued yen-for-yen but only for limited amounts. Both demand and savings deposits were also frozen. However, budgetary deficits of the Japanese government and credit creation by the Bank of Japan continued to be financed by an excessive printing of currency and expansion of bank credit.

Two important agencies of economic recovery and expansion were set up by the Japanese in late 1946, after the failure of the "new yen" experiment. These were the Keizai Antei Hombu, or Economic Stabilization Board (ESB; the present Economic Planning Agency), and the Fukko Kin'yu Kinko, or Reconstruction Finance Bank (RFB). The ESB planned and supervised a revived system of price controls and rationing and also subsidized increased production. The RFB made longer-term loans to public and private institutions to increase their productive capacities. A characteristic of Japanese planning was to select particular industries as keys to the next stage of economic expansion, and to concentrate assistance on such industries with little regard for short-term market forces. Priorities shifted from coal and food in 1946 to iron, steel, and fertilizer production in 1948.

The Reverse Course Period

The reverse course may be dated from 1 February 1947, the scheduled date for a general strike by a united front of government workers' unions. SCAP decided to forbid the strike, and a pattern of hostility between SCAP and the Japanese Left crystallized and continued for the remainder of the Occupation. Whereas SCAP had been antimilitarist, antinationalist, and antifascist before February 1947, anticommunism and antiunionism came to overshadow these earlier ideologies after that date.

With partial revival of Japanese production by 1948, international trade became increasingly important, but under SCAP's supervision all commercial imports as well as exports required licensed approval by the Japanese authorities. Only in 1948 did SCAP begin to permit the entry, and then the permanent residence, of foreign private traders.

The Dodge Line Period

In the fall of 1948 a Detroit banker Joseph M. Dodge was appointed a special adviser to SCAP on economic matters. The measures undertaken during this period were known collectively as the Dodge Line. Under the Dodge program, the price control system, production subsidies, and the RFB loans were terminated. Dodge advocated free-market economics, balanced budgets, lower taxes, stabilization of the exchange value of the yen (at ¥360 to the US dollar), and strict regulation of the money supply. His drastic anti-inflationary measures, combined with a recession in world markets for Japanese exports, brought on a severe decline in aggregate demand; the results were business failures and unemployment. By the spring of 1950 the short-term outlook for the Japanese economy was bleak.

The Korean War Period

The outbreak of the Korean War caught both SCAP and the Japanese authorities by surprise. After the war began on 25 June 1950 the semimilitary economy that Japan almost immediately became was dominated by *tokuju* (special procurement demand) for the United Nations forces in Korea; the Japanese economy thus returned to full capacity, boom conditions, and high growth. The money supply was freed from its Dodge line fetters. As for the Dodge line as a whole, three main pillars remained in place: an annually balanced budget, a stable yen-dollar exchange rate, and the dissolution of the price-control and rationing machinery.

Recovery and Growth

War procurements during the Korean conflict and a general expansion of world trade enabled Japan to earn the foreign exchange to pay for the imports so essential for growth. The Japanese rate of growth in the 1950s and 1960s was without historical precedent and came to be called an "economic miracle." Japan was the second largest borrower from the World Bank in the late 1950s, and it was classified as a less-developed nation in the early 1960s. Yet by 1964 it was recognized as one of the advanced industrial nations, and by 1968 it had surpassed West Germany to become the world's second largest market economy. Business optimism began to emerge as the economy moved beyond postwar recovery. Actual performance exceeded expectations, and the rates of growth and labor productivity accelerated. The average annual growth of the gross national product (GNP) rose, despite occasional slowdowns, from 7.1 percent between 1952 and 1957 to 9.8 percent between 1957 and 1962. Prime Minister Ikeda Hayato proposed a 10-year Income-Doubling Plan in 1960, only to see income double in 7 years. The size of the emerging Japanese economy in the 1960s and its concentration on exports and GNP growth provoked international complaints and retaliation (even from the United States), which played a major part in shaping Japan's economic policies and performance in the 1970s and 1980s.

Economic agencies

(*keizai kancho*). Government ministries and agencies concerned with economic policies, in particular, the Ministry of Finance, the Ministry of International Trade and Industry (MITI), and the Economic Planning Agency (EPA). The Ministry of Finance helps prepare the national budget and revisions to the tax system and also provides supervision and guidance to banks and securities companies. MITI supervises individual industries and is responsible for the formulation and enforcement of international trade policies. It influences the industrial world through its administrative guidance powers. The EPA coordinates economic policies and prepares long-term economic plans, annual economic forecasts, and the White Paper on the Economy.

Since the Japanese government often manipulates public works expenditures as a way to control business fluctuations, the Ministry of Construction and the Ministry of Transport also have important economic roles. The Ministry of Foreign Affairs, MITI, the EPA, and the Ministry of Finance divide the responsibility for overseas economic aid.

Budget, national

(*yosan*). The general account budget of the national government's revenues and expenditures is usually regarded as the most important of all government budgets. In addition to this budget, there are also individual budgets for a group of special accounts created to implement government policies. Thirty-eight special accounts were operative in 1992.

Social Security

Various outlays for public assistance programs, social welfare programs, social insurance programs, public health services, and unemployment measures are included in this category. Public assistance provides support to individuals who are unable to meet the cost of living. The national government provides 75 percent of this assistance and local governments 25 percent. Social welfare programs are intended to support those people for whom care is necessary, such as children, the aged, and the physically and mentally disabled.

Social insurance can be classified into health insurance, pensions, and unemployment insurance. The health insurance system consists of employee insurance and national health insurance. The pension system, similarly, has two classes. National pension insurance provides basic, mandatory coverage for all citizens, while other programs provide additional benefits for private- and public-sector employees. While these programs depend mainly on contributions made by employers and employees, subsidies from the general account are also substantial. Measures to combat tuberculosis, poliomyelitis, and other communicable diseases; cancer; and mental illness are carried out by the public health service. To cope with unemployment, there are unemployment insurance, unemployment relief works, and special measures to promote employment.

Public Works

One of the features of Japanese public expenditure is a relatively high level of government investment. The main emphasis since the late 1960s has been on public works aimed at increasing social overhead capital. Social capital includes erosion and flood-control projects; road construction; port, harbor, and airport facilities; housing; public service facilities; improvement of conditions for agricultural production; forest roads; and water supply for industrial use. Of these, the heaviest investment is in road construction, which is managed primarily through the Road Improvement Special Account. The expenditures in this special account consist of expenses for projects under the direct control of the national government, subsidies to local governments, and investments in public expressway corporations. The main sources of revenue for these expenditures are transfers from the general account. The gasoline tax revenue is also transferred to the special account.

Education

Schools for compulsory education (elementary schools and middle schools) are operated by local authorities; the national government is required by law to provide one-half of the teachers' salaries in these schools. Other government outlays are expenses for public school facilities, school education assistance, transfers to the National Schools Special Account, loans to students, and the promotion of science and technology. The revenue and expenditures of national universities and hospitals attached to national schools are managed through the National Schools Special Account.

Transfers to the Foodstuff Control Special Account

The Foodstuff Control Special Account was originally created to stabilize the prices of agricultural products by controlling the purchase and sale of rice, wheat, barley, and other commodities. However, sale prices of domestic rice and some other crops are not high enough to cover the government's purchase price and overhead expenses. As a result, a large deficit has developed in this special account, and funds are transferred from the general account each year to cover the deficit.

Economic Cooperation

In fiscal 1991 the government expenditure for economic cooperation was estimated at ¥846 billion (US $6.2 billion). Government economic assistance to developing countries has increased rapidly.

Local Allocation Tax

This expenditure which equals 30 percent of income, corporation, liquor, and consumption taxes is distributed by the national government to assist local governments through a special account for allotment of the local allocation tax and transferred tax. Local governments can use these grants at their discretion. The national government allocates these grants according to the financial needs of each local government.

National income

(*kokumin shotoku*). The national income measures used in international comparisons are gross national product (GNP) and gross domestic product (GDP). Japan's GDP in 1990 was ¥434.2 trillion (US $3.0 trillion), making it the second largest market economy in the world. In the same year per capita income was ¥2.8 million (US $19,242), comparable with that of Western nations after adjusting for Japan's high cost of housing and other goods. This high economic scale was achieved largely due to high economic growth from 1955 to the late 1960s, during which period the nation's average annual growth rate was around 10 percent, about double that of Western nations. Although Japan maintained this higher rate until the late 1980s, the bubble came to an end with its collapse in the 1990s.

Structure of National Income

The Japanese economy can be understood by examining three aspects of the national income: production, distribution, and disposition. Regarding production, primary industry (agriculture, forestry, and fishing), which accounted for 26.0 percent of the GDP in 1950, shortly after the war, fell to 2.4 percent in 1990, while the share of secondary industry (manufacturing) rose from 31.8 percent to 36.9 percent, and tertiary industry (services) rose from 42.3 percent to 60.7 percent in the same years. In recent years, the share of secondary industry appears to have reached a ceiling, and that of tertiary industry has continued to develop, creating a service-oriented economy.

As for distribution, the proportion of employee compensation has increased, whereas that of income from private corporations and private unincorporated entrepreneurial income has decreased. In 1950, employee compensation stood at 41.8 percent, while private unincorporated entrepreneurial income was 45.6 percent. In 1990, these figures were 69.0 percent and 9.1 percent, respectively.

When expenditures, or disposition of national income, are broken down into consumption and savings, the share of savings in national disposable income steadily increased from about 20 percent in the 1950s, peaking at 30.3 percent in 1970. It then fell to an average of 21.1 percent in the 1980s. Even now, however, this figure is higher than that of other advanced nations.

Foreign investment in Japan

(*zainichi gaishi*). Foreign investment in Japan includes whole and part ownership of companies or subsidiaries, the establishment of branch offices, capital ownership in Japanese firms, joint ventures, and technical and financial assistance agreements.

Early History

After the Meiji Restoration of 1868, both the government and newly formed enterprises sought technical assistance from overseas. Through technical tie-ups and the large-scale recruitment of American and European engineers and technicians, various industrial technologies were brought into Japan. Out of fear of foreign domination, however, Japan resisted the introduction of direct subsidiaries. When the Japanese had acquired the expertise or technology they desired, the foreign instructors were sent home.

From the Sino-Japanese War of 1894–1895 until the outbreak of World War I, emerging Japanese firms in the heavy manufacturing and chemical industries required closer access to proprietary technologies held by the Western industrial firms. At this juncture, American and European firms began to extend specialized technical assistance to Japanese firms through technical licensing agreements. This was sometimes done in exchange for part ownership of the Japanese licensee's voting capital. General Electric of the United States and the predecessor of Toshiba Corporation entered into such a relationship for manufacturing light bulbs, and Nippon Electric Co. was established as a joint venture with International Telephone and Telegraph of the United States.

Postwar Foreign Investment

Following the end in 1952 of the Allied Occupation of Japan, the Japanese government implemented a system of indicative economic planning that guided the pace and direction of the nation's growth. A key element in this planned growth was the control of foreign investment. Outright foreign operations by wholly owned or majority-owned subsidiaries were initially prohibited and only gradually decontrolled. The only permissible form of foreign investment was the technical licensing agreement, and even these were carefully screened by the government.

Until the early 1960s, Japan remained relatively unattractive to potential investors. Few foreign firms foresaw Japan's rapid industrial recovery from the devastation of World War II. Rather than setting up shop in Japan, many foreign firms chose simply to sell their standard technologies to the Japanese.

Japan's practice of freely engaging in international trade and investment while exercising strict control of such activities at home did not last long. As exports of manufactured goods increased, foreign pressure mounted for Japan to open its markets to foreign goods and services. After 1960 Japan began to liberalize imports by lifting nontariff barriers. The first industries to be opened to foreign investment were those unlikely to attract foreign capital.

After 1968, however, Japan expanded the number of industries in which foreign firms were permitted to establish subsidiaries. Foreign investment increased gradually in the 1970s and 1980s, but in the early 1990s entry into the Japanese market was still seen as a difficult process by many foreign companies. Some of the most common reasons given were the complicated Japanese distribution system, exclusionary tactics among affiliated Japanese companies, and the difficulty of finding qualified Japanese executives willing to work at a foreign company.

That it is possible, however, for a foreign company to establish profitable operations in Japan is evidenced by such success stories as IBM Japan, Ltd; Coca-Cola (Japan) Co, Ltd; and Procter & Gamble Co. IBM held the top share of the Japanese business computer market in the early 1990s. Coca-Cola, which entered Japan with the US Occupation forces just after World War II, now has about a 50 percent share of the Japanese market for soft drinks. Procter & Gamble is also considered a market leader.

In 1990 the country-by-country breakdown of 2,884 foreign companies operating in Japan was as follows: the United States, 46.8 percent; Germany, 11.4 percent; Great Britain, 10.2 percent; France, 6.7 percent; Switzerland, 6.0 percent; Asian countries, 4.8 percent; other countries, 14.1 percent. Of these companies, 1,379 were 100 percent foreign owned; 489 were between 50 and 100 percent foreign owned; 614 were 50 percent foreign owned; and 402 were less than 50 percent foreign owned.

Income distribution

(*shotoku bumpu*). Household income differentials in Japan narrowed sharply after World War II, especially in the high-growth period of the 1960s and 1970s. However, income differentials have started to widen in recent years. There are a number of factors accounting for this trend. First, wage levels of workers in large corporations often differ markedly from those of their counterparts in smaller firms. In the 1950s this situation was referred to as the dual structure of the economy, which was more or less eliminated in the high-growth period. In the 1980s, however, wage differentials based on corporate size began to expand again. The considerably higher levels of nonmonetary compensation provided by large corporations, including expense accounts and housing and other benefits, further exacerbate the effects of the dual structure.

A second feature of wage differentials in Japan is that they are far greater among different age groups than in other developed countries. This is primarily due to the seniority system followed by most Japanese corporations.

The third factor concerns the fact that an increasing number of Japanese women in households with lower incomes sought employment in order to supplement their husbands' limited incomes. This development originally served to equalize Japanese family incomes. Recently, however, supplementary incomes earned by working women have tended to widen income differences between families, as many women in high-income-bracket households are now also gainfully employed.

The wage gap between the sexes remains conspicuous in Japan. In 1988 the average monthly salary of a female worker amounted to only 61 percent of the salary of her male counterpart. This is primarily because the average working woman's career is only half as long as the average man's, a definite disadvantage in a wage system based on seniority; women are more often employed in comparatively low-paying industries and smaller firms; and many women are part-time workers.

Although income distribution in Japan is still relatively equal in terms of employment income, the gap between rich and poor is seen as much wider when considered in terms of asset ownership. The gaps in asset ownership have begun to widen markedly in recent years because of skyrocketing land prices. This trend is likely to further widen income differentials in the coming years as huge capital gains are generated by these assets.

Zaikai

(financial circles). Term used to refer to the Japanese business world, with special emphasis on the formal and informal associations linking leaders of the major corporations and financial institutions. The most important of the formal associations are Keidanren (Federation of Economic Organizations), a national alliance of major business firms; Keizai Doyukai (Japan Association of Corporate Executives), a business group whose members are individuals rather than companies; Nikkeiren (Japan Federation of Employers' Associations), which primarily deals with labor-management relations; and Nissho (Japan Chamber of Commerce and Industry), the central organization of chambers of commerce and industry linking all businesses throughout Japan. Referred to as the Four Key Economic Organizations, these four groups represent the opinions and interests of virtually all of corporate Japan and wield considerable clout with the government.

Informal groups take a variety of forms. Some, known as *keiretsu*, are enterprise-group-based associations, such as the Mitsubishi Kin'yokai of the Mitsubishi group and the Sumitomo Hakusuikai of the Sumitomo group. Other groups are formed around influential politicians and senior business leaders.

General trading companies

(*sogo shosha*). Large, highly diversified Japanese commercial houses that structure and facilitate the flow of goods, services, and money among client firms, operating both within Japan and globally. Nine firms (Mitsubishi Corporation; Mitsui & Co, Ltd; Itochu Corporation; Marubeni Corporation; Sumitomo Corporation; Nissho Iwai Corporation; Tomen Corporation; Kanematsu Corporation; and Nichimen Corporation) are considered to constitute the ranks of the general trading companies. The total sales of the nine firms equaled almost 29 percent of Japan's gross national product in 1990, and the imports and exports handled by them accounted for about half of the nation's foreign trade.

The sogo shosha have their roots in the development of industry and foreign trade during the Meiji period (1868–1912). Their functions include both financing and conducting trade. A firm may offer its clients a wide assortment of financing including trade credit, inventory financing, factoring, loan guarantees, and even equity participation as well as financial services such as foreign-exchange risk management. In Japan, the sogo shosha are very important sources of funds for business borrowing. They also play an important role in the establishment of large-scale projects by consortia of firms, especially overseas.

The trading firms compete vigorously with each other to maximize trading volume, while cutting their margins typically to 1 or 2 percent. The average pretax profit on sales of the nine firms was 0.33 percent in 1991. Nonetheless, since the firms deal in huge quantities, revenues are substantial. Even more than on price, sogo shosha compete on service, endeavoring to make themselves into "eyes and ears" for their clients, bringing opportunities to them.

Employment, forms of

(*koyo keitai*). There are three principal forms of employment in Japanese industry: permanent, temporary, and subcontract. Permanent employees account for the main body of a firm's labor force and are hired as regular employees on a long-term basis. Such employees are recruited with the expectation that they will eventually rise through company ranks to hold executive positions. Regular employees are largely selected from recent university graduates. Their wages are increased gradually through annual raises and promotions. Through the company welfare system, they also receive a number of benefits. Except in rare cases, it is very unusual for regular employees to be discharged before reaching the retirement age set by the company.

Temporary employees are hired to respond to fluctuations in labor demand; they are also hired to take advantage of low-cost labor. These workers are hired for a set period, after which their employment is terminated unless their contract is extended. In addition to temporary employees, there are part-time workers, students, and those on loan from employment agencies, who work a limited number of hours only. When regular employees reach retirement age, some are retained with the special status of "nonregular staff" (*shokutaku*), a kind of temporary employees. There is a strict demarcation between regular and temporary employees in terms of working conditions, job status, wages, and benefits.

Workers employed by subcontractors are called *shagaiko* (non-company workers) who work for the parent company. The shagaiko serve the same purpose as temporary employees but are employed indirectly through subcontractors.

Employment system, modern

(*kindai no koyo seido*). The employment system in the post-World War II period has been based on three essential institutions: lifetime employment (*shushin koyo*), the seniority system (*nenko joretsu*), and enterprise unionism.

Lifetime Employment

In the characteristic Japanese employment system, companies recruit workers immediately upon graduation from a school or university, and these workers continue in the same company until retirement. This is considered to be the ideal employment relationship, but it is mostly limited to larger firms.

Regular employees can expect to be employed until retirement unless they violate any of the rules of employment. When business is depressed, regular employees are dismissed only as a last resort. In return for this job security, employees are expected to accept transfers to other departments or to subsidiaries when business is bad and to respond positively by working overtime when the company is doing well. As long as employees maintain such a commitment, it is commonly understood to be the employer's responsibility to maintain stability of employment.

Seniority System

This system bases an employee's rank, salary, and qualifications within an enterprise on the length of service in that company. Wage increases and promotions are highly dependent on the employee's school background, sex, and type of work. This system can be traced to a period of serious labor shortages during World War I when the Yokosuka Naval Shipyard adopted it as a means of securing enough technical and skilled workers.

Enterprise Unionism

The third basic feature of the Japanese employment system is the prevalence of enterprise unions. This form of unionism was established after World War II, because of the following factors: (1) strong paternalism among postwar employers of all sizes and types; (2) a wide variety of working conditions, which prevented the development of a unitary wage structure based on technical qualifications and competence. These factors led Japanese union members to prefer to bargain with management at the level of the individual enterprise. Paternalistic management and enterprise unionism have both supported lifetime employment and promoted labor-management harmony.

Corporations

(*kigyo*). Japan has more than 1.3 million corporations. There is, however, considerable concentration of economic power in a small number of corporations. Of the 1,267,642 corporations existing at the time of the 1986 census, only 297 had more than 5,000 employees. These 297 companies, which represented 0.02 percent of all Japanese corporations, accounted for nearly 14 percent of all regular employees. Another indication of the number of major corporations is that 1,627 firms are listed on the Tokyo Stock Exchange.

Financial Characteristics

The huge capital requirements of many corporations during the period of rapid ecoonomic growth, which began in the 1950s, led to the dependence on debt financing. Since Japan's capital markets were still undeveloped at that time, companies were forced to rely on the banks for financing. Banks were then able to exert considerable influence over management decisions. Because banks, in turn, had to rely on the Bank of Japan, the country's central bank, for additional funds, the government was able to exercise a major influence on important corporate decisions using direct credit expansion controls known as *madoguchi shido* ("window guidance").

In the 1980s, however, development of the capital markets and substantial liquidity in the total economy led to a reduction in dependence on debt financing and a corresponding reduction in the use of this type of government influence.

Enterprise Groups and Subsidiaries

Following World War II, the *zaibatsu* (financial and industrial combines) were dissolved by Occupation fiat. Many groups later recombined, however, because of traditional ties and an urgent need for the capital that could be obtained from the banks of the group. Although mutual shareholding reinforces the connections, there is no central ownership, and group coordination is much looser than in prewar zaibatsu.

Of more importance to the operations of the corporation than its connections with other large companies is the pattern of subsidiaries and subcontracting firms that has developed. These smaller firms not only pay lower wages, but also provide a smaller package of benefits.

Hence a considerable economic advantage to using the smaller firm as a supplier of those components or subassemblies that require less-skilled labor. The subsidiary or subcontractor relationship also gives the parent company flexibility in scheduling and allows cyclic downturns in demand to be displaced onto the smaller firms.

Employment Practices

The pattern of Japanese employment has as its basis a mutual commitment by the corporation and the employee. The corporation undertakes to retain each person that it selects until retirement, despite later temptations to terminate employment. Employees undertake to remain in the employ of the corporation once they make their choice, however attractive alternative positions might appear. Large corporations recruit employees directly from school, and hiring is not for a particular skill or job. Each assumes that over time the individual will fill a range of positions. Compensation is based on seniority, with rank, performance, and other special conditions as additional considerations.

The effect of this pattern is to establish an unusual identity between the interests of the individual employee and the interests of the corporation itself. The employee's security and assurance of continued improvement in income depend directly on the success of the firm. Midcareer moves from one firm to another for more money are relatively rare. Besides, the enterprise union system peculiar to Japan tends to reinforce rather than dilute employee identification with the company.

It should be noted that this employment pattern applies only to regular, and not to temporary, employees. Changes in the pattern are occurring, but only slowly. Some companies have tried to shift the emphasis from seniority to performance when determining promotions and raises. Hiring of experienced personnel by foreign companies in Japan has opened up a limited number of opportunities for career changes.

Future Issues

With the increasing integration of the world economy, two issues have moved to a prominent position in the concerns of the Japanese corporation. The first is the need for innovative research and development that became evident in the late 1970s. Funding of research in Japan is largely by the corporation, in contrast to the economies of the West, where government plays a much larger role. As Japanese corporations have caught up to and even surpassed their Western counterparts in the area of technical expertise, there has been less and less chance to purchase or license technology from abroad. Corporate research funding has massively increased, along with a need to address organizational issues to allow for flexible use of younger researchers.

The second major issue is the need to move toward a global organizational structure—to establish worldwide positions in technology and manufacturing as well as trade. These extensions abroad of the Japanese corporation raise questions about the integration of non-Japanese nationals into the organization, about dealing with very different approaches to unionization, about the political consequences of the acquisition of substantial foreign assets, and about the development of worldwide product and personnel management systems—questions that the Japanese corporation is only beginning to address.

Corporate history

(*kigyo no rekishi*). An analysis of the development of Japanese business from the Meiji period (1868—1912) to the eve of World War II.

The Legacy of the Edo-Period Merchants

The activities of the merchants of the Edo period (1600—1868) facilitated the use of money throughout Japan and resulted in an increasingly unified market. Osaka became the commercial and financial center of the country, and developed highly advanced trading and financial techniques. Central to the commercial activities of the period was the concept of the household (*ie*), composed of the owner-family and all those employed by it, who, in exchange for absolute loyalty, were guaranteed permanent employment. Within the household each member had his place in a strictly ordered hierarchical system.

The Leaders of the Meiji Government as Modernizers

The leaders of the Meiji Restoration of 1868 superimposed selected Western-style institutions on traditional Japanese society. Class privileges and class restrictions were abolished, and former *samurai* were helped toward gainful employment; merchant guilds were prohibited; freedoms of enterprise and migration were proclaimed. In 1871 a unified currency, based on the yen, was established. The Ministry of Public Works (Kobusho), established in 1870, planned the importation of technology and the promotion of industry; it employed more than 500 foreign experts as technicians and instructors.

After 1884, most government enterprises were sold to private entrepreneurs. They were mostly the founders of *zaibatsu* such as Mitsui, Sumitomo, and Mitsubishi. Western-style businesses, notably factories and banks, were hailed as part of the new era of "Civilization and Enlightenment". The government, however, saw modern business primarily in terms of strengthening the state rather than in terms of satisfying consumer demands.

The Growth of Modern Business (1868 — 1937)

The overall growth of modern business passed through four major stages in Japan. There was a pioneering period from 1868 to 1884, when sound financial conditions were restored after the government initiated deflationary policies in 1881. Many firms collapsed during the period of deflation. The second period, from 1884 to 1919, was one of accelerated growth that was stimulated by Japan's policy of imperial expansion, notably after the Sino-Japanese War of 1894 — 1895 and the Russo-Japanese War of 1904 — 1905. The latter gave a particular impetus to the shipbuilding industry and to heavy industry in general. Industrial paid-up capital tripled during World War I, when the Asian market was left totally open to Japanese trade. Worldwide economic dislocation following World War I led to the prolonged depression that was the major feature of the third period, which ended in 1931. There were waves of bankruptcies, mass unemployment, and a growing concentration of capital in the hands of the zaibatsu. After 1931, the fourth period saw a reflation under the influence of war preparations. Exports were strongly promoted, and the economy reflated toward full employment.

Modern banks were launched in 1876 in the form of National Banks. The Bank of Japan as the central bank was established in 1882, and a few government-run banks granted long-term loans for foreign trade, industry, and agriculture. The main weakness of Japan's banking system was the large number of small banks that were tied to individual firms by continued extension of large loans. In periods of crisis, many such banks failed, and this in turn led to a heavy concentration of banking capital. Between 1926 and 1929 the number of banks decreased from 1,417 to 897, and, by 1935, 40 percent of all deposits were held by the "Big Five" (Dai-Ichi, Mitsui [now Sakura Bank, Ltd], Mitsubishi, Yasuda [now Fuji Bank, Ltd] and Sumitomo).

During the 1920s and 1930s general trading companies, notably those of the zaibatsu, played the key role in expanding Japan's international trade. The Mitsubishi, Kawasaki, Ishikawajima, and Hitachi shipyards grew and integrated vertically into large industrial enterprises that produced heavy machinery, railway engines and coaches, electric cables, and other related products. Shipping received some subsidy but was left to private initiative. Nippon Yusen Kaisha (controlled by Mitsubishi), Osaka Shosen, and Toyo Kisen emerged as the three major shipping companies.

By 1886 a total of 32 railway companies had come into existence, and by 1905, 67 percent of some 7,800 kilometers (4,846 mi) of railway lines were operated by private companies. Nationalization of all but 9 percent of the lines was carried out in 1906 — 1907. Sumitomo, Mitsui,

Mitsubishi, and Furukawa had operated mines since the 1870s.

Forms of Business

The joint-stock company (*kabushiki kaisha*) received strong backing from the government. The Commercial Code of 1899 distinguished three types of company: limited liability company (*yugen kaisha*), limited partnership company (*goshi kaisha*), and unlimited partnership company (*gomei kaisha*). The zaibatsu holding companies controlled the expanding network of financial and industrial companies through a system of direct and interlocking stockholdings and through the appointment of loyal top managers.

There were four main reasons for the growth of Japan's zaibatsu. First, they had large initial capital resources. Second, the holding-company system itself gave them ready access to financial resources (banks), raw materials (mines), and direct lines of foreign trade. Third, they were led by able individuals who were entrepreneurs and who actively secured new managerial talent. Fourth, they were family-based organizations that applied the concept of the household (*ie*) to the new business environment. They delegated decision making but demanded the unswerving loyalty of their managers and employees.

Corporate recruitment

(*saiyo*). Large Japanese corporations have adopted a general pattern of long-term employment for both workers and management. This has allowed firms to plan for their projected employment needs and hire on a highly systematic basis. Large companies recruit new employees (the company's future managers) almost exclusively from the finest universities. The graduates are hired on the assumption that they will be with the same company until they retire, are given on-the-job-training, and are promoted within the company. Most companies begin holding company information seminars for undergraduates about eight months to one year before college graduation in March; official hiring begins after graduation and employment begins in April. However, some companies have resorted to "decide" on students unofficially well before their actual graduation from college. This practice has been officially discouraged by universities and the Ministry of Labor, but many companies continue to recruit undergraduates secretly.

Small and medium-sized companies are generally more flexible in hiring executive staff and may hire people who have had prior work experience. The main reason for this is that almost all of the most promising new graduates are quickly snatched up by the large companies. Recently, more companies of all sizes have been filling white-collar positions through nontraditional means, such as headhunters. Also, growing numbers of workers are leaving their jobs of their own accord and looking for better opportunities at other companies. These changes reflect the increasing mobility in the Japanese labor market.

Corporate decision making

(*ishi kettei*). The *ringi* system, a process of decision making through the use of circular letters, is known as a system unique to Japanese enterprises. Top management decides fundamental managerial policy; proposals for and research on actual measures to be followed are assigned to each responsible division. Middle management takes a leading part in planning a measure, and after informal negotiations with other related departments the plan is formally presented in the form of a *ringisho*, a letter bearing the proposal that is circulated among the various departments of the organization. Since information is reported to the top level, the upper management, including the CEO, is well acquainted with the plan when it is finally submitted at a board of directors' meeting. Consequently the support of the plan in such a meeting is, in principle, unanimous.

As a company increases in size and the business diversifies, decision-making authority is passed down to each responsible division. Some examples of the resulting structures are the headquarters system (Sumitomo Bank, Ltd), divisional organization (Matsushita Electric Co, Ltd), and the divided-company system (Saison group). Even in these cases, however, at the very least fundamental plans for the corporate group and decisions on important matters are made at meetings of the parent company's top-level management. In addition, the CEO of the parent company controls the whole group by retaining control over important personnel appointments and budget allocations to each division or subsidiary. In Japan it is the company's main bank, its principal customer, and its employees' union, rather than its stockholders, that exercise outside influence on the decision-making process.

Corporate culture

(*kigyo bunka*). The unique style and policies of a company. Japanese corporate cultures tend to share certain basic understandings and managerial ideologies that differ from those of Western corporations, including conceptions of such crucial matters as profits, dividends, contractual obligations, and company personnel practices. These features reflect the values and characteristics of Japan's social and economic systems.

Background

In the early Meiji period (1868 – 1912) foreign influence was great on Japanese business community but it soon became only a part of larger and more complex developments, in which the legacies of premodern Japan and particular processes and markets played significant roles in shaping the character of emerging companies. Two sources of indigenous organizational influence were the official *han* (domain) and Tokugawa shogunate bureaucracies and the successful merchant houses (*shoka*). The supreme ideal of serving political authority and thus society was espoused by merchants as well as bureaucrats.

Confucianism with its conception of the social order as one of many parts working together for the common good, its acceptance of hierarchy, and its emphasis on social identity was easily adapted as an ideology for modern organizations. The close-knit agricultural hamlet (*buraku*) and the work-oriented forms of the patron-client (*oyabun-kobun*) relationship are two elemental social institutions influencing Japanese corporate consciousness.

Typical Corporate Ideology

The contemporary Japanese company generally possesses an official company ideology expressed in the company song, in essays by company elders, in catechismlike lists of primary goals and values, and in annual celebrations and public events. Each company's leader seeks to create a distinct ideology and company spirit which portray the company as a big family, or in terms that underline common interest, comradeship, and long-term relationships. Harmony, cooperation, and hard work will bring prosperity and growth despite a fiercely competitive and changing environment. The company is clearly the highest priority, and the morality of membership is judged in terms of loyal service to the company.

It is also common for company ideologies to contain lofty pronouncements stressing that business success must be honestly won with the best interests of society in mind. The company's work is seen as contributing to the glory and prosperity of Japan. The money, the people, the company's history, and the results of business are all seen as merged into one organic social entity.

Socialization and Reinforcement

Japanese have little trouble accepting that companies will try to mold their members to fit a particular ethos and style. The worker's character, attitudes, and values are properly subjects of company concern. Therefore, new employees usually undergo intensive corporate education and training programs.

Training represents a conscious effort on the part of management to reinforce corporate culture. Most employees are willing to participate in informal company-sponsored activities. Relations within small work groups are expected to be personal, warm, and actively developed outside working hours. The ideal boss is one who will aid subordinates in personal problems, give advice, and enter into a close association.

Corporate culture is reinforced by routine behavior. A prime example is the simple matter of morning greetings among workers. Typically company policy calls for a brief ceremony to begin the day in each office or workshop and, however seemingly mundane it may become, its absence can create difficulties.

One of the most characteristic qualities of Japanese corporate culture, in fact, is the degree to which it is managed. Japanese of all ages and stations in life tend to defer to the group, particularly its leaders. Due to the general absence of strong personal religious beliefs, the governance of daily social conduct has typically become a matter of rather particularistic group and institutional norms.

Seniority system

(*nenko joretsu*). System of employment in Japan in which an employee's rank, salary, and qualifications within a firm are based on the length of service in the company. Workers, upon hire, are expected to stay with the company until their retirement. Starting wages are determined by educational background, age, sex, and type of job, while wage increases are primarily governed by age and length of service; retirement pay is based on length of employment, position, and wage level at the time of retirement. Seniority is also an important factor in promotions.

The seniority system enables employees to benefit from stability of employment: the longer they work at a single company, even at comparatively low wages, the greater their overall remuneration. They can benefit from strong worker loyalty and stability and the resultant ease with which they can formulate personnel plans. Employers suffer, however, from the necessity of carrying along surplus workers and growing inflexibility within their organizations.

In the 1970s, with the steady increase in numbers of employees in higher age brackets, the pyramidal personnel structure started to crumble as Japanese corporations began to suffer from skyrocketing labor costs. A growing number of corporations started reviewing the seniority system in the late 1970s, and some even stopped giving pay raises to workers in their forties or older. Particularly since the 1980s, faced with a rapid obsolescence of technology and internationalized activities, Japanese corporations have been forced to place more emphasis on their employees' talents and abilities. Japan's seniority system has thus been placed at an important crossroads.

Settai

(entertaining; particularly entertaining of business clients). In Japan one of the most common ways of showing gratitude to a company's best customers is still to provide entertainment. This typically consists of an invitation to a substantial meal at a Japanese or Western restaurant, followed by one or more visits to Japanese-style hostess bars. Because of the high cost of these evenings, the less favorable tax treatment of such expenses, and the trend among younger persons to spend more time with their families, there has been a tendency toward less conspicuous consumption.

Settai is mainly carried out at expensive Japanese-style restaurants (*ryotei*). The typical *ryotei* is patterned after traditional Japanese houses, with, of course, waitresses dressed in *kimono*. The typical evening in *ryotei* for a valued client usually begins with a meal of 10 or more courses (all rather small in volume) lasting between two and three hours. If the guest is to be particularly honored, the host may call a group of *geisha* to play the *shamisen* (lute) and dance for the party.

The most common alternative to an evening of eating and drinking is an invitation to a round of golf. Since memberships in golf courses can run from nearly ten million yen for a new but distant course to several hundred million yen for courses convenient to Tokyo, golf is regarded as an appropriately prestigious activity with which to reward customers.

Trade

Foreign trade

(*boeki*). In the sense of international commerce, foreign trade can be considered to include financial or capital flows as well.

The Opening of Japan

Japan's modern foreign trade officially began in 1859. The Tokugawa shogunate (1603—1867) until then had maintained a policy of National Seclusion. However, with the signing of the Harris Treaty (United States-Japan Treaty of Amity and Commerce) in July 1858, Japan opened its doors to Western commerce. At the outset the most important Japanese export was raw silk, which was welcomed in the European market. Other exports were primarily raw material goods, semimanufactures, and foodstuffs; these included tea, copper ware, marine products, medicine, oil, and lacquer ware. Key imports were cotton thread, cotton and wool textiles, ironware, sugar, medicinal herbs, military ships, and guns. Approximately 80 percent of Japan's trade was with the United Kingdom, the next largest trading partners being the United States and the Netherlands.

In the initial stage, Japan maintained a continual surplus balance of trade. However, after lowering import tariffs by the signing of the Tariff Convention of 1866, imports of manufactured goods increased, and Japan entered a period of deficit trade balances. Trade treaties concluded during this period did not recognize Japan's right to set its own customs duties, and Japan did not obtain tariff autonomy until 1911.

From the Meiji Restoration (1868) to World War I

After the Meiji Restoration, Japanese foreign trade increased dramatically every year. As part of its efforts to increase production and modernize Japanese industry, the government actively worked to further foreign trade and promoted overseas such products as raw silk, tea, hemp, tobacco, camphor, and soy. Considering individual products, raw silk's percentage of total exports gradually declined from the level of more than 70 percent in 1863. Manufactured goods such as matches, silk products, and cotton textiles began to be exported around 1890. After 1900, raw cotton imports replaced cotton thread, iron became the primary metal import, and ship imports were supplanted by various types of machinery.

In the early Meiji period (1868−1912) almost all commercial trading rights were held by foreign merchants, primarily English traders. According to an 1877 study, 94 percent of all exports were handled by foreign firms.

Japan's trade volume, which in 1870 had been less than ¥30 million (US $84,000), exceeded ¥500 million (US $1.4 million) by World War I. During the 47 years from 1868 to 1915, there were only 12 years in which Japan had a surplus balance of trade.

From World War I Prosperity to a Wartime Trading System

World War I provided the opportunity for a major increase in export business. The war caused a sharp decrease in exports of European and US products and an increase in demand for Japanese products. There was also an increase in exports of military supplies to the countries at war. As a result, the structure of Japanese exports changed, with a decrease in the percentage of raw materials and semimanufactures and an increase in the percentage of finished goods. Compared to prewar statistics, Japan's exports doubled by 1916, and in 1918, the last year of the war, exports were three times prewar levels. The cumulative trade surplus during the four years of the war was ¥1.4 billion (US $3.9 million).

However, because of an increase in Japan's domestic demand, the foreign trade balance changed from a surplus to a deficit. The worldwide Great Depression, which began with the New York stock market crash of 1929, dealt a serious blow to Japan's foreign trade. The adverse effect was heightened by a steep increase in the value of Japanese currency resulting from Japan's ill-timed return to the gold standard in January 1930. Japan's 1930 exports declined 31.6 percent compared to the previous year, and 1931 exports declined another 46.6 percent compared to 1930. Import levels also dropped severely. Imports in 1930 declined 30.2 percent compared to the previous year, and 1931 imports declined 40.3 percent compared to 1930.

Following the Manchurian Incident (1931) Japan adopted foreign trade and exchange controls in the course of organizing its war economy. With the development of trading blocs within the world trading system, the 1930s were marked by a great expansion of Japan's trade with its colonies. After the outbreak of the Sino-Japanese War of 1937−1945, Japan's foreign trade began increasingly to take on a wartime character. While imports became a means of obtaining military materials, exports were promoted in order to acquire the foreign currency needed for imports.

Japanese trade controls were imposed progressively, and in 1941, with the issuance of the Trade Control Order, Japan began a program of general mobilization. Consequently, Japan became heavily dependent on trade within the "yen bloc," which included its colonies, and trade with countries outside this bloc was cut drastically. Japan had a trade surplus with respect to yen bloc countries and a large trade deficit with other countries.

Foreign Trade after World War II

Immediately following World War II, the devastation of Japan caused a continuing foreign trade deficit as well as a chronic lack of foreign currency. It is not until the high-growth period of the late 1950s and early 1960s that export power increased significantly because of dramatic advances in manufacturing capacity and technology. Japan's trade balance began to show a surplus starting in the second half of the 1960s. Although oil crises in 1973 and 1979 caused a temporary balance-of-trade deficit, in the second half of the 1980s, Japan's trade surplus soared, reaching a peak of US $96.4 billion in 1987, then fluctuated.

Postwar Exports

In the 1960s, Japan's average dollar-base export increase of 18.4

percent per year was 2.3 times the overall rate of increase in world trade. The makeup of Japan's exports continued to shift to the heavy-industry fields of steel, machinery, and chemical products and away from textiles and light-industry products. In the 1970s, exports of machinery and electronics jumped as increasing emphasis was placed on high-value-added products. As a result, the focus of trade friction shifted from textiles and steel to products such as color televisions and automobiles. In the 1980s, exports of advanced-technology-intensive products including computers, semiconductors, videocassette recorders, machine tools, and facsimile machines continued to increase sharply, and trade friction over these products began to occur. Developing nations, primarily countries in Southeast Asia are important destinations. In the 1980s, one-third of all exports went to the United States.

Postwar Imports

The relative importance of textile raw materials which made up the bulk of the imports in the postwar period decreased and that of mineral fuels and metal raw materials increased, while the price of oil dropped and development of Japanese heavy industry slowed down. In 1980 mineral fuels were approximately 50 percent of total imports. By 1990, however, mineral fuels had fallen to 24.2 percent of imports due to lower oil prices and the successful energy-conservation efforts of Japanese industry. During the same period imports of manufactured goods increased, and in 1990 they constituted more than 50 percent of Japan's imports.

Prior to the oil crisis of 1973, approximately one-third of Japan's imports came from the United States, approximately one-sixth from Southeast Asia, and only about one-eighth from the Middle and Near East. Following the oil crisis, the Middle and Near East, which supply 70 percent of Japan's imported oil, provided nearly 30 percent of total imports, and the US share fell to less than 20 percent.

In the 1980s, imports of manufactured goods from Europe, the United States, and the developing countries of Asia increased.

Foreign trade, government policy on

(*boeki seisaku*). Japan's modern trade policy began in the Meiji period (1868−1912), and its first major objective was the achievement of parity with the West. Until the end of the Unequal Treaties, tariffs and trade were in the hands of the Western powers, so the Japanese fovernment was limited in the measures it could take to improve the nation's trade position. The government promoted industrialization and economic development through subsidies, loans, and technical assistance. This necessitated the import of equipment, ships, steel, and other commodities that Japan itself did not make and that had to be paid for by exports. Thus evolved what has remained a fundamental part of Japan's trade policy: Japan exports in order to import.

After 1899 tariff protection of specific industries was undertaken. At the same time, tariffs on raw materials were kept low, increasing the effective protection and further stimulating manufacturing. The need to secure raw material and markets in a hostile international trading environment led to efforts to form the so-called Greater East Asia Coprosperity Sphere in the years immediately preceding World War II.

Following the war there was an immediate need to resuscitate the economy, especially trade. Specific trade-related measures were taken. Priorities for imports were set by the government in conjunction with business. There were protective tariffs on manufactured goods, while raw materials were allowed in essentially duty-free. Specific assistance was given or removed as industries developed or gained strength. Thus steel was given priority first, then automobiles in the 1950s, and computers in the 1960s and 1970s. Industries with either export potential or strategic economic importance were favored, and the government encouraged exports via special tax and credit incentives.

Fundamental economic policies have had as much of an impact on trade as trade-specific policies. The government's push to industrialize placed a premium on investment and growth. Financial resources were channeled through the city banks, the government development banks, the tax structure, and the government's expenditure patterns to such areas as steel, chemicals, shipping, and shipbuilding. The primary architect of the plan was the Heavy Industry Bureau of the Ministry of International Trade and Industry (MITI), along with the Ministry of Finance. The focus on growth and industrialization in turn led to rapid increases in manufacturing investment and productivity, which enhanced Japanese competitiveness.

Import liberalization continued slowly through the 1960s and 1970s as Japan's industrial strength and export surplus developed further. After 1968, Japan's export surplus developed rapidly due to the Vietnam War, rising US inflation, and Japan's improving productivity. In turn, external pressures, especially from the United States, for real and substantive liberalization increased markedly. But the government still did not embrace full liberalization quickly.

Beginning in the 1980s the major trade issue has been the growing trade surplus, and Japan's current trade policies are thus increasingly oriented toward encouraging imports while keeping the volume of exports down. This has created the need for major institutional reversals, which have been difficult to achieve. Some obvious policy steps have been taken to encourage imports, including unilateral tariff cuts, removal of import restrictions, reform of the system for standards certification, and import promotion campaigns. In addition, there have been periodic voluntary export restrictions on items such as automobiles to specific markets. Liberalization of agricultural imports, particularly rice, continued to be a politically sensitive issue, since almost all political parties' owe a considerable part of their support to agriculture. However, the coalition government of Prime Minister Hosokawa Morihiro (1938—)finally broke the taboo and decided at the end of 1993 that it would partially open the rice market to imports. The decision was a part of the last-minute agreement reached at the Uruguay Round as well as an emergency measure to make up for a poor rice crop that year. Still, much remains to be done to change ingrained procedures.

Trade friction

(*boeki masatsu*). Trade friction has been a recurring issue in Japan's relationships with other nations since the mid-1950s. Until the early 1980s, friction primarily involved efforts to control rising Japanese exports and to prevent alleged dumping of Japanese products. In contrast, during most of the 1980s Japan's trade disputes with the United States typically involved attempts to gain greater access to the Japanese market. The Structural Impediments Initiative talks, which began in 1989, marked a new phase by addressing so-called nontariff obstacles to trade between the United States and Japan.

The history of Japan's trade friction is both lengthy and broad in scope. For example, until about 1981 Japan placed voluntary limits on exports from cotton goods through steel to automobiles to the United States. Japan also agreed to restrain its steel exports to Europe in 1972. To counter dumping, the United States instituted a formula to trigger penalties on steel and machine tools imported at unfairly low prices (1978).

Through the late 1970s and the 1980s, as a result of the US objective of improving access to the Japanese market, the following accommodations were reached: increases in Japanese import quotas in beef and oranges, revision of Japanese import standards and certification procedures, the Japanese government's Action Program to Improve Market Access, the Japan-United States Semiconductor Agreement, and the Market-Oriented Sector Selective agreement covering Japanese markets for telecommunications equipment, electronics, pharmaceuticals, medical equipment, forest products, and transportation equipment.

Similarly, the "Super 301" clause of the US Omnibus Trade and Competitiveness Act (1988) was applied to improve access to Japan's supercomputer, satellite, and wood product markets (1988). In contrast with the market-opening approach adopted by the United States, Japan has had a number of disputes with the EC countries and Australia concerning Japanese exports of videocassette recorders and semiconductors.

Under the Structural Impediments Initiative agreement of 1990, Japan and the United States established a wide-ranging basis on which each country will address structural issues affecting bilateral trade. Specifically, Japan has agreed to investigate price differentials existing betwen Japan and other countries, Japanese distribution and business group practices, and other issues. For its part, the United States has agreed to address its fiscal deficit, the link between savings and investment, corporate capital spending and research-and-development practices, and other matters.

Disagreement among the nations of the European Community, the United States, and Japan over agricultural trade has stalled talks since the start of the so-called Uruguay Round of 1986. In Japan there is considerable domestic opposition to liberalization of its rice market, since major political parties were steadfast defenders of farmers. Under these circumstances, the Hosokawa coalition government, replacing the Liberal Democratic Party leadership which had been dominant of 38 years, carefully arranged the opening of the market and announced the decision of partial liberalization in December 1993.

The series of negotiated settlements covering Japan's trade friction has in turn spawned a number of significant economic developments. For example, Japan has responded to restrictions on exports by moving production of some products such as color televisions and automobiles to the United States. Japanese companies also increased the number of automobiles manufactured in Europe, notably the United Kingdom.

Trade balance

(*boeki shushi*). The difference over a period of time between the value of a country's exports and imports of merchandise.

Japan experienced a continuing deficit trade balance after World War II and also suffered from a chronic shortage of foreign currency. After about 1964, however, Japan's trade balance began to show a surplus. Earlier equipment investments contributed to the improvement. Another factor was lower commodity price increases in Japan than in the United States and Europe, which strengthened the international competitiveness of Japanese products. In 1974 Japan's trade surplus fell sharply due to a rise in the value of the yen (a result of the changeover to a floating exchange rate system) and steep increases in oil prices. However, Japan's trade surplus again expanded as a result of rapid progress in the development of Japan's industrial structure.

In the 1980s such factors as macroeconomic structural disparities between Japan and the United States, Japan's high savings rate, and excess consumption in the Western countries contributed to further increases in the Japanese trade surplus, which in 1984 reached US $44.0 billion, a dramatic increase over the previous year's figure of US $9.5 billion. Japan's yearly trade surplus continued to climb and in 1988 reached US $95.0 billion, of which US $47.6 billion was with the United States alone. Japan's one-sided trade balance with the United States is a major cause of continuing friction between the two countries.

Balance of payments

(*kokusai shushi*). A statistical record of all economic transactions between residents of the reporting country and residents of all other countries.

Merchandise Trade Balance

Defined as the difference between exports and imports, this is one of the most frequently used measures of a country's balance-of-payments performance. Japan ran a deficit in merchandise trade in the early postwar years through the mid-1950s, a time when the national economy did not achieve full recovery. By the mid-1960s Japan had increased its international competitiveness to the point where it began consistently to run a surplus in its merchandise trade balance. Expanding rapidly in the 1980s, reaching its peak in 1987, the surplus began to decrease in 1988 as a result of expanding domestic demand and the yen's appreciation following the Plaza Accord of September 1985. In 1990 Japan's total trade surplus was US $63.5 billion, including a surplus of US $38.0 billion with the United States, US $18.5 billion with the European Community, and US $28.1 billion with the developing economies of East and Southeast Asia.

Trade Balance in Invisibles

Invisible items include expenditures and receipts for transportation, insurance, business travel and tourism, investment income, and interest on loans. Data on Japanese transactions in invisibles since 1961 show a consistent trend toward larger and larger deficits. A number of factors account for the deficits. First, it took a long time for Japan to build up foreign assets to the point where earnings on those assets had a perceptible impact on the net invisibles account. Second, because of Japan's imports of raw materials, transportation payments tend to be high. Third, for years Japan has paid a considerable amount in licensing arrangements for technology to foreign firms. In the second half of the 1980s, Japan's deficit in invisible trade increased rapidly because of the rise in the yen's value and increases in overseas tourism. Japan's deficit in unilateral transfers, a part of invisible trade, also grew quickly during this period because of increases in official development assistance (ODA).

Current Account Balance

This balance combines net merchandise trade, transfer payments, and net invisibles. Japan's current account fluctuated between deficit and surplus in the mid-1950s and mid-1960s, reflecting the business cycle. It has since maintained a consistent current account surplus except for a few years of the two oil crises in the 1970s. In the first half of the 1980s the current account surplus grew due to a drop in oil prices and to increases in exports. However, after peaking as a percentage of the gross national product (GNP) at 4.3 percent in 1986 and peaking in absolute terms at US $87 billion in 1987, it has since fallen substantially. The fall can be attributed to several factors, including a sharp appreciation of the yen and increase in public investment that were designed to spur domestic demand. In 1990 the current account surplus was US $35.8 billion, or 1.2 percent of the GNP.

Trade liberalization

(*boeki jiyuka*). Immediately after World War II, Japan was allowed to maintain import restrictions. As a condition for joining international organizations such as the General Agreement on Tariffs and Trade (GATT) and the International Monetary Fund (IMF), however, Japan was required to liberalize substantially its trade policies. In 1955 the percentage of liberalized products was only 15 percent, but this figure rose to 90 percent by 1963. International trade was liberalized further in the 1960s as the result of multilateral tariff negotiations by GATT. In 1967 Japan instituted the across-the-board tariff reductions agreed to during the talks known as the Kennedy Round and removed tariffs from 2,147 items. Discussions in the mid-1970s known as the Tokyo Round removed more tariffs.

In the 1980s Japan adopted other measures to open its domestic market to imports. In the Action Program for Improving Market Access in 1985, tariffs were reduced on or removed from 1,853 items. Japan's tariff rates are the lowest among the advanced industrialized countries. As of 1992, Japan still protected 12 agricultural products through import quotas, but international pressures were moving Japan closer to removing restrictions.

JETRO

(Jetoro). Acronym of the Japan External Trade Organization (Nihon Boeki Shinkokai). Japan's official trade promotion association, supervised by the Ministry of International Trade and Industry. Established in 1958. Although originally set up to promote exports from Japan, JETRO's activities have stressed both import and export promotion in recent years. JETRO offices overseas provide information on overseas markets to Japanese exporters and information to foreign concerns interested in the Japanese market.

Industries

Industrial history

(*sangyoshi*). The country's modern industrial history can be roughly divided into two periods: first, the early modern era from the Meiji Restoration (1868) to the end of World War II, during which capitalism was established in Japan, and second, the contemporary period which has seen reconstruction and rapid economic growth.

Early Modern Industry (1868 − 1945)

Japan's industrial revolution began in the late 1880s. Light industry, notably the textile industry, grew rapidly between 1887 and 1896, while a second wave of industrialization between 1897 and 1906 led to the establishment of many heavy industries. The Meiji government took the lead in developing such basic industries as railroads and mining, as well as a number of manufacturing industries such as shipbuilding, iron and steel, and machine tool. Most of these enterprises were later turned over to the private sector.

During World War I Japanese industry experienced significant growth, as it benefited greatly from the inability of European suppliers, preoccupied with the war, to trade in Asian markets. Japan provided the Allies with military supplies, and there was great demand for Japanese shipping. An industrial boom took place during the period of the war as the values of Japanese exports rose threefold, and there was a rapid accumulation of capital. Industrial production overtook agricultural production during the war; capitalism in Japan had become fully entrenched.

Despite economic hardships caused by a depression in 1920, the Tokyo Earthquake of 1923, and the Showa Depression of the 1930s, the productivity of Japanese industry continued to increase as a result of technological progress, greater efficiency in production techniques, and the development of managerial techniques designed to secure employee loyalty. Japan's heavy industries, such as iron and steel and shipbuilding, grew rapidly in the 1930s. The output of the chemical industry and the machine tool, electric machinery, and ceramics industries all increased greatly during this period. Exports rose sharply, led by shipments of textile products and sundry goods. In the precision machinery industry, which became the foundation for Japan's munitions industry, domestic products were almost meeting domestic demand.

Throughout this period there was no antimonopoly policy in Japan. Since the Meiji Restoration the overriding concern of the nation's leaders had been Japan's national survival in the face of the political and economic threat of Western domination. Therefore, in the period before Japan's defeat in World War II it is not clear that the government placed a premium on economic competition in itself. Administrations considered rather that the national interest would best be served by supporting the interests of large, powerful, and well-established companies such as the Mitsui, Mitsubishi, and Sumitomo—the *zaibatsu* (financial cliques)—that had the resources to lead the nation's industrial progress. The zaibatsu dominated industry in this period, exercising an oligopolistic control over a wide range of industries such as manufacturing, mining, and transportation, as well as finance and overseas trade.

Meanwhile, a dual structure had developed within the manufacturing industry itself, between, on the one hand, the relatively small number of firms with capital-intensive production methods, and, on the other hand, vast numbers of low-capital, labor-intensive small firms and family concerns. In 1930, 60 percent of the nation's manufacturing labor force was employed by firms with fewer than 10 workers. Although this figure had fallen to just 9 percent by 1986, the "dual structure"—the high proportion of smaller-scale businesses in dependency relationships with larger firms—has continued to be a key characteristic of the Japanese economy in the post-World War II period.

A great many new industries emerged in the years between the world wars. For instance, the development of the electric power industry gave a great boost to the domestic aluminum-smelting industry. The development of the radio led to the beginning of vacuum tube production. Many new businesses entered this area, including the companies now known as Toshiba Corporation and Victor Co of Japan, Ltd. Many other major Japanese manufacturing companies of the present day were founded at this time, such as Toyota Motor Corporation, Nissan Motor Co, Ltd, and Mitsubishi Heavy Industries, Ltd.

Subsidies supported the production of military vehicles and the substitution of domestic production for the import of cargo ships. The birth of Nippon Seitetsu (Nippon Steel Co), an iron and steel trust, was the result of government guidance. Industrial growth was also fostered by laws enacted for individual industries, with emphasis placed on automobiles, the petrochemical industry, iron and steel, machine tools, and aircraft manufacturing. For example, the infant automotive industry was promoted by the Automobile Manufacturing Industry Law of 1935.

Contemporary Industrial History (from 1945)

During the reconstruction period following World War II, the recovery of key industries was aided by an industrial policy known as the Priority Production Program. Underdeveloped capacity in certain areas was seen as a bottleneck limiting overall growth, so the electric power, iron and steel, marine transportation, and coal industries were targeted for rapid reconstruction.

The Korean War (1950—1953) enabled Japanese industry to climb out of stagnation in which it was mired at the end of the 1940s. By supplying the United Nations forces serving in Korea with the vast quantities of matériel, Japan was able to earn the foreign exchange necessary to pay for vital imports; the war thus provided the stimulus for the economic recovery of the 1950s.

During the rapid-growth period from the late 1950s to the early 1970s, industries such as iron and steel, the construction industry, and the pharmaceutical industry grew quickly, and the household electrical products industry and the petrochemical industry developed. The international economic environment at this time was favorable for Japanese exports; in the 1960s, Japan's average export increase of 18.4 percent per year was 2.5 times the overall increase in world trade. This period saw the establishment of an industrial structure based on imported raw materials that were domestically processed for export.

In the wake of the export successes of the iron and steel and shipbuilding industries, other industries such as precision machinery and electronic and optical equipment also turned to export-led growth. Huge investments were made in production facilities for heavy industry, located in the Tokaido megalopolis that stretches along the Pacific coast from Tokyo to Osaka and Kobe. Total plant and equipment investments exceeded profits, and the ratio of borrowed capital increased.

Aggressive management created an increasing demand for funds, which banks satisfied using their large volumes of household savings deposits. Relationships between corporations and their main banks became closer, and industrial groups of affiliated companies formed around major banks (*keiretsu*). This aggressive corporate capitalism and strong reliance on indirect financing were characteristic of the Japanese industrial structure and were the basic mechanisms responsible for the strong economic growth. Japan's national income more than doubled in the 1960s, and in 1968 its gross national product became the second largest among the world's market economies. The spring labor offensive (*shunto*) became in the 1960s the established mechanism by which labor bargained for more equitable income distribution.

Efforts to reduce costs and increase efficiency in response to the oil crisis of 1973 strengthened the competitiveness of major export industries. Successful conservation efforts were made by both management and labor; as a result, energy demand fell by 37 percent in the chemical industry and by more than 20 percent in the iron and steel industry. In the automobile industry energy-saving efforts led to lighter automobiles and increased fuel economy, which further increased export competitiveness.

The oil crisis of 1979 also caused distinctive changes in the country's industrial structure. The heavy industries, which had supported rapid economic growth, stagnated, and the emphasis shifted to industries such as electronics and automobile that utilize high technology and sophisticated machinery. Productivity increased through innovations such as the mounting of small computers on machine tools to develop numerically controlled equipment. It was also during the late 1970s that the computer industry and the semiconductor industry began to grow rapidly.

Although the yen's appreciation later reduced the price competitiveness of Japanese exports, export volume remains high. Japan, which had relied on exports for its economic recovery, has been strongly criticized for not taking action to stimulate domestic demand, and trade friction has become a pressing issue.

Many outside observers tend to emphasize the role of the intimate relationship between business and government in increasing industrial competitiveness of Japan. Since the Meiji Restoration, Japanese administrations have indeed worked closely with industry to develop Japan's economy. It is argued that, particularly since World War II, the government has identified key industrial sectors for development and then actively encouraged major corporations to undertake the necessary research, investment, and development. Recent examples were the official encouragements in the early 1980s to Japanese manufacturers to overtake the US computer giant IBM. However, other observers have insisted that much of the credit for Japan's rapid economic growth must be given to the private sector rather than the government. They claim that the introduction of new technologies and the development of new products owe more to the mechanisms of market competition than they do to the leadership of government, and that in many key areas, such as robotics, the government was slow to respond to the challenge of the new technology.

Industrial structure

(*sangyo kozo*). National economies are conventionally divided into three sectors: primary industries (agriculture, forestry, and fisheries), secondary industries (mining, manufacturing, and construction), and tertiary industries (transportation, communications, retail and wholesale trade, banking, finance and real estate, business services, personal services, and public administration). In general, national economies in the early stages of development are dominated by primary production related to land. As the economy develops and income rises, the primary sector shares of output, capital, and labor tend to fall, and those of the secondary sector tend to rise. In late stages of development, the primary sector accounts for only a small fraction of total economic activities, the secondary sector begins to decline in relative terms, and the tertiary sector comes to the fore.

Historical Experience of Japan

Japan's economic development since the Meiji Restoration (1868) is an excellent illustration of these patterns. In the distribution of the labor force between agriculture and nonagriculture, changes were slow until the early 1900s, considerably accelerated from then up to World War II, and very rapid during the decades following disruption of the war. After 1960 the agricultural labor force began to contract in absolute terms, and even those who remained on farms worked only part-time as farmers.

In the secondary sector, statistics show a continued relative expansion in employment and production until the mid-1970s. The tertiary sector maintained a relatively stable share in net domestic product before World War II, although its share of the national labor force expanded. After World War II, its share of employment continued to increase, while its share of gross domestic product (GDP) remained stable until the early 1960s when it, too, started to rise.

Changes in Manufacturing

A broad comparison of light and heavy manufacturing reveals that light manufacturing accounted for as much as 85 percent of total production until 1900. From then on, the share steadily declined, and after 100 years the relative positions of light and heavy manufacturing were reversed. Textile output jumped above 25 percent of the total in the 1890s from less than 10 percent of the total of the 1870s and stayed close to 30 percent until World War II. Its continued expansion through the prewar period provided significant employment opportunities for surplus female labor in agriculture. This was a salient feature of prewar labor mobility. After World War II, the textile industry began to decline; by 1990 the industry accounted for only 3.1 percent of the national labor force.

In heavy manufacturing, the iron and steel industry began to expand in the decade beginning in 1910, but government protection was necessary to shield it from international competition. After World War II, basic metals maintained a stable share of manufacturing output. On the other hand, the machine tool industry, after making relatively slow progress in the pre-World War II period, experienced a spectacular expansion in the three decades after 1945; its share of manufacturing output exceeded 40 percent by 1972. Japan is now one of the world's leading exporters of machinery. The chemical industry maintained a comparatively stable 10 percent share before World War II and rose to 20 percent after the war.

The most recent stage in the development of national economies has been called postindustrialism, which is marked by a decrease in the employment share of the secondary sector, a shift from production of goods to services. This "service revolution" brings the continuing growth of tertiary industries; it seems to have begun in Japan in the mid-1970s, when manufacturing employment started to decline. In 1990 the tertiary sector accounted for 60.8 percent of total output and employed 59.0 percent of the national labor force.

Relationship to the Foreign Trade Structure

The composition of a nation's exports and imports closely reflects its stage of industrialization. Japan's main exports were tea and raw silk when the country opened its doors to foreign powers in the 1860s, and raw silk remained the most important export item until 1929. In the 1930s, cotton replaced raw silk as a major export of Japan. In the early postwar period, more than half of exports were in light manufacturing, but with the expansion of heavy industries Japanese exports continued to shift to heavy manufactured goods, which came to account for more than 87 percent of the total value of exports by 1990.

Japan's imports consisted almost entirely of manufactured products in the early Meiji period. Industrialization in the subsequent decades enabled Japan to increase imports of crude materials. Thus, in the 1930s, Japan's imports consisted of light manufactures (12 percent), heavy manufactures (30 percent), foodstuffs (18 percent), raw materials (33 percent), and fuels (7 percent). Comparable figures in 1988—1990 were 16, 31, 14, 14, and 22 percent (others 3 percent), respectively.

Agriculture

(*nogyo*). Prior to the Meiji Restoration of 1868, as much as 80 percent of the population of Japan was engaged in farming. Rice has been overwhelmingly dominant as the main crop. The emphasis has always been on improving productivity per unit of land area in rice and other plant crops. Highly labor-intensive farming methods were developed as a result of the limited acreage allotted to each farm household. These agricultural characteristics gave rise to farming practices and folk customs that in turn profoundly affected the nature of Japanese culture as a whole. Since the Meiji Restoration, industrialization and urbanization have had a significant impact on Japanese agriculture. The proportion of farmers to the total population, the proportion of cultivated acreage to the total area of the country, and the relative importance of agriculture in the total economy have all declined, while the importation of foodstuffs has increased. With these tendencies, many of the events and customs of Japanese rural life have begun to lose their importance.

History of Agriculture

Japanese agriculture began about 2,000 years ago with the cultivation of rice. Other crops cultivated in Japan since ancient times include wheat, barley, *awa* (Italian millet), *hie* (barnyard millet), soybeans, *azuki*, *daikon*, and cucurbits.

The oldest farm tools were made of wood or stone. When technology from the continent brought the manufacture of iron tools, rapid progress in agriculture was made and much wasteland was brought under cultivation.

From the end of the Heian period (794–1185) influential families emerged in the provinces and accumulated wealth through agricultural production. Taking control of the government in the Kamakura period (1185–1333), they showed greater concern about agriculture and encouraged improvements. With the emergence of a large number of cities and towns in Edo period (1600–1868), the percentage of the population not engaged in agriculture increased, and farmers were required to produce more and more. However, more than half of the rice produced was collected as land tax, and farmers were frequently left with insufficient amounts for their own needs. They made do with wheat, barley, or millet. Agricultural output was increased with endeavors in three major areas: reclaimed lands, fertilizers, and plant breeding.

During Japan's drive toward modernization after the Meiji Restoration, Western practices in agriculture were studied closely. However, since the natural condition in Japan is quite different from the West, mere transplantation of foreign technology often did not work well. Emphasis was shifted, therefore, back to rice as the main crop and to the development of intensive farming methods. Agriculture experimental stations, too, were built by the state to conduct most of the plant breeding of important crops.

Agricultural Modernization

Of all the reform programs that followed World War II, the Land Reforms of 1946 were perhaps the most successful in bringing about basic and far-reaching changes in Japan. A sweeping redistribution of land largely eliminated tenancy by 1949 and resulted in about 90 percent of cultivated land being farmed by owners. Postwar food shortages, high prices, a black market in rice, and general inflation all worked to the advantage of Japan's farmers. In most cases they were able to pay off the debts on their new land with relative ease and to begin investing the capital that was needed for the rationalization of agriculture. The government aided farmers by establishing price support programs, especially for rice. It also gave strong support to agricultural technical schools, experimental stations, and extension programs. Agricultural Cooperative Associations enhanced these government initiatives by extending low-interest loans and developing group marketing at the village level. The end result was a relatively affluent farming population with the education, incentive, and access to capital needed to purchase the new crop strains and fertilizers to increase yields, as well as the machinery to ease labor demand.

Japan began to experience labor shortages by the late 1950s after the beginning of economic growth. The demand for labor in the urban-industrial centers resulted in a growing exodus of people from rural areas. A large part of the present agricultural labor force is over 45 years of age. Part-time farmers are numerous, and well over half the labor force is female.

It seems unlikely that Japanese agriculture could have succeeded without the spread of machines, chemicals, and other labor-saving devices. Virtually all land is now cultivated by machine. Traditional methods of farming are rapidly giving way to power cultivators, tractors, and other machines. Due to all of these factors Japan's total rice crop increased from about 9.5 million metric tons (10.5 million short tons) in 1950 to over 13 million metric tons (14.3 million short tons) in 1975. Per capita rice consumption, however, has declined, and the government is now concerned with problems of overproduction and surplus storage. Farmers have been encouraged, and in some cases subsidized, to convert their rice fields to other crops. However, this governmental policy of production adjustment worked negatively in the face of an extremely poor rice crop such as one in 1993. Accompanying changes in Japanese eating habits, production of meat, dairy products, fruits, and vegetables has increased.

Japan's traditional labor-intensive agriculture has been transformed into a highly mechanized and capital-intensive system in less than a generation and much of its new technology serves as a model for other developing Asian nations. Yet some problems and questions remain for the future. Production costs, especially for rice, are very high, and Japanese agriculture requires heavy subsidies. Most farms are too small in scale for maximum utilization of land and capital. When and how Japanese farms will reach a more efficient size still remains to be solved.

Fish and shellfish farming

(*yoshoku; saibai gyogyo*). The artificial cultivation of marine products (also called aquiculture) plays an important role in the Japanese fishing industry. Japan has long been engaged in the farming of freshwater fish, *nori* (a type of seaweed), and oysters. In recent years the farming of such choice fish as yellowtail, red sea bream, and prawns has proliferated. In addition, a large number of fish and shellfish farming centers have been established along Japan's shores, where selected species of fish and shellfish are artificially bred and raised to a certain size, then released to the sea to grow to sizes fit for harvesting.

Freshwater Fish Culture

The climate in Japan ranges from near subarctic to semitropical, and intensive farming of a variety of species of both cold and warm water fish has developed through the use of sophisticated fish culture techniques.

Species that have been successfully farmed in Japan include tilapia. Experimental farming of a total of eight strains of tilapia was attempted, and the results showed that *T. nirotica* was best suited to the Japanese climate.

Saltwater Fish Culture

Nori and oyster farming are said to have started in Japan about 300 years ago. However, it was only in 1957 that saltwater fish (yellowtail) farming was started in earnest. Saltwater farming is also applied to shrimp, lobsters, prawns, octopuses, oysters, scallops, and seaweed (nori, *wakame*, and kelp).

Methods of Culture

Methods of culture are divided into lake, river, pond, paddyfield, reservoir, canal, and shallow saltwater cultures. Methods are also classified by type of facility as follows: fish preserve, net-enclosure, embankment, pond, reservoir, and raft cultures.

Typically, seeds are bred artificially and raised in a controlled environment to commercial sizes, then shipped to the farms. The method in which artificially bred seeds are raised to egg-bearing sizes and then harvested after bearing the eggs is called full-cycle culture.

In the case of freshwater fish, composite feed is used, while fish meat is used for feeding saltwater fish (except sea bream). Ingredients for composite feed are adjusted to the nutrition requirements of different species. Such abundant and inexpensive fish as sardines, mackerel, and saury pike are used as feed, either fresh or frozen. Oxygen is supplied by exchanging the water in the fish farm, so it is necessary to maintain the fish population at a level compatible with the water-exchanging capacity of the farm.

Fish Farming

Fish farming is carried out through public projects of the central and prefectural governments. The term "fish farming" refers to an operation in which fish seeds are produced in large quantity, released in a protected sea environment for growth, and harvested when grown to a commercial size. Fish and shellfish now being raised, including those in the experimental stage, cover about 100 species, including yellowtail, harvest fish, flounder, horse mackerel, hardtail, Spanish mackerel, grouper, rockfish, rock trout, black porgy, flatfish, king crab, northern sea shrimp, and cuttlefish.

Forestry

(*ringyo*). About 70 percent of Japan's total area is wooded. Forests play a particularly important role in land conservation in Japan, as steep mountain ranges run along the midline of the islands from north to south and the rivers are short and torrential. Japan is a great consumer of wood as well as the world's greatest importer of logs and wood chips (accounting for about 20 percent of the world's wood trade). It is also notable for its exceptionally high proportion of planted forests, which occupy about 40 percent of the nation's total forest area.

Forest Conditions in Japan

A great variety of trees grow in Japan because of the marked temperature differences from north to south and a high level of humidity brought about by warm ocean currents. Trees can be classified as evergreen broad-leaved types such as camellias and *kusunoki* (camphor tree), deciduous broad-leaved types such as *buna* (beech) and *tochinoki* (Japanese horse chestnut), and conifers such as *sugi* (cedar) and *hinoki* (cypress). Of the total forest area of about 24.7 million hectares (61.0 million acres), about 9.9 million hectares (24.5 million acres) support planted forests consisting mainly of cedar, cypress, and pines.

Forestry Operations

In the 18th century, exploitive forestry aiming at simply gathering wood from natural forests was replaced by sustained-yield forestry with artificial planting and cultivation of trees. After the Meiji Restoration of 1868 forestland was divided into privately owned and government-owned areas. National forests account for about 7.3 million hectares (18.0 million acres) of the total wooded area of Japan, private forests for 14.0 million hectares (34.6 million acres), and forests owned by local governments for the remainder. Private forests occupy 56 percent of Japan's entire forest area. The continued migration of young farm workers to urban areas and factories has greatly reduced the number of forestry workers.

History of Wood Utilization

Wood has been used for construction and fuel in Japan since early times, but the use of lumber for construction increased rapidly starting in the 8th century as wooden palaces and temples such as Todaiji and Toji were built. The city of Kyoto became Japan's center of wood consumption.

The flourishing of urban culture in the Edo period (1600−1868) accelerated an increasing demand for wood products for furniture, building, and fuel. Starting in the late 18th century, regional lumber markets developed along the lower reaches of the large rivers; these markets continued to grow in the 19th century. With the modernization of the Japanese economy following the Meiji Restoration, the demand for wood grew rapidly. Following the Tokyo Earthquake of 1923, imports, particularly from the United States, became an important factor in Japan's wood supply.

After World War II, the need for building materials escalated, as did the demand for such wood products as paper pulp and plywood. However, domestic production was on the decline. Finally, in recent years emphasis has been increasingly placed on forests as places of recreation and as natural environments in need of conservation. Thus Japan has had to rely more and more on outside sources of wood. In 1990 Japan's total wood consumption was 113 million cubic meters (4.0 billion cu ft), of which only 28 percent was domestically produced. Lumber made up 48 percent of the total, pulp and wood chips 37 percent, and plywood 13 percent.

Chemical industry

(*kagaku kogyo*). The Japanese chemical industry was created in the 1870s, when the government imported technologies for the production of glass, inorganic chemicals, cement, and other products from the West. The electrochemical industry was developed during the early 1900s. On the eve of World War II, production in the chemical fertilizer, rayon, and soda industries had reached international levels.

After the war, the first industry to recover was chemical fertilizers, because of the urgent need to increase food production. In the late 1950s, the Japanese petrochemical industry made its debut, spurred by two major factors. First, the conversion of energy production from hydroelectric and coal to oil resulted in a surplus of naphtha (a product of oil refining and an important material for petrochemical production). Second, the enactment of the Foreign Investment Law facilitated the introduction of foreign technology. The Japanese chemical industry accounted for 7.4 percent (¥22.1 trillion; US $160.5 billion) of the nation's industrial output in 1989, a full 42 percent of the industry's output being in petrochemicals. The fine chemicals sector (pharmaceuticals and cosmetics) has been steadily expanding since the mid-1980s. The industry was investing heavily in the research and development of new materials and biotechnology products, spending ¥687.4 billion (US $4.1 billion) in 1987. New materials are being used in many areas, and biotechnology applications have begun in such fields as medical products and horticulture.

Computer industry

(kompyuta sangyo). Japan has the second largest data-processing industry in the world after that of the United States, with large-scale subsectors producing mainframe computers, minicomputers, peripheral equipment, and software. Japan is the second largest computer market in the world after the United States, and accounts for about 20 percent of all computer sales worldwide. In 1989 the Japanese industry controlled 60 percent of the domestic mainframe market and 70 percent of the domestic market for office computer equipment. Total domestic production in 1990 reached ¥5.81 trillion (US $40.1 billion), and exports amounted to about ¥1.7 trillion (US $11.7 billion).

The market for personal computers was dominated by NEC's 50 percent share. Manufacture and sales of personal computers are particularly vigorous; over 2.9 million units were produced in 1989, and the market was valued at ¥798.9 billion (US $6.9 billion). On the technical front, research and development programs are currently under way for fifth-generation computer systems.

History

Although Osaka University launched Japan's first computer

development program in 1947, the first electronic digital computer was not constructed until 1956, 10 years after ENIAC, the first electronic computer was developed in the United States. Following the first exports of US computers to Japan in 1954, the Ministry of International Trade and Industry (MITI) organized the Research Committee on the Computer to coordinate computer industry development, but computers did not attain urgent priority in Japanese industrial policy until the mid-1960s.

In 1960 IBM was granted permission to manufacture in Japan in return for licensing basic patents to all interested Japanese manufacturers; 13 Japanese companies immediately entered cross-licensing agreements with IBM. RCA, TRW, Honeywell, General Electric, and Sperry Rand as well entered technical assistance agreements with Japanese makers.

The Japanese government's vigorous promotion of the computer industry dates from 1964. In that year IBM's introduction of its System 360 and its success at the Tokyo Olympic Games graphically demonstrated to Japanese political and business circles the strategic potential of computers. Interest was also stimulated by the purchase of the largest French computer manufacturer by the US firm General Electric. Computers came to be seen in Japan as a strategic industry whose fate held profound implications for Japan's future.

To achieve rapid advancement in domestic computer technologies, MITI launched several national priority projects. The FONTAC project (1962—1964), undertaken by Fujitsu, Oki and NEC, was the first prototype manufacturing project of a general-purpose large-scale computer system in Japan. Another project, aimed at prototype manufacture of a super-high-performance computer system, was undertaken from 1966 to 1972, based on the Electronics Industry Deliberation Council Report of 1966 and prepared under the aegis of MITI. As a result of the commercial agreements with US firms and the success of these vigorously coordinated domestic projects, the Japanese computer industry made rapid strides in the late 1960s. Epitomizing the new priority given to computers, government research and development (R&D) subsidies by 1967 were four times 1960 levels.

In the early 1970s, prior to liberalizing the Japanese computer market, MITI organized the six mainframe makers into three specialized R&D groups with the aim of developing a computer to match IBM's 370 series; the groups were provided with government R&D subsidies amounting to 50 percent (US $195.9 million) of the expenses incurred. When IBM brought out its fourth-generation computer utilizing VLSI (very large scale integration) technology, MITI responded by organizing another "national project": two new cooperative research groups consisting of Fujitsu, Hitachi, and Mitsubishi Electric in one group, and NEC and Toshiba in the other. The project was so successful that by the late 1970s Fujitsu and Hitachi were selling computers to their US and European rivals. By the early 1980s the Japanese computer industry had in many respects closed the 10-year gap in hardware sophistication that had existed in relation to IBM in the 1950s, although its software remained inferior in most applications. IBM was in Japan by the early 1990s no more than one among several major manufacturers; in 1990 it had to yield its leading position in the mainframe market to Fujitsu.

Structure of the Industry

In contrast to US and European patterns, there are virtually no specialized major computer makers in Japan. Except for Fujitsu, there is not a single major Japanese computer maker for which computers provide over 35 percent of total sales. Three of the six major producers, Fujitsu, NEC, and Oki, are telecommunications firms that diversified into computers. The other three, Hitachi, Mitsubishi Electric, and Toshiba, are general electronics firms that diversified into computers in the early 1960s.

For structural reasons, it has been the bureaucracy, especially MITI, that has been the constant initiator of policy on computers, rather than individual firms. MITI has frequently taken the initiative at key stages in the development of the computer industry by providing strategic direction and by organizing and subsidizing industry research groups.

The character of Japanese government R&D assistance to computers has been somewhat different from that of the United States. US manufacturers receive aid in connection with projects designed primarily for governmental end-use, especially in the defense and aerospace sectors. Japanese makers receive aid, often in the form of direct subsidies, for commercial R&D, although the amounts are relatively modest by international standards.

A further crucial factor greatly contributed to the development and competitiveness of the Japanese computer industry. During the so-called calculator war that began in the mid-1960s, a furiously competitive process of cost cutting and progressive miniaturization brought down the price of calculators from ¥400,000 (US $1,100) in the mid-1960s to a mere ¥1,000 (US $4) in the 1980s, 1/400th of their original price. In the same 20-year period calculators were reduced from the size of television sets to that of credit cards. It was this ferocious competition among the leading manufacturers that enabled them to develop the kind of high-quality, low-cost mass-production manufacturing techniques that served them so well when they moved into the computer market.

Construction industry

(*kensetsugyo*). Japan has the world's largest construction market, with 1988 domestic construction investment estimated at ¥67.1 trillion (US $523.6 billion), or 17.4 percent of the gross national product. This construction investment was 40 percent civil engineering works and 60 percent (building) construction works. Nationally there are some 510,000 construction companies, and the approximately 5.8 million construction industry workers represent 9.7 percent of all workers.

In 1983 overseas construction orders exceeded ¥1.0 trillion (US $4.2 billion). Although orders have increased from the industrialized countries, primarily the United States, 87 percent of the orders received from the United States are development investments and factory construction projects for Japanese companies operating there. Foreign construction companies have difficulty in breaking into the Japanese domestic market, but extended negotiations have produced some results: by 1989, 21 foreign companies had received construction licenses.

Science

Biotechnology

(*baiotekunoroji*). At the start of the biotechnology boom in Japan in 1981, Japanese researchers relied on cooperation with Western ventures for basic research technology and for information. Since that time the Japanese have developed considerable expertise in biotechnology. One reason for Japan's rapid advancement is the country's long experience in fermentation technology, which plays a significant role in biotechnology.

From 1986 efforts were concentrated on developing biotechnology as an industry in Japan, making use especially of recombinant DNA and cell fusion techniques, and in 1990 there were more than 200 Japanese companies in the field. However, business ventures that focus strictly on biotechnology, as do many US firms, are rare in Japan. Instead, research and development tends to be done by established firms. Biotechnology research is especially active in the medical, pharmaceutical, and chemical fields, notably in the production of insulin, growth hormones, and interferons, but research is also done by firms involved in food processing, agricultural chemicals, and livestock.

The Japanese government has also taken an interest in biotechnology and considers it to be a major element in the next, increasingly knowledge-intensive phase of industrial development. The Ministry of International Trade and Industry (MITI) and various other ministries play major roles in biotechnology research, and appropriate funds for biotechnological development. In 1989 Japanese investment in biotechnology totaled ¥117 billion (US $850 million), and MITI predicts that by the year 2000 total investment will reach ¥5 trillion (US $35 billion).

Electric power

(*denryoku*). Electric power was introduced to Japan in the form of thermal power in 1887; hydroelectric power followed in 1890. From 1887 to 1911, thermal power predominated. Most hydroelectric power plants were located far from cities, and electricity could be transmitted only over short distances, making hydroelectric power unsuitable for city use. Hydroelectric power became more important than thermal power after 1912 and continued to predominate during an almost 50-year period that spanned the two world wars. In the 1920s, electric utilities began selling surplus electricity inexpensively, encouraging the expansion of electrochemical and other industries.

During the reconstruction period that followed World War II, development of new power generating sites, both thermal and hydroelectric, rapidly increased. Large dam power plants began to be used in the development of hydroelectric power. In spite of these innovations, thermal power generating facilities took on more importance because construction of hydroelectric generating facilities required a good deal of time and capital.

After 1960, a period of high economic growth in Japan, iron and steel, chemical, machinery, and other heavy industries expanded rapidly. With the resulting rise in individual incomes, electric appliances became common household items and demand for electricity rose accordingly. Japan's first nuclear power plant for commercial use began operating in July 1966, and after the 1973 oil shock there was an upsurge in the development of nuclear power. As of December 1989, 37 nuclear reactors were in operation with a total output of approximately 187.9 billion kilowatt hours. The construction of 17 new reactors is planned as part of the government's program. In 1989 total generating capacity amounted to 791.2 billion kilowatt hours, of which oil-fired power stations supplied 32.0 percent; nuclear power plants, 23.1 percent; liquefied natural gas (LNG), 18.7 percent; hydroelectric power plants, 11.3 percent; coal, 14.7 percent; and alternative energy sources such as geothermal power, 0.2 percent.

In Japan maximum transmission voltage has been 500 kilovolts since 1974 because of the increase in the number of nuclear and other generating facilities built far from cities. Increasingly, safer under-ground transmission lines have replaced overhead power lines close to urban areas.

Nuclear power plants

(*genshiryoku hatsudensho*). As of December 1990 there were 39 commer-cial nuclear power plants operating in Japan, with a total of 21 boiling water reactors, 17 pressurized water reactors, and 1 advanced thermal reactor; total electrical capacity was 31.48 million kilowatts. In 1990 Japan was the world's fourth largest producer of nuclear power. With 181.9 billion kilowatt-hours produced (25.8 percent of the nation's total output), atomic energy was Japan's single largest source of electrical power. The average rate of operation of the nation's nuclear power plants in 1990 was 72.7 percent, the highest in the world.

Although Japan has depended on Britain, the United States, and France for all of the enriched uranium used as fuel, in 1991 Japan Nuclear Fuel Industries, Inc, completed construction of Japan's first nuclear fuel plant in the village of Rokkasho, Aomori Prefecture. The plant began operations in 1992, meeting a portion of Japan's demand for enriched uranium.

Following the catastrophe at the Chernobyl nuclear power plant in the Soviet Union, many Japanese expressed concern over the safety of such facilities. Although the Japanese government revised its safety inspection standards, it made no policy changes concerning the nuclear generation of electricity. It is estimated that by the year 2030 the demand for electricity will require the expansion of nuclear power output to 137 million kilowatts.

Ocean resource development

(*kaiyo kaihatsu*). Japanese government policy on ocean development is formulated by the Council for Ocean Development (Kaiyo Kaihatsu Shingikai), an advisory body to the prime minister. In 1979 the council published a 10-year plan that focused on the following areas of potential development: the cultivation of the biological resources of the sea; the development of technologies for the exploitation of sea minerals and metals, especially the recovery of uranium from seawater and the mining of manganese from the seabed; the generation of electricity from thermal sources, waves, and ocean currents; and the utilization of ocean areas for industrial projects, airports, and recreation. Japan has joined with 19 other nations in a cooperative effort (called WESTPAC) to study the western Pacific Ocean in order to make predictions regarding global changes in climate and marine food resources.

One step in guaranteeing the preservation of Japan's ocean resources was taken in 1970 with the passage of legislation setting up marine parks. Other development projects involve altering the natural state of the ocean. One Japanese proposal, for instance, foresees the building of man-made islands for recreational purposes. Today emphasis in government planning has shifted from ocean resources development to development of land reclaimed from the sea as living areas for people.

Natural resources

(*tennen shigen*). Japan's industrial complex is built on one of the world's weakest resource bases. Although in variety Japan's resources are surprisingly rich, their amount, availability, and quality limit domestic production to a fraction of the country's needs.

The degree of Japan's dependence on imported raw materials is illustrated by the following import figures from 1989: petroleum, 99.7 percent; coal, 91.4 percent; bauxite, 100 percent; nickel, 100 percent; iron ore, 99.8 percent; copper, 98.4 percent; and lead, 90.0 percent. Japan also relies on outside sources for 100 percent of its raw cotton, wool, and rubber, as well as large and growing amounts of forest products, agricultural commodities, and seafood. Japn's exceptionally high rate of economic and industrial growth since the 1960s has resulted in ever greater reliance on foreign sources.

Resources, especially sources of energy, have also been strained by the rising affluence of Japanese society. In addition to industrial growth rates of 20 percent or better during some years, the purchase of major household appliances by Japanese families has greatly increased the demand for energy. Periodic shortages along with sharp rises in production costs have given the energy industries top priority in government planning.

Coal

Japan's coal reserves were estimated at about 7 billion metric tons (7.7 billion short tons) in 1990, but the largest fields are located at opposite ends of the country in Hokkaido and Kyushu, adding transportation fees to relatively high production costs.

Japanese coal is generally low-grade bituminous of inferior heating value. High-grade coking coal supplies are negligible, so virtually all of the nation's needs must be imported. Coal seams are generally deep below the surface, steeply inclined, and plagued by inflammable gases, all of which make mechanization difficult. High production costs, bitter labor-management strife, dangerous operations, and competition from other energy sources have led to a sharp drop in output and in the number of mines and miners. Production in the 1950s and 1960s averaged 50 to 55 million metric tons (55 to 60.5 million short tons) annually; by 1990 it had dropped to 8.3 million metric tons (9.1 million short tons). Coal-mining labor has similarly declined from a force of roughly 244,000 in 1960 to about 5,000 in 1990, and the number of operating mines has dropped from 682 to 26. Despite greatly improved productivity, the domestic coal industry has a doubtful future, notwithstanding government subsidies.

Petroleum and Natural Gas

Japan's petroleum-refining industry is the third largest in the world, but virtually all crude oil must be imported from China, Indonesia, and the Middle East. A trickle of domestic oil comes from the Niigata fields along with smaller fields scattered through northern Honshu and Hokkaido.

Small natural gas fields and wells are also scattered, with the largest concentrations in Hokkaido, northern Honshu, and Chiba Prefecture. But as with coal, most of Japan's increased demand for petroleum and liquefied gas will have to be met by foreign sources, often through joint development projects with countries having surplus energy resources.

Hydroelectric Power

Rugged terrain, abundant precipitation, and fast-flowing streams have made it possible for Japan to develop one of the world's largest hydroelectric industries. Numerous small hydroelectric plants once produced the largest share of Japan's electricity, but in 1991 they accounted for only a little over 20 percent, while thermal power supplies almost 80 percent.

Nuclear Power and Alternative Energy Sources

Japan is among the world leaders in the development of nuclear power plants. Despite growing concern and an increasingly vigorous anti-nuclear-energy movement, the government has pressed ahead with its nuclear power program. By 1990, 39 atomic reactors had been built, supplying 25.8 percent of its total electrical power output through nuclear generation. Japanese electrical power producers have signed agreements with suppliers in Canada, the United Kingdom, Australia, and Niger to secure reserves of unprocessed uranium amounting to a total of 200,000 metric tons (220,000 short tons).

Alternative sources account for only a small fraction of the nation's energy supply, but research and development proceed in such areas as solar and geothermal power, gasification and liquefaction of coal, and the separation of hydrogen from seawater.

Metal and Minerals

Japan's metal resources have become almost totally inadequate for such a large industrial complex. In 1991 Japan ranked third in steel production and it also has the world's third largest aluminum industry. The small size of Japan's deposits of metal ores, coupled with the scale of production for both export and domestic consumption, makes it impossible to reduce the nation's dependence on overseas supplies.

In the steel industry, for example, Japan imported 99.8 percent of its iron ore requirements in 1989, mainly from Australia and Brazil; it also imports 99.5 percent of the coking coal essential to steel production.

Similarly, though more than 3 million metric tons (3.3 million short tons) of aluminum is produced annually in Japan, production is totally dependent on imported bauxite, mainly from Australia. Japan in 1989 imported 98.4 percent of the materials used in making copper and 82.2 percent of those used by the zinc industry. Domestic supplies of lead meet only 10.0 percent of the demand. In other minerals, Japan is virtually wholly dependent on foreign sources.

Wood and Pulp

Even though Japan's forests cover about 60 percent of the land, lumber supplies have grown tight, forcing Japan to look to outside sources for over half of its lumber supply. Nor are domestic supplies adequate for one of the world's largest producers of pulp, paper, and other wood products; pulp imports now constitute roughly 20 percent of consumption.

With the growth of tourism, Japan's forest lands have become valuable as parks. But heavy demands have led to overcutting. Any further expansion of domestic wood and pulp production would result in heavy environmental damage to Japan.

Future Outlook

Without continued access to foreign resources, Japan has no chance for economic survival. Virtually all its natural resources are of such small quantities as to make it impossible to expand production without quickly exhausting them. In addition, Japan also faces the challenges of increasing international competition for resources and rising global concern over ecological issues, factors that are likely to have a significant impact on Japan's resource policies in the years to come.

SOCIETY

Omote Sando at Harajuku, Tokyo. Lined with cafes and boutiques, this avenue forms the main approach to Meiji Shrine.

Aging population

(*koreika shakai*). The aging of Japan's population is expected to become an increasingly acute problem as the number of elderly grows at the rate of approximately 650,000 per year. Longevity for both sexes first exceeded 50 years in 1947, 60 years in 1952, and 70 years in 1971. Figures for 1989 show a life expectancy of 82 years for women and 76 years for men. These figures are expected to increase to 84 years for women and 78 years for men by 2025. Due to the growing number of elderly within the working population, most large corporations have raised their mandatory retirement age to 60 years or above since the mid-1980s. In 1986 a more unified pension system, based on revisions of the National Pension Law, the Employees' Pension Insurance Law, and laws affecting other types of public pensions, was put into effect to respond to problems created by the aging population. Revisions were designed to assure the long-term stability of the nation's pension system and establish 65 as the uniform starting age for public pensions.

It is estimated that by 2020 only three workers will be supporting each retiree. Due to the disproportionately large burden that health care for the elderly was beginning to place on the medical care system as a whole, existing provisions for a national system of free health care for the elderly were replaced in 1983 by the Law concerning Health and Medical Services for the Aged. The law stipulated that health care expenses for the elderly were to be covered partly by fixed rate contributions from local governments, the National Health Insurance program, employee insurance plans, and the individual. A 1986 amendment further increased costs borne by the elderly for health care. In 1986 and 1988, however, expenses began to rise again, and by 1989 more than 25 percent of national medical care expenditure was devoted to caring for the elderly.

Other issues that are expected to accompany Japan's growing elderly population include the development of facilities and resources to care adequately for the senile and bedridden and the projected drop in economic vitality and tax revenues. Finding acceptable solutions to these problems will be one of Japan's greatest challenges as it approaches the 21st century.

Women in the labor force

(*fujin rodo*). Women were traditionally an important part of Japan's agrarian labor force, but the industrialization that followed the Meiji Restoration of 1868 initiated the flow of female workers into the textile industry. Most received very low wages; some even were indentured by their families in return for a lump-sum payment. Buttressed by growing nationalism, their working conditions deteriorated while their numbers increased.

The textile industry's poor working environment and over-crowded dormitories first received widespread attention with the 1903 publication of *Shokko jijo*, a report by the Ministry of Agriculture and Commerce, and *Nihon no kaso shakai* (1899, Japan's Lower Classes) by Yokoyama Gennosuke. A movement for legislation to protect women and minors, begun in the 1890s but stalled during the Russo-Japanese War (1904−1905), revived as part of a budding labor movement. The Factory Law of 1911, implemented in 1916, limited workdays for women to 12 hours, forbade night work between 10 pm and 4 am, and required a minimum of 2 days off per month.

Although concentrated in the textile industry, women outnumbered men in the total labor force until about 1930. Women also moved into other manufacturing jobs and skilled occupations as growing numbers of men joined the military.

After World War II, with many women left single and impoverished by the war, women's participation in the labor force remained necessarily high. Before World War II, most working Japanese women were young and single, but with rapid economic growth many companies began to offer part-time employment, and the number of married women employees rose considerably. Since 1955 the percentage of married women in the female labor force has almost tripled, rising to 64.9 percent in 1990.

Until about 1950, over 60 percent of working women were "family workers," mainly in agriculture. By 1990, family workers had declined to 16.7 percent. Conversely, women's entry into "prestige professions" such as law and medicine has been slow, and fewer than 1 percent of female civil servants occupy managerial posts.

In 1990 clerical and related jobs accounted for the largest percentage of female employees (34.4 percent, excluding self-employed and family workers), followed by craft and production workers (20.6 percent), professional and technical workers (13.8 percent), sales workers (12.5 percent), service workers (10.7 percent), and other occupations (8.0 percent). The order of distribution has not changed for some time, although the number of women in each occupation has varied, increasing in professional and technical fields while decreasing in manual labor.

The treatment of women in Japan's labor force resembles their treatment in other industrialized countries. In both Japan and the West, female workers make up more than one-third of the total labor force and earn lower wages than men. Residual prejudice against women, however, has resulted in somewhat more discrimination against them in Japan than in the West. Tradition holds that women should devote themselves to the home after marriage, a view that causes the length of uninterrupted employment at the same firm to be rather short. Japanese court decisions have ruled against forcing women to retire upon marriage or upon having passed the "appropriate" age for marriage (commonly set at 30).

Japan's Labor Standards Law of 1947 stipulates equal pay for equal work, but this is rare in practice because of continuing tendencies to channel women into dead-end jobs and favor men at promotion time. According to one survey, the average monthly wage paid to female employees in 1990 was somewhat over 60 percent of that paid to male employees. The difference in Japan between men's and women's wages is still the greatest in the industrialized world, although it has narrowed slightly.

This disparity is due largely to the seniority system that presupposes "lifetime" employment of men, whereas the length of uninterrupted employment, average age, and educational level of women have tended to be considerably lower than those of men. Very few women attain positions of high responsibility in business. Businesses still generally employ women only in low-level or temporary jobs because of the view that they should work only until marriage or childbirth.

The Equal Employment Opportunity Law for Men and Women of 1985 removed all restrictions for management and specialist positions except certain regulations applying to women workers in the period prior to and following childbirth. It is anticipated that the new law will encourage the employment and advancement of women on merit.

Sarariman

Loanword derived from the English "salaried man." The term was coined in the Taisho period (1912—1926) to distinguish the emerging class of white-collar workers, who received a regular salary, from blue-collar workers, usually paid an hourly wage. Today, sarariman is often used in reference to middle-class, white-collar workers employed by private companies or government agencies. The sarariman usually works for the same company or organization until he reaches retirement age, although midcareer company changes have become increasingly common. Status is strongly influenced by the employee's academic background, and advancement is a gradual upward movement within the company. The model sarariman is expected to be intensely loyal to his employer, putting company considerations before those of family and personal life, working many hours of overtime, and taking only the minimum number of holidays each year.

Nuclear family

(*kaku kazoku*). The nuclear family has become far more common in Japan with the changes in industrial structure and increased urbanization of the country after World War II. The traditional pattern in Japan was that of the extended family, in which the head of the household (*kacho*) lived not only with his wife and children but with his parents, grandparents, and occasionally other relations as well. After the end of the war the concept and the legal system supporting it gradually lost their power, and the nuclear family has come to predominate. The shift away from primary industries, which involved the labor of all family members, toward secondary and tertiary industries in which the husband became the sole breadwinner has also accelerated this trend. In 1955 nuclear families constituted 45.3 percent of all households, a figure that rose to 59.6 percent by 1991.

Marriage

(*kon'in*). Marriage in Japan has been characterized as centering on arranged marriage (*miai kekkon*), in which a man, a woman, and their families are formally introduced to each other by a go-between, or *nakodo*. Allied to this is the traditional Japanese concept of marriage as the creation of links between two households rather than the joining of two individuals. Put simply, marriage has traditionally been more of a family affair in Japan than it has in most Western cultures.

In recent years, however, the Japanese attitudes to marriage have changed in response to a host of new social situations, some of which are the result of influence from the West. While traditional ideas concerning the mechanics of making a match in Japan have not been completely abandoned, marriage in contemporary Japan is much more of a private decision between two people than it was before World War II. Households, in particular the parents of a couple contemplating marriage, do not have as final a say in the matter as they did 50 years ago; and the function of the nakodo, while still important, has in many cases shrunk to a largely ceremonial role.

Marriage in the Premodern Period

During the Nara and Heian period (710–1185) among the court

aristocracy marriage was essentially matrilocal, with a man moving into his wife's house after they were married. Men of rank and importance could divide their time between two or three different houses, and marriage practices among the ruling elite are thought to have been largely polygynous.

An aristocratic woman usually conducted herself with discretion, since her pregnancies needed recognition by a man for her children to have any importance in society. Children might be confirmed to the rank of their father, or they could be adopted into other households to achieve rank.

It was much more difficult for lower classes to follow the marriage practices of the Heian elite. Farmers, artisans, and low-ranking warriors had a better chance of maintaining their status through permanent marriage with one wife.

Change to Permanent Marriage

By the late 12th century the *samurai* class had become the ruling elite in both central and provincial affairs throughout Japan. The political imbalances, warring factions, and military reprisals had brought the samurai to power and frequently involved households related through marriage. It was during this politically unsettled time that marriage, that is, *seiryaku kekkon* (marriage of convenience) began to assume importance as a means of ceremonially establishing military alliances between families, reaching the height of its importance in the period of intense inter-family political struggle known as the Sengoku period (1467–1568).

Among samurai families the practice of maintaining multiple wives became less common. Samurai marriage customs also stressed the immediate transfer of the wife from her parents' home to her husband's residence. Family concerns became important in the selection of a spouse, intensifying the need for professional nakodo to ensure an appropriate match.

The marriage practices of rural commoners were less affected by the rise of the military elite. Practices that lent a more casual air to marriage customs, such as night visiting (*yobai*) and multiple liaisons, continued in the provinces.

With the establishment of the Tokugawa shogunate in 1603 and the return of political stability, the samurai emphasis on arranged marriage continued throughout the Edo period (1600–1868) and urban commoners increasingly emulated samurai custom. The miai, a formal meeting of prospective marriage partners and their families, became popular. The *yuino*, a ceremonial exchange of engagement gifts between families, also became an important part of marriage practice among urban commoners.

Legally, marriage in the Edo period was subject to a number of rules and regulations designed to preserve the status quo of the ruling military elite. Central among the many laws created was the mandatory reporting of proposed marriages before any ceremonies took place. Marriages had to be cleared through officials and the appropriateness of the match confirmed.

Marriage and Industrialization

After the Meiji Restoration of 1868, Japan began an all-out effort to industrialize and catch up with the West. Cities, the centers of industry, also became centers of migration from all parts of Japan, further increasing the need for a nakodo to ensure the appropriateness of a marriage.

The increased mobility of the population during the Meiji period (1868—1912) was a key factor in changing attitudes toward marriage in many rural areas. As in urban centers, the miai, yuino, the use of nakodo, and other practices that had originated with the samurai became more common in rural areas. Parental arrangement of and authority over marriages increased.

By the Meiji period, under the Civil Code of 1898 marriage was legally conducted under the so-called *ie* (household) system, which had necessitated the agreement of the heads of the two households involved in a marriage, rather than the man and woman to be married. Under Meiji civil law husband and wife were far from equal: through marriage, the wife lost her legal capacity to engage in property transactions; management of her own property came under her husband's control; and only the wife had the duty of chastity. The Meiji Civil Code remained the law of the land until after World War II, when the new Civil Code of 1947 abolished the *ie* system and eliminated the legal inequality of husband and wife.

Post-World War II Japan

Though the legal requirements of marriage in Japan changed radically after the war, marriage practices were slower to respond to outside influence. The traditional marriage pattern continued relatively unchanged, especially in high-status families. Very few Japanese of the mid-20th century expected to find a spouse through casual meeting or dating.

Even in contemporary Japan, where Western marriage practices seem to have affected a sizable number of Japanese, the traditional system has not completely disappeared. Rather, Western influence has worked its way into a traditional system that has modified itself to meet contemporary preferences. Many people still seek the advice of a nakodo on a potential spouse; dating then confirms or disallows previous judgments concerning the individual's suitability. The nakodo is especially useful when a person is near or past what is considered the "appropriate" age for marriage (statistically, the average age at marriage has been on the rise since 1970; in 1990 it was 25.9 for females and 28.4 for males). Additional examples of the ways in which the traditional system has opened itself to modern-day preferences are the matchmaking networks that operate among large companies and their affiliates, as well as many college alumni associations.

More Japanese now say they prefer a *ren'ai kekkon*, or "love marriage," over the traditional arranged marriage. Individual choice has in many cases become the deciding factor in settling on a marriage partner, and the level of familial involvement in the marriage process has come to resemble that found in Western countries; that is, not completely absent, but not nearly as deep as it was in prewar Japanese society.

Housing problems

(*jutaku mondai*). Urban housing problems in Japan arose as the country entered the stage of industrialization and urbanization around 1900. Before the end of World War II, no public measures were taken, but in the 1950s three major pieces of legislation established a general framework for Japanese housing policy. The Government Housing Loan Corporation (Jutaku Kin'yu Koko) founded in 1950 was a means of channeling public funds for low-interest, long-term loans for owner-occupied housing. Under the Public Housing Law (Koei Jutaku Ho) of 1951 local authorities were empowered to build public housing for rental to low-income households with subsidies from the central government. Finally, the Japan Housing Corporation (Nihon Jutaku Kodan) was founded in 1955 as a public nonprofit developer to supply housing units for urban dwellers.

In 1966 the Housing Construction Planning Law (Jutaku Kensetsu Keikaku Ho) was enacted to coordinate public policy measures for housing. The act mandated that the central government formulate five-year comprehensive housing construction plans at five-year intervals starting in 1966. The first Five-Year Housing Construction Plan aimed at constructing a total of 6.7 million housing units.

The second Housing Construction Plan, initiated in 1971, aimed at achieving "one room for each member of the household." Although the plan was to construct 9.6 million housing units in five years, only 8.26 million units were actually built.

The third Housing Construction Plan, approved in 1976, stated explicitly that the main priority of housing policy should be shifted from an emphasis on quantity to the improvement of quality. The purpose of the fourth Housing Construction Plan, begun in 1981, was to continue to improve housing quality, especially in urban areas.

High prices for land have forced many people to buy housing at a considerable distance from their workplaces. Particularly in the Tokyo metropolitan region, the average price increase of 1988 was 68.6 percent over the previous year. In all of Japan's intensely crowded urban areas it is becoming increasingly difficult for the average "*sarariman*" (middle-class workers) to purchase a single-family dwelling. Multistory buildings with individual units for sale, similar to condominiums in the United States, have become the standard form of urban housing.

The fifth Housing Construction Plan (1986−1991) set forth a number of guidelines, including new standards for residential housing floor space and facilities. Other issues also remain, including the problems of the nearly 24.5 percent of all Japanese families who live in substandard private rental housing, as well as the difficulties faced by the aged, the handicapped, and other socially disadvantaged members in securing adequate housing.

Foreigners in Japan

(*zainichi gaikokujin*). The number of foreign nationals resident in Japan steadily increased throughout the 1980s to 1,075,317 in 1990, 26.4 percent increase over 1985. This figure includes only foreigners registered in accordance with the Alien Registration Law; tourists in Japan for less than 90 days, children under the age of two months, and members of foreign diplomatic services are not included. The largest national group, accounting for 64 percent of the total, is composed of North and South Koreans (687,940), followed by citizens of China and Taiwan (150,339), Brazil (56,429), the Philippines (49,092), and the United States (38,364).

Since the revision of the Immigration Control Law in 1990, regulations governing employment of foreigners have been more strictly enforced; however, the revised law also makes foreign nationals of Japanese descent eligible for permanent resident status, and their numbers have suddenly increased. For example, the number of Brazilians of Japanese descent residing in Japan increased almost 29 times between 1985 and 1990.

Fifty-five percent of all foreigners in Japan live in the four prefectures of Tokyo, Osaka, Hyogo, and Aichi, with the highest concentration in Tokyo, where there are 213,056 foreign nationals. Of registered aliens in Japan, 60.0 percent were permanent residents in 1989; the rest were temporary residents, drawn to Japan by increasing foreign direct investment, by employment opportunities offered by the growing demand of Japanese firms for foreign workers, and by the chance to study in Japan. The influx of workers from South America, South and Southeast Asia, and the Middle East, a significant number of whom are employed illegally, has become a much-discussed trend.

The number of international marriages increased 3.5 times between 1965 and 1985. From 1975 onward, the number of marriages involving Japanese men and foreign women, many from China, Korea, or the Philippines, surpassed the number of Japanese women marrying foreign men.

A number of Japanese local governments have begun to implement new services to respond to the needs of foreign residents, such as the publication of information pamphlets in English, Chinese, and Portuguese and the assignment of English-speaking personnel to provide assistance. Since many foreign nationals of Japanese descent bring their families with them to Japan, special courses are being set up in elementary schools in areas where their numbers are especially concentrated.

Alien registration

(*gaikokujin toroku*). The Alien Registration Law (Gaikokujin Toroku Ho, 1952) requires all foreigners residing in Japan for more than one year to apply for registration to the mayor or headman of the village, town, or city where they live and to present a passport and copies of a photograph within 90 days from the date of entry into Japan. The information required on the application form includes the applicant's name, date and place of birth, sex, nationality, occupation, port of entry, passport number, and address while in Japan.

Upon registration by the local government official, registrants are issued a Certificate of Alien Registration that must be renewed every five years or whenever visa status changes. Each registrant, excluding children under the age of 16, is required to carry this certificate at all times and to present it upon demand to police officers, maritime safety officials, railway police officers, or other public officials.

A growing number of noncitizens in Japan have objected strongly to the requirement that fingerprints be taken as part of the registration procedure, arguing that fingerprinting is the treatment given to criminals. By December 1991, 156 people had refused to be fingerprinted, and several prosecutions had resulted in guilty verdicts and fines. In response to growing protests the Ministry of Justice abolished the fingerprinting requirement for persons with permanent resident status, effective January 1993.

Foreign students in Japan

(*gaikokujin ryugakusei*). In 1949 the Japanese government began granting scholarships to students from Asian countries. In 1954 Japanese government scholarships for foreign students (the so-called Mombusho scholarships) were established. At present Japan accepts foreign students in two categories: those receiving Japanese government scholarships and those receiving government or private support from their own countries. Students receiving Japanese government scholarships are themselves divided into two categories: research students, who pursue graduate-level studies, and undergraduate students, who enroll in university departments, technical colleges, or special training schools. Government scholarship students in fiscal 1990 numbered 4,961, of whom more than 90 percent were Asians. Students not on Japanese government scholarships numbered 36,386 in 1990.

Since 1980 the total number of foreign students in Japan has grown each year, increasing from 6,572 in 1980 to 52,405 in 1993. However, these figures are still small when compared with the 343,780 foreign students in the United States in 1985; with West Germany's 79,354 in 1985; and with France's 133,848 in 1984. Hoping to admit 100,000 foreign students into Japan by the year 2000, the Ministry of Education is increasing the number of Japanese government scholarship recipients.

Foreign workers

(*gaikokujin rodosha*). Paid employment of workers who are citizens of foreign countries is strictly regulated by the Immigration Control Law, the revisions of which were implemented in 1990. Except for spouses of Japanese nationals and people of Japanese descent, permission to work is granted to foreigners only in 28 skilled employment categories such as education, communications, medicine, finance, and computer software design. In principle, manual workers are not allowed entry, and students from overseas who work part-time are also subject to restrictions.

The majority of illegal foreign workers in the early 1980s were women who had entered the country with tourist visas and worked in bars and entertainment districts. However, severe shortages of labor triggered by the economic boom of the late 1980s have attracted a large influx of male foreign workers, mostly from Asian countries such as the Philippines, Bangladesh, and Iran. In recent years Japanese have been avoiding the so-called "3K" jobs (those that are *kitsui, kitanai, kiken;* "difficult, dirty, dangerous"), and there has been a significant increase in the number of construction and small engineering firms that are prepared to

Society

employ foreign manual laborers illegally.

The revision of the Immigration Control Law extended the right of long-term residence to descendants of Japanese emigrants and removed restrictions on their ability to work in Japan. Due to high inflation in Brazil, many Brazilians of Japanese descent have sought to take advantage of this change in the law; twice as many were working in Japan in 1990 as in the previous year. However, the serious depression which assailed the Japanese economy in the early 1990s has resulted in fewer jobs for foreign workers.

Environment

Environmental quality

(*kankyo mondai*). Environmental pollution in Japan has accompanied industrialization since the Meiji period (1868−1912). One of the earliest and well known cases was the copper poisoning caused by drainage from the Ashio Copper Mine in Tochigi Prefecture, beginning as early as 1878. The subsequent development of the textile and paper and pulp industries led to water pollution, and the use of coal as the major fuel for industry in general contributed to widespread but still localized air pollution. In the period of rapid growth following World War II, however, the isolated cases coalesced into a national crisis, with Japan becoming one of the most polluted countries in the world.

As regards environmental protection, at first there was widespread ignorance on the part of the public and apathy on the part of the government. Thus, although the pollution-related Minamata disease was first reported in May 1956, the existence of the disease had been concealed and patients secretly hospitalized in municipal isolation wards. Although a Kumamoto University research team identified mercury from the Chisso Corporation plant as the cause of the disease in 1959, the government did not officially recognize this as the cause until 1968. By the late 1960s, however, the degradation of the environment had deeply struck the national consciousness, and a series of strict environmental protection measures were taken.

These were quite successful in some areas, most notably in the removal of toxic substances from the water and the reduction of sulfur oxides in the air, measures that helped to dull the public's sense of urgency. At the same time other concerns came increasingly to the fore, especially such economic issues as the sharp increase in oil prices following the oil crisis of 1973, the prolonged slump in industries such as steel and shipbuilding, and the ending of the period of rapid growth. Under these conditions, public pressures for a clean environment became subdued and the government weakened its standards. Thus, whereas in May 1973 the Environment Agency set a maximum permissible level for nitrogen oxides (a major contributor to photochemical smog) of 0.02 ppm (parts per million), the world's strictest standard, it agreed in June 1978 to a request by the Ministry of International Trade and Industry (MITI) and business circles to relax the standard to 0.06 ppm in cities and 0.04 ppm elsewhere. Still, much of the struggle against pollution had already been institutionalized, and further moderate improvement seemed in store, although the long-range outlook remained uncertain.

In four major lawsuits regarding pollution-related diseases, the right of the victims to compensation was established. The decisions in cases involving *itai-itai* disease (1971), Niigata Minamata disease (1971), Yokkaichi asthma (1972), and Kumamoto Minamata disease (1973) eased the burden of proof on the victims. These decisions clarified the responsibility of the companies to ensure that their activities were non-polluting and to prevent pollution from actually taking place.

Four major factors have especially contributed to the emergence in Japan of water-pollution problems: rapid industrialization, rapid urbanization, the lag in constructing such social overhead capital facilities as sewage systems, and the fact that water pollution in Japan emerged from a public policy that heavily favored economic growth over public health and a clean environment.

As a consequence of the increased concern with pollution problems, there has been an overall improvement in water quality, but the progress has been uneven. Strict emission controls on waste industrial waters have reduced cases of toxic-substance pollution to a very small number. On the other hand, rivers and coastal waters within metropolitan districts continue to suffer considerable pollution from organic substances. The problem is even more severe in bays, inland seas, lakes, and other water areas, including Tokyo, Ise, and Osaka bays and Lakes Biwa, Kasumigaura, and Suwa. In these areas there is relatively little "transfusion" of water, so the enormous amounts of nutritive salts of nitrogen and phosphorus poured into them lead to a multiplication of plankton or algae and eutrophication.

Another water-pollution problem is that of thermal pollution. As an increasing number of power plants are being built on an ever-larger scale, their heating of surrounding waters poses a threat to marine life and the fishing industry. Although heavy-metal pollution is no longer a serious problem, Japan's coastal waters remain highly polluted; in addition to household and industrial wastes discharged, oil dumped by ships, often deliberately, is a significant source of maritime pollution.

A number of measures have been taken to improve the quality of the water in Japan. These include the setting of national standards for toxic substances and of variable standards for the living environment (depending on the use and type of water area) and the establishing of strict effluent controls and of a comprehensive surveillance and monitoring system. Also, many laws fixing responsibility for pollution damages have been passed, court decisions favorable to victims have reinforced these, and projects to improve sewers have extended sewer service to a greater proportion of the population.

Japan's efforts to control air pollution have also met with mixed results. The greatest success has been attained in limiting pollution by sulfur oxides and carbon monoxide. The relatively successful control of sulfur oxides reflects a long-term commitment on the part of the government to reduce their concentrations. In the case of nitrogen oxides, the overall relaxation of standards in 1978 suggested that the delay in significantly reducing nitrogen oxide concentrations in the air could be prolonged indefinitely. Photochemical smog, to which nitrogen oxides are a principal contributor, first appeared in Tokyo in July 1970; since then it has appeared regularly in different parts of Japan.

In addition, the government has taken measures to cope with a variety of other forms of pollution or environmental disruption, including noise, vibration, waste disposal, ground subsidence, offensive odors, soil pollution, and pollution by agricultural chemicals. The number of complaints about noise is greater than for any other type of pollution. The greatest number of complaints concerns noise from factories, but construction, traffic, airport, and railroad (especially the high-speed Shinkansen line) noise have all generated a considerable number of complaints.

In response to the sharp deterioration in the natural environment caused by the postwar period of rapid economic growth, the Nature Conservation Law was passed in 1972 to serve as the basis for all legal measures to protect the natural environment. To protect nature and promote recreation, an extensive system of national parks, quasi-national parks, and prefectural natural parks was established. In urban areas, the government has sought to expand city park areas.

Environmental deterioration has led to sharp decreases in the number of such birds as hawks and owls, while various species, including the Japanese crested ibis, the stork, and the red-crested crane, have become threatened with extinction. Since 1972, however, the observed number of migratory birds—ducks, swans, and geese—has generally been increasing, suggesting that environmental protection measures are bringing favorable results.

The Pollution Countermeasures Basic Law in 1967 sought to

create common principles and policies for pollution control in all government agencies and to promote an integrated effort to clean up the environment. The Basic Law indicates the responsibilities of the central government, local governments, and business firms with regard to controlling pollution. In addition, the Basic Law laid the framework for establishing environmental quality standards, drafting pollution-control programs, and aiding victims of diseases caused by pollution.

Although antipollution policies are mainly national, much of the enforcement is done at a prefectural or municipal level. Moreover, the designation and classification of pollution or environmental protection zones are often done by local governments, which are also empowered to adopt standards stricter than national ones if necessary. In the 1970s Japan adopted the Polluter Pays Principle, according to which polluting enterprises had to accept financial responsibility for damages they inflicted on the community. Even so, the tolerable limits remained high for many substances, and when environmental goals conflicted with "stable" growth, the latter would prevail.

By the 1980s new environmental issues, such as groundwater contamination by organic solvents in the effluence from semiconductor factories, the pollution of rivers and streams by agricultural chemicals used to maintain the grounds of golf courses, and acid rain, have aroused concern. The attendant damage to the natural environment caused by large-scale land development has also spurred increasing attention to conservation issues.

In the late 1980s a growing body of scientific evidence suggested that the ozone layer of the atmosphere is being destroyed by chlorofluorocarbons and that an increase in carbon dioxide in the atmosphere is causing a general rise in world temperatures. Concern over these findings in Japan, which produces 10 percent of the annual world supply of chlorofluorocarbons, led to the passing of the Ozonosphere Protection Law of 1988.

AIDS

(acquired immune deficiency syndrome; J: *eizu*). The first confirmed case of AIDS in Japan was reported in May 1985. As of February 1991 the Ministry of Health and Welfare had confirmed the existence of 374 AIDS patients and 1,640 carriers of the virus. Among patients, 280 were hemophiliacs who had contracted AIDS through infected blood preparations that had been imported, largely from the United States. Blood preparations are now sterilized by heating and are no longer a source of infection. Medical costs of hemophiliac patients of AIDS are borne by the firms that sold the infected blood preparations. The Law concerning the Prevention of AIDS, effective in 1989, was created as a part of efforts to arrest the spread of the disease.

AIDS, Law concerning the Prevention of

(Eizu Yobo Ho). A law was enacted in 1988 to prevent the spread of the AIDS virus in Japan and became effective in 1989. The law requires doctors to explain to anyone who tests positive for the AIDS virus, and who, in the judgment of the doctor, is considered likely to spread the disease, the methods necessary to prevent its transmission. Doctors are further required to report the patient's name, age, and address, and information about the manner in which the virus was contracted, to the prefectural governor within seven days. If a patient fails to follow the doctor's instructions, the governor will urge or order the patient to undergo a second medical examination, during which methods to prevent transmission will again be explained. A report to the prefectural governor is not required in the case of a patient who has contracted the AIDS virus from imported blood preparations. Critics have, however, pointed out that the law represents a danger to the human rights and to the right to privacy of AIDS patients.

National Health Insurance

(Kokumin Kenko Hoken). National Health Insurance covers the self-employed and their dependents, retired persons, and various other categories of individuals ineligible for employees' health insurance or any of the other medical and health insurance plans. In 1958 a new law gave the responsibility of overseeing the insurance to local governments. Under the present system premiums are paid solely by the insured; they consist of a fixed portion and a means-proportional portion. The amount of the premium varies from one municipality to another. The system also receives financial assistance from the national treasury. The insurance covers 70 percent of medical costs incurred by the principal insured or the principal's dependents (the rate is 80 percent for an insured retiree). As of 1992 there were 42.6 million people enrolled in National Health Insurance plans.

Pensions

(nenkin). The Japanese pension system centers on public pensions administered by the national government, providing old-age, disability, and survivor benefits. Public pensions are supplemented by individual pension plans provided by private enterprises. By law, all Japanese citizens of working age must subscribe to a public pension plan.

Japanese pensions started in 1875 with the *onkyu* system for retired army and navy servicemen. This system was later expanded to cover government officials, schoolteachers, and policemen. In 1939 the first pension program for private-sector employees, the Seamen's Insurance Law, was enacted. From 1942 Laborers' Pension Insurance provided coverage for general workers; this was the precursor to the current Employees' Pension Insurance. In 1959 the National Pension Law was passed; it covers farmers, the self-employed, housewives, and other categories of people who had been excluded from employees' pensions.

In 1986 the pension system was greatly simplified and was reorganized into a two-tiered system. The National Pension was extended to provide basic, mandatory pension coverage to all Japanese citizens. Spouses of employees' pension subscribers are now required to enroll in the National Pension program. As of 1992, 68.4 million citizens were enrolled in this program, 30.6 million of whom depended on it as their sole pension coverage. Two supplemental programs provide additional coverage and benefits. The Employees' Pension Insurance program provides coverage for 32.0 million private-sector employees. Mutual Aid Association Pensions enroll an additional 4.9 million public employees and teachers. A declining number (now under 3.0 million) still receive *onkyu* pensions. Additional coverage for employees of certain companies is provided by privately funded corporate pensions.

The National Pension and Employees' Pension Insurance are administered by the Ministry of Health and Welfare. The smaller mutual-aid-association programs are under the jurisdiction of various ministries. One-third of the costs of contributory National Pension benefits are provided by the national treasury, with the rest supplied by contributions from the insured and from other pension plans. The costs of employee insurance are usually covered by equal contributions of employer and employee proportionate to the employee's wage rate.

National Pension

(Kokumin Nenkin). Introduced in 1959, the National Pension was originally designed for those not covered by other existing pension programs, especially farmers and the self-employed. Since reform of the pension system in 1986, joining the National Pension program is mandatory for all Japanese citizens between the ages of 20 and 60. Employed persons also receive additional benefits from Employees' Pension

Insurance or Mutual Aid Association Pensions. In 1992, 68.4 million people were covered under the National Pension system.

The National Pension consists of three components: a basic old-age pension, a disability pension, and a basic survivor's pension. Contributions from insured persons and employers cover two-thirds of the cost of National Pension benefits, with the remainder paid by the national treasury. In 1991 the monthly payment required of all individual contributors to the National Pension system was ¥9,700 (US $72.00). The basic old-age pension of ¥60,441 (US $449) per month (as of 1991) is paid to people aged 65 and over who have fulfilled the minimum contributory requirement of 25 years.

Police system

(*keisatsu seido*). Japan's approximately 220,000 police officers are organized into prefectural forces coordinated and partially controlled by the National Police Agency in Tokyo. They enjoy wide community support and respect.

Historical Development

During the Edo period (1600−1868), the Tokugawa shogunate developed an elaborate police system based on town magistrates, who held *samurai* status and served as chiefs of police, prosecutors, and criminal judges. The system was augmented by citizens' groups such as the *goningumi* (five-family associations), composed of neighbors collectively liable to the government for the activities of their membership.

After the Meiji Restoration (1868), the Home Ministry was established in 1873. With jurisdiction over the Police Bureau, it effectively controlled the police. This new, centralized police system had wide-ranging responsibilities, including the authority to issue ordinances and handle quasi-judicial functions. It also regulated public health, factories, construction, and businesses and issued permits, licenses, and orders. To help control proscribed political activities, the Special Higher Police were established in 1911 and strengthened in 1928 with the introduction of the Peace Preservation Law (Chian Iji Ho) of 1925. With the outbreak of the Sino-Japanese War in 1937, the police were given the added responsibilities of regulating business activities for the war effort, mobilizing labor, and controlling transportation. Regulation of publications, motion pictures, political meetings, and election campaigns also came under police direction.

After World War II, leaders of Allied Occupation required the Diet to enact a new Police Law. This 1947 law abolished the Home Ministry. It also decentralized the system by establishing about 1,600

independent municipal police forces in all cities and towns with populations of over 5,000. Smaller communities would be served by the
National Rural Police. Popular control of the police was to be ensured
by the establishment of civilian public safety commissions.

This attempt at decentralization was unsuccessful. In June 1951,
the Police Law was amended to allow smaller communities to merge
their police forces with the National Rural Police. Eighty percent of the
communities with autonomous forces did so. The system was further
centralized with passage of a new Police Law in 1954.

Present Structure

Today the Japanese police system is based on prefectural units
that are autonomous in daily operations yet are linked nationwide
under the National Police Agency. Prefectural police headquarters,
including the Tokyo Metropolitan Police Department, control everyday
police operations in each prefecture. In effect, the prefectures pay for the
patrolman on the beat, traffic control, criminal investigation, and other
routine functions but have little control over domestic security units,
which are funded by the national government, as are the salaries of
senior national and prefectural police officials.

Prefectures are divided into districts, each with its own police
station under direct control of prefectural police headquarters. There are
about 1,250 of these police stations nationwide. Districts are further subdivided into jurisdictions of urban *koban* (police boxes) and rural *chuzai-
sho* (residential police boxes).

The mainstay of the Japanese police system is the uniformed
patrol officer (*omawari san*). The patrol officers man the police boxes and
patrol cars and comprise 40 percent of all officers. They are the general-
ists who usually respond first to all incidents and crimes and then
funnel them to the specialized units for further investigation.

The scope of police responsibilities remains broad. Besides
solving ordinary crimes, criminal investigators establish the causes of
fires and industrial accidents. Crime prevention police bear added
responsibility for juveniles, businesses such as bars and Mah-Jongg par-
lors, and the enforcement of "special laws" regulating gun and sword
ownership, drugs, smuggling, prostitution, pornography, and industrial
pollution. Public safety commissions usually defer to police decisions .

Police contact with the community is augmented by the requirement that koban-based police visit every home in their jurisdiction to
gather information, pass on suggestions regarding crime prevention,
and hear complaints. Neighborhood crime prevention and traffic safety
associations provide another link between police and community, further promoting extensive public involvement in law and order.

Education, history of

(*kyoikushi*). Education in the sense of reading and writing began in Japan after the introduction of the Chinese writing system in the 6th century or before. The aristocracy was educated in Confucian thought and Buddhism in the Nara (710–794) and Heian (794–1185) periods. Buddhist priests were the first teachers in ancient Japan, and temples became centers of learning. Education spread to the military class during the Kamakura period (1185–1333); at the same time, through the growth of popular forms of Buddhism, the peasantry was also increasingly exposed to education. During the Edo period (1600–1868) both the shogunal and domainal governments established schools; the official systems were supplemented by private schools at shrines and temples. Education was widely diffused by the time of the Meiji Restoration of 1868.

Nationalism and the drive toward modernization were strong influences on education during the late 19th century. The nationalist influence was predominant after Japan militarized in the 1930s, while the post-World War II period brought decentralization and new democratic influences to education. The postwar system provides nine years of compulsory schooling, and high school education is also nearly universal. Some 40 percent of Japanese students continue their education in universities. The schools are administered by local autonomous bodies under the broad supervision of the Ministry of Education. Education plays a critical role in preparing students for employment, and career opportunities are determined largely according to school performance.

EDUCATION BEFORE 1600

Prior to the introduction of written language to Japan, education was carried out primarily through an oral tradition of stories concerning history and customs. The introduction of writing to Japan necessitated a more conscious and systematic form of education.

Ancient Japan

Education in ancient Japan was fostered by the imperial family. Prince Shotoku (574–622) constructed Horyuji, a temple in Nara, as a place of learning. The emperor Shomu (701–756; r 724–749) constructed temples in each province; monks were sent to these temples by the government as instructors. Of particular importance in the period was the education of clergy, who were among the leaders of society.

The role of priests in spreading education among the masses

during the Nara and Heian periods was considerable. Gyogi (668−749) built places of training (*dojo*) in the various regions he visited. Other priests, including Kuya (903−972) and Ryonin (1073−1132), continued this tradition of teaching.

With the establishment of the Chinese-inspired *ritsuryo* (legal codes) system of centralized government in the late 7th century, two types of schools for the nobility were established: the Daigakuryo, to educate the children of the nobility in the capital, and the *kokugaku*, to educate the children of the provincial nobility.

Medieval Education

During the Kamakura period (1185−1333) when political power shifted to the provincial military class, *samurai* drew up *kakun* (house laws) to educate their children and ensure family solidarity.

The Christian missionaries who came to Japan in the 16th century founded schools where both general and vocational education were conducted. By this time the Daigakuryo and the provincial kokugaku had declined. The most representative educational institution of this period was the Ashikaga Gakko, where monks made up a large part of the students body and the curriculum concentrated on Confucian learning. The school flourished during the late 1500s, when enrollment reached 3,000.

EDO-PERIOD EDUCATION

The civilizing effect of two and a half centuries of peace and modest economic growth during the Edo period (1600−1868) was nowhere more apparent than in the field of formal education. At the beginning of the period literacy rate was very low. Tutors, mostly priests, could be found for the children of noble families, but there were virtually no schools.

The contrast at the end of the period was great. Large schools organized by the domainal authorities gave a graded instruction in the Chinese classics to almost every samurai child, and local *terakoya*, the schools for commoners, taught reading and writing to villagers as well as townsmen. Other private schools and academics called *shijuku* provided more advanced instruction in a variety of disciplines and schools of thought to both samurai and commoners. Books abounded. Japan had almost certainly reached the 40 percent literacy threshold that some consider a prerequisite for modern growth.

For the Japanese of the Edo period the Chinese classics were the repository of wisdom and knowledge. Learning painfully to "construe" these classics was the central business of the schools operated by the feudal clans in the Edo Era. In contrast to the powerful Christian church, the Buddhist temples yielded moral authority to the Confucian schools. The school during the Edo period thus came to combine the functions shared in Western society between school and church.

Confucian Scholarship and School Formation

The establishment of Confucian scholarship as a separate branch of learning, and of the role of the Confucian scholar-governmental adviser-teacher as a distinct profession, was the work of a number of distinguished men of the 17th century: Fujiwara Seika (1561–1619), Hayashi Razan (1583–1657), and Ito Jinsai (1627–1705). Fujiwara was the first to cut himself off from his temple roots and to declare himself an adherent of the philosophy and ethic of Confucianism as something incompatible with Buddhism.

By the end of the 17th century the idea was generally established that every self-respecting *daimyo*'s band of retainers should include a *jusha* (Confucian adviser) to advise on tricky questions of historical precedent or political morality, and to tutor the daimyo's heir. Some daimyo gave financial assistance to help transform the band of disciples who gathered at the feet of any scholar into the framework of a formal school. Some 20 domains had founded schools by 1703. The number was over 200 by 1865.

Heterodoxy and New Orthodoxy

An emphasis on moral virtue developed, becoming the dominant but by no means the only strand of Confucian thought or of educational philosophy in the Edo period. The leader of a reaction against this trend away from mastery of ancient Chinese texts and commentaries was Ogyu Sorai (1666–1728). He rejected the entire Neo-Confucian notion that the purpose of study was the moral cultivation of the individual. He took the Legalist view that one kept men in order not by winning over their individual hearts and minds to virtue but by establishing institutions that channel their self-interest in socially beneficial directions. Scholarship was the rigorous, intellectual study of such institutions but in addition to that practical purpose it was also an end-in-itself pursuit of intellectual and literary excellence.

For over half a century the followers of Sorai coexisted with the Neo-Confucianists until Matsudaira Sadanobu's (1758–1829) famous Ban on Heterodox Learning (Kansei Igaku no Kin) of 1790. Henceforth, it ruled that the teachings of Zhu Xi's Neo-Confucian school should be adhered to at the shogunate's own school (the Shoheiko). The ban was part of Matsudaira's plan to revitalize the Hayashi school, which he expected to play an important role in his attempts to reform the shogunate. As other domains followed suit, the "Sorai school" practically disappeared, but the new orthodoxy was in fact a relatively tolerant and eclectic one that had room for political economy as well as for moral improvement.

Other Edo-Period Schools

There were two other forms of education. The first was Japanese studies. About 15 domains, those most influenced by the National Learning (Kokugaku), had established schools of national studies around the end of the period. The other much more consequential innovation was the establishment of schools that specialized in Dutch, later Western, studies. From the first spurt of interest in Dutch science—particularly medical science—in the 1770s until the mid-1850s, these exotic studies were largely carried on by individual doctors and low-ranking samurai. A number of special schools for Western studies were begun in the 1850s, notably the shogunate's Bansho Shirabesho, which rapidly developed into a flourishing school that admitted pupils from all over Japan.

Parallel to these developments was the laying of foundations for mass literacy by the simple private reading-and-writing schools (terakoya) that helped prepare the way for Japan's transition to an industrial society.

Convinced that knowledge would enhance the strength of the nation, the Meiji government decreed an entirely new educational system based upon imported models. Almost none of Japan's great schools and colleges can trace direct links of institutional continuity back to the schools of the Edo period.

MODERN EDUCATION

The history of education in Japan since the Meiji Restoration (1868) can be divided into the following five periods: the period of establishment (1868–1885), when the initial framework for a modern educational system was created; the period of consolidation (1886–1916), when various school orders were issued and a systematic educational structure was established; the period of expansion (1917–1936), based upon the recommendations of the Extraordinary Council on Education (Rinji Kyoiku Kaigi; 1917–1919); the wartime period (1937–1945) of militaristic education; and the present period (from 1945), which was ushered in by educational reforms during the Allied Occupation.

The Period of Establishment (1868–1885)

The Education Order of 1872 (Gakusei) established the foundation for a modern public education system. Many Edo-period schools were incorporated into the new educational system. Terakoya and shijuku, schools for the common people, became primary schools; the shogunate-controlled, elite school called Kaiseijo developed into a university that later became Tokyo University, while many domain schools became public middle schools, which eventually developed into universities. Most of the schools of Western Learning developed into private *semmon gakko* (professional schools).

The educational reform effort based on the Gakusei was overambitious and was thus revised two times, in 1879 and 1880. A significant development was the 1879 issuance of the Kyogaku Taishi (Outline of Learning), which emphasized Confucian values of humanity, justice, loyalty, and filial piety. Education in *shushin* ("moral" training) took on new importance. The utmost priority came to be placed on nationalistic moral education. This formed the basis for national educational policy until the end of World War II.

The Period of Consolidation (1886—1916)

In 1885 the cabinet system was created, and Mori Arinori (1847—1889) became the first minister of education. In 1886 he issued in quick succession the Elementary School Order, the Middle School Order, the Imperial University Order, and the Normal School Order. The Imperial Universities were intended to be the institutions that would create capable leaders who would absorb advanced Western Learning necessary for the modernization of the nation. Middle schools (especially the higher middle schools that became higher schools in 1894) were designed to prepare students for the Imperial University.

In these ways a comprehensive school system was established for the purpose of modernization on one hand and the spiritual unification of the people on the other. In 1890 the Imperial Rescript on Education (Kyoiku Chokugo) was issued in the name of Emperor Meiji. The rescript served as a powerful instrument of political indoctrination and remained in effect until the end of World War II. The text states that the fundamental principles of education are based upon the historical bonds uniting its benevolent rulers and their royal subjects. The Rescript was given ceremonial readings at all important school events. Later, with the development of industry after the Sino-Japanese War (1894—1895) and the demand for industrial education, Inoue Kowashi (1844—1895), who became minister of education after Mori, established systems of vocational and girls' schools. In this period a variety of private semmon gakko (later to become universities) was also established. In 1898 the attendance rate for compulsory education reached 69 percent. Compulsory education was extended to six years in 1907.

The Period of Expansion (1917—1936)

Stimulated by the Russo-Japanese War and World War I, capitalism developed rapidly in Japan. During this period the governmental Rinji Kyoiku Kaigi (Extraordinary Council on Education) issued several reports that formed the basis for the expansion of the education system over the next decade or so to meet the need of the development. Until 1918 universities had been limited to the imperial universities, but the reforms contained in the University Order of 1918 extended recognition to colleges and private universities. In accordance with this order many national, public, and private semmon gakko were raised to the status of university.

On the other hand, with the inflow into Japan of new currents of thought, including socialism, communism, anarchism, and liberalism, the teachers' union and student movements rose up in opposition to nationalistic education. These trends intensified in the late 1920s with the deepening of economic crisis and political confrontation. The government attempted to counteract the influence of leftist ideology by promoting the so-called Japanese spirit.

The Wartime Period (1937 – 1945)

After the Manchurian Incident of 1931, educational policy soon became ultranationalistic; after the beginning of the Sino-Japanese War of 1937 – 1945, it became militaristic. Elementary schools were changed to *kokumin gakko* (national people's schools), which were to train subjects for the empire, and *seinen gakko* (youth schools, for vocational education) became obligatory for graduates of elementary schools. Normal schools were raised in status to semmon gakko. After Japan entered World War II, militaristic education became even stronger. In order to enhance nationalistic indoctrination, control over learning, education, and thought was strengthened.

Educational Reforms after World War II (1945 –)

After defeat in 1945 Japan was placed under the Occupation of the Allied forces until the San Francisco Peace Treaty of 1952. Reports of the United States education missions to Japan, which came to Japan in 1946 and 1950, became the blueprints for educational reform. The core of the reform was the Fundamental Law of Education (1947), which took the place of the Imperial Rescript on Education as the basic philosophy of education. Based on this law, the School Education Law of 1947 was promulgated in the same year, and a new school system was established. The essential elements of the new system were the replacement of the existing dual-track (popular and elite) system with a single-track 6-3-3-4 system (six years of elementary school, three years of middle school, three years of high school, and four years of university), compulsory education in elementary and middle schools, the establishment of the principle of coeducation and the creation of the board of education system. There have been calls for further educational reforms in response to the social and economic changes that have occurred in Japan since the late 1940s, and in 1984 the Nakasone cabinet established its own advisory council, the Provisional Council on Educational Reform (Rinji Kyoiku Shingikai; also called Rinkyoshin), which presented a final report in 1987. It stressed the principle of respect for and encouragement of individuality as a fundamental goal.

Education system reforms

(*kyoiku seido no kaikaku*). The Japanese education system has undergone numerous reforms since modern education was introduced soon after the Meiji Restoration (1868).

The Ministry of Education was established in 1871, and the Education Order of 1872 set up an education system patterned after European and American models. The Imperial Rescript on Education (1890) stressed loyalty to the nation and a Confucian-oriented ethical education. In the first half of the 1890s, in the wake of rapid industrial progress, vocational schools and professional schools (*semmon gakko*) were established for graduates of elementary schools. Secondary schools for girls were set up after 1899.

Elementary school education spread rapidly during the first decade of the 20th century, and the duration of compulsory education was increased from four years to six years. The government also strengthened national controls over content and reinforced the teaching of ethics. The Rinji Kyoiku Kaigi (Extraordinary Council on Education), formed in 1917, introduced several new measures, such as the recognition of colleges and universities outside the imperial university system. It also proposed emphasizing military training at school to promote the concept of national polity (*kokutai*). *Seinen gakko* (youth schools), which mixed vocational and military education, were made compulsory for elementary school graduates in 1939, and in 1941 the elementary school system was reorganized under the name *kokumin gakko* (national people's schools). After World War II, the educational reforms of 1947 resulted from the advice of the first of the United States education missions to Japan and from the Japanese Education Reform Council. Militaristic education was abolished and an emphasis on peace and democracy was introduced. The complicated, multitrack, prewar system was replaced by a unified system with a six-year elementary school, three-year middle school, three-year high school, and four-year university. The first nine years of the system were made compulsory. Coeducation and equal opportunity in education were promoted. Curriculum was developed under school course guidelines of the Ministry of Education. Since 1952 all education policies have been developed by the Central Council for Education (Chuo Kyoiku Shingikai), an advisory council attached to the Ministry of Education.

Educational expenses

(*kyoikuhi*). The School Education Law (Gakko Kyoiku Ho) of 1947 guarantees free primary and middle school education to all Japanese citizens. However, each family must pay supplementary expenses, including kindergarten and high school tuition, field trips, supplies, transportation to and from school, school lunches, extracurricular lessons at *juku* (private tutoring schools) and cram schools, and private lessons in calligraphy, piano, etc.

The total cost per child for a family in 1987 averaged out to ¥179,723 (US $1,242) for public kindergarten and ¥339,767 (US $2,349) for private kindergarten (attended by 76 percent). In the public schools the average per student was ¥184,000 (US $1,275) for elementary school and ¥225,407 (US $1,558) for middle school. Costs in public high schools averaged ¥294,471 (US $2,035) and in private high schools ¥605,481 (US $4,186). Of the 94.3 percent of middle school graduates who went on to high school, 72 percent attended public schools.

Since academic records have a strong influence on social status, parents spare no expense to prepare a child for the entrance examinations for high school and college. The pressure to send students in middle or high school to *juku* or cram schools is acute. Although Japan's consumer price index for 1987 rose only 0.1 percent over the previous year, educational expenses increased by 2.9-4.5 percent, saddling parents of competing children with a great burden, exacerbated by the fact that scholarship grants are rare and educational loans are small.

Entrance examinations

(*nyugaku shiken*). Entrance examinations are given great weight in Japan's educational system. Although nursery, primary, and middle schools also conduct such tests, Japanese society attaches the most importance to entrance exams for high schools and universities.

High school is attended by 94 percent of middle school graduates, so the function of high school entrance tests is not to weed out unqualified applicants, but to determine which school a student may attend. Private high schools design their own tests and conduct applicant interviews to select students, while public high school entrance standards are determined by the local school system. Generally, achievement test results in five categories (English, mathematics, Japanese, social studies, and science) are evaluated, along with the student's junior high school records.

Objective achievement-test performance is the key factor in university applicant selection, but certain universities may include essay-writing tests, or performance tests for applicants in music or physical education, in their evaluation process. All national and other public universities (and a few private ones) require prospective applicants to take the University Entrance Examination Center Tests—a series of standardized multiple-choice examinations measuring competence in the Japanese language, social studies, mathematics, science, and foreign languages. Based on the results, students may then make a more informed choice as to which schools to apply to. Ultimately, admission is based on the combined results of the general test plus the independent examination offered by the university in question. Entrance examinations for both high schools and universities are administered each year during the period from January through March. Students may apply to more than one high school or university.

The Japanese entrance examination system does not establish in advance a target score that, if achieved, assures admission; those applying at the same time compete for a limited number of openings. In Japanese society it is generally accepted that the school one attends will decisively influence the course of one's life and career (gakureki shakai). Entrance tests are therefore regarded as major events in determining one's fate, and the battle to qualify for the best schools is waged with fierce intensity. The competition is seen as having assumed excessive proportions in the 1980s. This has not only led to enormous prosperity for the operators of *juku* (private tutoring schools) and cram schools, but is also thought to have helped precipitate many education-related problems. These include increasing juvenile delinquency, apathy on the part of students not targeted as high achievers, and school allergy, a phenomenon whereby some students are unable to attend school for emotional reasons.

Gakureki shakai

("credential society"). Term used in Japan to refer to the great emphasis the Japanese place on a person's educational background. In Japan an individual's social and occupational status is generally considered to be determined not only by the level of education completed, but also by the rank and prestige of the particular universities attended. Factors such as class, race, religion, and personal wealth, which are important determinants of social status in other societies, are not quite as significant in Japan because of the country's high level of homogeneity and lack of extreme inequalities in the distribution of wealth. A person's educational career, on the other hand, provides a convenient determinant of status. With a high percentage of students attending universities, the status distinctions among schools have become increasingly pronounced. As a result of this, the competition to gain entrance to the most prestigious schools has intensified markedly.

Hensachi

(*deviation*). Statistical term frequently used in Japanese education to express a student's performance on a standardized examination relative to a mean average score. Since the early 1960s hensachi figures have been used in Japan to calculate an individual's percentile ranking for practice entrance examinations. Guidance counselors often base their assessment of how likely a student is to gain admission to certain schools by comparing the student's hensachi with the average hensachi of other students applying to the same schools. The industry of private tutoring schools (*juku*) and cram schools also calculates hensachi figures for students, based on the results of large-scale practice examinations, to advise them on test-taking strategies.

Cram schools

(*yobiko*). Schools whose primary purpose is preparing students to pass the high competitive entrance examination of Japanese universities. Most cram school enrollees are recent high school graduates who are seeking admission to colleges and universities and failed in their first sitting for the entrance examination. In 1989 there were 165 yobiko with a combined enrollment of about 205,510.

Recently competition among those hoping to pass college entrance examinations has become intense, and large numbers of students commute to cram school while still in high school. The information regarding university entrance examinations provided by the major yobiko is indispensable not only to their enrolled students but to all prospective test takers.

Juku

(private tutoring schools). In the Edo period (1600−1868) the term juku referred to small schools for the teaching of martial arts or the doctrines of a particular school of philosophy. Modern juku may offer lessons in nonacademic subjects such as arts and sports or in the academic subjects that are important in school entrance examinations. Juku for high school students must compete for enrollments with *yobiko* (cram schools), which are solely geared to helping students pass university entrance examinations. According to a 1989 survey, 38.2 percent of elementary school students, 74.9 percent of middle school students, and 37.6 percent of high school students in Tokyo were attending juku. Recently there has been a trend toward expanding the major juku into chain or franchise operations. At the same time, a number of smaller, innovative juku have sprung up to help students who are unable to keep up with classwork or who have had problems.

English language training

(*eigo kyoiku*). English is the most widely studied foreign language in Japan. During the Meiji period (1868–1912), the study of English was considered essential for importing the Western technology necessary for modernization. Language training was chiefly based on reading ability and not on conversation.

Because the written entrance examinations for universities and high schools test for English ability, grammar and reading comprehension are stressed in the English classes offered by most high schools and middle schools. However, there is a growing awareness that neglecting speaking and listening during the first six years of English language training leads to problems. The school course guidelines introduced in 1992 stress spoken communication, and the Ministry of Education has brought in native English speakers as assistant teachers of middle and high school English classes. In 1990 there were 2,146 such assistant teachers invited to Japan.

English conversation schools, courses on television and on radio, and company-run classes for employees offer further training in English. In 1988, some 2,361,982 people took the Test in Practical English Proficiency (offered by the Ministry of Education since 1963).

School lunch in a Tokyo elementary school.

School lunch program

(*gakko kyushoku*). During the post-World War II food shortage the Allied Occupation started a nationwide school lunch program. With the School Lunch Law of 1954 the practice was established on a permanent basis. The school lunch menu was based on bread until 1976, when a rice-based menu was introduced. In 1989, 98.0 percent of elementary schools and 85.4 percent of middle schools had lunch programs.

School textbooks

(*kyokasho*). In Japan all elementary, middle, and high schools are obliged to use government-approved textbooks. Textbooks are compiled by private publishers, who are given a certain amount of freedom in the style of presentation, but are also required to conform to government-issued school course guidelines. Authorization is given only after evaluation of the texts by Ministry of Education specialists and appointed examiners and a final review by the Textbook Authorization and Research Council, an advisory organ of the ministry.

A system of free distribution of textbooks for compulsory education was established in 1963. The textbooks used in each school district are chosen by the local board of education from among those authorized by the central government; in the case of private schools the responsibility lies with the school principal.

The purpose of the official authorization of textbooks, a system that has been in effect in Japan since 1886, is the standardization of education and the maintenance of objectivity and neutrality on political and religious issues. The textbook approval process has engendered considerable controversy and has led to one famous court case, a suit brought against the government by a historian Ienaga Saburo (1913−) in 1965, charging that the authorization process was both illegal and unconstitutional.

Transportation

Transportation

(*kotsu*). Japan has a highly developed domestic and international transportation network. The system as it now exists was developed in the century following the Meiji Restoration of 1868, but even earlier the transportation system was relatively sophisticated for a preindustrial society.

Premodern Transportation

During the early periods of Japanese history, and especially during the 7th to 9th centuries, goods and people traveled extensively by ship between Japan and the Asian mainland. Within Japan, the establishment of a rice tax system and legal system in the late 7th century was accompanied by the construction of the first major roads. The Inland Sea was a major transportation route between settlements in Japan from early times.

After the establishment of the Tokugawa shogunate (1603−1867), international transportation activity was halted by the National Seclusion policy, which was in force from 1639 to 1854. Domestic transportation, on the other hand, grew and improved greatly during the Edo period (1600−1868). Coastal shipping routes were extended to support the expanding commodity trade, and the road network was also improved.

Meiji Period (1868 – 1912) to World War II

Following the Meiji Restoration of 1868, Japan absorbed Western technology at a rapid pace. The first steam-powered train ran on a narrow-gauge track between Tokyo and Yokohama in 1872, the first automobile was imported in 1899. Western vessels quickly replaced most Japanese sailing ships, as the government subsidized the shipbuilding industry. From the 1880s onward the rail network expanded rapidly and in 1906 major portions of it were nationalized. In 1927 the first subway in Tokyo began operation. Bus service and trucking companies began in 1910s, with rapid expansion after the Tokyo Earthquake of 1923. During the 1930s taxis developed into an important means of urban transportation.

By the 1940s the mainstay of the passenger transportation system was the railroads, while freight transportation was conducted primarily through coastal shipping and the railroads.

Postwar Transportation Network

The postwar era was characterized by an explosive growth in moter vehicles and airlines. By 1990 the rail share of total domestic passenger transportation had fallen to 30 percent, with automobiles increasing from less than 1 percent in 1950 to 66 percent in 1990. Buses also compete with the railroads to some extent, but they mainly provide feeder service to train stations or operate in rural areas where there is no rail service. Subways are an important means of urban transportation, with a total length of 523.6 kilometers (325.3 mi) in 1991. In addition to the vast network in Tokyo, there are also subway systems in Fukuoka, Kobe, Kyoto, Nagoya, Osaka, Sapporo, Sendai, and Yokohama.

Scheduled domestic airlines have grown rapidly but still occupy a small share (4 percent in 1990) of total passenger transportation. International air travel has also grown at a tremendous pace: the number of passengers carried by scheduled Japanese airlines was only 112,000 in 1955 but reached 11.3 million in 1991.

For freight transportation, the rail share of total ton-kilometers fell to 5 percent by 1990, while trucks expanded from 8 percent in 1950 to 50 percent in 1990, and coastal shipping went from 39 percent to 45 percent.

Coordination of the transportation system has been a problem because different modes of transportation are governed by separate laws and represented by different bureaus within the Ministry of Transport. In addition, certain transportation-related activities are under the jurisdiction of other ministries.

Railroads

The network of railways consists of the JR (Japan Railways) group

and a number of private railways. The JR group is made up of six passenger railway companies, a freight railway company, and several other
affiliated companies, all of which were created when long-term financial
difficulties led to the privatization of the Japanese National Railways
(JNR) in 1987. In 1990 the rail system comprised 26,895 operation-kilome-
ters (16,710 mi), of which JR companies operated 20,175 or 75 percent of
the total. JR passenger service includes intercity trunk lines, urban feeder
service, and a large number of rural lines. It also operates Japan's fastest
passenger trains on the Shinkansen "bullet train" lines of standard gauge.
In 1950 the JNR alone generated 59 percent of all passenger-kilometers,
but this figure had fallen to 18 percent for the JR in 1990. The JR group's
Japan Freight Railway Co. provides almost all of the rail freight service in
Japan, but railroads can no longer effectively compete with trucks for
most freight business.

In addition to the JR group companies, there are 16 large railway
companies and 58 smaller railways. Unlike the JR, the other large railway companies have evolved into conglomerates of related activities,
operating sports stadiums, baseball teams, department stores, amusement parks, and real estate. More of their profits often come from these
related businesses.

Motor vehicles

Private automobiles have been one of the fastest growing segments of passenger transportation because of three factors that became
conspicuous in the 1960s: the rapid growth of income to a point where
families could afford automobiles; the development of a domestic automotive industry geared to the specific needs of the domestic market
(small-sized vehicles); and the improvement of roads. The number of
registered motor vehicles increased from only about 1.5 million in 1960
to over 43 million in 1990. Paving on national highways was extended
from 29 percent in 1960 to 98 percent in 1991. Japan also had developed
a total of 4,869 kilometers (3,025 mi) of expressways by 1991. Even as
late as 1960, 20 percent of all automobiles were business vehicles, but by
1990 private automobiles were 97 percent of total registrations. Despite
the popularity of automobile ownership, problems such as urban traffic
congestion, lack of parking, and the high cost of fuel continue to restrict
the actual day-to-day use of private vehicles in Japan.

As roads have improved, trucks have increased in size. Whereas
most commercial trucks did not exceed a 5-ton capacity in the mid-
1950s, 18-ton trucks are now common and the number of trailer trucks is
also increasing.

During the 1980s the parcel delivery service business grew
rapidly. Small parcels such as gifts and catalog purchases are delivered

on the day of or following their dispatch.

Highway safety continues to be a major problem. Although major safety campaigns led to a steady decline in traffic deaths between 1970 and 1980, since then the trend has reversed, and in 1988 highway fatalities exceeded 10,000.

Marine transportation

Seaborne freight is the primary means of transporting Japan's huge volume of raw-materials imports and finished-goods exports. Total tonnage handled by Japanese ports grew at an annual rate of 15 percent from 1980 to 1990. The most important of Japan's 121 international ports are the Tokyo Bay area (Tokyo, Yokohama, Kawasaki, and Chiba), Nagoya, the Osaka Bay area (Osaka and Kobe), Kita Kyushu, and Wakayama Shimotsu (a major oil port).

Since the Oil Crisis of 1973 an oversupply of ships worldwide has hurt the shipping industry as a whole. Japanese shipping companies have lost international competitiveness because of rising wages and the continuing high value of the yen since 1985. Japanese-owned vessels under flags of convenience have been increasing to gain the advantage of lower-cost labor. By 1990 the total gross tons of vessels flying the Japanese flag had fallen about 42 percent from its peak of 35 million tons in 1982. The industry has responded to the difficult business environment by trying to increase efficiency through mergers and large-scale reductions in capacity.

View of Tokyo bay from Tokyo Tower.

Along with the increases in maritime freight through the mid-1970s, Japan's shipbuilding industry expanded to a point where Japan became the world's largest shipbuilder. Japan pioneered the construction of supertankers, which were instrumental in supplying Japan's energy needs at substantially reduced transportation costs. However, the oil crisis and ensuing severe recession brought depression to the shipbuilding industry. Since then the government has taken measures to reduce capacity and employment in the industry.

Air transportation.

After World War II, passenger airlines were prohibited by SCAP (the supreme commander for the Allied powers) until 1951, when the Ministry of Transport was given control over licensing airline routes and fares. Japan Airlines Co, Ltd (JAL), was established in 1953 as an international airline (including domestic trunk lines) with 50 percent government capital participation. At the same time approval was also given to two private regional firms, which later merged to become All Nippon Airways Co, Ltd (ANA). JAL became a private company in 1987.

As of January 1991 there were 5 scheduled international airlines in Japan, including JAL and ANA, as well as 6 scheduled domestic airlines and 49 unscheduled air service companies. To handle the increased air traffic, airports have also expanded. In the spring of 1978, the New Tokyo International Airport (Narita) replaced Tokyo International Airport (Haneda) as the main international airport for Tokyo. Kansai International Airport is expected to open in 1994 in Osaka.

Railways

(*tetsudo*). Railways in Japan date from 1872, only four years into the country's modern period, but almost four decades from the time that railways first appeared in Europe and the United States. Progress was rapid after the late start, however, and in the 20th century Japan's railways have compared favorably with those of any other nation in the world. In the post–World War II period, and especially since the development of the Shinkansen "bullet train," Japan has been at the forefront of railway technology.

History and Early Development

The first line, begun in 1870 and completed in 1872, was of modest proportions, running 28 kilometers (17.4 mi) from Shimbashi in Tokyo to Yokohama on the track of narrow gauge. Financing for the first state lines was obtained partly by floating bonds on the London money market, and British technicians and technology figured prominently in the early construction of both public and private railways. Domestication of technical expertise and equipment was relatively rapid and thorough, and one of the few lasting reminders of British influence is that Japanese trains run on the left, a practice that has carried over to highway traffic control.

In the Kinki region, a state-constructed line between Kobe and Osaka was opened in 1874. Following initial government plans calling for a trunk line between Tokyo and Kyoto, running through a coastal route, the Tokaido was first spanned by rails in 1893. Two years later the nation's first electric railway began operating in Kyoto. By 1901 tracks had been laid the entire length of the main island of Honshu, and each of the other three main islands also had some trackage by this time. By and by, gaps in the system were filled in gradually, so that, in effect, a nationwide network was in place by the eve of nationalization in 1906–1907.

Nationalization

Although the earliest lines had been constructed by the government, after about 1885 the apparent profitability of railways was sufficient to attract a flood of private entrepreneurs into the field. During the period prior to nationalization, however, the wars with China (1894–

1895) and Russia (1904 – 1905) raised the question of the desirability of private control of such a key national resource. The importance of foreign loans in financing railway development was thought to raise the specter of foreign control of the private lines, and this possibility was a key element in arguments in favor of nationalization. Finally the measure of nationalization was put into effect in 1906 – 1907. The resulting system was known as the Japanese National Railways from 1949 until denationalization took place in 1987.

Postwar Developments

The extension of urban commuter systems, including subways, has been a major accomplishment of the postwar period, but the most spectacular development has been the routes of the world-famed Shinkansen "bullet trains" and the infrastructure that has been created to extend these routes throughout Japan. The original section of the Shinkansen was opened in 1964 as a route between Tokyo and Osaka. Since then, extensions have been opened to Okayama (Okayama Prefecture) in 1972 and Hakata (Fukuoka Prefecture) in 1975. Two more new lines, connecting Tokyo with northern Japan, were put into operation in 1982: the Joetsu Shinkansen, from Tokyo to Niigata (Niigata Prefecture), and the Tohoku Shinkansen, from Tokyo to Morioka (Iwate Prefecture). Also the "Mini" Shinkansen, using the conventional narrow-gauge track partially broadened into standard gauge by addition of a third rail, started operation between Fukushima (Fukushima Prefecture) and Yamagata (Yamagata Prefecture) in 1992. New Shinkansen routes are planned for other parts of the country as well.

Overnight trains with sleeping car service are available on non-Shinkansen routes. Approximately 2,300 limited express and ordinary express trains operate on principal lines every day, along with about 23,300 local trains.

Unlike those in many countries, the Japanese rail system can be characterized as passenger oriented. Especially suburban residents, for their part, have been so dependent on the spread of commuter railways that land values for lots within walking distance of stations are correspondingly higher.

Denationalization

The basic form of the railway system remained the same from nationalization in 1906 – 1907 until 1987, when the Japanese National Railways was privatized and broken up into six regional private passenger services and one rail freight company, known collectively as the JR (Japan Railways) group. The JNR had been suffering an increasing burden of debt and operating deficits since the 1960s. Most of the new JR companies returned to profitability within two to three years of privatization by cutting staff, by reducing services on loss-making lines or abolishing them altogether, and by buying into service industries such as restaurants and hotels.

In addition to the main JR network—20,175 kilometers (12,535 mi) of track—and the private local lines, subway systems serve the main cities of Japan. In these densely populated urban centers, the subways provide important feeder services to the aboveground rail lines. As crowding increases even further, subways should become an even more important component of the urban transportation system.

Shinkansen

(New Trunk Line). The Shinkansen, a high-speed passenger railroad system operated by companies of the JR group provides first-class, or "Green Car," service as well as reserved and unreserved ordinary-car service. There are no sleeping facilities and few dining facilities on Shinkansen trains, since most runs can be made in a few hours.

The Nozomi Shinkansen.

The first line to be completed was called the Tokaido Shinkansen, because it was a new trunk line on the route of the Tokaido between Tokyo and Osaka. The San'yo line has since been constructed from Osaka west to Hakata in Kyushu. The combined route, with a total length of 1,069 kilometers (664 mi), is known as the Tokaido-San'yo Shinkansen. The train has a maximum speed of 270 kilometers per hour (168 mph), and the minimum trip time between Tokyo and Hakata is 5 hours 4 minutes. A Shinkansen train departs Tokyo for Osaka or some point further west about every seven minutes throughout most daytime schedules, lasting from approximately 6 AM to 12 PM. In 1991, 278 trains were scheduled on the route per day, each with a uniform 16 cars. Between the inauguration of service on the line in 1964 and early 1991, the Tokaido San'yo Shinkansen had carried 3 billion passengers.

The Tohoku Shinkansen and Joetsu Shinkansen commenced service in 1982. The former connects Tokyo and Morioka in northern Japan, with a route length of 535.3 kilometers (332.6 mi) and a minimum trip time of 2 hours 36 minutes. On average 115 trains are scheduled daily and passengers number over 30 million per year. The latter connects Tokyo and Niigata on the coast of the Sea of Japan, with a route length of 333.9 kilometers (207.5 mi) and a minimum trip time of 1 hour 40 minutes. On average 85 trains are scheduled daily and passengers number 20 million per year. From the inauguration of service to 1991, the two lines carried over 400 million passengers.

Development of the System

The railroad that serves the 500-kilometer (311-mi) corridor between Tokyo and Osaka has always been considered the main artery of Japan. Located on the Pacific coast of central Honshu, this zone is the industrial and socioeconomic nucleus of the country; almost half the population and two-thirds of the nation's industry are concentrated there.

In the 1950s innovations on the conventional Tokaido rail line, which served this district, were given priority over other lines in an effort to meet steadily increasing demand. Because of the significance of the line, it became imperative to increase the capacity. The eventual solution was to construct a high-speed railroad on a separate double track of standard gauge—the Shinkansen. Ground was broken for the project in April 1959, and construction was completed in July 1964. Service was begun on 1 October 1964, 10 days before the opening of the Tokyo Olympic Games, with initial daily service of 60 trains with 12 cars each. The total construction cost was ¥380.0 billion (US $1.1 billion), double the original estimate.

The Shinkansen reduced the minimum trip time between Tokyo and Osaka from 6 hours and 30 minutes to 2 hours and 30 minutes. A business trip between the two cities was no longer an overnight journey, a fact that considerably altered business activities. The Shinkansen was enthusiastically welcomed by the public because of its high speed, short trip time, good ride comfort, and superb on-time operation. In the 1960s and 1970s the image of the Shinkansen speeding past a snowcapped Mt. Fuji was seen as a symbol of modern Japan.

The line's popularity and the rapid growth in traffic volume brought about a need for the westward extension of the Shinkansen system. The San'yo Shinkansen opened for service with a 160.9 kilometer (100-mi) stretch between Osaka and Okayama in March 1972. The project had taken five years to complete at a cost of ¥224.0 billion (US $739.0 million). The line was extended to Hakata in Kyushu through the Kammon undersea tunnel in March 1975. The construction for this stretch of 392.8 kilometers (244 mi) also took five years, and the cost was ¥729.0 billion (US $2.4 billion).

In 1971 the construction of two new lines was begun from Omiya in Saitama Prefecture north to Niigata and northeast to Morioka. These lines were completed in 1982 and extended from Omiya to Tokyo in 1991. Additional routes are under construction, and others are being planned.

Technical Aspects

The Shinkansen track is a conventional ballasted track between Tokyo and Osaka. This track structure, however, requires a great deal of time and labor to maintain the track geometry. Consequently, concrete slab track, which is maintenance free, was adopted for further line extensions. The Shinkansen has a DC series traction motor installed on each single-wheel axle, allowing dynamic brakes to be applied to all axles at once, and uses electric multiple-unit trains fed by AC 25 kilowatts. This system was selected for a number of reasons: the even distribution of axle load results in less strain on track structure; the turnaround operation is simple; and a failure of one or two units does not interrupt the operation of the entire train. The car body is streamlined and the cars are air-conditioned and airtight. Windows cannot be opened, but the train is well ventilated throughout. Automatic Train Control (ATC) is used to prevent collisions by maintaining a safety distance between trains and to prevent excess speeds by applying brakes automatically. All trains are continuously monitored and controlled from computer-aided traffic control systems in two central control rooms in Tokyo. Electric power supply to the trains is also monitored and controlled from the same rooms by electric power dispatchers. In case of accidents or other problems, the dispatchers act promptly to secure alternative power to restore the failure.

Since it was inaugurated in 1964, the Shinkansen has had a remarkable record of high-speed operation, safety, volume of transport, and punctuality. The success of the Shinkansen revolutionized thinking about high-speed trains. It has been described as the "savior of the declining railroad industry" since its example has stimulated many other countries to take on the new construction or the modernization of railroads as national projects, among which are the French TGV, the English HST, and the Northeast Corridor Rail Improvement Project in the United States.

Expressways

(*kosoku doro*). Construction of expressways in Japan began in the 1960s. Intercity expressways are designed for a maximum speed of 120 kilometers (75 mi) per hour, although legal speed limits are usually lower. These four-lane, limited-access, divided highways have a 3.6-meter (11.8-ft) lane width.

Since the opening in 1965 of the Meishin Expressway between Nagoya and Kobe, the first part of the expressway system, 4,869 kilometers (3,025 mi) had been completed by March 1991, and construction of the projected 11,520-kilometer (7,157-mi) network is expected to be finished early in the 21st century. Because of the nature of the terrain and the high concentration of housing, cultivated land, and factories along the routes, the cost of highway construction has been high in Japan relative to that in other countries, and expressway tolls are also proportionately high. However, expressways are used extensively; in fiscal 1990 average daily traffic between Tokyo and Komaki in Aichi Prefecture was 366,917 automobiles. Of the total traffic in that year, 75 percent consisted of passenger cars and 25 percent of other vehicles. Measures are being taken to protect residents along routes against highway noise and exhaust fumes. Expressways are administered by the Japan Highway Public Corporation.

Drivers' licenses

(*unten menkyo*). They are of two kinds, Class I for drivers of private vehicles and Class II for drivers of commercial passenger-carrying vehicles (taxis and buses), and must be renewed every three years. Anyone 18 years of age (20 for trucks over 5 tons and noncommercial buses, 16 for motorcycles) may obtain a Class I driver's license by passing an examination given by the Public Safety Commission in the prefecture where he or she lives. Applicants for a Class II license and for a Class I license permitting operation of trucks over 11 tons must be 21 years old. The examination is in three parts: a test for vision, color blindness, and hearing; a road test of driving skills; and a written test on traffic regulations. Anyone certified by an accredited driving school is exempt from the road test. The possessor of a foreign driver's license is exempt from the road test and the written test. A foreign national who holds an international driver's license may drive in Japan for one year after arrival without applying for a Japanese license.

Aviation

(*koku*). The first airplane flights in Japan were made on 19 December 1910 at Yoyogi drill ground in Tokyo. Other efforts followed, but aviation technology was still considerably behind that of the advanced nations of the West. When the Japanese army and navy established air units, they imported equipment from Western nations and produced planes under international licensing agreements at military arsenals. After World War I broke out, planes were developed at a rapid pace in Europe, but Japan fell even further behind aviation technology.

Japanese manufacturers soon succeeded in developing their own designs, and in the late 1920s domestic production of military airplanes began with planes such as the Mitsubishi shipboard attack plane Model 13 (1924) and the Kawasaki reconnaissance plane Model 88 (1928). Around 1935 Japanese aeronautical technology began to produce solely Japanese-made planes with features not to be found in European and American aircraft. Japanese-made planes dating from this period were chiefly warplanes.

While the European and American air forces preferred heavy fighter planes with relatively high-wing loading capacities and high-horsepower engines, capable of striking one blow and making a high-speed escape, the Japanese military rated more highly light varieties of fighter planes with low-wing loading capacities, easy maneuverability in circular flight, and the capability of sharp turns. In the first half of World War II, these flight characteristics contributed appreciably to the early air war victories scored by Japan. The representative Japanese fighters were the navy's Model 96 (Mitsubishi, 1936), Model Zero (commonly called Zerosen or zero fighter; Mitsubishi, 1940), and Shiden-modified (Kawanishi, 1944) and the army's Model 97 (Nakajima, 1937), Hayabusa (Nakajima, 1941), and Hayate (Nakajima, 1944). Long-distance high-speed reconnaissance planes, called command reconnaissance airplanes by the army, were a type unique to Japan. Japan did not build any large strategic bombers.

With defeat in 1945, Japan was completely prohibited from the production and use of airplanes, and all facilities for aviation research and production were either dismantled or converted to other purposes. This proscription lasted until April 1952, when Japanese aviation activities were resumed with the conclusion of the San Francisco Peace Treaty. In the seven years of Japanese aviation industry inactivity, the world switched from propeller to jet planes and aircraft construction changed greatly in all areas, including performance, structure, and equipment. The Japanese aircraft industry rapidly absorbed the new technology, however, and in January 1956 a Lockheed T-33A jet trainer, manufactured by Kawasaki Aircraft Co under license, made the first flight of a postwar Japanese-made jet plane. The first purely domestic airplane was the T1 jet trainer developed and built by Fuji Heavy Industries, Ltd for the Self Defense Forces; the prototype made its first flight in January 1958. In the area of civil aviation, the YS11, a twin-engined turbojet type was developed by Nihon Kokuki Seizo Co and made its debut in 1962.

Until 1977 nearly 90 percent of the postwar gross sales of the Japanese aircraft industry was accounted for by the demand for national defense, a strikingly high dependence on military demand in comparison with other countries. This imbalance has been redressed to some extent by the civil demand for the Boeing 767, which Fuji Heavy Industries, Kawasaki Heavy Industries, and Mitsubishi Heavy Industries began building in 1978 in the joint-development YX project with Boeing Aircraft. The 767 entered service in 1982, and production is continuing.

Mass Communications

Mass communications

(*masukomi*).

Historical Development

The Edo period (1600—1868) left Japan with a superb social base for modern mass communications in its geographically compact, culturally homogeneous, politically centralized, education-oriented, and increasingly urbanized population. The spread of democratic institutions, university education, and urban lifestyle in the 20th century created enormous markets for newspapers, magazines, and books and for the electronic media.

Structures and Functions

In organization, scale, and allocation of functions, the Japanese mass media have developed uniquely out of the indigenous economic and social structure and philosophical bent. Both newspapers and book publishing display the same intensive oligopolistic competition among gigantic, tightly knit enterprise groups that is characteristic of modern Japanese business as a whole.

Competitive pressures in a basically unitary national newspaper market have led to a striking uniformity of format, content, editorial viewpoint, and reportorial style for each prefectural paper and three regional "bloc" papers as well as the five national dailies (the *Yomiuri shimbun, Asahi shimbun, Mainichi shimbun, Sankei shimbun,* and *Nihon keizai shimbun*). With a total daily publication of 52 million, Japan ranked first in the world in per capita circulation of newspapers in 1991.

As for radio broadcasting, in 1926 the Japan Broadcasting Corporation (NHK) was granted a broadcasting monopoly under the firm control of the Ministry of Communications. In 1950 the new Broadcasting Law made provision for a commercial sector and reorganized NHK as a strictly public service organization. Since television broadcasting started in 1953, there has been much competition between the public and private sectors of Japan's dual system. NHK is the most popular news source and provides lavish cultural and informational programming on both its general and educational channels. The five commercial chains are Nippon Television Network Corporation (NTV); Tokyo Broadcasting System, Inc (TBS); Television Tokyo Channel 12, Ltd; Fuji Telecasting Co, Ltd; and Asahi National Broadcasting Co, Ltd. These five have been strengthened by tie-ups with the five national newspapers.

The functions of wire services, weekly magazines, and monthly journals in Japan have all been affected by the character of the newspapers. With the national dailies relying mainly on their own domestic and foreign news bureaus, Japan's two news agencies, Kyodo News Service and Jiji Press, play a supplementary role except for the local press.

Journalists and Their Audience

The journalists in Japan's major media firms enjoy high professional status, and they are joined by a broad public forum (*rondan*) of intellectual critics (*hyoronka*) who fuel debate through daily columns and television symposia. Japan's highly literate public, deferential toward intellectual authority and eager for information and guidance in the pursuit of personal and corporate uplift, sustains an extensive high-grade sector of "mass quality" newspapers and television programs. The surprising homogeneity, especially in news coverage, derives from the unique organization of news gathering in Japan. The typical reporter writes not so much independent stories as raw material for reprocessing at the departmental desk, and the correspondents themselves are organized into exclusive press clubs (*kisha kurabu*) attached to all major government institutions and public figures.

News, Opinion, and Politics

The Japanese press was under constant regulation and periodic suppression from the time of the Press Ordinance of 1875 through the militaristic regime of the 1930s, the war years, and then the censorship of the Allied Occupation authorities. Democratization during the Occupation nevertheless left the press in 1952 in a far more liberated state than it had ever before experienced. Today, Japanese journalism continues to enjoy great freedom from statutory restraint, but the press has often failed to attack government and business promptly and head-on over major evils such as graft or pollution. The collaborative ties between the press and its sources in the press clubs, among club members, and between media management and big business have all joined with general group psychology to produce a more comfortable relation between journalism and established power.

Education, Culture, and Society

Mass communications has contributed to political and social stability in postwar Japan. Television has virtually eliminated the urban-rural cultural gap, a divisive factor in the prewar period. The mass media and educational system together have greatly reduced the potential for class cleavage by spreading a uniform, middle-class culture throughout Japan. Recent social concerns have included information glut and "data pollution," technological threats to privacy and individual freedom, and the gradual loss of psychological space in a postindustrial society dominated by computers, telecommunications, and hyperproductive mass media. The Japanese have done a great deal to develop the concept of the "information society" (*johoka shakai*) both as a popular notion and as a new academic discipline.

In a continuing effort to reduce the depiction of sex and violence, standards of ethics, decency, and taste are monitored by the Newspaper Content Evaluation Center, the Japan Advertising Review Organization, several broadcasting program consultative committees for television, the Motion Picture Code Committee, and the National Mass Communications Ethics Council.

Recent Trends

The 1980s saw Japan enter the so-called New Media Age, a term that refers to the development of new information technology through the use of computer and telecommunications hardware. A major stimulus for this was the deregulation of the telecommunications industry in April 1985.

In the late 1980s major dailies computerized page production by inputting articles into computers and editing them on video display terminals. Telecommunications systems could then be used to forward these articles in the form of digital signals for print publication anywhere in the world. Japanese newspapers were thus able to bring out same-day editions by satellite in Europe and the United States. Newspaper companies developed new enterprises utilizing this information as videotex and data bases.

Broadcasting industry developments included satellite broadcasting, multiplex broadcasting, high-definition television, and digital broadcasting. As of April 1991, three satellite broadcast channels were being operated, two by NHK, and one by Japan Satellite Broadcasting, Inc (JSB). Cable television (CATV) has also been made available via satellite relay, and 77 stations were operating in 1990 with a further 26 planned. In the public sector, as of 1991 there were 109 television channels, 1 satellite channel, 47 AM channels, 35 FM channels, 1 commercial shortwave channel, and numerous cable television channels.

The publishing industry has shifted from metal type to computerized word processing and typesetting, and most editorial and production functions are also fully computerized. The use of new electronic hardware has enabled publishers to produce varieties of nonprint publications such as audiocassette books and videocassette "magazines." Up-to-date dictionaries have also been made available on compact disc.

Publishing

(*shuppan*).

Development of Modern Publishing

Newspapers, magazines, and books underwent a process of Westernization after the Meiji Restoration. Following the practice in Europe and the United States at that time, the Japanese press and newspapers formed their own unique sphere from the beginning. The rest of the printed media, such as books and magazines, formed a separate world of publishing. This division has exercised a great influence on the formation of the character of Japanese journalism.

Before World War II, freedom of the press was greatly restricted by the Publications Law, the Newspaper Law, the Peace Preservation Law, and other repressive laws and regulations. A large number of publishers, editors, scholars, and writers were punished and imprisoned under these laws. After World War II, however, article 21 of the 1947 constitution guarantees freedom of speech and the press, prohibits censorship, and abolishes all the laws and regulations that had controlled the press. In 1992 Japan published 42,257 new book titles. As of 1989 Japan ranked second in the world behind the United States in the consumption of printing and writing paper.

Until 1955 weeklies had been put out by newspaper companies, but beginning with *Shukan shincho* (1956), publishing companies began to issue their own weeklies. With government, scholarly, and corporate publications included, the total number of magazine titles in Japan is estimated to be over 10,000. Magazine sales for 1990 totaled ¥1.26 trillion (US $8.73 billion).

The Publishing Industry

As in the publishing industry throughout the world, the majority of Japanese publishers operate on a small scale. According to the 1990 edition of *The Almanac of Publishing*, the total number of publishers in Japan was 4,282, of which publishers with capital of less than ¥5 million (US $38,910)—or whose capital was not known—numbered 2,763 (64.5%) and those with 10 employees or fewer (or with unknown numbers) totaled 2,929 (68.4%). According to the same source, more than half of the new titles in Japan were published by 120 publishers. In other words, less than 3 percent of all publishers accounted for more than half of all publishing activities. This oligopolistic situation was even more clearly reflected in the respective share of sales.

Top-ranking publishers have been moving into nonprint media such as radio, television, and motion pictures, and newspaper and broadcasting companies have also been active in publishing activities.

The basic route of the distribution for publications in Japan is from publisher to agent to bookstore. The basis of the sales system is fixed-price sales and consignment sales, by which the majority of publications have been traded.

As of 1990 about 12,556 bookstores belonged to the Association of Booksellers; when nonmember stores are added, the total number exceeds 20,000. A distribution agent connects a bookstore with a publisher and handles the distribution and return of books. Books and magazines traded by this route are considered to account for 50 percent of the total; about 70 percent are handled by the two major agencies, Tokyo Shuppan Hambai (abbreviated Tohan) and Nippon Shuppan Hambai (abbreviated Nippan).

The buying and selling of published material by the so-called regular route has been characterized since the 1920s by strict observance of fixed retail prices and consignment sales. An antitrust law prohibits producers from compelling agents or retailers to sell at fixed prices. From its inception, however, this law exempted so-called cultural items and daily necessities and in 1953 extended exemptions to include published material as well. As a result, published materials in Japan have been sold according to price maintenance agreements. The Japanese Fair Trade Commission has begun reviewing the price maintenance system because of growing consumer pressure.

Postwar Reforms

In prewar Japanese publishing circles, a clear line was drawn between publications for intellectuals and those for the masses. Since the end of the war, however, the movement toward a mass society has been symbolized by television, as well as the numerous weekly magazines created by publishing companies, and the so-called masses are no longer distinguished from the intellectual elite in the prewar sense. After 1950 best-seller fiction was neither infraliterature nor subliterature but books of quality intended for the masses. Equality of the sexes, improvement of labor conditions, and an increase and leveling in income also stimulated the creation of a new class of readers.

What played the decisive role for the postwar publishing boom, however, was the spread of secondary-school and university education. Only 3 percent of all youths attended universities in 1940, while in 1975, 30 percent attended a university or junior college.

When the conditions for the development of the publishing business in Japan are reviewed, it may be concluded that favorable growth as a whole may be expected for some time to come. But it cannot be denied that the conditions that hitherto supported the publishing business may turn into brakes: the growth of the economy has slowed since the 1970s, the proportion of students wishing to go on to universities has peaked, and individual households have been hard pressed economically. Furthermore, the full-scale arrival of the television age and the revival of motion pictures are contributing to a departure from the written media. Yet there are also signs that these visual media are forcing written media forms to undergo a kind of transformation, including the popularization of "cassette books" since 1987 and the fact that one-third of all types of magazines in Japan are comics. This revolution within the publishing industry will in all probability continue for some time.

Freedom of the press

(*shuppan, hodo no jiyu*). Under the 1889 Meiji Constitution and other laws, the Japanese media were severely restricted before World War II. After the war, Japanese media came under the protection of article 21 of the 1947 constitution, which guarantees "[freedom of] assembly and association as well as speech, press and all other forms of expression" and prohibits censorship. However, the act of soliciting the disclosure of secrets from public officials is prohibited by the Public Employee Law. Regulations also exist to control violations of reputation and privacy, and others prohibit the use of obscene expressions. In addition to these general restrictions, the Broadcasting Law of 1950 regulates broadcasting on such matters as the principle of political impartiality.

Newspapers

(*shimbun*). In the vanguard are several colossal national newspaper organizations that publish either morning or evening editions of their newspapers or both morning and evening editions. In addition to these major national media companies, there is a host of local and special-interest newspapers that also help cater to the diverse interests of the world's most literate readership.

History

The first modern newspaper was the *Nagasaki Shipping List and Advertiser*, an English paper, published twice a week beginning in 1861 by the Englishman A. W. Hansard in Nagasaki. In 1862 the Tokugawa shogunate (1603—1867) began publishing the *Kampan Batabiya shimbun*, a translated and re-edited edition of *Javasche Courant*, the organ of the Dutch government in Indonesia. These two papers contained only foreign news. Newspapers covering domestic news were first started by the Japanese in Edo (now Tokyo), Osaka, Kyoto, and Nagasaki in 1868. Yanagawa Shunsan's *Chugai shimbun*, a model for later papers, carried domestic news as well as abridged translations from foreign papers. The first Japanese daily paper, the *Yokohama mainichi shimbun*, was launched in 1871. The *Tokyo nichinichi shimbun* (predecessor of the *Mainichi shimbun*), the *Yubin hochi shimbun* (predecessor of the *Hochi shimbun*), and the oldest existing local newspaper, the *Kochu shimbun* (predecessor of the *Yamanashi nichinichi shimbun*), were all begun in 1872.

Most papers published at this time were referred to as "political forums" because they demanded the establishment of a national Diet and printed political opinions at the time of the Freedom and People's Rights Movement (Jiyu Minken Undo). However, after the establishment of the Diet, the newspapers virtually became organs of the newly formed political parties. These newspapers were called *oshimbun* (large newspapers). *Koshimbun* (small newspapers) were popular newspapers containing local news, human interest stories, and light fiction. The *Yomiuri shimbun*, which began publishing in 1874, is a typical example. Partially because strong government pressure caused the *oshimbun* to fail, new newspapers printing impartial news started springing up around 1880. The *Asahi shimbun* was launched in 1879 in Osaka, and the *Jiji shimpo* in 1882 in Tokyo. The sudden increase in circulation made possible in the 1890s by the widespread use of rotary presses and the growth of advertising turned Japanese newspapers into large business enterprises.

When the Tokyo Earthquake of 1923 destroyed much of Tokyo, the Osaka-based *Asahi* and *Mainichi* became the two largest national newspapers overnight, virtually dominating the Japanese newspaper industry. The opinion-shaping activity of Japanese newspapers gradually declined as the papers became interested in profits and had to respond to a broader readership. The heavy pressures from the government and the military authorities also weakened the papers' capacity for strong editorial policy.

The press was placed under complete government control from the outbreak of the Sino-Japanese War in 1937 until the end of World War II in 1945. Newsprint was rationed, and many newspapers were forced to merge. The number of newspapers dropped from 848 in 1939 to 54 in 1942.

Free competition among newspapers revived after the abolition of wartime regulations and the lifting of controls on newsprint in 1951. The system of morning and evening editions of the same paper, which had been suspended, also revived, and major papers started printing local editions. When weekly magazines, comic magazines, and television became popular, most general newspapers began to concentrate on news and advertising. As in other countries, progress in broadcast media such as radio and television deprived the newspapers of their edge in prompt reporting, which forced the press to turn to in-depth articles and news commentary. In the late 1970s and 1980s Japanese newspapers greatly increased the efficiency of their operations by full computerization of all aspects of their work—reporting, editing, typesetting, and printing—and by utilizing satellite communications.

Circulation

According to statistics of the Japan Newspaper Publishers and Editors Association, the total circulation of daily papers as of 1991 was 52,026,372, or an average of 1.24 newspapers per household. General papers accounted for 88.5 percent and sports papers for 11.5 percent.

The five major daily general papers in order of their circulation are: *Yomiuri shimbun*, *Asahi shimbun*, *Mainichi shimbun*, *Nihon keizai shimbun*, and *Sankei shimbun*. Maintaining their own nationwide home-delivery networks, they account for 52.6 percent of the entire circulation of daily general papers. The two leading newspapers, the *Yomiuri* and the *Asahi*, had circulations of 9,764,551 and 8,255,902, respectively, in 1991 (morning editions). Their readers are concentrated in the Tokyo and Osaka metropolitan areas, where publishing offices are located. Many prefectural papers enjoy more than 50 percent of the newspaper circulation in their areas.

Monopoly Dealership

The *Tokyo nichinichi shimbun* initiated a home delivery system that was soon followed by other papers. The *Hochi shimbun* started exclusive dealerships in 1903 to distribute only its own papers nationwide. The dealers not only were responsible for delivery but also acted as subscription salesmen. News of the increase in circulation for the *Hochi* prompted other papers to set up their own news dealerships, and the system of monopoly newspaper dealerships peculiar to Japan was created in 1930.

Journalists

Would-be journalists in Japan are selected from among new university graduates through examinations conducted by the individual newspaper companies. The examinations are notoriously difficult, and hundreds of applicants may compete for a single job. Once accepted, however, they can look forward to lifetime employment. Japanese companies more often than not shift the journalists to administrative positions by the time they become senior reporters. Press clubs are a significant characteristic of Japanese journalism. They function both as social clubs for journalists and as locations for important press interviews and political announcements. It is widely recognized that there exists the danger of such clubs' becoming too closely associated with the government and other public bodies to which nonmembers have difficulty gaining access.

Broadcasting

(*hoso*). Broadcasting is defined in Japan's Broadcasting Law (Hoso Ho, 1950) and Radio Law (Dempa Ho, 1950) as "wireless communication intended for direct reception by the general public."

History of Broadcasting in Japan

On 20 August 1926 the Communications Ministry (Teishinsho; now the Ministry of Posts and Telecommunications) established the Nippon Hoso Kyokai (NHK; Japan Broadcasting Corporation). NHK monopolized the country's broadcasting industry until after World War II, but NHK was placed under the strict supervision of the Communications Ministry.

After World War II all legislation suppressing freedom of speech and the press was abolished in an effort to further Japan's democratization. When the Broadcasting Law came into effect in June 1950, NHK was reorganized, and a new corporation was formed. This law also paved the way for private commercial broadcast stations. In April 1950 preliminary licenses were issued to a total of 16 private broadcast stations in 14 districts of the country. Despite early pessimism about their commercial viability, these ventures soon showed large profits. The way was opened for television broadcasting with the granting of a preliminary license to Nippon Television Network Corporation (NTV) on 31 July 1952. The first actual telecast in Japan was made by NHK's Tokyo station on 1 February 1953.

Present-Day Broadcasting in Japan

Japan's broadcasting system consists of two types of broadcast enterprise: NHK, which is a government-sponsored venture, and the various commercial companies. As a special corporation, NHK is neither a state-operated enterprise nor a public corporation. However, unlike the private companies, NHK's activities are subject to restrictions by the government and the Diet. The Management Commission makes major decisions regarding NHK, including the content of programs, and is a governing organ with the authority to appoint the president and other high officials of NHK. The members of the Management Commission are appointed by the prime minister after obtaining the approval of the Diet.

Programming   The Broadcasting Law stipulates the types of programs to be broadcast domestically. NHK is required to (1) broadcast high-quality programs that will both satisfy the demands of the public and elevate the country's cultural level, (2) broadcast local as well as national programs, and (3) contribute to the preservation of traditional culture and foster and publicize modern cultural events. Programs shown by both NHK and private commercial broadcasting firms are required by the Broadcasting Law to (1) guard against disturbing public peace and order and damaging morals, (2) maintain political impartiality, (3) include truthful news broadcasts, and (4) present all sides of complex issues and maintain a balance among educational, cultural, news, and entertainment programs.

Networks   NHK operates a nationwide broadcasting network. Private broadcasting stations licensed in their respective local regions also have their own networks. As of 1992, commercial television broadcasting consisted of five networks centered on the following key stations: Tokyo Broadcasting System, Inc (TBS) (28 stations), Nippon Television Network Corporation (30 stations), Fuji Telecasting Co, Ltd (27 stations), Asahi National Broadcasting Co, Ltd (22 stations), and Television Tokyo Channel 12, Ltd (5 stations). At the center of each of these networks is a news network. General programming other than news is also distributed through these networks. In 1992 there were 115 commercial television stations, 47 commercial AM radio stations, 39 FM stations, and 1 shortwave station.

There are two major commercial radio broadcasting networks: the Japan Radio Network and the Nippon Radio Network, both established in 1965. Commercial FM broadcasting is dominated by the Japan FM Broadcasting Association, which operates a nationwide network with FM Tokyo as its key station.

Financing   The ordinary operating revenues of NHK are obtained from viewer fees, government subsidies, and miscellaneous revenues from other sources, with some 98 percent of the entire revenue represented by viewer fees. The distribution of television sets, however, has almost reached the saturation point, so that it is difficult to foresee any large increase in revenue from future fees. (Radio fees were abolished in 1968.)

Private television broadcasting companies are showing large profits with the tremendous increase in revenue from television advertising. Advertisement expenditures paid to television firms exceeded those paid to newspapers in 1975, and television has been the top advertising medium ever since.

In 1993, 34.3 million households were paying reception fees to NHK. Television sets are owned by practically all Japanese families, and according to a recent survey television ownership now averages two sets per household.

New media   New broadcast technology made possible the introduction of multiplex sound broadcasting in 1978 for stereo and bilingual programming and also text multiplex broadcasting for captioned news and other programs. High-definition television (HDTV) and extended definition television (EDTV) technologies have been developed to improve picture quality. Videocassette recorder ownership expanded rapidly beginning in the mid-1980s, reaching a total of 66.8 percent of the population by 1990. In 1984 NHK began direct satellite broadcasting, and in 1989 the launch of a communications satellite made possible the establishment of a commercial network combining satellite and cable transmission. Cable television has also begun to make significant inroads into urban areas. Japanese television programs are also broadcast directly to the United States and other countries via satellite.

Television

(*terebi hoso*). Including public, commercial, and satellite stations, 111 television stations were broadcasting throughout Japan in 1990. More than 99 percent of Japanese households have one television set, and many have two or more sets. The average length of time Japanese spend watching television is three hours a day.

Television broadcasting was begun in Japan in 1953 by Nippon Hoso Kyokai (NHK), the national public broadcasting system. Black-and-white televisions spread rapidly at the time of the 1959 wedding of the present emperor and empress. Color televisions sold similarly well at the time of the Tokyo Olympics in 1964 and replaced black-and-white sets by the mid-1970s.

In the early days of television in Japan, the television set was a focal point of family gatherings. However, with the diversification of lifestyles and the number of sets per household increasing to two or more, television viewing has increasingly become an individual activity. In response, programs have increasingly been tailored to the interests and tastes of specific viewer age groups.

Especially in the 1980s, the number of after-midnight viewers sharply increased. In 1987 NHK commenced 24-hour satellite broadcasting, which was soon followed by all-night programming on commercial television stations. After midnight, information-oriented programs for young people, movies, and all-night debate shows are broadcast. Around 1985 prime-time programming, which had until then been devoted to entertainment programs, began to feature long news programs and documentaries, with considerable success. Television has also become a major advertising medium, accounting for ¥1.65 trillion (US $13.0 billion), or about 30 percent of total advertising expenses in 1992.

NHK broadcasts throughout Japan and private stations broadcast on a local basis. Private stations in different parts of the country, however, generally belong to one of the nationwide networks centered on key stations headquartered in Tokyo, so programs seen in Tokyo can be seen elsewhere. The number of original programs produced by local stations is very small, but creating locally centered programming has become increasingly important for local stations.

In the second half of the 1980s, television reached an important turning point: videocassette recorders came into wide use in homes, direct satellite broadcasting began, and cable television broadcasting services using communication satellites have created a multichannel television age. The development of high-definition television (HDTV) is expected to greatly increase the pleasures and potentials of television broadcasting.

Broadcasting, commercial

(*minkan hoso*). Japanese commercial broadcasting, as distinguished from public broadcasting, dates from 1 September 1951, when the first privately owned radio stations went on the air in Nagoya and Osaka; commercial television followed on 28 August 1953. Beginning about 1960 radio fell on difficult times because of the rise in popularity of television. To win back their audience, radio stations changed their format, incorporating live programs that ran for several hours, celebrity shows, late-night broadcasts, and traffic reports, and began making a comeback in the late 1960s. Commercial FM broadcasts began in 1969.

It is not until around 1957 that commercial television broadcasting spreads throughout Japan. Coverage of spectacular events such as the Crown Prince's wedding in 1959 and the Tokyo Olympic Games in 1964 served to increase the number of television owners. Technological developments such as color programming and satellite-relay broadcasts paved the way for further growth of the television industry.

In 1990 there were 83 radio stations (47 AM, 35 FM, 1 shortwave) and 109 television stations (48 VHF and 61 UHF) licensed for commercial broadcasting. Advertising revenue for 1992 amounted to ¥235.0 billion (US $1.8 billion) for radio and ¥1.65 trillion (US $13.0 billion) for television. There were some 28,000 people employed in commercial broadcasting. NHK, by comparison, had 15,000 employees.

Commercial radio and television networks operate as cooperatives under the leadership of certain key stations. Among AM radio networks are the Japan Radio Network (JRN), led by Tokyo Broadcasting System, Inc (TBS), and the National Radio Network (NRN), with

Nippon Cultural Broadcasting, Inc, and Nippon Broadcasting System, Inc, as key stations. Television networks include the Japan News Network (JNN), again led by TBS; the Nippon News Network (NNN), led by Nippon Television; the All Nippon News Network, led by Asahi National Broadcasting Co, Ltd; and the Fuji News Network (FNN), led by Fuji Telecasting Co, Ltd.

The prime viewing hours between 7:00 and 10:00 PM, when advertising is most effective, are referred to as the "golden hours," and during these hours there is fierce competition among stations for viewers. In 1978 Japan led the world in developing multiplex television sound broadcasts, which made possible stereo and bilingual broadcasts.

CULTURE

Floats are the highlight
of the Gion Festival
which is sponsored every
July by the Yasaka Shrine
in Kyoto.

Religion

(*shukyo*). Religious life in Japan is rich and varied, with a long history of interaction among a number of religious traditions. Most of the individual features of Japanese religion are not unique; the distinctiveness of Japanese religion lies in the total pattern of interacting traditions.

Many traditional Japanese beliefs and practices hark back to prehistoric customs, and most of these form the core of Shinto, the only major religion indigenous to Japan. Indian Buddhism, the Chinese contributions of Confucianism and Taoism (transmitted first through the cultural bridge of Korea), and, much later, Christianity were introduced to Japan from outside. All these foreign traditions have undergone significant transformations in a process of mutual influence with the native tradition.

The Historical Formation of Japanese Religion

In Judaism and Christianity religion entails faith in one supreme deity; revelation of the will of this deity in a sacred book; concern with sin as disobedience to the deity; relation of man to divinity through a conscious decision or act of faith; specific ecclesiastical organizations, involving regular attendance and worship; and ethical behavior linked directly to this religious commitment.

Japanese religion differs significantly on each of the aforementioned points: there are not one but many deïties; there is no one sacred book, but many religious scriptures; rather than emphasis on sin as disobedience to the deity there is a concern with ritual impurity and purification; one person usually participates in more than one religious tradition; there is no regular worship day comparable to the Sabbath but many seasonal festivals; and ethical codes are more closely related to family life and philosophy than to organized religion, while ethical shortcomings are not linked directly to divine will but are considered in terms of human imperfection.

In early Japan religious life was closely related to rice agriculture. Religious rites focused on seasonal celebrations anticipating and giving thanks for agricultural fertility and on venerating ancestral spirits who were considered directly responsible for fertility. From about 500 BC to AD 500, southwest Japan was developing into a centralized kingdom headed by an imperial family. From about AD 500, the high culture of China— including written language—entered Japan and immediately became a major influence upon the elite class and eventually upon the common people. The tendency in Japanese history has not been "either-

or" exclusivity, but rather "both-and" inclusivity, in adopting foreign cultural elements. Therefore, instead of rejecting Buddhism, the Japanese eventually incorporated it into the life of the family, making Buddhist memorial rites central to the veneration of family ancestors and directly linking Buddhist divinities to Shinto gods. Confucian notions were adopted to encourage loyalty to the emperor.

By the 8th century, local myths and traditions were largely unified around one account of creation and the descent of the emperor from the gods as seen in the *Kojiki* (712, Record of Ancient Matters) and *Nihon shoki* (720, Chronicle of Japan), the two earliest Japanese historical chronicles. Partly in reaction to the highly organized Buddhist religion, Japanese rituals and practice came to be organized as Shinto, "the Way of the gods." From this time on, Buddhism and Shinto were the major organized religions and gradually penetrated more into the lives of ordinary people. Many Shinto shrines that originated as family institutions developed into territorial shrines and eventually expanded to include branch shrines in other locales. Buddhist temples for the common people also gradually arose to fulfill the need for funerary and memorial services. From about 800 to 1400, various Buddhist sects and Shinto schools developed. In the Edo period (1600−1868) Buddhist temples became closely allied with the power of the state, and families were required to belong to a specific temple; at about the same time, Confucian thought became important for providing the rationale for the state. With the Meiji Restoration of 1868, however, Shinto became prominent in justifying and maintaining the new nation-state under its emperor and was influential even in education.

The Major Features of Traditional Japanese Religion

The seven major features that characterized Japanese religion until about 1900 overlapped and interlocked to form the general pattern of what is now considered traditional Japanese religion. These features can be identified briefly as follows:

Mutual interaction among several religious traditions Typical of religious history in Japan is both a plurality of religious traditions and simultaneous or alternate participation by one person (or family). In recent times a person might be married in a Shinto shrine, live his life according to Confucian social teachings, hold some Taoistic beliefs about "lucky" and "unlucky" phenomena, participate in folk festivals, and have his funeral conducted by a Buddhist temple.

Intimate relationship between man and the gods and the sacredness of nature In Japan the relationship between man and the sacred (*kami*) is very close. In addition to the specific deities represented in mythology, natural phenomena and emperors and other special human beings were also considered to be sacred or kami. The spirits of the dead of each family, as revered ancestors, were termed either *hotoke* (Buddhas) or kami. In Japanese religion kami and Buddhas are not conceived as being in another world so much as they are thought to exist within the world of nature and in the lives of human beings.

The religious significance of the family and ancestor The ancient Japanese emphasis on lineage or family carried with it devotion to clan kami (*ujigami*), and Confucianism, with its insistence on filial piety and social harmony, provided a philosophical rationale for strong family ties. The home was always a center of religious practice, and this became more formalized during the Edo period, when it became customary for most homes to possess both Shinto family altars (*kamidana*) and Buddhist altars (*butsudan*) for venerating ancestors. Traditional Japanese religious life was conducted by family participation rather than by individual choice.

Purification as a basic principle of religious life Notions of purity and impurity (*kegare*) and procedures of ritual purification (*harae; misogi*) in Japan have assumed an extraordinary importance and have pervaded the culture as a whole. The Japanese people have not conceptualized sin (*tsumi*) as a violation of divine commandments, but they have had a clear sense of the impurity or defilement that separates one from one's fellowmen and especially from the kami. The traditional observance at a Shinto shrine is to rinse the hands and mouth ceremonially as a symbolic act of purification before coming into contact with the kami. In Japan no one tradition dominates ethical concerns; rather each tradition contributes its concepts of ideal behavior: for Shinto, ritual purity and sincerity; for Buddhism, compassion and liberation from desire; for Confucianism, loyalty to superiors and benevolence toward inferiors.

Festivals as the major means of religious celebration The pattern of religious activities was determined by each religious institution observing its own special festival days, in addition to annual festivals celebrated by families and the nation as a whole. Festivals at shrines and temples often celebrate the particular kami or Buddhist divinities enshrined there, but more often festivals are part of a seasonal drama reenacted every year. Shrines usually have both a spring festival and fall festival roughly coinciding with the transplanting and harvesting of rice. The time surrounding the New Year is a long festival period marked by large crowds visiting both Shinto shrines and Buddhist temples. The summer Bon Festival in honor of the returning spirits of the dead is observed in most Japanese homes.

Religion in daily life In traditional Japan, religion was not an organization apart from everyday life but closely related to every aspect of economic and social life. Rituals followed a person throughout life, from birth to marriage and death. Aesthetic pursuits such as the tea ceremony and flower arranging also embodied religious notions concerning veneration of the forces of nature.

Close relationship between religion and state In Japan the general rule has been for religious authority to be subservient to political power. From the beginnings of Japanese history, myth has sanctioned the unity of ritual and government (*saisei itchi*) through the notion that the kami created the Japanese islands as a sacred land to be ruled by a sacred emperor who was a descendant of the supreme kami, the sun goddess Amaterasu Omikami. Cultural influence from China, especially Confucianism and Buddhism, strengthened and modified this basic pattern.

Religion in Modern Japan

Religion has undergone gradual and significant change throughout Japanese history. After the remarkable changes in national life of the late 19th and early 20th centuries, religion changed even more drastically.

During the Edo period, both Shinto and especially Buddhism became more highly formalized, and the still vital folk traditions tended to attract more of the attention and enthusiastic participation of the people. In the 19th century, popular movements formed around pilgrimage associations (*ko*) and charismatic leaders. Such groups often expanded to form the so-called new religions (*shinko shukyo*). Until 1945 the government controlled religion closely, but new religious movements continued to arise and expand, and after 1945 they became the most conspicuous development of the religious scene. With urbanization and centralization, folk customs generally and folk religion in particular declined. Social mobility, especially immigration to cities, tended to weaken both local ties and family relationships, in turn impinging upon organized religion.

Buddhism

(J: Bukkyo). According to tradition, the founder of Buddhism, Gautama Siddhārtha, was born about 446 BC as the first son of King Śuddhodana of the Śākya clan at the castle Kapilavastu, located in the center of the clan's domain in what is now Nepal. Some scholars, however, place the birthdate as much as a century earlier. Although raised in luxury, at age 29 he left home to seek an answer, through renunciation, to the problem of human existence. After completing six years of asceticism, he experienced enlightenment at Buddhagayā beneath the bo tree, becom-

Culture

ing the Buddha ("one who has awakened to the truth"). Thereafter, until his death at Kuśinagara at the age of 80, he traveled throughout central India sharing his wisdom. He became known by the honorary name Śākyamuni (the sage or holy one from the Śākya [J: Shaka] clan).

Early Buddhism

In the central Ganges River Basin and eastern India at the time Gautama lived, affluence had led to a decay in the traditional caste system, less reliance on the priestly Brahmin class and the authority of the Vedas, and a decline in public morality. Philosophers became involved in endless metaphysical discussions of problems that had no solutions, but Gautama asserted that such metaphysical questions were meaningless. Buddhism attempted to point to and teach dharma, the "true eternal law" or "perennial norm" that would be valid for humanity for all ages. Buddhist doctrine is not specific, established dogma, but a practical wisdom or ethic that promises us the ideal state of humanity.

In Gautama's view, life is suffering (Skt: *duḥkha*), in the face of which man is helpless. We experience suffering because everything is the result of ever-changing, interrelated conditions and causes; human existence is always in flux and in transience (Skt: *anitya*; J: *mujo*). Therefore, it is impossible to claim anything as belonging to oneself, or to assert that there is a self (Skt: *ātman*). By denying the existence of *ātman*, Buddhists also rejected the dichotomy between the subjective and objective worlds. Our perplexing and painful existence stems from various causes, and if those causes are extinguished, the confusion and suffering will also dissolve. In Japanese this chain of causality is called *engi* (dependent origination; Skt: *pratītyasamutpāda*).

A five-storied pagoda at Horyuji temple in Nara Prefecture.

Those who wish to be free from suffering must come to a clear understanding (enlightenment) concerning suffering, impermanence, nonself (Skt: *anātman*), and reality. To attain true knowledge (Skt: *prajñā*), all lust and attachment—the root of illusion—must be extinguished. In order to achieve this, one must undergo spiritual discipline, abide by the precepts, and practice meditation. Only then will one be able to free oneself from myriad restrictions and attain that freedom called *nirvāṇa* (J: *nehan*). The two extremes of hedonism and self-mortification are rejected; the Middle Way of no suffering and no pleasure is to be taken. Buddhism also emphasized compassion, teaching that it should be extended to all sentient beings.

Upon attaining enlightenment, the Buddha gathered around him a group of disciples; this community adopted the organizational principles of the saṃgha, which generally referred to a confederate form of government or a guild. The religious saṃgha was composed of both mendicant monks and lay believers, male and female. The mendicants were expected to be celibate and to refrain from secular occupations and economic transactions.

Later, rules for the religious life were stipulated: 250 precepts for males (*bhikṣu*; J: *biku*) and 500 for females (*bhikṣuṇī*; J: *bikuni*). Lay believers were instructed to maintain a good household, engage in proper work, strive to help others, and secure honor and fortune through diligent effort so that, upon death, they would be reborn in heaven. Five precepts were particularly emphasized: (1) do not kill; (2) do not steal; (3) do not act immorally; (4) do not lie; (5) do not drink liquor. Sorcery, magic, and divination were strictly forbidden, and believers were told to reject the authority of the Vedas and to eschew ceremonies involving sacrifice. While monks and nuns sought the ultimate goal of *nirvāṇa*, the laity aimed at a better rebirth.

Spread of Buddhism

In the 3rd century BC, under King Aśoka, India was united as one country. Aśoka supported the Buddhists, and Buddhism spread throughout the country. Around that time Buddhists split into two groups: the conservative elders (Theravādin), whose purpose was to maintain traditional rules; and others, who called for various changes within the religious order. By the 1st century BC there were as many as 20 factions. These groups tended to be self-righteous and aloof from the needs of the common people and in time came to be called the "lesser vehicle" (Hīnayāna; J: *Shojo*) by their opponents.

Mahāyāna ("greater vehicle"; J: Daijo) Buddhism developed among the common people. Mahāyānists believed in a series of Buddhas (apart from the historical Buddha)—Buddhas from the cosmic past and also Buddhas-to-be, or bodhisattvas (J: *bosatsu*)—who had deferred their own salvation until the salvation of all mankind. Mahāyāna stressed that the path of the bodhisattva was open to both monks and laity.

Several Mahāyāna texts were compiled. First to appear were the *Prajñāpāramitā* sutras (J: *Hannyakyo*), which taught that all things are empty (Skt: *śūnya*; J: *ku*). These were followed by the *Vimalakīrti-nirdeśa-sūtra* (J: *Yuimakyo*) and the *Śrīmālādevī-siṃhanāda-sūtra* (J: *Shomankyo*), which propagated lay Buddhism; the *Avataṃsaka-sūtra* (J: *Kegonkyo*), which taught the altruistic way of the bodhisattva and idealism; the Pure Land sutras, which advocated belief in the Buddha Amitābha (J: *Amida*); and the Lotus Sutra (*Saddharma-puṇḍarīka-sūtra*; J: *Hokkekyo* or *Hokekyo*). The latter taught that various Buddhist practices would lead practitioners to perfection and that ultimately there is one eternal Buddha.

Two major philosophical schools also arose in the Mahāyāna

branch during this period. The Mādhyamika school (J: Chuganha), founded by Nāgārjuna (J: Ryuju; ca 150-ca 250), emphasized śūnyatā (emptiness). The second school, Yogācāra (J: Yugagyoha), brought to doctrinal completion by Vasubandhu (J: Seshin; 4th century), taught that the basis of our existence is a spiritual principle, *ālayavijñāna*, from which all things become manifest.

In 320 the Gupta dynasty was established. Buddhists developed the esoteric teachings of tantrism, known as Vajrayāna or Mantrayāna (J: *Mikkyo*), which incorporated elements of Brahmanism and folk religion. Esoteric Buddhism, however, tended to be absorbed by Hinduism. At the beginning of the 12th century, when India was conquered by Muslims, many Buddhist monasteries were destroyed, and Buddhism all but disappeared from India.

The Diffusion of Buddhism in Asia

King Aśoka had sent out numerous Buddhist missionaries. A branch of Theravādin Buddhism was transferred to Ceylon (now Sri Lanka) and then to Burma, Thailand, Cambodia, and other Southeast Asian lands. The Buddhist tradition in these areas is generally called "Southern Buddhism."

In the Kashmir and Gandhara regions in northwest India, the Theravādin lineage, especially the Sarvāstivādin teachings (J: Setsu Issai Ubu), was popular. Later, Mahāyāna Buddhism became prevalent and from here spread throughout the western region. In Nepal as well, Mahāyāna Buddhism, especially the esoteric branch, was disseminated.

From the 8th century, Mahāyāna Buddhism, predominantly esoteric Buddhism, was transmitted to Tibet and, upon fusion with indigenous folk beliefs, developed into what is popularly known as Lamaism. In Lamaism, or Tibetan Buddhism, some lamas ("superior ones") were worshiped as incarnations (*tulkus*) of their predecessors. Lamaism eventually spread even throughout Mongolia and the Rehe (Jehol) region of northeastern China.

Buddhism was introduced to China in the 1st and 2nd centuries. Buddhist literature was subsequently translated into Chinese from Sanskrit (or its vernacular) originals. The Buddhism that came to flourish in China was chiefly Mahāyāna and reflected the influence of Taoism and Confucianism. Among the more important Chinese schools are the Pure Land (Ch: Jingtu; J: Jodo), Chan (J: Zen), Tiantai (J: Tendai), and Zhenyan (J: Shingon), all of which were transmitted to Japan.

Buddhism in Japan

According to one of Japan's earliest chronicles, the *Nihon shoki* (720, Chronicle of Japan), Buddhism was officially introduced into Japan from Korea in 552, when the king of Paekche sent a mission to the emperor of Japan bearing presents including "an image of Śākyamuni in gold and copper" and "a number of sutras." However, current scholarship favors another traditional date for this event, 538.

The Soga family argued that Japan should accept Buddhism. Others, particularly the Mononobe family and the Nakatomi family, claimed that the native gods would be offended by the respect shown to a foreign deity. Buddhism was publicly accepted after the Soga family's political and military defeat of the Mononobe and became prominent in the 7th-century reign of the empress Suiko (r 593 — 628). Her regent, the devout Prince Shotoku, is considered the real founder and first great patron of Buddhism in Japan. He established a number of important monasteries, among them Horyuji and Shitennoji.

Studies of Buddhist teachings began in earnest as six prominent schools were introduced from China during the 7th and the early 8th centuries. These were the Ritsu Sect, the Kusha School, the Jojitsu School, the Sanron School, the Hosso Sect, and the Kegon Sect. In the Nara period (710 — 794), especially under the aegis of Emperor Shomu (r 724 — 749), Buddhism was promoted as the state religion. Official provincial monasteries (*kokubunji*) were established in each province. At Todaiji, the head monastery, an enormous image of the Buddha was erected.

Early in the Heian period (794 — 1185), the Tendai sect and Shingon sect were introduced to Japan. They received support principally from the ruling aristocratic class. At the beginning of the Kamakura period (1185 — 1333), Zen Buddhism was introduced from China and was especially favored by the dominant military class. The popular sects of Nichiren and Pure Land Buddhism emerged around the same time.

Under the Tokugawa shogunate (1603 — 1867), Buddhism and its network of temples were used to eradicate Christianity, but Buddhism also came under the strict regulatory power of the shogunate. While sectarian divisions that had been established in previous times continued, there were also modernizing tendencies, such as Suzuki Shosan's (1579 — 1655) occupational ethics and the popularization of Zen by Shido Bunan (1603 — 1676), Bankei Yotaku (1622 — 1693), and Hakuin (1685 — 1769). Another sign was the movement to return to the true meaning of Buddhism as revealed in the original Sanskrit texts, led by Fujaku (1707 — 1781), Kaijo (1750 — 1805), and Jiun Onko (1718 — 1804). After the Meiji Restoration (1868), the government sought to establish Shinto as the national religion, and many Buddhist temples were disestablished. Since then, Buddhist organizations have survived by adjusting to the developments of the modern age.

After World War II, many religious groups among the so-called *shinko shukyo* (new religions) were organized as lay Buddhist movements. Several of the largest of these groups (Soka Gakkai, Rissho Koseikai, Reiyukai, Myochikai, etc) draw upon Nichiren's teachings and the Lotus Sutra.

Several characteristic tendencies can be seen in the history of Japanese Buddhism: (1)an emphasis on the importance of human institutions; (2)a nonrational, symbolic orientation; (3)an acceptance of the phenomenal world; (4)an openness to accommodation with ancient shamanistic practices and Shinto; and (5)the development of lay leadership.

Statistically, Japan is a country of Buddhists. More than 85 percent of the population professes the Buddhist faith. Buddhism in Japan maintains some 75,000 temples with nearly 200,000 priests.

Christianity

(Kirisutokyo). Christianity was introduced into Japan in the middle of the 16th century. The religion was generally tolerated until the beginning of the 17th century, but the Tokugawa shogunate (1603−1867) eventually proscribed it and persecuted its adherents. When relations with the West were restored in the middle of the 19th century, Christianity was reintroduced and has continued to exist in Japan with varying fortunes.

Martyrdoms

In 1596 the Spanish ship *San Felipe* foundered off Shikoku and the Japanese confiscated its rich cargo. A controversy among Japanese, Jesuits, and friars resulted; Toyotomi Hideyoshi (1537−1598)once more turned anti-Christian and condemned to death the Franciscans and their parishioners in Kyoto. Twenty-six Christians—both foreigners and Japanese—were crucified at Nagasaki in 1597. No further hostile action was taken, and missionary work continued unobtrusively. By this time the Church had reached its greatest expansion, with the number of Christians being estimated at about 300,000. Tokugawa Ieyasu (1543−1616), who became the de facto ruler in 1600, was at first willing to tolerate the missionaries' presence for the sake of the profitable Portuguese trade, but the arrival of Protestant Dutch and English merchants allowed him to act more freely against the Catholic missionaries. As the final showdown between Ieyasu and Toyotomi Hideyori, son of the late Hideyoshi, approached, Ieyasu turned against the Church, knowing that his rival commanded considerable support in western Japan, where Christian influence was strongest. Ieyasu was victorious, and in 1614 the Tokugawa shogunate ordered missionaries to leave the country; most of them departed, but some 40, including a few

Japanese priests, remained to continue their work under cover.

Persecution and Suppression

Within a few years organized persecution commenced. In 1622, 51 Christians were executed at Nagasaki, and two years later 50 were burned alive in Edo (now Tokyo). A total of 3,000 believers are estimated to have been martyred; this figure does not include the many who died as a result of sufferings in prison or in exile. In 1633 some 30 missionaries were executed, and by 1637 only 5 were left at liberty. The Shimabara Uprising of 1637−38 prompted the government to sever contacts with the West, except for some merchants of the Dutch East India Company, confined to Dejima. Subsequent missionary attempts to enter and work in the country were unsuccessful.

The Japanese are noted for their religious tolerance, and the persecution was occasioned by social and political rather than purely religious factors. Christian exclusivism, with its unwillingness to tolerate other religions, aroused resentment in some circles. Missionaries were regarded as a potential fifth column preparing the way for Iberian colonialism. More significantly, the shogunate was on the alert for any coalition of disaffected elements that might threaten its hegemony, and Christianity was viewed as a possible catalyst. Finally, Christian insistence on the primacy of the individual's conscience was regarded as subversive in a society that attached overwhelming importance to unconditional obedience to superiors.

Reintroduction

Japan's period of isolation ended in the mid-19th century, when Westerners were again allowed to enter the country. In 1859 a Catholic priest took up an appointment as interpreter for the French consulate in Edo, and in the same year representatives of three Protestant churches reached Japan. Ostensibly these ministers came to serve foreign residents, but their true aim was to begin direct work among the Japanese.

Social Activity

At the beginning of the 20th century Christians made a notable contribution to the foundation of the socialist and trade union movements in an effort to solve the grave social problems caused by rapid industrialization. Many of the founding members of the Social Democratic Party (Shakai Minshuto; 1901) were active Christians. A Christian, Suzuki Bunji, founded the Yuaikai or Friendship Association, in 1912; this later developed into the Nihon Rodo Sodomei, or Japan Federation of Labor. The Nihon Nomin Kumiai (Japan Farmers' Union) was founded in 1922 by two Christian socialists. Despite this contribution at the time of their foundation, many of these movements were later split by disputes and much of the initial Christian influence was weakened or lost.

War and Recovery

The growing spirit of nationalism in the 1930s raised problems of conscience for Christians, especially when the authorities urged attendance at Shinto shrines as "a civil manifestation of loyalty." Foreign missionaries of all churches were interned or repatriated at the outbreak of World War II or at best allowed limited freedom. In 1941 government pressure led to the formation of the Nihon Kirisuto Kyodan, or United Church of Christ in Japan, a union of some 30 Protestant churches. After the war some churches withdrew from the union, but it is still regarded as the most influential Protestant body today.

Christianity Today

At present Christianity in Japan is characterized by unobtrusive activity, with emphasis still placed on education as a means of spreading the gospel message. In recent years there has been a growing ecumenical spirit between the Protestant and Catholic churches, although contacts at the grass-roots level are often still tenuous. Discussions have been held between Christian and Buddhist scholars to reach a better mutual understanding and appreciation of the two religions. In 1990, Christians numbered some 1,075,000, or less than 1 percent of the population. There were 436,000 Catholics with some 800 parishes in 16 dioceses, while Protestants numbered 639,000 with nearly 7,000 churches.

Conclusion

In popular estimation Christianity is still regarded as a "foreign" creed, preaching admirable ideals but unsuitable for ordinary Japanese. Because of its "foreign" nature, the religion has been persecuted when demands for national identity were strong; it has been widely accepted during periods of social instability (the 16th century, the early Meiji period, and the immediate postwar period), but once social equilibrium was restored interest rapidly waned. Apart from the Nagasaki region, Christianity has yet to make any appreciable impact on rural communities; it draws its strength from the urban, professional classes.

Shinto

Japan's indigenous religion. The word Shinto is written with two Chinese characters; the first, *shin*, is also used to write the native Japanese word *kami* ("divinity" or "numinous entity"), and the second, *to*, is used to write the native word *michi* ("way"). The term first appears in the historical chronicle *Nihon shoki* (720, Chronicle of Japan), where it refers to religious observance, the divinities, and shrines, but not until the late 12th century was it used to denote a body of religious doctrines. The worship of kami slowly emerged at the dawn of Japanese history, crystallized as an imperial religious system during the Nara (710–794) and Heian (794–1185) periods, and subsequently was in constant interaction with Buddhism and Confucianism, which were introduced from the Asian continent. This interaction gave birth to various syncretic cults that combined the worship of kami with the imported religions. In the Muromachi (1333–1568) and Edo (1600–1868) periods, however, there was a revival of Shinto as the "Ancient Way," and an attempt was made to pare away all foreign influences. This expurgated system became the state religion of Japan during the Meiji period (1868–1912), but in 1945 Shinto was disestablished and again became one among other forms of worship.

Shinto can be regarded as a two-sided phenomenon. On the one hand it is a loosely structured set of practices, creeds, and attitudes rooted in local communities, and on the other it is a strictly defined and organized religion at the level of the imperial line and the state. These two basic aspects, which are not entirely separate, reflect fundamental features of the Japanese national character as it is expressed in sociopolitical structures and psychological attitudes.

Origins and Formative Period

Archaeological evidence of the Jomon period (ca 10,000 BC-ca 300 BC) has yielded scant information concerning religious practices. However, artifacts of the Yayoi period (ca 300 BC–ca AD 300), during which important population movements occurred and contacts with the continent intensified, show that religious life was becoming complex. Wetland agriculture necessitated stable communities, and agricultural rites that later played an important role in Shinto were developed. Metal implements, such as weapons and mirrors, were deposited in burial sites as emblems of political legitimacy. Cups and jars for food offerings have been found, a significant matter in the light of later practice in which the primary form of worship consists in offering food. Oracular bones show the increasing importance of divination.

The gate to the Shinto Shrine at Tsurugaoka Hachimangu in Kamakura.

The Kofun period (ca 300–710) was marked by influences from the continent and by the emergence of Japan as a nation. The 100 or so Japanese "kingdoms" mentioned in the late-3rd-century Chinese chronicle *Wei zhi* were gradually unified as relationships of clientage and allegiance were formed around the leaders of the powerful Yamato clan, from which developed the imperial line. Not only the Yamato kings, but also the chiefs of major clans (*uji*)—each worshiping its own tutelary divinity (*ujigami*)—were buried in stone chambers covered by earthen mounds (*kofun*) and accompanied by swords, curved gemstones (*magatama*), and mirrors, suggestive of the myth of the three imperial regalia (three sacred objects that are the symbols of the legitimacy and authority of the emperor). It was during this period that the Ise Shrine and Izumo Shrine, the most important shrines of the imperial tradition of Shinto, were established. The introduction of Confucianism contributed to the formalization of the Shinto moral precepts *tsumi* (hindrance of the life force) and *kegare* (ritual impurity).

On the one hand religious activity was grounded in each community and was concerned with agriculture and seasonal acts of worship, while on the other hand it was central to the ritual and political life of the leading clans. Imperial legitimacy, based on mythical, ritual, and religious coherence, was established through the compilation of the histories *Kojiki* (712, Record of Ancient Matters) and *Nihon shoki*. In the chapters of these works that recount mythology, the structure of the pantheon is connected to the structure of early society: the relationship of major clans to the imperial family is stated to be the result of relationships established between their respective ancestors. The centrality of religious practices to the *ritsuryo* (legal codes) system of government, created after the Taika Reform (645) and under which all the lands and people of Japan belonged to the emperor, is reflected in the fact that the Office of Shinto Worship (Jingikan) was in form, if not in practice, preeminent over the Grand Council of State (Dajokan). The Jingikan, presided over by the Nakatomi, Imbe, and Urabe clans, administered a system of shrines (some 3,000 in the early 10th century) at which prayers were offered for the benefit of the state. The Shinto rituals surrounding the imperial family and its satellite clans were codified at the end of the 9th century in the Jogan Gishiki and in the early 10th century in the Engi Shiki. Imperial Shinto thus achieved the status of a coherent religion, with a system of myths, rituals, sacerdotal lineages, and shrines.

The official recognition of Buddhism by Empress Suiko (r 593 – 628) in 594 and its acceptance by the upper strata of society not only contributed to the systematization of the traditions that later came to be known as Shinto, but also initiated a process of syncretism that was formalized in the medieval period (mid-12th – 16th centuries). At the beginning of the 8th century, Buddhist temples were already being built on or next to the grounds of Shinto shrines and were called *jinguji* (literally, "shrine-temples"). Buddhist monks considered the Shinto divinities (kami) to be in need of salvation and read and lectured on the Buddhist sutras in front of Shinto shrines. In 741, members of the emperor's court offered up a set of Lotus Sutra scrolls to the Usa Hachiman Shrine, and in 745 the shrine sent funds for the completion of the state-sponsored temple Todaiji. This service, among others, resulted in the granting of the Buddhist title "bodhisattva" to the kami Hachiman in 783.

Crucial developments in the interaction between Shinto and Buddhism occurred during the Heian period, following the introduction from China of the Tiantai (J: Tendai) sect by Saicho (767−822) and esoteric Shingon teachings by Kukai (774−835), founder of the Shingon sect. The Tendai sect was permeated by Shingon doctrines after Saicho died, and the two sects established a close relationship with Shinto, resulting in the development of syncretic ritual and philosophical systems in the medieval period. The facility with which esoteric Buddhism adapted itself to Shinto worship can be explained in part by the fact that it incorporated numerous syncretic practices that had developed in India and that its fundamental teaching was that all things in the phenomenal world are emanations of the Buddha Mahavairocana (J: Dainichi).

The Medieval Period: Syncretism

Of several pivotal theories of amalgamation introduced by Buddhism, the *honji suijaku* ("original prototype and local manifestation") theory played a key role in the evolution of Shinto-Buddhist relationships. At its core lies the notion that Shinto divinities are manifestations of Buddhas and bodhisattvas. Hence worship of a kami was worship of a Buddha in its kami form. Associations between Shinto divinities and Buddhas, such as that which obtained between Amaterasu Omikami, chief divinity of the Ise Shrine, and Dainichi, were established at the level of particular shrines and temples, and each devised its own system of rituals and practices surrounding its syncretic pantheon. Legends explaining the origin of these associations and descriptions of ritual systems were recorded in *engi-mono*, a type of picture scroll (*emakimono*). While these were for proselytization among the masses, there also developed between the 13th and 19th centuries a vast body of mythicohistorical and philosophical treatises composed by scholarly monks and priests. Its major categories are treatises based on schools of Buddhism, especially the Tendai and Shingon sects; treatises based on shrine traditions; and treatises written by Shinto priests. Examples of the first category are works dealing with Sanno Shinto and Sanno Ichijitsu Shinto, which arose from the Tendai sect, and Ryobu Shinto, which arose from the Shingon sect. The second category includes works of cults that originated at major shrines, such as the Kumano Sanzan Shrines, Iwashimizu Hachiman Shrine, and Kasuga Shrine. The third category is represented by works of the imperial tradition of Shinto, such as Watarai Shinto at the Ise Shrine and Yuiitsu Shinto at the Yoshida Shrine, that evince a reaction to Buddhist influence.

The Edo Period

There developed in the Edo period a shift of Shinto away from Buddhism and a rapprochement with Neo-Confucianism. At the same time scholars of the Kokugaku (National Learning) movement attempted, through rigorous philological study of old texts, to gain new insights into the culture and religious beliefs of ancient Japan as they had existed before the introduction of Confucianism and Buddhism.

The Meiji Period and After

The 19th century was a crucial turning point in Shinto history: on the one hand a number of religious movements emerged to form Sect Shinto, and on the other the expurgated imperial tradition of Shinto became the state religion, giving to the Meiji Restoration of 1868 the superficial appearance of a return to the Age of the Gods. The system of national shrines was reinstated, as well as the classical Office of Shinto Worship. Shrines were supported by the government, and Shinto, whose doctrines were taught in schools, took on an increasingly nationalistic coloration. Buddhism came under attack after the government decreed the separation of Shinto and Buddhism, but quickly reacted with its own brand of scholarship. After Japan's defeat in World War II, State Shinto was disestablished and replaced by shrine Shinto, which represents the bulk of Shinto shrines at the regional and local levels.

The religious picture of Japan today is complex. Statistics fail to suggest the numerous layers of interaction that have emerged, disappeared, and reemerged through history; syncretic tendencies and a general nonchalance concerning religious phenomena make it impossible for the uninitiated to come up with a clear image. There is no doubt that the identification of imperial Shinto with nationalism has hurt the tradition considerably, even though in many ways the essence of Shinto has been preserved only at the local shrines, which have had little to do with the imperial tradition. Industrialization and fundamental social changes are now confronting Shinto with what may be its greatest challenge.

Kasuga Taisha shrine in Nara Prefecture.

Shinto Worship and Ritual

Shinto practice is circumscribed within the context of sacred space and sacred time. The oldest known form of sacred space is a rectangular area covered with pebbles, surrounded by stones, and marked off by a rope linking four corner pillars; in the middle of this area is a stone (*iwasaka* or *iwakura*), a pillar, or a tree (*himorogi*). This ritually purified place where divinities were invoked (*kanjo*) was located in the midst of a sacred grove. The typical shrine (*jinja*) is located near the source of a river at the foot of a mountain. Surrounded by a fence (*tamagaki*), its entrance is marked by a wooden gate (*torii*) of simple style, on which a rope (*shimenawa*) has been fixed.

The etymology of the term kami, which is often rendered as "deity" or "god" but is translated here as "divinity," is unclear. The

Shinto pantheon, which is structured only at the level of the imperial tradition, consists of the *yaoyorozu no* kami (literally, "800 myriads of divinities"). Therefore, the presence of the kami is overwhelming and pervades all aspects of life. Natural phenomena—wind, sun, moon, water, mountains, trees—are kami. Specialized kami overlook and patronize human activities and even dwell in man-made objects. Certain kami are divinized ancestors or great figures of the past, and until 1945 the emperor was regarded as divine.

Each kami is endowed with an efficient force called *tama*, which is the object of religious activity and may be seen as violent (*aramitama*) or peaceful (*nigimitama*). Tama, the force that supports all life, dwells in human beings as *tamashii* and departs at the time of death. The tama of a kami is called upon at the outset of a ceremony to listen to the praise of the community and to its wishes. It is then offered food, praised again, and sent back. During ceremonies the tama of a divinity is thought to invest itself in the sacred tree or stone described above, or, more commonly, in a stone, root, branch, sword, mirror, or other object that is kept out of sight in a shrine. As the tama is inexhaustible, it may be invoked at many different locations.

Sacred time is that of the myths of the origin of the gods and of the land, as well as the time during which these origins are commemorated. Rituals and ceremonies are performed at each shrine by priests or by a rotating group of community members, on a cyclical and yearly basis. Each word uttered, each gesture and movement, and each ceremony is prescribed in ritual codes that are today set for all shrines in the *Saishi kitei*, published by the National Organization of Shrines (Jinja Honcho).

The other central aspect of Shinto ritual is purification. Grounded in mythology, it takes two forms: *misogi*, purification from contact with sullying elements (kegare) such as disease or death, and *harae*, the restoration of proper relationships after wrongdoing, through the offering of compensation. Misogi is held to have originated in the myth of the deity Izanagi no Mikoto, who, having followed his consort Izanami no Mikoto to the Land of Darkness (Yomi no Kuni; the netherworld) and seen her in a state of decomposition, returns to the world and cleanses himself in a stream. As he does so, the purification of his left eye results in the birth of the solar divinity Amaterasu Omikami, the purification of his right eye results in the appearance of the lunar divinity Tsukuyomi no Mikoto, and the purification of his nose causes the appearance of the storm divinity Susanoo no Mikoto.

The second form of purification, harae, is held to derive from the myth of Susanoo no Mikoto, who, after rampaging through the palace of his sister Amaterasu, is compelled to make recompense by offering up a great quantity of goods and having his beard cut and nails pulled off. Ritual implements, such as the folded paper strips (*shide*) that are affixed to ropes, gates, and sacred trees, and offerings of hemp, ramie, salt, and rice derive from the tradition of harae and serve the function of misogi; hence the origin of the general term misogi harae for purificatory practices. The emphasis on purity in Shinto worship is also manifested in the custom of undergoing a period of interdiction (*imi* or *kessai*) of as long as 30 days, which requires avoidance of contact with death, disease, menstruating women, and disfigured persons and abstention from sexual activity and the eating of meat, as well as adherence to conventions in food preparation, clothing, and bathing.

Shinto and the Arts

Important objects of Shinto art are the artifacts found in archaeological sites, such as polished gemstones (tama, magatama), mirrors, swords, earthenware statuettes (*dogu*), and other ritual implements. It has been suggested that wooden sculptures representing anthropomorphic divinities owed their appearance to the introduction of Buddhism, or, perhaps, to Chinese influence in general. In any case, a number of statues that have been preserved are of extreme beauty, characterized by august simplicity (those in the Matsunoo Shrine and Kumano Hayatama Shrine), or by stern but refined elegance (Tamayori Hime of the Yoshino Mikumari Shrine). A type of painting used in syncretic ritual is the shrine mandala. Depicting shrine-temple complexes, such mandalas served as maps for mental pilgrimages and as objects of meditation. Famous examples are the Fuji mandala of the Fuji Hongu Sengen Shrine, the Kasuga Jodo mandala of the Noman'in, and the Kumano Nachi mandala of the Tokei Shrine. Because anthropomorphic images are generally alien to Shinto practice, shrines did not support schools of painting as the ritsuryo government and later schools of Buddhism did, and, outside of syncretic iconography, one cannot find what could be called Shinto painting.

Shrines

(*jinja*). A Shinto shrine is an enclosed area containing a wooden sanctuary and several auxiliary buildings where Shinto rites are performed and prayers offered. The shrine is the focal point of organized Shinto religious practice, including annual festivals and *kagura* (sacred dance and music). In urban areas it provides a sense of community to those living within its parish. In rural areas it tends to create a feeling of kinship among villagers by stressing the common tie that all have to the shrine deity.

A typical medium-size shrine might be laid out as follows: Toward the rear of the shrine precinct, which is often rectangular and surrounded by a fence marking it off as a sanctified area, stands the *honden* (main sanctuary), which houses the *shintai*, a sacred object in which the spirit of the deity (*kami*) is believed to reside. Usually more than one deity is enshrined. Directly in front of the honden is the *haiden* (hall of worship or oratory), where the priests conduct their rituals and individuals make their offerings. Worshipers announce their presence to the deity or deities enshrined in the honden by clapping their hands and tugging on a heavy bell rope hanging from the eaves of the haiden. A wooden box stands in front of the haiden to receive money offerings. The interior of the haiden may be entered by laymen only on special ritual occasions, and the honden only by priests on rare occasions. At the entrance to the shrine stabds a *torii*, the characteristic shrine gateway. A pair of highly stylized stone lions called *komainu* stand guard in front of the gate or haiden.

Customs

New Year

(Shogatsu). New Year observances are the most important and most elaborate of Japan's annual events. Although local customs differ, at this time homes are decorated and the holidays are celebrated by family gatherings, visits to shrines or temples, and formal calls on relatives and friends. In recent years the New Year festivities have been officially observed from 1 January through 3 January, during which time all government offices and most companies are closed.

Preparations for seeing in the New Year were originally undertaken to greet the *toshigami*, or deity of the incoming year. These began on 13 December, when the house was given a thorough cleaning; the date is usually nearer the end of the month now. The house is then decorated in the traditional fashion: A sacred rope of straw (*shimenawa*) with dangling white paper strips (*shide*) is hung over the front door to demarcate the temporary abode of the toshigami and to prevent malevolent spirits from entering. It is also customary to place *kadomatsu*, an arrangement of tree sprigs, beside the entrance way. A special altar, known as a *toshidana* (literally, "year shelf"), is piled high with *kagamimochi* (flat, round rice cakes), *sake* (rice wine), persimmons, and other foods in honor of the toshigami. The night before New Year's is called Omisoka. Many people visit Buddhist temples to hear the temple bells rung 108 times at midnight (*joya no kane*) to dispel the evils of the past year. It is also customary to eat *toshikoshi soba* (literally, "year-crossing noodles") in the hope that one's family fortunes will extend like the long noodles.

Traditional sacred straw rope making.

Culture

New Year's Days

The first day of the year (*ganjitsu*) is usually spent with members of the family. People also throng to Buddhist temples and Shinto shrines. In the Imperial Palace at dawn or early on the morning of 1 January, the emperor performs the rite of *shihohai* (worship of the four quarters), in which he does reverence in the directions of various shrines and imperial tombs and offers prayers for the well-being of the nation. On 2 January the public is allowed to enter the inner palace grounds; the only other day this is possible is the emperor's birthday. On the second and third days of the New Year holidays, friends and business acquaintances visit one another to extend greetings (*nenshi*) and sip *toso*, a spiced rice wine.

Oshogatsu and Koshogatsu

Shogatsu refers to the first month of the year as well as to the period of the New Year's holidays. The events described above concern what is commonly referred to as Oshogatsu (literally, "Big New Year"). There is, however, another traditional New Year called Koshogatsu (literally, "Small New Year"). The former follows the date calculated by the Gregorian calendar, and the latter is set according to the lunar calendar. Koshogatsu thus starts with the first full moon of the year or more commonly on about 15 January and is largely observed in the rural areas of Japan, where the toshigami have been traditionally considered as agricultural deities.

New Year display of *kagamimochi*.

Hatsumode

("first shrine or temple visit"). Word used to refer to a person's first visit to a Shinto shrine or Buddhist temple during the New Year. Because it was customary to visit the shrine or temple located in the direction from one's home considered to be the most auspicious that year (*eho*), this practice was also called *ehomairi* ("visiting the shrine or temple in the eho"). Today, however, it has become more common to visit well-known shrines and temples, regardless of their location. These visits, which begin at midnight on New Year's Eve, are made annually by large numbers of Japanese. Tokyo's Meiji Shrine, Kamakura's Tsurugaoka Hachiman Shrine, and Kyoto's Yasaka Shrine each receive several million visitors over the first three days of January.

Hatsumode at Meiji Shrine, Tokyo.

Setsubun

Traditional ceremony to dispel demons, now observed on 3 or 4 February. The practice of scattering beans (*mamemaki*) to drive away demons is one of a number of magical rites performed to ward off evil.

On Setsubun, beans (usually soybeans) are scattered inside and outside the house or building to the common chant of *oni wa soto, fuku wa uchi* ("Out with demons! In with good luck!"). It is customary for family members to eat the same number of beans as their age.

Doll Festival

(Hina Matsuri). Festival for girls held on 3 March. Tiered platforms for *hina ningyo* (hina dolls, a set of dolls representing emperor, empress, attendants, and musicians in ancient court dress) are set up in the home, and the family celebrates with a meal, eating *hishimochi* (diamond-shaped rice cakes) and drinking *shirozake* (made with rice malt and *sake*). Also called Joshi no Sekku, Momo no Sekku (Peach Festival), and Sangatsu Sekku (Third Month Festival).

Holidays, national

(*kokumin no shukujitsu*). As of 1992, there were 13 national holidays authorized under Japanese law. Nine of these were established under the Law concerning National Holidays (Kokumin no Shukujitsu ni kansuru Horitsu), which was enacted in 1948. Four additional holidays were created by revision of this law. The 13 national holidays are as follows:

Display of traditional hina ningyo.

Ganjitsu (New Year's Day). 1 January.

Seijin no Hi (Coming-of-Age Day). 15 January. This holiday honors people who attain the age of 20 years anytime between 2 April of the previous year and 1 April of the current year. This is specified in the Japanese Civil Code as the age at which adulthood is reached.

Kenkoku Kinen no Hi (National Foundation Day). 11 February. Nationalistic commemoration of the legendary enthronement of Japan's first emperor, Jimmu.

Shumbun no Hi (Vernal Equinox Day). 21 March. Visits to family graves and family reunions occur on this day, the central day of a seven-day Buddhist memorial service (*higan*). A similar holiday is celebrated at the time of the autumnal equinox.

Midori no Hi (Greenery Day). 29 April. In 1989 this was designated as a day for nature appreciation. Prior to that the birthday of Emperor Showa was celebrated on this day.

Kempo Kinembi (Constitution Memorial Day). 3 May. Commemoration of the day the Constitution of Japan became effective in 1947.

Kodomo no Hi (Children's Day). 5 May. Day set aside for praying for the health and happiness of Japan's children.

Keiro no Hi (*Respect-for-the-Aged Day*). 15 September. Day honoring Japan's elderly and celebrating their longevity. Established to commemorate the enactment of the Law concerning Welfare for the Aged (Rojin Fukushi Ho) in 1966.

Shubun no Hi (*Autumnal Equinox Day*). 23 September. Visits to family graves and family reunions occur on this day, the central day of a seven-day Buddhist memorial service (higan). A similar holiday is celebrated at the time of the vernal equinox.

Taiiku no Hi (*Sports Day*). 10 October. Day on which good physical and mental health are fostered through physical activity. Established to commemorate the Tokyo Olympic Games, which were held 10−24 October 1964.

Bunka no Hi (*Culture Day*). 3 November. Day on which the ideals articulated in Japan's postwar constitution—the love of peace and freedom—are fostered through cultural activities.

Kinro Kansha no Hi (*Labor Thanksgiving Day*). 23 November. Day on which people express gratitude to each other for their labors throughout the year and for the fruits of those labors.

Tenno Tanjobi (*Emperor's Birthday*). 23 December. Celebration of the birthday of Japan's present emperor, Akihito.

Festivals

(*matsuri*). Japanese festivals, holidays, and other ceremonial occasions fall into two main categories: matsuri (festivals) and *nenchu gyoji* (annual events; also pronounced *nenju gyoji*). Matsuri are essentially native Japanese festivals of Shinto origin, held annually on established dates. Nenchu gyoji is a larger category of annual and seasonal observances, many of which are of Chinese or Buddhist origin. Nenchu gyoji are arranged seasonally to form an annual calendar of events. Matsuri are often included in this calendar, and there is some overlapping between the two categories.

Matsuri are chiefly of sacred origin, related (at least originally) to the cultivation of rice and the spiritual well-being of local communities. They derive ultimately from ancient Shinto rites for the propitiation of the gods and the spirits of the dead, and for the fulfillment of the agricultural round. Some of these Shinto rites were incorporated, along with Buddhist and Confucian rites and ceremonies imported from China, into the imperial calendar of annual observances (nenchu gyoji).

The word matsuri includes the rites and festivals practiced in both Folk Shinto and institutionalized Shinto. A matsuri is basically a symbolic act whereby participants enter a state of active communication with the gods (*kami*); it is accompanied by communion among participants in the form of feast and festival. In a broad sense, matsuri may also include festivals in which the playful element and commercial interests have all but obliterated the original sacramental context.

Hare and *Ke*

The Japanese have a concept of two dimensions of life, hare and ke. Hare correlates with the out of the ordinary, ke with the routine, and this duality extends over time, space, and things. Shinto shrines have special festival days set aside for matsuri; these, as well as such occasions as New Year's Day, the Bon Festival, birthdays, and weddings, are termed hare. Hare and ke thus resemble the idea of the sacred contrasting with the profane, but it is perhaps more accurate to define them in terms of special and everyday.

The Matsuri and the Seasons

Matsuri are in origin and tradition closely related to rice-centered agriculture, especially the growing cycle of rice. Among annual rites, spring and autumn matsuri are the most important. The spring festivals invoke a rich harvest or celebrate an anticipated good harvest; the autumn festivals are held in thanksgiving for a plentiful harvest.

Besides spring and autumn fetes, there are summer festivals (*natsu* matsuri) and winter festivals (*fuyu* matsuri). In farming areas the summer matsuri have the role of driving away natural disasters that might threaten the crops. In the cities, especially since the medieval period (mid-12th—16th centuries), the role of such festivals has been to ward off plague and pestilence. The winter matsuri, held between the harvest and spring seeding, have elements of both the autumn and spring matsuri. Thus, Japanese matsuri are synchronized with seasonal changes and are classified according to the four seasons.

Essentials of the Matsuri

Monoimi, or purificatory asceticism   In the center of the Shimane Peninsula on the coast of the Sea of Japan is the Sada Shrine. Each year at the end of September the shrine celebrates the Gozakae Matsuri (literally, "seat-changing rite"). In a midnight ceremony Shinto priests change the seat on which the god is to sit. Priests participating in these rites must confine themselves to the shrine for a week of purificatory asceticism prior to the rite. Monoimi serves as the symbolic gate by which the participants in a festival leave the everyday world (ke) to enter into the special realm (hare) of the matsuri. The purification rites have been greatly simplified in recent years. In premodern Japan, however, people were not allowed to participate in the matsuri unless they had undergone this purification process.

Culture

Offerings Another essential element of the *matsuri* is the offerings made to the gods. Typical items include regular and glutinous (*mochi*) rice, *sake* (rice wine), seaweed, vegetables, and fruits. In Japan there are no sacrifices of living creatures during matsuri, nor is there any offering of broken bread.

Communion The *naorai*, in which participants in the matsuri partake of the food offerings at the place of celebration together with the gods, is another essential element of the matsuri. In recent years the word naorai has also come to include the eating of offerings at a place separate from the matsuri site after the festival has ended, but this is essentially a banquet and not a true naorai.

The Matsuri and the Group

The matsuri presupposes the existence of a definite group of people to act it out. Generally speaking, in both the cities and villages of Japan every local community has a shrine that is its religious symbol. The members of a community, and thus of a certain shrine, are known as *ujiko*, and they in turn refer to their shrine as the *ujigami*.

Most matsuri are conducted by a ceremonial organization consisting of Shinto priests and a small group of laymen selected from the ujiko community.

Village and City Festivals

Although village festivals and city festivals resemble each other in several ways because they developed from the same origin, there are differences: village festivals tend to center on agricultural rites in the spring and autumn, and city festivals occur mostly in the summer; village festivals emphasize a man-god communion, and the city festivals stress human camaraderie. The most famous of all summer festivals is Kyoto's Gion Festival.

The Matsuri and Modern Society

After World War II, Japan underwent rapid changes in population distribution and the structure of traditional communities. These changes had direct and indirect effects on the matsuri. Although many of the traditional patterns are still evident on closer scrutiny, human interaction has become the framework of new events, showing a move from the closed and vertical order of communion between man and god to the more open and horizontal order of interpersonal relationship.

Summer fireworks in Tokyo.

Fireworks

(*hanabi*). Fireworks, along with firearms, were introduced to Japan by the Portuguese at the end of the 16th century. The first recorded fireworks display was held by shogun Tokugawa Ieyasu in 1613.

Eventually fireworks were adopted by the common people for their own amusement. Commercial fireworks manufacturers appeared, and specialty shops, such as the Tamaya and Kagiya in Tokyo, became widely known. Occasionally fireworks displays were prohibited because of the danger of fire. With improved manufacturing techniques, innovative Japanese projectile types and set pieces were constructed. The summer fireworks on the banks of the Sumida River (Sumidagawa) in Tokyo have been famous since they were first staged in 1733. Toy fireworks originated in the 18th century. Many varieties, including sparklers and "mouse" fireworks that dart about on the ground before they expire with a bang, are popular diversions for children on summer evenings.

Hanami

(literally, "flower viewing"; generally, cherry-blossom viewing). Excursions and picnics for enjoying flowers, particularly cherry blossoms; one of the most popular events of the spring. In some places flower-viewing parties are held on traditionally fixed dates according to the old lunar calendar. The subject of flower viewing has long held an important place in literature, dance, and the fine arts.

Today radio and television stations regularly broadcast reports on the blossoming of local cherry trees. Popular viewing spots include Yoshinoyama in Nara Prefecture and Ueno in Tokyo.

Crowds flock to see the cherry blossoms at night in Ueno Park, Tokyo.

Seibo

Custom of giving year-end gifts and the gifts themselves; presented as an expression of appreciation for favors received in the past year. The Chinese characters for seibo mean "year end." The custom is said to have arisen from the practice of sharing with others offerings initially made to ancestors. Those in a socially superior position, such as a marriage mediator (*nakodo*), are typical recipients of seibo, as well as of midyear *chugen* gifts. Gifts are presented by those in inferior positions and are usually considered to be from family to family or from business to business. There is some discontent with the custom of seibo, probably because it is obligatory, but of all calendrically determined gift-giving occasions, seibo is by far the most important. Traditionally, seibo were personally delivered, but today people often will have stores deliver or send the gifts through the mail.

M*iai*

The formal meeting, arranged by a *nakodo* (go-between) of a man and a woman seeking a marriage partner. Miai have a strong association with pre-World War II Japanese customs, in which marriage was seen as a link between two families rather than a joining of two individuals.

The miai process usually begins when the nakodo informally approaches one party (who has previously asked the nakodo's help in finding a marriage partner) and proposes a match. A formal written request is then made, accompanied by a photograph and a brief personal history of the prospective bride or groom. If the response is favorable, negotiations can proceed.

After the nakodo has decided on a suitable place or occasion for the miai, all parties concerned gather for a chance to observe and assess each other. Although most miai are group affairs, the prospective couple are usually given a chance to talk privately at some point in the proceedings. After the miai both parties must decide whether or not to continue negotiations. If the man and the woman decide that they would like to see each other again, they usually date for a while. This can lead to engagement and the formal exchange of betrothal gifts (*yuino*). However, if either party feels that the match is not right, and the nakodo cannot overcome their objections, it is permissible to end negotiations after the miai. Many people go through a number of miai before finding a suitable partner.

W eddings

(*kekkonshiki*). Weddings, perhaps the most important of the Japanese rites of passage, are one of the four major ceremonial occasions referred to as *kankon sosai* (coming-of-age, marriage, funerals, ancestor worship). For a marriage to be official, a new family register (*koseki*) must be compiled for the couple at the local administrative office. However, social and public recognition of a marriage in Japan is still often sought through the holding of extravagant weddings with elaborate formal costumes and large receptions.

Traditional Weddings

The "traditional" wedding of today was established as a pattern during the Meiji period (1868–1912). Although the marriage procedure varied a great deal with locality, most weddings included the customs described here. The day of the wedding was chosen carefully to avoid inauspicious days as determined by Chinese and Japanese astrological traditions. Traditional wedding rituals began the day before the wedding, when the bride prayed at the family shrine or temple or had a parting banquet with neighbors and parents. The wedding-day rituals primarily took place at the household of the groom, or at the household of the bride if the groom was adopted into her family in the kind of marriage called *mukoirikon*. In cases where the bride entered the groom's household, she dressed in white as she took formal leave of her parents. The white was symbolic of the death of her natal ties to them. At the household of the groom she appeared wearing a colorful *furisode*-style *kimono* and a cotton or silk head covering called *tsunokakushi* (literally, "horn-hiding"), which was supposed to suppress and hide the feminine "horns of jealousy." The groom wore a kimono with family crests and the loose trousers called *hakama*.

Modern Weddings

Traditional weddings were basically secular rites decided upon by local customs and personal preference. Weddings today are still determined by these considerations but are more likely to include a religious ceremony, even when the couple has no particular belief or religious affiliation. Shinto weddings, which became popular after the Shinto marriage ceremony held for the crown prince in 1900, are more common than Buddhist or Christian weddings, although Christian ceremonies have become increasingly fashionable. The trend has shifted from weddings at home to weddings in shrines, temples, and (since World War II) hotels, restaurants, churches, or special wedding halls, which are often furnished with special wedding chambers of Shinto or Christian design. Although the custom of *satogaeri* (the wife returned to her family home, bringing gifts for relatives and friends) might still be observed by some, most Japanese try to take a honeymoon of at least a week. The couple may make their ritual trip after settling into their new home. Although large-scale, expensive weddings directed and financed by the parents are still common, there are also an increasing number of weddings that more closely reflect the personal wishes of the couple.

Shinto wedding ceremony.

Funerals

(*sogi*). About 90 percent of the funerals in Japan are conducted according to Buddhist rites. Upon death the body is washed with hot water (*yukan*), then dressed by family members in white garments (*kyokatabira*) or in his favorite clothes. More recently it has become the practice for physicians and nurses to cleanse the body and for morticians to dress it. In many cases the entire process of funeral rites is entrusted to a mortuary.

The body is laid out with the head toward the north without a pillow and is covered with a sheet of white cloth. A priest from the Buddhist parish temple recites sutras at the bedside and gives a posthumous Buddhist name (*kaimyo*) to the deceased. The body is then placed in an unpainted wooden coffin.

A notice of mourning, written on a piece of white paper with a black frame, is posted on the front door or gate of the house throughout the mourning period (*kichu*). An all-night wake (*tsuya*) or a briefer "half wake" (*hantsuya*) is held. Refreshments are served and mourners present gifts of "incense money" (*koden*). The day after the wake the funeral service is held at home, the parish temple, or a funeral hall. There are both Buddhist and Shinto forms of service.

After cremation pieces of the bones of the deceased are gathered, placed in a small jar (*kotsutsubo*), and brought home for later burial. Every 7th day until the 49th day, rites are held around the altar where the kotsutsubo is kept. The family members of the deceased express their gratitude to mourners by sending acknowledgment notes and return gifts (*kodengaeshi*) valued at about half of the koden. The kotsutsubo is buried at the grave site during this period.

E*nkai*

Japanese-style banquet usually held in a *tatami*-floored room (*zashiki*). Originally court ceremonial parties held at specific times of the year, enkai were later adopted by the general populace for the celebration of important occasions such as New Year parties (*shinnenkai*) and year-end parties (*bonenkai*). The year-end parties (*bonen* means "to forget the year") in late December offer an opportunity to forget the trials and misfortunes of the past year as well as to welcome the New Year in a cheerful mood. Year-end parties usually take the form of drinking parties among close friends or coworkers.

Literature

L*iterature*

(Nihon *bungaku*). The written literature of Japan is one of the more venerable of the literary traditions of the Orient. Moreover, the oldest works in the standard canon, the histories *Kojiki* (712, Record of Ancient Matters)and *Nihon shoki* (720, Chronicle of Japan), provide in their myths, legends, and songs ample evidence of an ancient tradition of oral literature that, for the lack of a native system of writing, was not recorded until the introduction of Chinese characters.

Contact with the Asian mainland, the source of much of the material culture of the Yayoi period (ca 300 BC — ca AD 300) of Japanese history, became increasingly close during the 4th and 5th centuries. By the late 6th or early 7th century a small number of Japanese had gained an incipient mastery of Chinese writing and had developed the rudiments of a system whereby the Japanese language could be transcribed, using Chinese characters semantically to denote corresponding Japanese words or phonetically by the assignment of a Japanese sound value to individual characters. The pervasive influence of Chinese literature and its system of writing persisted until the mid-19th century, and most educated men considered it the literary language of Japan. Consequently over the course of more than a millennium a vast number of literary works were written in classical Chinese; these, as well as writings in high-classical Japanese and in hybrid forms of Sino-Japanese, of which modern Japanese is one, are all considered by the Japanese people to be elements of their literary heritage. For a discussion of aspects of the tradition of Japanese oral literature.

Official embassies to Sui (589−618) and Tang (618−907) dynasty China, initiated in 600, were the chief means by which Chinese culture, technology, and methods of government were introduced on a comprehensive basis in Japan. The *Kojiki* and the *Nihon shoki*, the former written in hybrid Sino-Japanese and the latter in classical Chinese, were compiled under the sponsorship of the government for the purpose of authenticating the legitimacy of its polity. However, among these collections of myths, genealogies, legends of folk heroes, and historical records there appear a number of songs—largely irregular in meter and written with Chinese characters representing Japanese words or syllables—that offer insight into the nature of preliterate Japanese verse.

The first major collection of native poetry, again written with Chinese characters, was the *Man'yoshu* (late 8th century), which contains verses, chiefly the 31-syllable *waka*, that were composed in large part between the mid-7th and mid-8th centuries. The earlier poems in the collection are characterized by the direct expression of strong emotion but those of later provenance show the emergence of the rhetorical conventions and expressive subtlety that dominated the subsequent tradition of court poetry. Although the *Man'yoshu* is today considered the great monument of early Japanese verse, contemporary literati, invariably men, chose to write their public verse in Chinese, and between the mid-8th century and the early years of the Heian period (794−1185) four imperial anthologies of Chinese poetry written by Japanese were compiled.

A revolutionary achievement of the mid-9th century was the development of a native orthography (*kana*) for the phonetic representation of Japanese. Employing radically abbreviated Chinese characters to denote Japanese sounds, the system contributed to a deepening consciousness of a native literary tradition distinct from that of China. The waka, now written with kana, was an indispensable element of social relations, and the practice arose of holding poem contests (*uta-awase*) at which pairs of verses were set against one another. Poets compiled collections (*shikashu*) of their verses, and, drawing in part on these, the *Kokinshu* (905), the first of 21 imperial anthologies of native poetry, was assembled in the early 10th century.

The introduction of kana also led to the development of a prose literature in the vernacular, early examples of which are the *Utsubo monogatari* (late 10th century), a work of fiction; the *Ise monogatari* (mid-10th century), a collection of vignettes centered on poems; and the diary *Tosa nikki* (935). From the late 10th century the ascendancy of the Fujiwara regents, whose power over emperors depended on the reception of their daughters as imperial consorts, resulted in the formation of literary coteries of women in the courts of empresses, and it was these women who produced the great prose classics of the 11th century. Written in high-classical Japanese with only the rare intrusion of Chinese characters, such works as *The Tale of Genji* (early 11th century), a fictional narrative by Murasaki Shikibu, and the *Makura no soshi* (996−1012), a collection of essays by Sei Shonagon, are considered by Japanese to be a watershed in the development of the native literary tradition. A distinctive feature of these and of many of the best of later Japanese prose works is their tendency to disregard formal structure in favor of a series of discrete scenes or discourses that present in the aggregate a comprehensive and richly detailed vision of a time and place.

Calligraphy of The Bell Cricket (1), from *The Tale of Genji*.

Medieval Literature

The chief development in poetry during the medieval period (mid-12th−16th centuries) was linked verse (*renga*). Arising from the court tradition of waka, renga was cultivated by the warrior class as well as by courtiers, and some among the best renga poets, such as Sogi, were commoners. A major development in prose literature of the medieval era was the war tale (*gunki monogatari*). The *Heike monogatari* relates the events of the war between the Taira and Minamoto families that brought an end to imperial rule; it was disseminated among all levels of society by itinerant priests who chanted the story to the accompaniment of a lutelike instrument, the *biwa*. An increase in travelers along the highway connecting Kamakura, the seat of the military government, with the old capital of Kyoto gave rise to a number of travel diaries, such as the *Izayoi nikki* (ca 1280), and the social upheaval of the early years of the era led to the appearance of works deeply influenced by the Buddhist notion of the inconstancy of worldly affairs (*mujo*). Not only does the theme of mujo provide the ground note of the *Heike monogatari* and the essay collections

Hojoki (1212) and *Tsurezuregusa* (ca 1330), it is also an element of the theoretical framework of the historical work *Gukansho* (ca 1220). The writing of literary works in Chinese continued in the hands of aristocrats and Zen Buddhist priests of the Gozan temples.

Edo Literature

The formation of a stable central government in Edo (now Tokyo), after some 100 years of turmoil, and the growth of a market economy based on the widespread use of a standardized currency led to the development in the Edo period (1600−1868) of a class of wealthy townsmen. General prosperity contributed to an increase in literacy, and literary works became marketable commodities, giving rise to a publishing industry. Humorous fictional studies of contemporary society by Ihara Saikaku and Ejima Kiseki were huge commercial successes, and prose works, often elaborately illustrated, that were directed toward a mass audience became a staple of Edo-period literature. Commercial playhouses, patronized by commoner and *samurai* alike, were established for the performance of puppet plays (*joruri*) and *kabuki*, whose plots often centered on conflicts arising from the rigidly hierarchical social order that was instituted by the Tokugawa shogunate and underpinned by Neo-Confucian moral precepts.

Portrait of Ihara Saikaku.

The 17-syllable form of light verse known as *haikai*, whose subject matter was drawn from nature and the lives of ordinary people, was raised to the level of great poetry by Matsuo Basho, who applied to its composition the standards of classical aesthetics. Some of the most evocative of native poetry in Chinese appeared during the Edo period; moreover, government adherence to the principles of Neo-Confucianism led to the writing in Chinese of a great number of prose works that dealt with the Neo-Confucian philosophical system. The waka, long stultified by functionless compositional conventions, was given new life when it was taken up by townsmen. A number of philologists, among them Keichu, Kamo no Mabuchi, and Motoori Norinaga, wrote scholarly studies on early literary texts, such as the *Kojiki*, the *Man'yoshu*, and *The Tale of Genji*, in which they attempted to elucidate the native Japanese world view as it existed before the introduction of Buddhism and Confucianism.

Modern Literature

The imperial restoration of 1868 was followed by the wholesale introduction of Western technology and culture, which largely displaced Chinese culture. As a result the novel, which during the Edo period had been considered a base form of literature appropriate only for the titillation or, in some instances, the moral edification of the masses, became established as a serious and respected genre of the literature of Japan. A related development was the gradual abandonment of the literary language in favor of the usages of colloquial speech, fully achieved for the first time in *Ukigumo* (1887–1889) by Futabatei Shimei. Although the *tanka* and the *haiku* remained viable poetic forms, notably in the hands of Ishikawa Takuboku, Yosano Akiko, Masaoka Shiki, and Takahama Kyoshi, there developed under the influence of Western poetry a genre of free verse, the first great achievement of which was the collection *Wakanashu* (1897) by Shimazaki Toson. Early stylistic influences on Japanese literature were romanticism, introduced in the 1890s by Mori Ogai; symbolism, introduced in Ueda Bin's *Kaichoon* (1905), a collection of translations of French poems; and naturalism, which reigned supreme from 1905 to 1910 and out of which developed the enduring genre of the confessional novel (I-novel or *watakushi shosetsu*).

Kawabata Yasunari, winner of the 1968 Novel Prize for literature.

Until the 1950s a distinctive feature of the Japanese literary community was the publication of coterie magazines by writers of like mind. The humanist Shirakaba school of writers, including Mushanokoji Saneatsu and Shiga Naoya, published the journal *Shirakaba* from 1910; the early writings of Yokomitsu Riichi and Kawabata Yasunari appeared in *Bungei jidai* (1924–1927), the organ of the modernist Shinkankaku school; and works of the proletarian writers Kobayashi Takiji and Sata Ineko were published in *Senki* (1928–1931), a Marxist-oriented periodical. The serial publication of novels in newspapers has also been a common practice, and some of the best Japanese novelists, from Natsume Soseki to Nagai Kafu, Tanizaki Jun'ichiro, and Kawabata Yasunari, have written for the newspapers. Translations of Japanese literary works have appeared in rapidly increasing numbers since the 1970s, and the best creations of Soseki, Ogai, Kafu, Akutagawa Ryunosuke, Shiga, Tanizaki, Kawabata, Ibuse Masuji, Dazai Osamu, Enchi Fumiko, and Mishima Yukio are available in English versions. Among the foremost writers of fiction in the early 1990s were Oe Kenzaburo, Abe Kobo, Endo Shusaku, Tsushima Yuko, Murakami Ryu, Nakagami Kenji, and Murakami Haruki.

W*aka*

("Japanese poetry"). A genre of verse of various prosodic types that began to take form in the hands of the court aristocracy in the mid-6th century. By the late 8th century the term was used synonymously with *tanka* ("short poem"), a type of verse that consists of five lines in 31 syllables in the pattern 5-7-5-7-7 and that is still composed today. Early Japanese song, from which waka arose, and the derivative genres *renga* ("linked verse") and *haikai* (later known as *haiku*) are distinguished from waka, as is modern free verse. The sinicized term waka, in use by the Heian period (794—1185), replaced the previous term Yamato *no uta* (poetry of the land of Yamato), but both imply the distinction of native verse from *kanshi*, or verse composed in Chinese by Chinese or Japanese poets.

Prosody and Rhetorical Devices

The primary sources of our knowledge of early Japanese poetry are the annals *Kojiki* (712, Record of Ancient Matters) and *Nihon shoki* (720, Chronicle of Japan) and the late-8th-century anthology of poetry *Man'yoshu* (Collection of Ten Thousand Leaves or Collection for Ten Thousand Generations), most of the more than 4,000 poems which were culled from earlier anthologies that are no longer extant. The oldest poems display little prosodic regularity, although there was a tendency to alternate longer and shorter lines. In the 7th century, however, possibly arising from the influence of the five-character and seven-character lines of Chinese verse, the number of syllables per line became standardized at five and seven. From the mid-7th century the tanka form appears to have been paramount, but until the middle of the 8th century it was rivaled by the *choka* ("long poem"), consisting of an indefinite number of pairs of five- and seven-syllable lines with an extra seven-syllable line at the end. The longest choka, by Kakinomoto no Hitomaro, is one in 149 lines. Other forms were the *katauta* ("half poem"), of 3 lines of five, seven, and five syllables, to which another poet replied to form a set; the *sedoka* ("head-repeated poem"), of 6 lines in the syllable pattern 5-7-7-5-7-7; and the *bussokuseki no uta*, also of 6 lines but in the syllable pattern 5-7-5-7-7-7, the chief examples of which are inscribed on an ancient stela erected beside a stone (bussokuseki) on which the Buddha's footprints are incised.

Alliteration, consonance, and assonance are found in the earliest Japanese verses and were used by poets of all periods to provide sonority and rhetorical complexity. Until the mid-8th century the dominant cadence of waka was 5-7, but thereafter the 7-5 cadence gained the ascendancy. It also became common for the cadence to be broken, usually at the end of the third line, by a caesura. In the following 12th-century poem by the priest Jakuren, the third line terminates with a conclusive verb inflection and is followed by a noun phrase:

> *Sabishisa wa*
> *Sono iro to shi mo*
> *Nakarikeri*
> *Maki tatsu yama no*
> *Aki no yugure*

To be alone—
It is of a color that
Cannot be named:
This mountain where cedars rise
Into the autumn dusk.

Imagery and Subject Matter

Classical waka employed a high proportion of images drawn from nature, personification of which led increasingly to allegory. However, unlike Western allegory, with its personified conceptual abstractions, allegory in waka tended to be concrete and personal (e.g., a poem about an orange tree that awaits the arrival of the cuckoo in early summer might also represent a lady awaiting her dilatory lover). The conventions of waka militated against the innovative use of natural images—the stock of which, in the case of insects, included the cicada and the cricket, but not the butterfly, the bee, or the firefly—and a consequence of this narrowing of content was that a new poem inevitably alluded to earlier poems in the tradition.

Waka poets concentrated on a handful of subjects, primarily human affairs (celebration, separation, grief, and especially love) and nature (natural beauty and the changing aspects of the seasons), avoiding war, physical suffering, death, and all that was ugly or low. The themes of beauty and sadness, infused by an awareness of the overarching effects of time, increasingly dominated waka. With the growing influence of a Buddhist world view holding all life to be ephemeral and all human attachment to be an impediment to enlightenment, nature poetry came typically to express a lyric melancholy, while poetry of love expressed a poignant consciousness of the impermanence of personal ties.

Historical Development

Following the *Man'yoshu*, the next major collection of waka was the *Kokinshu* (905, Collection from Ancient and Modern Times), the first of 21 imperial anthologies. These anthologies varied considerably in size and quality, but each was considered the most important literary enterprise of its day. Among the chief sources from which poems were drawn for inclusion in the imperial anthologies were the *shikashu*, collections of poetry written and compiled by individual poets. Other important repositories of classical waka—and of critical judgments—are the records of poetry matches (*uta-awase*).

Calligraphy from the *Kokinshu*.

Waka of the *Kokinshu* was much influenced by the mannered elegance and precious conceits of Chinese poetry of the late Six Dynasties period (222–589), in particular the monumental *Wen xuan* (J: *Monzen*). Nevertheless, the *Kokinshu* also displays in its verse, as well as in the vernacular preface written by one of its compilers, Ki no Tsurayuki, a strong consciousness of a native poetics. Tsurayuki distinguishes between the essence or "heart" (*kokoro*) of a poem and the construct of language (*kotoba*) by means of which it is embodied. The ideal toward which the poet strives, Tsurayuki declares, is a harmony of kokoro and kotoba, of individual feeling and sincerity with rhetorical elegance and purity of diction.

The eighth imperial anthology, *Shin kokinshu* (1205, New Collection from Ancient and Modern Times), one of whose editors was Fujiwara no Teika, brought to fulfillment the organizational concepts, already apparent in the *Kokinshu*, of association and progression. Adjacent poems were linked by such devices as similarity of image or common allusion to an older poem, while all of the poems of the major divisions of the anthology, such as those devoted to individual seasons or to love, were ordered on the basis of the appearance of seasonal phenomena or the progress of a love affair. The principles of association and progression were among the influences that contributed to the development of the genre of linked verse (renga).

The last imperial anthology, *Shin shoku kokinshu* (New Collection from Ancient and Modern Times, Continued) was completed in 1439. Following the *Shin kokinshu*, imperial anthologies displayed an increasingly sterile style, marked by a slavish veneration of the conventions of the Heian period, and by the Edo period (1600−1868) the center of waka composition had passed from the court to society at large.

Early in the Meiji period (1868−1912), the influential poet-critics Yosano Tekkan and Masaoka Shiki called for a break with the past and, following their practice, the custom arose of referring to the art of 31-syllable poetry as tanka, rather than waka. In 1899, with other young tanka poets, Tekkan founded the Shinshisha (New Poetry Society), which in 1900 initiated the publication of the literary magazine *Myojo* (Bright Star). One of the leading contributors was Yosano Akiko, whose passionate lyricism brought a new vigor to the genre.

Tanka continues in the post−World War II period to be a widely practiced form of verse; nevertheless, though today hundreds of societies and millions of practitioners carry on the tradition, the best Japanese poets have increasingly chosen to work in the genre of free verse. Moreover, the importance of convention in waka has led to the preservation of classical grammar in tanka composition, thus vitiating the immediacy of its effect on the majority of Japanese. A notable exception, however, is the vastly popular tanka of Tawara Machi (1962−), who has preserved the subtlety of feeling and expressive grace of classical waka while employing colloquial diction.

Culture

Haiku

A 17-syllable verse form consisting of three metrical units of 5, 7, and 5 syllables, respectively. One of the most important forms of traditional Japanese poetry, haiku remains popular in modern Japan, and in recent years its popularity has spread to other countries.

Haiku, *Hokku*, and *Haikai*

Loose usage by students, translators, and even poets themselves has led to much confusion about the distinction between the three related terms haiku, hokku, and haikai. The term hokku literally means "starting verse." A hokku was the first or "starting" link of a much longer chain of verses known as a haikai *no renga*, or simply haikai, in which alternating sets of 5-7-5 syllables and 7-7 syllables were joined. Hokku gradually took on an independent character. Largely through the efforts of Masaoka Shiki (1867–1902), this independence was formally established in the 1890s through the creation of the term "haiku." Haiku was a new type of verse, in form quite similar to the traditional hokku but different in that it was to be written, read, and understood as an independent poem, complete in itself, rather than as part of a longer chain.

Portrait of Matsuo Basho.

Strictly speaking, then, the history of haiku begins only in the last years of the 19th century. The famous verses of Edo-period (1600–1868) masters such as Matsuo Basho (1644–1694), Yosa Buson (1716–1784), and Kobayashi Issa (1763–1827) are properly referred to as hokku even though they are now generally read as independent haiku.

Development of Haikai

Renga, or linked verse, which began to be written in the Heian period (794–1185), was originally considered a diversion by which poets could relax from the serious business of composing waka poetry. By the time of the renga master Sogi (1421–1502), however, it had become a serious art with complex rules and high aesthetic standards. Haikai no renga, or simply haikai, was conceived as a lighthearted amusement in which poets could indulge after the solemn refinements of serious renga.

When haikai began to emerge as a serious poetic genre in the early 16th century, two characteristics distinguished it from serious *renga*: its humorous intent and its free use of *haigon* (colloquialisms, compounds borrowed from Chinese, and other expressions that had previously been banned from the poetic vocabulary). However, the erudite Matsunaga Teitoku (1571–1653) succeeded in establishing a more conservative and formalistic approach to haikai. For Teitoku, humor implied a sort of intellectual wit, and the distinction between haikai and renga lay ultimately only in the use or nonuse of haigon. He established strict rules concerning the composition of haikai and sought to endow the form with the elegance and aesthetic elevation of waka and serious renga.

After Teitoku's death his formalistic approach was challenged by the more freewheeling Danrin School of haikai led by Nishiyama Soin (1605–1682). Soin emphasized the comic aspects of haikai. Characteristic of the Danrin style of poetry was the practice of yakazu haikai, in which a single poet would reel off verse after verse as quickly as possible in a sort of exercise in free association. The most renowned example of this is the legendary performance by Ihara Saikaku (1642–1693) in 1684 at the Sumiyoshi Shrine in Osaka, where he composed 23,500 verses in a single day and night.

Basho was not only the greatest of haikai poets, he was also primarily responsible for establishing haikai as a true art form. Having received instruction in both the Teitoku and Danrin styles of haikai, he gradually developed in the late 17th century a new style that, through its artistic sincerity, transcended the conflict between serious renga and comic haikai and could express humor, humanity, and profound religious insight all within the space of a single hokku.

Uejima Onitsura (1661–1738) wrote haikai of exceptional quality, and his notion of makoto or "sincerity" represents one of the high points of Japanese poetic theory. Other notable poets of the time include Konishi Raizan, Ikenishi Gonsui, and Yamaguchi Sodo. Basho also had a great number of disciples. Of these, the so-called Ten Philosophers are particularly well known. They are Naito Joso, Mukai Kyorai, Sugiyama Sampu, Morikawa Kyoroku, Hattori Ransetsu, Kagami Shiko, Ochi Etsujin, Takarai Kikaku, Shida Yaba (1663–1740), and Tachibana Hokushi. Nozawa Boncho, another of Basho's disciples, is also worthy of mention.

After Basho's death many of his disciples set up their own schools of haikai. In general these poets sought special effects—with some writing enigmatic, puzzlelike verse and others satisfying themselves with witty wordplay—and at times their haikai became virtually indistinguishable from zappai and senryu, popular comic verse forms that had come into vogue in the Genroku period (1688–1704). In the late 18th century, however, there arose a movement of poets who sought to restore high aesthetic standards. The principal figure in this haikai reform was the talented painter-poet Buson, and the main cry of the movement was "Return to Basho!" Buson possessed great imagination and culture and a painter's eye for vivid pictorial scenes. Other important haikai poets of the period include Tan Taigi, Kato Kyotai, and Oshima Ryota.

The number of composers of haikai grew rapidly in the early 19th century. This popularization, however, was accompanied by a general decline in quality. The most notable exceptions were Iwama Otsuni (1756—1823) and Kobayashi Issa. Issa's poems about his poverty and about his love for small animals and insects are particularly memorable, and today he ranks with Basho and Buson as one of the most beloved haikai poets.

Modern Haiku

The history of modern haiku dates from Masaoka Shiki's reform, begun in 1892, which established haiku as a new independent poetic form. It is a history that features constant experimentation and the confluence of various literary trends such as naturalism, romanticism, symbolism, and proletarianism. Basic to the modernization of haiku was Shiki's most important concept, *shasei*, or sketching from life—a term borrowed from the critical vocabulary of Western painting. The magazine that Shiki began in 1897, *Hototogisu*, became the haiku world's most important publication.

Shiki's reform did not change two traditional elements of haiku: the division of 17 syllables into three groups of 5, 7, and 5 syllables and the inclusion of a seasonal theme. Kawahigashi Hekigoto, who succeeded his mentor Shiki as haiku editor of the newspaper Nihon, carried Shiki's reform further with a proposal that haiku would be truer to reality if there were no center of interest in it. The logical extension of this idea was free-verse haiku, since the traditional patterning was seen as another artificial manipulation of reality. Hekigoto also urged the importance of the poet's first impression, just as it was (*sono mama*), of subjects taken from daily life and of local color to create freshness. Other poets associated with Hekigoto's Shinkeiko haiku (New Trend Haiku) movement were Anzai Okaishi (1886—1953), Osuga Otsuji, and Ogiwara Seisensui.

Protesting against the prosaic flatness characteristic of much of the works of Hekigoto's school, Seisensui maintained in 1912 that free-verse haiku must also discard the seasonal theme. He held that haiku must capture in its rhythms not the object perceived but the poet's perception. The work of many able poets appeared in his magazine *Soun*. Notably successful among them were Taneda Santoka and Ozaki Hosai, who both led wandering lives of poverty, like the beggar-priests of the past.

In 1912 Takahama Kyoshi began in the pages of *Hototogisu* (which he had edited since 1898) his lifelong defense of the traditional 17-syllable form, the seasonal theme, and the descriptive realism of Shiki. He outlined his views in a collection of essays published under the title *Susumubeki haiku no michi* (1915—1917, The Path Haiku Ought to

Take). The first flowering of the traditional school was in the Taisho period (1912—1926) and featured such gifted poets as Iida Dakotsu, Kawabata Bosha, Murakami Kijo, and Watanabe Suiha (1882—1946).

By 1920 a second generation of poets clustered about *Hototogisu*, including Mizuhara Shuoshi, Awano Seiho, Yamaguchi Seishi, and Takano Suju. The first Showa-period (1926—1989) poet to break away into subjects previously avoided was Hino Sojo, who wrote verses on romantic and sensuous love. *Hototogisu* continues to represent the central position in haiku to the present day.

Mizuhara Shuoshi broke away from *Hototogisu* in 1931, two years after having assumed the editorship of the magazine *Ashibi*. Shuoshi's talent for making imaginative use of the historical past shines in his collection *Katsushika* (1930). *Ashibi* was an important outlet for such poets as Yamaguchi Seishi, Ishida Hakyo, and Hashimoto Takako (1899—1963), the foremost woman haiku poet.

In the early Showa period the term *shinko haiku* (new haiku) loosely identified all groups that deviated from the traditional *Hototogisu* school. In addition to the *Ashibi* poets and the modernistic school of Hino Sojo's magazine *Kikan*, the term also included the proletarian school, headed by Kuribayashi Issekiro (1894—1961), originally of Seisensui's group. Other prominent proletarian poets were Hashimoto Mudo (1903—1974), Shimada Seiho (1882—1944), and Yoshioka Zenjido (1889—1961). Another politicizing group centered around the liberal publication *Kyodai haiku*, which appeared during the period 1933—1940 and accepted both conventional and free-verse haiku.

Joining *Hototogisu* in 1933, Nakamura Kusatao deplored the shinko haiku movement for its emphasis on technique and methodology. By 1939 he was identified along with Ishida Hakyo, Kato Shuson, Shinohara Bon (1910—1975), Ishizuka Tomoji (1906—1986), and Nishijima Bakunan (1895—1981) as a member of the *Ningen Tankyu Ha* ("Humanness" school).

During the military-dominated prewar and World War II period, haiku was controlled by government censorship. The immediate postwar period saw an effort by the leftist union Shin Haikujin Remmei to "break the hold of feudalism in haiku and to expose war collaborators," a pronouncement aimed at *Hototogisu* and other traditional schools. In 1947 many leading poets withdrew from this union. The Modern Haiku Association (Gendai Haiku Kyokai) was formed in July 1947 to "enhance modern haiku" with the inclusion of all groups from the political left to the literary traditionalists.

The effort to unite all factions was stimulated by a widely discussed 1946 article entitled "Daini geijutsuron" (On a Second-Class

Art), in which the critic Kuwabara Takeo maintained that modern haiku was not a serious literary genre but only a pleasant pastime. A number of efforts to "modernize haiku"—to make it relevant to contemporary experience—were stimulated by the publicity given Kuwabara's article.

One such effort was *Tenro*, a magazine begun in 1948 under Yamaguchi Seishi's editorship and supported by the prewar liberal Kyoto University haiku association together with some former *Ashibi* poets. *Tenro* and the prewar *Ashibi*, which continues to appear, are the two most important vehicles of the nontraditional haiku. Other prewar magazines that continue to appear are Ishida Hakyo's *Tsuru* and Kato Shuson's *Kanrai*. Iida Dakotsu's *Ummo* ceased publication in 1992. The extreme haiku fringe of symbolism and surrealism is found in such magazines as *Taiyokei*, founded in 1946 by Mizutani Saiko (1903—1967) and Tomizawa Kakio (1902—1962), and *Bara*, started in 1952 by Tomizawa Kakio and Takayanagi Shigenobu (1923—1983).

Haiku Abroad

The West's first introduction to haiku came in B. H. Chamberlain's pioneer work, *Japanese Poetry* (1910), in a chapter entitled "Basho and the Japanese Epigram." William Porter's early anthology of translations was entitled *A Year of Japanese Epigrams* (1911). Haiku was first introduced to France by Paul-Louis Couchoud at the time of the Russo-Japanese War. The title of his introduction to haiku was *Les Epigrammes Lyriques du Japon*. The use of the term "epigram" in these titles is indicative of how haiku was first intepreted abroad.

Ezra Pound quickly noticed and appropriated the haiku technique of cutting up the poem into two independent yet associated images. In France Paul Eluard wrote poems in the haiku style. Haiku has rapidly become naturalized both in Europe and in the United States, and magazines of original haiku are published. Haiku magazines in the United States include *Modern Haiku*, *byways*, *Tweed*, and *New World Haiku*.

Folktales

(*minwa*). Narrative literature of the people, handed down orally from generation to generation. Some tales can be traced back even before writing was introduced to Japan. The term *mukashi-banashi* (tale of yore) is assigned by Japanese folklorists to denote the "folktale" as against the *densetsu* or "legend"; the latter is defined as a marvelous incident that is believed by the folk to have actually happened.

Written History

Outside of the oral tradition, there is rich documentation of folk material throughout the ages. The 8th century saw the first written records of the imperial history with the *Kojiki* (712, Record of Ancient Matters) and *Nihon shoki* (720, Chronicle of Japan), which contain many tale motifs. The *Nihon ryoiki, Konjaku monogatari,* and *Uji shui monogatari* of the following centuries are collections of traditional narratives, Buddhist and secular, totaling well over 1,000 in number. Also, the classic dramas of the 15th century, the No and *kyogen,* as well as *kabuki,* which originated in the early 17th century, are examples of how dramatists based their plots and themes on folk material, resulting in the preservation of tale motifs today.

Collecting Folktales

Systematic collecting of folktales was started in the 1930s, following the precepts of a list of 100 major story types devised by Yanagita Kunio, who wrote *Mukashi-banashi saishu techo* (1936, Manual for Collecting Folktales).

The first attempt to tabulate the collected material in classified order was *Nippon mukashi-banashi meii* (1948, A List of Japanese Folktales). Listing the outlines of various tale types in one volume, it is useful as a handbook for tale collecting. In 1958 the original classification system of Yanagita was expanded sevenfold by Seki Keigo in a classified anthology of 8,600 folktale synopses entitled *Nippon mukashi-banashi shusei,* published in six volumes.

Diffusion Routes to Japan

In prehistoric times Japan seems to have had closer contact with the Eurasian continent than is commonly thought. It was an era of dynamic migration from east to west along many routes. One that intimately concerns Japan was the circumpolar route that eventually populated the Americas. Situated adjacent to this route, Japan shares many cultural features with the races along this grand migration route, including the Fox-Bear Cycle, which originated and still thrives in northern Europe.

The warm tides washing the shores of Japan suggest another far-reaching route of diffusion. Because many Japanese myths and legends correspond to those of ancient Greece, there is a strong possibility of an overseas route that connected the two areas by way of ports of call dotting the southern fringe of the Eurasian continent.

Again there are Japanese tales and legends that are shared by cultures on the perimeter of the Pacific Ocean. This circumpacific diffusion route follows the Japan Current, which circulates clockwise about the Pacific, north from Taiwan along the east coast of Japan, then across to the western shores of North and South America, and returns west through the Southern Pacific Ocean.

With the advent of the Yayoi period (ca 300 BC — ca AD 300), an entirely new sort of culture complex came into Japan from the southern part of Korea. A considerable number of migrants arrived with the technology of rice cultivation, weaving, the use of iron tools, bronze weapons, dolmens, pot coffins, and the making of Yayoi pottery. Yayoi culture flourished in northern Kyushu for some time and then spread eastward. From about the 3rd to the 5th centuries, the present emperor's ancestors consolidated their power in central Honshu. The *Kojiki* and *Nihon shoki* trace the imperial family history back to the mythical era and incorporate many preexistent tale motifs.

With the introduction of writing and Buddhism to Japan, first from Korea and then directly from China, Japanese folk literature gained yet another overland route to sources in Central Asia and down to India through Tibet. Tales recorded in the *Nihon ryoiki* and *Konjaku monogatari* belong to this group.

Well-known folktales of Japan include "Peach Boy"(Momotaro), "The Wen Removed" (Kobutori jijii), "The Tongue-Cut Sparrow" (Shitakiri suzume), and "Kachikachi Mountain" (Kachikachi yama). Standardization of the repertory and form of tales is chiefly the result of compulsory schooling since the 1870s, when government-compiled textbooks were used uniformly throughout Japan. The textbook adapted several popular folktales from chapbooks for children published during the Edo period (1600 – 1868).

Fine Arts

Art

(Nihon *bijutsu*). Over the centuries, a wide variety of social, economic, political, cultural, and environmental factors have had an influence on the development of Japanese art. The temperate climate and four distinct seasons provided an abundance of seasonal symbols and motifs, such as the plum, the cherry, the maple, and the chrysanthemum, which appear again and again in Japanese art. The Japanese love of nature is reflected in the use of such raw materials as lacquer, wood, bamboo, and paper throughout Japanese architecture. The high humidity and frequent earthquakes and typhoons common to Japan discouraged the use of more permanent materials such as stone in architecture and ensured the preference for the more readily mendable and available materials that dominate the Japanese aesthetic.

At the same time, the influence of China, whose culture rests at the heart of East Asian creativity, was particularly felt in Japan; Chinese artistic styles and larger segments of Chinese culture, including the great international tradition of Buddhist art, reached Japan either directly or filtered through the Korean peninsula. Even the famous secular style of the Heian court (794 – 1185) received notable inspiration from continental shores.

Despite Japan's contact with and absorption of foreign aesthetics from prehistoric times to the present, Japanese art had little, if any, influence on outside cultures, especially Western cultures, until the last half of the 19th century, when European artists discovered its beauties and developed a passion for *japonaiserie*. Exposure to and consciousness of Japanese art through, for example, Japanese ceramics and woodblock prints played a major role in the development of a modern European painting aesthetic, as well as influencing the aesthetic course of the decorative arts. Present-day Japanese artists are making an increasingly active contribution to the development of contemporary international art.

Buddhist art

(Bukkyo *bijutsu*). Like Japanese Buddhism itself, Japanese Buddhist art was a national variant of an international tradition. In Japan the Buddhist art forms that were periodically introduced from China and Korea were tempered in the crucible of local custom and usage, to yield a rich tradition of religious art and architecture.

The Buddhist Mainstream

Buddhism was formally transmitted to Japan from China and Korea in the 6th century. The forms of Buddhism and Buddhist art that first arrived in Japan were chiefly those of the Mahāyāna (J: Daijo Bukkyo) tradition, a theistic and catholic system of belief that stressed universal salvation and that was to remain the underlying framework of most sects of Buddhist belief and practice in Japan through the modern era.

From its inception Buddhism in Japan engaged the concern and patronage of ruling interests and became virtually a state creed. Temples and monastic compounds usually consisted of at least seven typical structures, including a *to* (pagoda), a main hall called the *kondo* ("golden hall"), a lecture hall called the *kodo*, and a *kyozo* or sutra repository. They were built as the seats of Buddhist worship and instruction. In the first wave of such construction, numerous temples were erected from the late 6th to the early 7th century in what is now the Kyoto-Osaka region, most notably Asukadera, Shitennoji, and Horyuji. After Heijokyo (Nara) was designated the national capital in 710, a new wave of temple construction in the early 8th century produced the great Nara-period (710 – 794) metropolitan monasteries, among them Kofukuji, Daianji, and Yakushiji.

A tremendous amount of Buddhist art was commissioned for the halls and chapels of these temple complexes. Paintings and sculptures representing various Buddhas, bodhisattvas, and guardian deities were the icons to which worship and ritual were directed.

The construction of Todaiji from 747 marked the apex of classical Buddhist art and architecture in Japan. The temple's *honzon*, or principal object of worship, is a colossal gilt-bronze image—measuring some 15 meters (49 ft) in height—of the cosmic Buddha called Birushana (Skt: Vairocana). A technical feat, this giant sculpture—called the Nara Daibutsu ("Great Buddha of Nara")—came to symbolize the power, wealth, and intrusiveness of state-sanctioned Buddhism.

Esoteric Buddhism

In part as a reaction to the state Buddhism symbolized by Todaiji and the Nara Daibutsu, a new regime moved the capital to Heiankyo (now Kyoto) in 794. Largely coincidental with this move was the emergence into prominence of *mikkyo*, "the secret teachings," a system of esoteric Buddhist belief and practice that was to be articulated in the Shingon sect and the Tendai sect.

The Buddha Dainichi (Skt: Mahāvairocana), a cosmic force that was already evident in Buddhist ideology by the time of the Nara Daibutsu, became the organizing principle of esoteric Buddhism and the focus of worship. Esotericism also involved a vastly enhanced pantheon of deities, many culled from non-Buddhist traditions, and an increased emphasis on elaborate ritual as a means of harnessing the power inherent in this pantheon.

Key to Shingon and Tendai practice were the paired mandalas of the Diamond or Thunderbolt Realm and the Matrix or Womb Realm, together referred to as the "Two Mandalas."

The paintings and sculptures that filled Shingon and Tendai temples, in keeping with their function as iconic representations of esoteric deities, displayed an aesthetic and stylistic tenor appropriate to the mystery of ritual and meditation at a remote temple in mountain setting. An important example of this tendency is seen in the 9th-century set of five statues of the Bodhisattvas of the Void (Go Dai Kokuzo Bosatsu), each in painted wood, at Jingoji. Also coincidental with the development of esotericism was a trend in sculpture toward the carving of votive statues out of single blocks of wood, their surfaces left unadorned with paint or lacquer in deference to the inherent sanctity of the sacred tree (*shimboku*). The principal examples of this "plain wood" style are the Yakushi figures at Gangoji (early 9th century) and at Jingoji (ca 783).

Pure Land Buddhism

Even though esotericism remained a major element in Japanese religious life, by the close of the 10th century it had begun to give way as a system of popular belief to Pure Land faith and practice. In the Pure Land tradition worship focused on the Buddha Amida (Skt: Amitābha) and on rebirth in his Western Paradise, or Pure Land, called Gokuraku (Skt: Sukhāvatī).

A celebrated example of Pure Land art and aesthetics is the *amidado* (Amida hall), now called the Phoenix Hall (Hoodo), at Byodoin in Uji, which was constructed in 1053 by Fujiwara no Yorimichi (992—1074), who, with his father, Fujiwara no Michinaga (966—1028), was one of the great patrons of Pure Land Buddhism and art. Like other temples of its day, which were much influenced by descriptions in Pure Land scripture of Amida's palatial residence, Byodoin was at the same time a detached residence in the *shinden-zukuri* mode, where Yorimichi might live as well as pray.

One of the principal treatises of Japanese Pure Land Buddhism—one that had a major impact on art production—was a work by the Tendai monk Genshin (Eshin Sozu; 942—1017) called *Ojoyoshu* (985, The Essentials of Pure Land Rebirth), in which was set forth an exhaustive account of Amida's nine sectors of paradise and the nine degrees of rebirth (*kubon ojo*) therein.

In painting, a key Pure Land genre was the so-called *raigozu* ("welcoming pictures"), in which Amida and his heavenly entourage are shown arriving to welcome and guide the dying to paradise. The raigozu genre was heavily influenced by Genshin's work. An important example is the mid-12th-century triptych *Amida shoju raigozu* (Descent of Amida and the Heavenly Multitude) at Mt. Koya.

In *Ojoyoshu* Genshin did not limit his discussion to paradise; the first part of this treatise provides a horrific vision of the six realms of existence (*rokudo*), and especially various hells, as a means to awakening faith and penitence. This, too, was reflected in contemporary Pure Land painting, particularly in the *emakimono* format; by the 12th century an imagery of hell and karmic retribution was fully developed. Celebrated examples of this genre are the *Gaki-zoshi* (Scrolls of Hungry Ghosts) and *Jigoku-zoshi* (Scrolls of Hells). Another *emakimono* genre, that of temple histories (*engi*) and biographies of saints and monks, was also developed. An example of this popular genre is *Shigisan engi emaki* (The Legends of Mt. *Shigi*).

Zen Buddhism

In the 13th century the Zen (Ch: Chan) sect, disseminated by Japanese and Chinese monks, took hold among the ruling military elites and introduced new currents in art. Zen monasteries, such as Kenchoji and Engakuji, emerged as both seats of religious discourse and centers for the secular cultural activities for which the Zen monks became increasingly known: literary studies, poetry, painting, and calligraphy.

Zen temples were strongly continental in flavor and differed significantly from the architectural models used in other sects. Layout, nomenclature, furnishings, and even structural details were derived from the Buddhist architecture of south central China. The typical Zen monastic compound, especially the semiautonomous subtemple known as *tatchu*, usually incorporated a carefully composed small garden. In keeping with the austerity of Zen taste, some of these gardens, in a format called "rock and sand garden" (*karesansui*), were landscaped without the standard pond or stream; the flow of water was evoked through the raking of smooth sand and gravel.

The impact of Zen aesthetics and doctrine was by no means limited to the monastic compound. The development of a pure landscape painting genre in Japan, as well as the emergence of a mature *suibokuga* (ink painting) tradition, owes much to the influence of Zen and Zen monk-painters.

Buddhism under the Tokugawa Shogunate

The spread of Neo-Confucian orthodoxy in China and Korea also affected Japan, where the unifying ideology of the Tokugawa shogunate (1603—1867) and its widespread educational system constituted an official state Confucianism. As Buddhism lost its centrality to politics and culture, Buddhist art gave way to secular forms, although Buddhist values remained visible in much of Japanese taste and aesthetics.

The arts, however, were not entirely devoid of Buddhist genres. While not organized into a formal school, the tradition of the Zen monk—amateur painter flourished to the end of the 19th century and has recently been given the name *zenga*, "Zen painting."

Painting

(*kaiga*). Japanese painting is characterized by a wide range of styles in a wide array of formats, from horizontal and hanging scrolls to album leaves, fans, walls, and free-standing and sliding screens. Like the history of Japanese art in general, Japanese painting has been dominated by two components, continental and indigenous, in the development of style and technique.

PREMODERN PAINTING

Until the 19th century, China was the principal source of innovation. Much of the history of painting in premodern Japan can be described as a dialogue between Chinese and native styles.

Painting through the Nara Period (710—794)

The origins of painting in Japan can be traced to the simple stick figures found on Yayoi-period (ca 300 BC—ca AD 300) bells and the murals, both geometric and figural, on the inner walls of Kofun-period (ca 300—710) tombs. With the introduction of Buddhism and Buddhist culture from Korea and China in the 6th century, painting began to flourish as the production of Buddhist art and architecture became a major concern of the ruling class.

A number of paintings from the late 7th and early 8th centuries are preserved at the temple Horyuji. In Horyuji's museum a votive shrine called the Tamamushi Shrine, or "Beetle-Wing Shrine," bears a series of 7th-century paintings on its panels, whose bronze filigree frames were backed originally by the iridescent wings of the *tamamushi* beetle. These paintings illustrate episodes from the life of the Buddha as well as depicting figures of bodhisattvas and other deities. Their style of execution is reminiscent of painting styles in late-Six-Dynasties (222—589) China.

Painting of the Heian (794— 1185) and Kamakura (1185— 1333) Periods

With the rise in the early 9th century of esoteric Buddhism as developed by the Shingon sect and the Tendai sect, the painted mandala emerged into prominence. Important examples of this genre are the Diamond Realm (*Kongokai*) and Womb Realm (*Taizokai*) mandalas, dated 824—833, at the temple Jingoji, and the 11th-century *Kojima Mandala* at Kojimadera in Nara. The five-story pagoda at Daigoji, constructed in 952, contains a number of murals depicting various esoteric deities in a mandala format.

After the 10th century, the influence of Pure Land Buddhism—popularized by the Jodo sect and its predecessors—became increasingly apparent in painting. An important new genre was the *raigozu*, a depiction of the Buddha Amida arriving to welcome the dying to paradise.

By the mid-Heian period, Chinese modes of painting (*kara-e*) had begun to give way to a distinctly indigenous style known as *yamato-e*. The earliest paintings in this style were sliding screens and folding screens. Two new painting formats evolved as the native style was developed: the album leaf (*soshi*) and the illuminated handscroll (*emakimono*).

Painting of the Muromachi Period (1333— 1568)

During the 14th century, scroll painting declined as *suibokuga*, or ink painting, took hold in the great Zen monasteries of Kamakura and Kyoto. An austere monochrome style, introduced from Song (960— 1279) and Yuan (1279—1368) China, was favored by Zen painters and their patrons. The styles of the Chinese monk-painters Muqi (J: *Mokkei*; fl ca 1250) and Liang Kai (1140?—1210?) were particularly influential.

By the end of the 14th century, a monochrome landscape painting genre had emerged as the preferred medium among Zen painters and their Ashikaga family patrons in Kyoto. Artists whose works helped form the landscape genre include Mincho (1352—1431) and Josetsu (early 15th century). During the 15th century, Tensho Shubun (d ca 1460) and Sesshu Toyo (1420—1506) developed the Chinese-inspired monochrome landscape style into a fully Japanese format. A key work by Sesshu is *Amanohashidate* (ca 1501, Kyoto National Museum), which depicts the famous scenic spot of that name.

In the last years of Ashikaga rule, a new genre of ink painting was developed largely outside the Zen community by artists of the Ami school and the Kano school. The Kano school was initiated by the layman painter Kano Masanobu (1434—1530) and continued by his son Kano Motonobu (1476—1559). Although Chinese styles and themes remained their model, Kano-school artists introduced a more decorative and plastic sensibility that would come to dominate the landscape painting of the succeeding centuries.

Painting of the Azuchi-Momoyama (1568—1600) and Edo (1600—1868) Periods

The Kano school, promoted by Oda Nobunaga (1534—1582), Toyotomi Hideyoshi (1537—1598), and other powerful patrons, dominated painting in the late 16th century and developed a grandiose polychromed style for screen and wall painting. Kano Eitoku (1543—1590) was commissioned by Nobunaga to decorate Azuchi Castle (1576—1579; destroyed 1582) near Lake Biwa and by Hideyoshi to decorate Jurakudai Palace (1587; destroyed 1595) in Kyoto. Eitoku is believed to be the first painter to have introduced the dramatic use of fields of gold leaf in large mural compositions. Eitoku's pupil and adopted son Kano Sanraku (1559—1635) continued this style into the early Edo period. By the time that Eitoku's grandson Kano Tan'yu (1602—1674) was active, the Kano school was firmly established as the painting academy of the Tokugawa shogunate (1603—1867).

Another genre, one belonging to the yamato-e tradition, was developed by painters of the Tosa school, whose small-scale works often illustrated the literary classics of earlier generations. The yamato-e tradition also gave rise to the decorative painters of the group called Rimpa. The principal artists of this school were Tawaraya Sotatsu (d 1643?) and Ogata Korin (1658—1716), whose works—taking classical styles and themes and presenting them in a new, boldly decorative format—have come to symbolize the lavish tastes of Edo (now Tokyo) society in the 17th and 18th centuries.

Fuzokuga, or genre paintings, became popular in the late 16th century and gave rise to *ukiyo-e*, "paintings of the floating world," which captured the transient experiences of the pleasure quarters of Edo and other urban centers. The woodblock print as a significant Edo-period medium emerged out of this tradition.

The late Edo period was one of eclecticism in painting. The influence of European painting, earlier represented by the "southern barbarian" *namban* art of the late 16th century, was increasingly apparent. The port city of Nagasaki acted as the conduit for both Chinese and Western influence in painting. Major artists of this period include Maruyama Okyo (1733−1795) and Matsumura Goshun (1752−1811), founders of the Maruyama-Shijo school, and Ito Jakuchu (1716−1800). The works of these painters show a mixture of Japanese, Chinese, and Western elements and often evidence a heightened concern with naturalistic depiction.

Another major trend in late-Edo-period painting was that of *bunjinga*, "literati painting," whose artists took their inspiration from a tradition of Chinese scholar−amateur painters who, since the Yuan dynasty, had worked in a style called *nanga* ("Southern painting"). This style entered Japan in the 18th century via Nagasaki, where it was introduced by Chinese immigrant painters and described in Chinese painting manuals.

MODERN PAINTING

During the Meiji period (1868−1912), political and social change was effected in the course of a modernization campaign by the new government. Western-style painting (*yoga*) was promoted officially, and a number of painters such as Harada Naojiro (1863−1899), Yamamoto Hosui (1850−1906), and Asai Chu (1856−1907) traveled abroad for study under government auspices. However, the initial burst of enthusiasm for Western art soon yielded to renewed appreciation of traditional Japanese art, promoted by the art critic Okakura Kakuzo (1862−1913) and the American educator Ernest Fenollosa (1853−1908). Japanese-style painting (*nihonga*) rose to prominence as its conservative advocates gained control of art institutions. By the 1880s, Western-style painters were barred from exhibitions and widely criticized.

Confronted by the resurgence of traditionalism, Western-style painters formed the Meiji Bijutsukai (Meiji Fine Arts Society) and began to hold their own exhibitions. Prominent among these painters was Kuroda Seiki (also known as Kuroda Kiyoteru; 1866−1924), who introduced pleinairism and established the influential White Horse Society (Hakubakai).

Painting of the Taisho Period (1912−1926)

The Taisho period saw burgeoning Western influence in the arts. After long stays in Europe the painters Yamashita Shintaro (1881−1966), Saito Yori (1885−1959), and Arishima Ikuma (1882−1974) introduced impressionism and early features of the postimpressionist movement to Japan; Yasui Sotaro (1888—1955) and Umehara Ryuzaburo (1888—1986), whose careers would span the modern period, returned to promote the styles of Camille Pissarro, Paul Cézanne, and Pierre Auguste Renoir. The eclecticism that informed Taisho-period painting came as a direct result of the rapid infusion of the full range of contemporary European styles.

Although on a limited scale, Japanese-style painting too was affected by European styles, especially neoclassicism and, later, postimpressionism. Modernizing trends first appeared among second-generation nihonga members of the Japan Fine Arts Academy (Nihon Bijutsuin), which had been reorganized in 1914 to compete with the Bunten. Its founding members, Yokoyama Taikan (1868—1958), Shimomura Kanzan (1873—1930), and Hishida Shunso (1874—1911), all to some degree adopted Western-style atmospheric treatment of space and light, for which they were called the Moroha ("Dim and Hazy school"). The second wave of academy painters, while emphasizing yamato-e traditions, embraced certain features of postimpressionism.

Painting of the Showa Period (1926—1989)

The painters Yasui Sotaro and Umehara Ryuzaburo stood at the forefront of pre-World War II Showa painting. In recognition of their importance, the period 1925—40 is termed the "Yasui-Umehara era." While incorporating notions of pure art and abstraction, both succeeded in surmounting the heretofore largely derivative character of Western-style painting in Japan. Umehara in particular brought aspects of the nihonga tradition to his work and launched Western-style painting on a more interpretative path.

However, neither artist completely dominated Western-style painting of the 1930s. A far more international contemporary of Yasui and Umehara was Fujita Tsuguharu (also known as Fujita Tsuguji, Léonard Foujita; 1886—1968). The Nika Society widened its sphere of influence by absorbing surrealism and abstractionism, and the essentially fauvist Dokuritsu Bijutsu Kyokai (Independent Art Association) was formed in 1931.

Prominent painters' circles formed during the late Taisho and early Showa periods, such as the Nika Society, weathered the war years to emerge as leading interests among painters today. The government-subsidized Japan Art Academy (Nihon Geijutsuin) was formed in 1947 and contains both yoga and nihonga divisions. Government-sponsored art exhibitions like the Bunten have disappeared, replaced by privately sponsored exhibitions on a large scale. The Nitten (Nihon Bijutsu Tenrankai; Japan Art Exhibition) in particular has functioned as the modern counterpart of the Bunten. Initially the exhibition of the Japan

Art Academy, the Nitten since 1958 has been run by a corporation, Nitten, Inc. Exhibition of works in the Nitten can lead to membership in the Japan Art Academy and, for a few, decoration with the Order of Culture. Only a handful of non-Nitten artists have received this award, among them Munakata Shiko (1903–1975).

Today Japanese artists are active members of a worldwide artistic community. By the 1960s, avant-garde notions of art had been embraced, and an internationalization of Japanese art followed. Postwar trends in the West have been taken up rapidly in Japan, from the abstract expressionism of the 1950s to later developments such as the antiart movement, assemblage, pop and op art, primary structure, minimal art, and kinetic art. After a largely derivative past, modern Japanese painters have emerged as significant contributors to international movements in art.

Ukiyo-e

(literally, "pictures of the floating world"). A genre of art, chiefly in the medium of the woodblock print, that arose early in the Edo period (1600–1868) and built up a broad popular market among the middle classes. Subject matter tended to focus on the brothel districts and the *kabuki* theaters, and formats ranged from single-sheet prints and greeting cards to albums and book illustrations. Ukiyo-e flourished throughout Japan, attaining their most characteristic form in the prints produced in Edo (now Tokyo) from about 1680 to the 1850s.

Early Ukiyo-e

The distinctive milieu from which ukiyo-e would emerge was flourishing as early as the Kan'ei era (1624–1644). Genre paintings (*fuzokuga*) of the time depict pleasure seekers of every social class thronging the entertainment district beside the river Kamogawa in Kyoto. It was in such districts, in Kyoto, Osaka, and Edo, that there developed the freewheeling way of life of the *ukiyo*, or "floating world," and the genre of art, ukiyo-e, that glorified it.

Sex manuals (*shunga*; literally, "spring pictures") and courtesan critiques (*yujo hyobanki*) were among the earliest types of printed ukiyo-e. Shunga were either books or albums that depicted highly explicit love scenes, though rarely are couples completely naked. Few of the sex manuals from the 1660s and early 1670s have survived and none are signed; the earliest attributions are to Hishikawa Moronobu and Sugimura Jihei, who were active in the late 17th century, and thereafter shunga remained a genre at which most ukiyo-e artists tried their hand. The critiques of courtesans, essentially picture books with commentary, contained stylized portraits of the leading courtesans of the day, engaged in some casual activity such as reading or adjusting their hair. The interest of such scenes is chiefly in the poses and the draping of *kimono*. A similar type of picture was the *bijin-e* ("beautiful-woman picture"), in which courtesans of the highest rank (*tayu*) were depicted, often with their entourages. Pictures of courtesans remained popular throughout the history of ukiyo-e; the Kaigetsudo school (early 18th century) of ukiyo-e painters rarely turned to any other subject, and many of Kitagawa Utamaro's most memorable prints were of these stylish beauties.

Edo Ukiyo-e

By the late 17th century, the center of ukiyo-e had shifted from Kamigata (the Kyoto-Osaka area) to Edo, where the single-sheet print, probably initially intended for mounting on scrolls (*kakemono-e*), seems to have become a specialty in the closing years of the Genroku era (1688–1704).

A woman portrayed by Utamaro.

It was the development of the single-sheet print, however, that marked a turning point in the history of ukiyo-e, the coming of age of which was closely joined to that of kabuki. A major role in the development of kabuki was played by Ichikawa Danjuro I, who invented a bombastic style of acting known as *aragoto* that became immensely popular in Edo. Portrayals of actors (*yakusha-e*) in popular roles had already become standard subject matter of ukiyo-e, but it was the Torii school that achieved the greatest success in rendering the pyrotechnics of an aragoto performance in graphic terms. Torii Kiyonobu I and Torii Kiyomasu I perfected a style that, with its vigorous use of line and robust forms, was particularly appropriate for theatrical subjects, and their school soon acquired a virtual monopoly over commissions in Edo for painted theatrical posters (*kamban*) and illustrated program notes (*ebanzuke*). The finest of the Torii school prints, recording a pose or entrance popularized by a particular actor, are in the large *kakemono-e* format, and provided a visual catalog of theatrical conventions that reinforced kabuki tradition. A separate theatrical print style arose in Osaka.

Later ukiyo-e, especially those of Utagawa Toyoharu, included landscapes. Another important ukiyo-e artist of the second quarter of the 18th century was Nishikawa Sukenobu, a native of Kyoto, whose illustrated books presenting scenes from daily life or from classical poetry gained extraordinary popularity throughout the country. His work displayed a delicacy that set it apart from Edo ukiyo-e of the time and influenced the subsequent development of the genre.

Color Prints

In about 1745, a technique was conceived for registering successive blocks, each printing a different color on a single sheet. The resulting prints, called *benizuri-e* (pictures printed in red) because the most striking color was a red derived from the petals of the safflower (*benibana*), were produced only in two or three colors. It was not until 1764 that the first full-color prints appeared, a development that is closely associated with the sudden popularity of the work of Suzuki Harunobu. By 1766 almost every ukiyo-e artist was working in Harunobu's style. These new prints, called *nishiki-e* (brocade pictures) or *edo-e* (Edo pictures), represented the final stage of technical advancement in color printing achieved in the Edo period.

The stylistic revolution brought about by the development of full-color printing soon affected the traditional genre of yakusha-e. From about 1770, in the work of the major innovators Katsukawa Shunsho and Ippitsusai Buncho, actors were for the first time presented as individuals with distinctive features, whereas previously they could be distinguished only by the crest (*mon*) on their kimono. Shunsho had particular influence as the teacher of Katsukawa Shun'ei and Katsushika Hokusai, and the changes he set in motion laid the foundation for the work of Toshusai Sharaku.

In the 1770s poets of kyoka, a type of comic verse, and artists began to collaborate in the production of some extraordinarily handsome books combining kyoka with ukiyo-e illustrations. The success of these works, particularly Utamaro's *Ehon mushi erami* (1788, Insect Book), helped give rise to surimono. Popular in the 1790s, surimono, which combined kyoka or *haikai* and ukiyo-e, were prints that were produced on commission and issued in limited editions for use as announcements, invitations, or gifts. The printing was quite elegant, making frequent use of burnished metallic pigments and of embossing, which gave texture and depth to the surface of prints. Some kyoka poets also wrote *kibyoshi* and *sharebon* stories, which were customarily illustrated by ukiyo-e artists.

The Golden Age of Ukiyo-e

The late 18th century was largely a period of consolidation rather than innovation; however, development of the more generous *oban* format and the introduction of diptychs and triptychs led to more complex composition. After 1790, ukiyo-e images acquired a new intensity and styles began to succeed one another with greater rapidity. Utamaro and Sharaku achieved a heightened closeness to their subjects by using the format of the *okubi-e* or bust portrait: Utamaro's women are extremely sensuous and the masculinity of Sharaku's female impersonators (*onnagata*) infuses his portrayals. Utamaro was one of the first to isolate his figures against a brilliant mica background, and did so with a flair that other artists of the time, among them Hosoda Eishi and

Utagawa Toyokuni, only rarely managed to equal.

After 1800, there appears to have been a radical change in taste, accompanied by a faltering of inspiration in design and a deterioration in the quality of printing. Short figures with hunched shoulders and sharp features replaced the tall, elegant figures of the 1770s and 1780s, kimono patterns became coarser and more strident, and pictures of actors tended toward the exaggerated and grotesque. One reason for this was change in the print-buying public, which had grown larger and presumably less discriminating, resulting in prints that were produced hastily—many showing faulty registration of colors—and in great numbers.

Landscape

The emergence of the landscape print was a relatively late phenomenon in the history of ukiyo-e. Prior to Hokusai's *Fugaku sanjurokkei* (1823, Thirty-Six Views of Mount Fuji), landscape as independent subject matter for ukiyo-e was largely unknown. Other artists soon followed Hokusai's lead, and landscape achieved a popularity that rivaled the established genres of portraiture. Active as an artist for some 60 years, Hokusai developed a style that was highly individual, combining Chinese and Western influences with elements drawn from the native Kano school, the Tosa school, and the Rimpa tradition. He was also a prolific draftsman who employed a variety of techniques to create the astounding array of images in his famous 13-volume *Hokusai manga* (1814−1849, Hokusai's Sketches).

Hokusai's only true rival in landscape was Ando Hiroshige, whose great *Tokaido gojusantsugi* (1833−1834, The Fifty-Three Stations of the Tokaido Road) brought him fame and a host of imitators. Hiroshige displays in this and other works a greater concern than Hokusai with atmosphere, light, and weather. Drawing on the style of certain of the landscape paintings of the Southern Song dynasty (1127−1279), his work was also influenced by the contemporaneous Maruyama-Shijo school and by Western realism.

As an integral element of the Edo-period culture that it mirrored, ukiyo-e was unable to survive that society's demise in the wake of the radical Westernization that transformed Japan during the Meiji period (1868−1912).

Ceramics

(*tojiki*). Ceramics in Japan has a long history, stretching over 12,000 years. The Japanese archipelago is abundantly supplied with the raw material for ceramics, and an appreciation for clay and its multitude of possible uses has been a steady force in Japanese culture for millennia.

In the development of ceramic materials, China was the great innovator, and all of Japan's advanced technology came directly or indirectly from there; more often than not, China also set the style. Yet also typical of Japan's attitude toward ceramics was the fact that, while newer wares representing advanced technology might be accorded a position of highest status, they by no means obliterated existing wares and techniques, which for the most part continued unaffected. As a result, Japanese ceramics became steadily richer in variety, and the ceramic articles produced in Japan today cover the full range from earthenware directly descended from neolithic precedents to the most demanding Chinese-style glazed wares.

Early Earthenware

It seems to have been almost 12,000 years ago that people in Japan began to use sedimentary clay to form vessels. Jomon Pottery, characterized by its "cord-impressed" patterns, dates from as early as 10,000 BC. Its earliest forms resemble deep cylindrical baskets with pointed bottoms.

With the introduction of rice cultivation to Japan in the succeeding Yayoi period (ca 300 BC–ca AD 300), the heavy, elaborate Jomon style gave way to the smooth, thin, symmetrical, minimally ornamented Yayoi style. The change reflected a shift of habitation centers from highlands to river deltas where rice was grown: whereas Jomon clay is usually stiff, requiring considerable temper, and too coarse to take a fine finish, pots of the Yayoi period are formed from the plastic, fine-grained clay found in such deltas. Whereas ceramics in the Jomon period seems to have been the primary form of artistic expression, Yayoi culture had access to other materials introduced from the continent—most significantly bronze—and this is reflected in the pottery. Certain design elements in Yayoi pots, such as raised horizontal ridges, suggest the aesthetic influence of cast metal.

Sue and *Haji* Wares

During the Kofun period (ca 300–710) influences from the Korean peninsula wrought radical changes in Japanese culture and technology. By the mid-5th century a method of making high-fired stoneware ceramics known as sue ware had been introduced and was rapidly developed by Korean craftsmen residing in what are now the Nara and Osaka regions, eventually superseding earthenware in production and status. Sue vessels, produced in through-draft or tunnel kilns (*anagama*), were of superior quality for storing liquids.

Earthenware, however, now known as haji ware, remained indispensable for cooking purposes and also for ritual. Pottery grave goods, such as portable clay stoves and tall flanged pots, were placed in the conspicuous aboveground tombs (*kofun*) after which the period is named, and by the 6th century elaborate grave offerings of metal weapons and armor had been replaced with pottery replicas. Clay cylinders, or *haniwa*, were arranged around raised tomb mounds; eventually these cylinders were rendered as figurines and placed atop the tombs.

Medieval Ceramics

Under the patronage of the Kamakura shogunate (1192 – 1333) and Zen temples, Seto began by copying newly introduced Southern Song (1127 – 1279) Chinese forms—four-eared jars, flasks, ewers—with amber or green ash glaze applied over carved, stamped, or sprigged designs. By the 14th century Seto had also perfected use of the iron-brown *temmoku* glaze inspired by brown-glazed teabowls brought back from China.

Seto kilns reached their peak in the mid-15th century, but their development was cut short by the outbreak of the Onin War (1467 – 1477). The center for glazed wares shifted to Mino (now part of Gifu Prefecture), which had also produced first sue, then Sanage-type, and finally Seto-type glazed wares. At the beginning of the 16th century a change occurred in the kiln, as the through-draft or tunnel kiln introduced with sue ware was replaced by the larger, more reliable *ogama* ("great kiln"). Efforts to imitate porcelains from Ming (1368 – 1644) China led to the development of the opaque, white feldspathic glaze with underglaze iron decoration that became popular as Shino ware late in the century.

Although glazed as well as unglazed wares continued to be produced at Seto, Mino, and other medieval kilns, from the 12th through the 16th century the principal Japanese ceramic product was a sturdy, unglazed stoneware, called *yakishime* or *sekki*, that was made in a limited set of shapes primarily for utilitarian storage. The most important kilns to produce this type of stoneware were those at Tokoname in Owari (now part of Aichi Prefecture). Potters used the clay without alteration, employing simple coiling and scraping construction methods. Tokoname potters probably also spread the medieval kiln (a variation of the tunnel kiln but at a steeper angle and with a flame-diverting pillar behind the firebox) and encouraged the shift from reduction to oxidation firing. The Tokoname kilns were part of the so-called Owari kiln group, which also included Seto and Sanage and which manufactured a full range of ceramics for its clients.

With the growing commercial significance of ceramics in the Muromachi period (1333 – 1568), when unglazed stonewares in particular emerged as valuable sources of cash income, potters became more professional as output increased. Beginning with tea jars, everyday wares began to be glazed, resulting in further improvements in kiln structure. Mino potters were most influential in dispersing glazing technology to stoneware kilns.

Nevertheless, the same kilns that were striving to develop glazes were also influenced by the interest of the tea masters in unglazed pieces (particularly in ceramics imported from Southeast Asia, known as *namban* ware) for use as tea ceremony vessels. This interest reflected an increasing appreciation of simplicity and rusticity, aesthetic values that came to a peak in the tea ceremony school founded by Sen no Rikyu (1522−1591). Bizen produced the outstanding early pieces in this mode. Around 1600 the conscious manipulation at the Iga kilns of the features of unglazed medieval stonewares, including "natural" ash glaze, represented the epitome of the artificial naturalism espoused by many tea ceremony adherents.

Edo-Period Ceramics

The Edo period (1600−1868) saw a continuation of innovative stylistic and technological developments in stonewares and in glazed and unglazed ceramics—fueled not only by the aesthetic tastes of tea masters but also by the by-now-enormous commercial market for pottery. Innovations involved not only the popular decorated wares, such as Shino ware, Oribe ware, and Karatsu ware, but also the more austere wares, such as Raku ware, Iga ware, and Bizen ware, which underwent more subtle changes in form and design.

Japan's Invasions of Korea in 1592 and 1597 gave military leaders the opportunity to bring Korean potters, with their superior skills of throwing and glazing, to Japan to work in their domains. The introduction from Korea of the *noborigama* ("climbing kiln") revolutionized the firing of stonewares and made possible the successful firing of porcelain after suitable clays were discovered in the Arita area of northern Kyushu by Korean potters in the early 17th century.

The desire to make porcelain had been stirred by imported Ming porcelains, and Chinese ware had provided the earliest models, but by the mid-17th century a second crucial influence was added in the form of the European market. The Dutch East India Company not only placed enormous orders but also provided explicit models. Special preference was accorded an Arita-produced decorated ware called Kakiemon ware, which was characterized by application of polychrome enamels and underglaze cobalt to a milk-white porcelain body.

An Edo-period Kakiemon bowl.

The second half of the 17th century saw the full flowering of such decorated wares. Colorful Imari ware and Kakiemon ware were shipped to Europe from Kyushu in great quantities; the finer Kakiemon and Nabeshima ware porcelains were reserved for local rulers. In Kyoto, a popular form of decorated earthenware or stoneware known as kyo-yaki was developed by such potter-decorators as Nonomura Ninsei (fl mid-17th century) and Ogata Kenzan (1666–1743). Only isolated ventures, such as Himetani ware and Kutani ware, attempted the production of porcelain in competition with the dominant kilns in Arita.

Modern Ceramics

The opening of Japan to the West brought new opportunities for ceramics export and the development of porcelain centers at Kyoto and Yokohama. Through the work of the German technician Gottfried Wagener (1831–1892) in Arita, Kyoto, and Tokyo, and through Japanese participation in international expositions in Europe and the United States, Western ceramic technology and taste were introduced. Major ceramic centers opened training laboratories and began the process of transforming the workshop into the factory.

Contemporary Japanese ceramics may be said to have begun shortly after 1900 with the emergence of the "studio potter" with an individual name and style. Although precedents for the artist-potter reached back in Kyoto as far as the Raku family, Nonomura Ninsei, or Ogata Kenzan, most traditional potters were anonymous artisans following precedents. The studio potter of the 20th century came to ceramics by choice rather than by birth, and the typical eclectic style was based on a strong knowledge of Japanese ceramic history. Itaya Hazan (1872–1963), for example, was trained as a sculptor, and Kitaoji Rosanjin (1883–1959) began making pottery to supply his own gourmet restaurant.

From 1926, the folk crafts movement led by Yanagi Muneyoshi (1889–1961) began to foster interest in the aesthetic value of traditional craftwork and skillfully made simple objects of daily use—among them ceramics. The potters Kawai Kanjiro (1890–1966) and Hamada Shoji (1894–1978) participated in this movement, and it was through the latter, who established his workshop in Mashiko, that the town became famous as a center of folk-style pottery.

Swords

(*nihonto*). The origins of the Japanese sword go back to the 8th century and the earliest development of steel in Japan. Japanese swords are particularly impressive because of the early technical mastery achieved in Japanese steelmaking and because of the elegant shape, lines, texture, and shades of color of the steel fabric. For more than 12 centuries the sword has had a spiritual significance for the Japanese; along with the mirror and jewels, it is one of the three Imperial Regalia.

Swordsmiths

The Japanese swordsmith was traditionally held in high regard. The earliest swordsmiths were often *yamabushi*, members of the Shugendo sect, who with their apprentices lived an austere and religiously dedicated life. The approximately 200 schools of Japanese swordsmith-artists were scattered throughout Japan, each with its own history and its own identifiable and surprisingly consistent blade characteristics that can be traced down through the centuries.

Forging

Iron-working technology was introduced to Japan from about the 3rd to the 5th century AD, and, as early as the 8th to 10th century, sword blades of high-quality steel were being made in Japan. After the steel was forged, the "skin steel" (*kawagane*) was some 10 to 20 times hammered into plates, which were then hardened, broken into coin-sized pieces, stacked, and welded. This hardened steel was later welded onto the surface of the less brittle inner steel (*shingane*). This repeated folding and welding gave the Japanese blade one of its unique qualities—a texture (*jihada*) like that of the grain of wood.

Tempering and Polishing

The *hamon*, or temper pattern of the blade, is one of the most noticeable and beautiful features of the sword and also an important means of identifying its origin. By the early Kamakura period (1185−1333), this hamon was made to exhibit many shapes and forms. Generally a specific type of temper or group of types was employed by an individual school or smith.

Jokoto (Ancient Sword) Period

Jokoto, or ancient swords, have come down to us almost exclusively from the ancient burial mounds of the Kofun period (ca 300−710) and are badly rusted. Swords preserved in the 8th-century Shosoin imperial art repository in Nara have been kept in nearly perfect condition for centuries. These ancient blades were nearly always straight, with a very small and sharply angled slanted point (*boshi*). Swords of the Nara period (710−794) and the early Heian period (794−1185) were similar to those found in the mounds. Being rather short and lightweight, they were probably used for thrusting rather than slashing.

Koto (Old Sword) Period

In the Muromachi period (1333−1568), as a result of prolonged strife and feudal combat, the production of swords increased in number but quality declined. Swords became somewhat heavier and less curved, wider and considerably shorter, so that they could cut through the heavier armor then coming into use. This new blade was called *katana* and was upward of 60 centimeters (2 ft) in length. It was soon accompanied by a somewhat shorter blade, *wakizashi*. The katana and wakizashi were worn thrust through the sash, edge up and parallel to or crossing each other in the sash. These swords were called *daisho*, "long and short."

Shinto (New Sword) Period

During the Azuchi-Momoyama (1568—1600) and Edo (1600—1868) periods individual swordsmiths founded new schools, and an interest developed in the largely lost skills of the Kamakura period. They attempted to copy the swords of the past but were restricted by the requirements of hand-to-hand combat. Many swords had extraordinarily brilliant tempering patterns, a substantial structure of well-hammered and well-tempered steel, and beautiful chiseled engravings (*horimono*) and grooves. Sword guards (*tsuba*) and other fittings (*koshirae*) for the *samurai*'s long and short swords and for daggers became highly ornate.

Modern Period

In 1868 the emperor Meiji promulgated regulations forbidding the making or wearing of swords but permitted a small number of smiths to continue their work in order to keep the art alive. A further quickening of interest occurred during the Russo-Japanese War of 1904—1905 and before and during World War II. For the most part these later military swords are not genuine art swords (nihonto) but are made from machine-made steel.

After World War II, the Allied Occupation forces ordered all swords destroyed, but the order was modified to exclude swords of artistic, religious, or spiritual significance belonging to museums, shrines, or private collections.

Folk crafts

(*mingei*). The term mingei refers to objects handcrafted for daily use, as well as to the movement begun by Yanagi Muneyoshi (1889—1961), who coined the term in 1926. Yanagi himself preferred to translate mingei as "folk crafts," which emphasizes the utilitarian aspect, rather than "folk arts," although both terms have been used.

The Folk Craft Movement

Collecting examples of folk crafts from the Korean Yi dynasty (1392—1910) led Yanagi to realize that the most beautiful objects were the products not of individual artists but of the collective genius of the Korean people. He concluded that the approach of modern European art history, which emphasized the creativity of individual artists, was inadequate in understanding mingei.

Instead, Yanagi turned his attention to the work of a Japanese priest, Mokujiki Gogyo (1718−1810), who had carved tens of thousands of rough Buddhist images while traveling throughout Japan. To Yanagi these figures, created in response to the hopes and aspirations of the masses, were more beautiful than the Buddhist images by famous sculptors displayed by great temples. Around this time Yanagi also discovered Tamba ware, with its rich patterns of glaze formed during firing from wood ash randomly falling and fusing with the ceramic surface. Reflecting on this process, he concluded that beauty was not the result of any conscious intent but was born of chance and the cumulative skill of generations of unknown artists. Yanagi saw this process as akin to the Buddhist concept of *tariki*, the attainment of salvation not through one's own merits but through complete reliance on the Buddha's mercy.

Based on these theories Yanagi coined the term mingei to differentiate between *bijutsu*, or fine art, which he saw as created for aesthetic appreciation alone, and *kogei*, or utilitarian craftwork made for practical use. Yanagi saw kogei as a broader term than mingei: kogei included objects made by machine and by individual artists, as well as "aristocratic" works. But he also claimed that the best of kogei belonged to the category of mingei. According to Yanagi, the character of kogei was defined, first, by *yo* (use or function): kogei objects must be simple and sturdy to function effectively. Second, kogei objects must be produced on a large scale at low prices. Third, the beauty of authentic kogei is created by anonymous laborers who have honed their skill by turning out large numbers of articles without thought of self-expression. Fourth, handcrafted kogei objects are superior to those made by machine.

History of Japanese Folk Crafts

Tracing the history of folk crafts following the canons laid down by Yanagi is difficult because so few examples survive. Some scholars consider the earthenware of the Jomon (ca 10,000 BC−ca 300 BC) and Yayoi (ca 300 BC−ca AD 300) periods to be the first folk art in Japan. The "six old kilns" (*roku koyo*) were established in Echizen, Shigaraki, Seto, Tokoname, Tamba, and Bizen during the Heian period (794−1185), each producing pottery with distinct local characteristics. However, pottery then was considered precious and rare. Most of what is today considered mingei survives from the Muromachi period (1333−1568). This is doubtless partly because the traditional Japanese style of living, as presently understood, became widely established at that time: the *shoin-zukuri* type of architecture was perfected, and techniques for making lacquer ware (*negoro-nuri*; *kamakura-bori*) and pottery were highly developed. This, along with increased production, led to wider distribution of articles. The popularization of the tea ceremony from the Muromachi period through the Azuchi-Momoyama period (1568−1600) was another important factor. Local pottery and textile producers flourished in the latter half of the Edo period (1600−1868). Many examples from this period can still be found, and they set the standards of beauty in Japanese folk crafts. By the early 20th century, however, with the introduction of synthetics and increasing reliance on machinery, folk crafts began to decline. Folk crafts in Yanagi's sense of the term have nearly become extinct in Japan.

However, folk traditions in a broader sense are thriving. Under the Cultural Properties Law of 1950 the concept of cultural assets (*bunkazai*) was revised and broadened, encouraging governmental participation in the preservation of folk knowledge, folk performing arts, games, and folk utensils (*mingu*) used for making clothing, food, and shelter and in trade or communal life.

Classification of Folk Crafts

Folk crafts are generally classified in the categories of ceramics; wood and bamboo articles; metal and leather objects; dyeing and weaving; paper; and painting, sculpture, and calligraphy.

With regard to the first category, the kilns of Okinawa produce various types of ceramics called Tsuboya ware. In Kyushu, such ceramics as Karatsu ware, Agano ware, and Takatori ware are produced by techniques learned from Korean potters. Imari ware is also famous for its excellent quality. Other superior ceramics are Koishiwara ware and Onta ware. In the Shikoku region, the only well-known ceramic ware is Tobe ware. In the Chugoku region, some of the most ancient Japanese kilns are found in Fushina, Ushinoto, and Bizen. The Kinki region is noted for Tamba ware, Kyoto ceramics, Shigaraki ware, and Iga ware. The Chubu region, largest of Japan's ceramics centers, is famous for Seto ware and Mino ware. The Kanto region produced unglazed pottery such as *imadoyaki*. The center of the folk crafts movement is Mashiko. Much pottery is also produced in the Tohoku region.

Wood and bamboo craftworks include lacquer work inlaid with gold from Okinawa; dolls from Hakata (Fukuoka Prefecture); lacquer ware and *ikkambari uchiwa* (fans made by painting lacquer over a paper frame) from Shikoku; *yanagi-gori* (wicker trunks made of willow branches) from the San'in region; *funadansu* (ship trunks) from Niigata Prefecture used on ships (*kaisen*) traveling between Osaka and northern Japan during the Edo period; Wakasa and Wajima lacquer ware from Fukui and Ishikawa prefecture; woodcrafts from Hida (Gifu Prefecture) and Matsumoto (Nagano Prefecture); birch, bamboo, and other woodcrafts, including *kago* (woven basket), *magemono* (round containers), and *kabazaiku* (birch woodcrafts), from the Hokuriku region; lacquer ware such as *aizu-nuri* (Fukushima Prefecture), *shunkei-nuri* (Akita Prefecture), and *tsugaru-nuri* (Aomori Prefecture); and Ainu woodcrafts from Hokkaido.

Metalwork includes *kiseru* (smoking pipes), made by town craftsmen in various regions of Japan; tableware made in Tsubame (Niigata Prefecture); hardware and carpentry tools from Miki (Hyogo Prefecture); razors and other cutting instruments from Seki (Gifu Prefecture); metal fittings made in Sendai (Miyagi Prefecture); and iron pots and kettles produced throughout Japan.

Textiles include *bingata* (surface-dyed textile) and *basho* (abaca) cloth from Okinawa; Satsuma *jofu* (linen cloth) from Kagoshima Prefecture; *kurume-gasuri* (Kurume ikat cloth) from Fukuoka Prefecture and *iyo-gasuri* (Iyo ikat cloth) from Ehime Prefecture; indigo (*ai*) from Tokushima Prefecture, which was once valued throughout the country as *awa-ai*, a natural dye; cotton cloth from Tamba (Hyogo and Kyoto prefectures); *saki-ori* (woven from strips made from old clothes) from the Hokuriku and Tohoku regions; *habutae* silk from Fukui Prefecture and *chijimi* (crepe) from Niigata Prefecture; *mikawa momen* (Mikawa cotton) from Aichi Prefecture and *kaiki* (Kai silk) from Yamanashi Prefecture; silk weaving from the Kanto region at Kiryu (Gumma Prefecture), Ashikaga (Tochigi Prefecture), and Hachioji (Tokyo Prefecture); *kogin* from the Tsugaru region; *hishizashi*, distinguished by their embroidered patterns in white cotton thread, from Aomori and Iwate prefectures; and *sashiko* (quiltings) made by the Ainu in Hokkaido.

Washi (Japanese paper), once produced throughout the country, is now rarely used in everyday life. Japanese papers still produced today are *tosa-gami* from Kochi Prefecture and Sekishu *hanshi* and *izumo-gami* from Shimane Prefecture. Washi made in Kyoto and Nara has been famous for centuries. Dyed pattern paper is still produced in Mie Prefecture. Echizen *hosho* and *torinoko-gami* from Fukui Prefecture are well known, as is Yao paper made in Toyama Prefecture. Surviving washi products include kites from Nagasaki Prefecture and *shibuuchiwa* (fans) from Kutami in Kumamoto Prefecture.

Numerous types of paintings and religious sculptures are considered representative of Japanese folk crafts, although in these categories there are different opinions about what is and what is not folk craft. (According to Yanagi's somewhat personal and subjective criteria, *otsu-e* are included among folk arts whereas *ukiyo-e* are not.) Present designations of what can be considered mingei should not be accepted as final, since scholars may develop a more comprehensive method of categorization in the future.

Architecture

Architecture, modern

(*kingendai no kenchiku*). As Japan launched its modernization drive following the Meiji Restoration of 1868 and began to import Western science and technology as part of its national policy, the government invited foreign engineers and experts to train Japanese and oversee initial construction projects.

At first, Western methods and designs were incorporated into traditional Japanese methods of wood construction.

In 1877 Josiah Conder of Britain arrived in Japan to teach at the Industrial College (forerunner of the Department of Engineering at Tokyo University); he trained many architects, including Tatsuno Kingo and Katayama Tokuma. The Akasaka Detached Palace (1909) by Katayama and the main office of the Bank of Japan (1896) and Tokyo Station (1914) by Tatsuno are typical of the kind of Western-style buildings designed by Japanese at this time.

In the 1880s there was a general reaction against excessive Westernization in many fields, including architecture. Architect and art historian Ito Chuta was among the first to advocate Asian models for Japanese architecture; he was later responsible for the design of the Meiji Shrine (1920). After World War I architects like Frank Lloyd Wright and Antonin Raymondh of the United States and Bruno Taut of Germany came to Japan, contributing to the reevaluation of traditional Japanese architecture. Through their work, Japanese architecture influenced Western architecture, in much the same way that *ukiyo-e* had influenced Western painting. The renewed interest in tradition also led to the development by Yoshida Isoya of a new style in residential architecture that assimilated traditional *sukiya-zukuri* techniques.

Since World War II the activities of Japanese architects have increasingly attracted attention overseas. The reconciliation of modern and traditional architectural forms was one of the major issues during the postwar years.

One of the best-known and most influential modern Japanese architects is Tange Kenzo (1913–). He developed a methodology linking Japanese traditional elements with the achievements of science and technology in architectural form and established his reputation with a number of dramatic buildings in the 1950s and 1960s such as the futuristic Yoyogi National Stadium (1963), built for the 1964 Tokyo

Olympics, and the Dentsu head office building (1967). These were built at a time when there was a rush, propelled by a new wave of technological innovation and the dynamism of rapid economic growth, to construct very large buildings. The 1960s were a period both of pioneering work by individual architects and of the industrialization and depersonalization of architecture, as fast-working design and construction companies specializing in building groups of standardized, characterless structures came to dominate the field. Cities in Japan as in many other countries were rapidly filled with boxlike buildings.

The reevaluation of architectural priorities was led by Isozaki Arata (1931 –), who worked under Tange early in his career. Rejecting the tendency toward the total commercialization of architecture and construction, Isozaki argued that architecture had to regain its independence from commercial and technological imperatives. Examples of his work such as the Museum of Modern Art in Gumma Prefecture (1975) and his many critical writings had an immense impact on the rising younger generation of architects in the 1970s. It was about this time that architects who regarded themselves primarily as artists (as opposed to technicians or builders) began to make their appearance, among the most distinguished being Ando Tadao (1941 –), Shinohara Kazuo (1925 –), and Kurokawa Kisho (1934 –). During this period Japanese architects were preoccupied with reassessing the functional and utilitarian aspects of postwar Japanese architecture and its relationship to Japanese traditions. These more introspective concerns paralleled the relative contraction in the growth and dynamism of the Japanese economy as a whole after the expansion of the 1960s.

In the 1980s, however, the economy once again began to boom, and this was reflected in architectural circles by a union between new commercial imperatives, prompted by government deregulation of the construction industry, and the emphasis on pure design that had resulted from the introspection of the 1970s. The demand of business for imposing buildings with the power to impress customers—which had, for example, led to the construction of the first skyscrapers in the Shinjuku area of downtown Tokyo in the early 1970s—reasserted itself in the 1980s, but now architects responded with buildings that incorporated more artistic design features. Tange Kenzo's Tokyo Metropolitan Government Offices (1991) are a good example of the monumental style that resulted.

The 1980s and early 1990s also saw a rapid increase in the number of works by Japanese architects being built in other countries. Works like Isozaki's Museum of Contemporary Art in Los Angeles (1986) and Tange Kenzo's OUB Center in Singapore (1986) marked the advent of active two-way international exchange in the field of architecture.

Architecture, traditional domestic

(*dentoteki* Nihon *kenchiku*). Traditional residential architecture in Japan is perhaps best viewed as a response to the natural environment. Traditional Japan was a primarily agricultural society, centering on activities associated with rice planting. A feeling of cooperation, rather than an antagonistic relationship, developed between the Japanese and their natural surroundings. Instead of resistance or defense, accommodation and adaptation became the basic stance. Traditional Japanese architecture is characterized by the same attitude toward the natural environment, responding in particular to climatic and geographical conditions.

Japan's climate is distinguished by long, hot, humid summers and relatively short, cold, dry winters, and the Japanese house has evolved accordingly to make the summers more bearable. Since in the past the only relief from the oppressive heat and humidity was found in the cooling movement of air, the choice was toward light and open structures much like those found in Malaysia and other tropical areas. The traditional Japanese house was raised slightly off the ground and the interior opened up to allow for unrestricted movement of air around and below the living spaces. Associated with the heat and humidity of summer were sun and frequent rain. This necessitated a substantial roof structure with long, low overhangs to protect the interior.

With its open structure, the traditional Japanese house is vulnerable to all kinds of intrusion, including dirt, dust, and insects. Noise and lack of privacy are also problems, though screens and *shoji* (translucent paper-covered sliding panels) offer a measure of visual privacy to the inhabitants.

Materials and Construction

The choice of building materials has been determined by the climate, wood being preferred to stone. Stone is uncomfortable and unhealthy in hot, humid weather, restricting airflow and closing off the structure; it also requires a longer period of time in preparing materials and in building. In contrast, wood responds more sensitively to the climate, being much cooler and absorbing moisture in summer and not as cold to the touch in winter. Wood is also more suited to withstand earthquakes, almost daily occurrences in Japan.

The choice of wood and an open structure allows for flexibility in living arrangements according to seasonal changes and the needs of the family. Inner partitions such as shoji and *fusuma* (opaque paper-covered sliding panels) can be removed to open up the interior, and, except for the roof's supporting columns, a clear space can be exposed.

Apart from the use of wood, the apparently little consideration given to earthquake protection in the structure itself is striking. Diagonal bracing, for example, is hardly ever seen in walls or roof structure. Rigidity, however, is not the only way of protecting a structure against earthquakes. Wood is flexible and can take more shear and torque for its weight than most other materials. The joinery makes use of the strengths of wood. The walls, consisting essentially of bamboo lattices heavily plastered with clay, are not at all substantial by Western standards but are surprisingly resistant to earthquakes. One room of the traditional house is plastered heavily on four walls in this way, with only a minimal entrance in one. This is directly connected to some of the main supports and helps to strengthen the building. The diagonal was not unknown, for wood diagonal compression braces have been found beneath the plaster walls of a few very old structures, but for some reason it was not used generally. In older structures the joint between a foundation stone and the support post or column was not fixed, so that when the earth moved, the column sometimes simply slid off its foundation stone. After the earthquake, the house could be lifted up and the support placed on another stone with no real damage to the structure.

Spatial Concepts in Architecture

A basic spatial concept in Japan is *ma* (written with a Chinese character that is also pronounced *ken* or *aida*). It has no exact English equivalent, variously meaning space, relationship, interval, period, luck, or pause, depending on the context. In architecture the term is applicable to the distance between two posts or the space between two or more walls, rocks in a garden, buildings, people, or other things with a possible relationship.

In constructing a house, the first step is to raise posts and beams until a skeletal structure stable enough to support a roof is completed. The space is organized by the roof and by the modular placement of the posts and columns. From this point on, design concerns itself with filling in the spaces or intervals between the posts and columns. Two things happen as this filling-in process occurs. First, a relationship is developed between the filled-in wall planes, and subdivisions— rooms—are created. Second, the wall itself alters the relationship of the posts by the kinds of materials used in its construction and its value as a barrier. In both cases, one is adjusting ma, or relationships that already exist—a process that lies at the heart of traditional Japanese design. Once the structure is given, design is concerned with the realignment and alteration of already existing relationships. Consequently, in

Japanese design the wall has a different conceptual basis than that of Western design. Japanese walls are not defensive. In the West, by contrast, the wall is conceived as defensive, acting as a barrier between two opposing environments, such as winter cold and house warmth.

An important aspect of traditional design is the relationship of the house to its specific environment, particularly the garden; the two are continuous. The Japanese do not see exterior and interior as two separate entities; in other words, there is no definite point at which exterior ends and interior begins. The lack of barriers in Japanese designs has already been discussed. The Japanese veranda (*engawa*) is a concrete expression of this concept, serving as a transition space from inside to outside. Its function is further expressed by the materials used in its construction. Whereas the floors of the interior of the house are covered with *tatami* mats and the exterior is made of earth and rock, the engawa is made of unfinished wood planks, belonging neither to the soft and accommodating interior nor to the harsh and more primitive materials on the outside.

The development of the individual spaces within the house was a gradual process of breaking down the larger open space that was available into smaller, more human-scaled spaces. Individual rooms were later defined by shoji and fusuma, "sliding doors" that could still be removed to form a single large space.

Gardens

(*teien*). Japanese gardens possess a unique beauty derived from the combination and synthesis of various elements. There is a compositional beauty derived from a blending of natural plantings, sand, water, and rock, made unique by the natural beauty of Japan's landscape, seasonal change, and a symbolic beauty arising from the expression of Shinto beliefs and Buddhist intellectual conventions.

History

It has been said that the use of groupings of rocks is a distinguishing feature of the Japanese garden and provides its basic framework. The ancestors of the modern Japanese referred to places surrounded by natural rock as *amatsu iwasaka* ("heavenly barrier") or *amatsu iwakura* ("heavenly seat"), believing that gods lived there. Dense clusters of trees were also thought to be the dwelling places of gods and were called *himorogi* ("divine hedge"). Moats or streams that enclosed sacred ground were called *mizugaki* ("water fences").

The first gardens amidst the mountains of Yamato (now Nara Prefecture), where the Japanese state was established during the 6th and

7th centuries, imitated ocean scenes with large ponds rimmed by wild "seashores" and dotted with islands. During this period Buddhism was transmitted to Japan, and immigrants from Paekche on the Korean peninsula contributed continental influences to the Japanese garden.

In 794 the capital was moved from Nara to Kyoto. Here several rivers converged, and channels were dug to carry water through the city. In order to provide some relief from the summer heat, waterfalls and ponds were fashioned, and narrow streams (*yarimizu*) were made to pass between buildings and flow through the gardens of the *shinden-zukuri* mansions. The ponds were of simple shape yet were large enough for boating, and at their edges, jutting out over the water, were erected fishing pavilions (*tsuridono*) connected by roofed corridors to the other structures of the mansion. The large area between the main buildings and the pond was covered with white sand and used for formal ceremonies.

With the rise of the cult of the Buddha Amida in the 10th century, the shinden style of garden, modeled on the image of the Pure Land (Jodo) as described in scripture and religious tracts, was developed. A good example of this is the garden of the Byodoin, a temple at Uji near Kyoto that was originally the country residence of Fujiwara no Michinaga.

The Muromachi period (1333—1568) has been called the golden age of Japanese gardens. Skilled groups of craftsmen known as *senzui kawaramono* ("mountain, stream, and riverbed people") were active, and the new *karesansui* ("dry mountain stream") style of garden appeared. Waterless rock and sand gardens (karesansui) arose under the influence of Zen Buddhist doctrine, *shoin*-style architecture (*shoin-zukuri*), and Chinese ink painting, together with potted dwarf trees (*bonsai*), and tray landscapes, the ideal being the symbolic expression of the universe within a limited space.

The tea ceremony (*sado*) as taught by Sen no Rikyu emphasized a quiescent spirituality. The approach to a teahouse was through a tea garden (*roji* or *chaniwa*), the ideal of which Rikyu sought in the desolate tranquility of a mountain trail. Among the contributions of the tea garden to the contemporary Japanese garden are stepping-stones, stone lanterns, and groves of trees, as well as stone washbasins and simply constructed gazebos for guests being served tea.

During the Edo period (1600—1868) a synthesis of preceding forms took place. The garden of the Katsura Detached Palace, which achieved considerable renown through the writings of the German architect Bruno Taut, is made up of a number of tea gardens. This is an example of the *kaiyu* or "many-pleasure" style, which became fully established in the mid-Edo period. A representative garden designer of this period was Kobori Enshu, whose work included the gardens of the Sento Palace in Kyoto.

Performing Arts

Theater, traditional

(*koten geino*). The five major genres of Japanese traditional theater, all still in performance, are *bugaku*, No, *kyogen*, *bunraku*, and *kabuki*. Although different in content and style, they are linked by strong aesthetic relationships, derived from a confluence of sources both inside and outside Japan. The assumption of an integral relationship among dance, music, and lyrical narrative governed the evolution of performing arts throughout Asia. These three elements were held to be an extension of the poetic art in classical Sanskrit treatises on dance and drama, which strongly influenced traditional stage practices throughout Asia. The synthesis of the disparate elements of speech, music, and dance led to highly developed styles, of which the five Japanese genres represent supreme examples.

Among the five Japanese genres, bugaku stands apart as a ceremonial dance associated only with court ritual, in which the theatrical element is minimal and music predominates. Ceremonial dance was common in ancient Chinese ritual, and as far back as the Zhou dynasty (1027 BC – 256 BC) dance in China was divided into civil and military styles performed for propitiation. Bugaku incorporates aesthetic and structural principles current in the 8th century—admixtures of Central Asian, Indian, and Korean elements assimilated by China and adopted by Japan during a period of cultural borrowing.

No, kyogen, bunraku, and kabuki, by contrast, are indigenous forms representing successive periods of political and social change in Japan. The first two belong to an age when Chinese influences were still potent; the latter two come from a time when Japan was politically isolated. But all adhere to Asian dramatic principles emphasizing symbolism and allusive imagery, as opposed to the Aristotelian concept of mimesis, the imitation of reality, which dominates Western dramatic theory. Japanese theater, whatever the genre, strives to induce a mood, to create an immediate aesthetic experience drawing an instantaneous response from the spectator.

No drama, for example, seeks to reveal the ephemeral nature of reality through stage techniques stressing imagery, metaphor, and symbolism. Medieval Buddhist thought, which profoundly influenced No, rejected factual reality as illusory: in Buddhist theory it is only at the moment of perception that anything exists; thus, all existence is fleeting.

Kyogen, the comic interludes that are an integral part of No performance, poke fun at human frailties as did the traditional Asian storytellers, jesting at social pretensions, marital discord, quackery, and so forth. Through stylized vocal forms, pantomime, and spatial control, kyogen preserves some of the formal elegance of No. In its artless humor and oral techniques there is also a great deal that is reminiscent of traditional Chinese stage clowning, for the Chinese comic actor is also descended from a long storytelling tradition. In both kyogen and Chinese performance the comic action is physical and situational, playing off the discrepancies between what people would be and what they really are. In both, the comic actor becomes a catalyzing agent, relieving tension through the arrangement of his appearance between (or, in the case of the Chinese comic, within) the serious plays.

Bunraku, or puppet theater, is unique in being accepted in Japan as the equal of orthodox drama. Indeed, it is impossible to speak of bunraku without mentioning kabuki, since a sizable part of the latter's repertoire consists of plays originally written for puppet drama, which has also greatly influenced the style of kabuki acting. In turn, bunraku has taken much from the sophisticated technical presentation of kabuki and has incorporated some of its popular dance dramas into its own repertoire. Bunraku puppets bear a family resemblance to puppets once common in southern China, although they are more technically complex and are characterized by a degree of realism not found elsewhere in Asia. The artistry involved in the unique bunraku practice of using three puppeteers to manipulate a single character in coordination with a sung narrative and *shamisen* music produces a theatrical experience of considerable emotional intensity.

Kabuki carries even further the deployment of speech, sound, movement, and space as equal contributory forces. Theatrical synthesis reaches a powerful degree of instantaneous communication by using visual and aural techniques cumulatively to assail the playgoer's senses and emotions. Stylization conditions every level of performance. Narrative musical forms are used constantly to convey mood, emphasize emotional tensions, and provide exposition.

No

The oldest extant professional theater; a form of musical dance-drama originating in the 14th century. No preserves what all other important contemporary theater has lost: its origin in ritual, reflecting an essentially Buddhist view of existence. The performance looks and sounds more like solemn observance than life. The actors are hieratic,

Culture

playing their ancient roles of intermediaries between the worlds of gods and men. To the bare stage come soberly dressed instrumentalists, the six-or-eight-member chorus, then the supporting character (*waki*), handsomely robed, often as a priest. Finally, out of the darkness at the end of the long passageway leading to the stage proper, evoked by drums and flute, the resplendently caparisoned (usually masked) leading character (*shite*) materializes. In strict rhythms, out of music, voice, and movement rather than the artifice of stagecraft, time and space are created and destroyed. Language is largely poetic. Costumes are rich and heavy, movement, even in dance, deliberate. The shite seeks intercession by the waki and, having attained it at the end, returns to the darkness freed of karma.

Origins

At the middle of the 14th century professional theater was based in Kyoto and Nara, and the actors organized into troupes under the patronage of Shinto shrines and Buddhist temples. They raised money, piously and commercially, with subscription No (*kanjin* No), their performances at religious festivals serving both to propagate doctrine and to entertain.

Some troupes presented *dengaku* No, others *sarugaku* No. At this time little distinguished the two kinds, for both had a common theatrical inheritance. Their masks had origins in the ancient dance-drama called *gigaku*. Their music came from Shinto ritual dance (*kagura*), the Buddhist liturgy (*shomyo*), popular 10th-century songs (*imayo*), and 13th-century "party music" (*enkyoku*). Their dance was influenced by 7th-century dance music (*bugaku*); by *furyu*, an 11th-century dramatic dance accompanied by flute and drum; and by *shirabyoshi*, a type of 12th-century song-and-dance performance. Their plots were drawn from legend, history, literature, and contemporary events, given some literary refinement by the influence of *ennen* No. The players distinguished between comic and serious materials, the comic pieces, kyogen, being played as interludes between serious ones. In spite of their similarities, however, sarugaku eventually emerged as dominant, replacing dengaku in popularity.

The transformation of sarugaku into No, in basically the same form it has today, was accomplished by Kan'ami and his son Zeami, both prodigious actor-dancers and playwrights of the Muromachi period (1333–1568).

In 1374 Kan'ami and Zeami performed before the shogun Ashikaga Yoshimitsu, who, greatly taken by the performance and by Zeami, thereafter sponsored the troupe. Never before had actors attained such social esteem. Kan'ami's troupe, the Kanze school, was preeminent, and three other troupes that now survive, the Komparu school, the Hosho school, and the Kongo school, adopted the Kanze style of performance. It was on the Zen artistic principles of restraint, economy of expression, and suggestion rather than statement that Zeami fashioned his 40 or so plays, his acting, and his productions. His ideas on every aspect of the theater were set down in a series of essays that remain the essential documents of the No.

Evolution

A civil war, the Onin War, started in 1467 and was fought in and around Kyoto until 1477, when the battles shifted to the provinces. By the end of the century the entire country was engaged in a period of conflict known as the Sengoku, or Warring States, period, which lasted until 1568. The shogunate had little time for No, but for others the war whetted the desire for entertainment and culture. Toward 1500, amateur performances became widely popular. The study of No music and dance spread not only among aristocrats but also among priests, soldiers, and commoners, who wanted professional instruction, which the troupes gladly gave them for a fee. Written copies of the songs and chants (*utaibon*) of the Kanze and Komparu troupes appeared in 1512. By disseminating the performances throughout the country, civil war made No an increasingly integral part of the culture.

No returned to the center of political power when in 1571 the Kanze troupe was summoned to the military headquarters of Tokugawa Ieyasu. But it found its most enthusiastic support when Toyotomi Hideyoshi came to power in 1582. Hideyoshi bolstered his soldiers' morale by having all four troupes perform for them, and he commissioned 10 plays written about himself, in which he played the lead. When Tokugawa Ieyasu became shogun in 1603 he celebrated the occasion with No performances, and in 1609 he employed all of Hideyoshi's performers and established them in Edo (now Tokyo). The Kita school, which still exists today, was added to the original four in 1618. No became the official property and ceremonial art of the Tokugawa line. In 1647 Tokugawa Iemitsu issued regulations for its governance, as stringent as those by which he ran the country: tradition must be maintained, the troupe leader brooking no deviations. Over more than two centuries No became more and more codified, even surpassing Zeami's refined art in solemnity. Performances that took half an hour in Zeami's day take an hour and a half or more today.

During the Edo period (1600−1868) favored commoners were invited to performances at the shogun's castle on auspicious occasions. They were forbidden to learn No music and dance, but they did nonetheless. As the economic life of the military class worsened in the 19th century, that of many commoners improved, and they were able to pay well for No instruction. Large numbers of them also became attracted to the popular kabuki theater. When the shogunate fell in 1867 and government subsidy of No stopped, some of the nobility kept No alive. Their support ended with the end of World War II, however, and the public became No's sole sponsor. Today No has a small but dedicated following, many members of which belong to No study groups.

Stage

Tokugawa formalization of No also standardized the stage, and today that architecture is requisite for the correct performance of the plays. Although the stage is now usually inside a concrete building, it retains its original appearance as an exterior structure. The elaborate, carved, cypress-bark-covered roof of Shinto shrine architecture extends over the main stage (*butai*), which measures 6 by 6 meters (19.7 by 19.7 ft), as well as the side stage (*wakiza*), the rear stage (*atoza*), and the bridge (*hashigakari*). The bridge joins the main stage at an oblique angle, connecting it with the "mirror room" (*kagami no ma*), the actors' dressing room. Musicians (*hayashikata*) and actors enter and exit on the bridge. The only other entrance to the stage is a 1 meter (39 in) high sliding door (*kirido*), upstage left on the main stage, used by stage assistants (*koken*) and the members of the chorus (*jiutai*).

No stage.

Along the front of the entire structure, at audience level, is a strip of pebbles. In front of the bridge in this area are three equidistantly placed pine trees. A stylized pine tree, the only scenic background, is painted on the back wall (*kagamiita*) of the main stage. The entire structure is built of polished Japanese cypress (*hinoki*).

Performers

All performers are male, and their organization is that established in the Edo period. Each of the five schools of No, mentioned earlier, trains its own shite, his "companion"(*tsure*), the child actor (*kokata*), the chorus, and the stage assistants. The waki and his "companion" have their own separate schools, such as Fukuo and Takayasu. Each instrument—the flute, small and large hand drums, and the large drum standing on the floor—is taught in a number of different schools.

The actors' children, trained in the traditional manner beginning at the age of seven, appear in performance in children's roles. Training is strictly by rote, vocally and physically. Each unit of movement, including the No style of walking in which the heel never leaves the floor, is called a *kata* ("form"). Some 200 kata exist, each having a name, but only about 30 are commonly used.

Properties, Masks, and Costumes

The expressiveness of the shite and the waki is enhanced by

hand properties, among them letters, umbrellas, rosaries, and the bamboo branch signifying derangement, but most of all by the folding fan (*chukei*). Closed, partly closed, or open, it may represent any object suggested by its shape and handling—dagger, lantern, rising moon. In other kata it represents not objects but actions—listening, moon viewing, sleeping. The abstract or pictorial design painted on the fan is conventionally associated with a type of character such as a ghost, old woman, or demon. Only the shite and waki use them. The other actors and the chorus carry fans (*ogi*) bearing the crest of the school. The chorus place their fans, always closed, on the floor in front of them and pick them up to signal the beginning of a chant.

Only the shite and his companions wear masks, carved of wood and painted, though not in plays in which the characters they portray are living men. Each mask is a variation on a general type—holy old men, gods, demons or spirits, men, women—and in many plays the shite changes masks midway through the play, the second mask revealing the character's true being. The shite chooses the mask he prefers for the role, and his choice determines, by association and custom, his costume.

Han'nya (female demon) mask.

Many of the costumes (*shozoku*) used today were constructed in the 18th and 19th centuries when the patterns, colors, and materials to be worn by a given character were systematized. Costume creates an effect of luxurious elegance but also a bulky, massive figure, that of the shite looming largest. This is effected by at least five layers of clothing, the outermost richly figured damask, brocade, or embroidered silk gauze. No garment completely conceals the one beneath it; surfaces and textures are multiple. Wigs, hats, and headdresses heighten the figure.

Plays

Okina, the oldest item in the repertory, consists principally of three dances extant in the 10th century that are prayers for peace, fertility (the basis of Shinto), and longevity. Scarcely a play, it is performed only on ceremonial occasions and always first on the program. The usual program today consists of two or three No plays with half-hour comic pieces, kyogen, between them.

The other 240 or so plays now performed, most dating from the 15th century, are grouped into five categories, corresponding to the five parts of the traditional No program called *goban-date*. *Shobamme-mono* (part-one plays) are sometimes called *wakino-mono* or *kami* (god) plays. *Nibamme-mono* (part-two plays), or *shura-mono*, are often about men or warriors. *Sambamme-mono* (part-three plays) are also called *katsura-mono* ("wig" plays) and are usually about women. *Yobamme-mono* (part-four plays) are also called *zo-mono* ("miscellaneous No") or "madwoman"

Culture

plays. Some of these are referred to as "present-day" or "realistic" plays. *Gobamme-mono* (part-five plays) are also called "demon" plays, or *kirino-mono* ("final No'").

Kabuki

One of the three major classical theaters of Japan, together with the No and the *bunraku* puppet theater. Kabuki began in the early 17th century as a kind of variety show performed by troupes of itinerant entertainers. By the Genroku era (1688—1704), it had achieved its first flowering as a mature theater, and it continued, through much of the Edo period (1600—1868), to be the most popular form of stage entertainment. Kabuki reached its artistic pinnacle with the brilliant plays of Tsuruya Namboku IV (1755—1829) and Kawatake Mokuami (1816—1893). Through a magnificent blend of playacting, dance, and music, kabuki today offers an extraordinary spectacle combining form, color, and sound and is recognized as one of the world's great theatrical traditions.

Origin of Kabuki

The creation of kabuki is ascribed to Okuni, a female attendant at the Izumo Shrine, who, documents record, led her company of mostly women in a light theatrical performance featuring dancing and comic sketches on the dry bed of the river Kamogawa in Kyoto in 1603. Her troupe gained nationwide recognition and her dramas—and later the genre itself—became identified as "kabuki," a term connoting its "out-of-the-ordinary" and "shocking" character.

The strong attraction of *onna* (women's) kabuki, which Okuni had popularized, was largely due to its sensual dances and erotic scenes. Because fights frequently broke out among the spectators over these entertainers, who also practiced prostitution, in 1629 the Tokugawa shogunate (1603—1867) banned women from appearing in kabuki performances. Thereafter, *wakashu* (young men's) kabuki achieved a striking success, but, as in the case of onna kabuki, the authorities strongly disapproved of the shows, which continued to be the cause of public disturbances because the adolescent actors also sold their favors.

Kabuki after 1652

In 1652 wakashu kabuki was forbidden, and the shogunate required that kabuki performances undergo a basic reform to be allowed to continue. In short, kabuki was required to be based on *kyogen*, farces staged between No plays that used the spoken language of the time but whose style of acting was highly formalized. The performers of *yaro* (men's) kabuki, who now began to replace the younger males, were compelled to shave off their forelocks, as was the custom at the time for men, to signify that they had come of age. They also had to make representations to the authorities that their performances did not rely on the provocative display of their bodies and that they were serious artists who would not engage in prostitution.

In the 1660s a broad platform, the forerunner of the *hanamichi* in use today, extending from the main stage to the center of the auditorium, was introduced to provide an auxiliary stage on which performers could make entrances and exits. In 1664 two theaters located in Osaka and Edo (now Tokyo) introduced the draw curtain, which brought unlimited theatrical possibilities to the previously curtainless stage by permitting the lengthening of plays through the presentation of a series of scenes and providing the freedom to effect complicated scene changes unobtrusively. In the meantime the roles played by the *onnagata* (female impersonator) gradually increased in importance; mastery of them came to require many years of training. By the mid-17th century, the major cities, Kyoto, Osaka, and Edo, were permitted to build permanent kabuki playhouses.

Genroku Era Kabuki

By the beginning of the Genroku era in 1688 there had developed three distinct types of kabuki performance: *jidai-mono* (historical plays), often with elaborate sets and a large cast; *sewa-mono* (domestic plays), which generally portrayed the lives of the townspeople and which, in comparison to jidai-mono, were presented in a realistic manner; and *shosagoto* (dance pieces), consisting of dance performances and pantomime. In the Kyoto-Osaka (Kamigata) area, Sakata Tojuro I (1647–1709), whose realistic style of acting was called *wagoto*, was enormously popular for his portrayal of romantic young men, and his contemporary Yoshizawa Ayame I (1673–1729) consolidated the role of the onnagata and established its importance in the kabuki tradition. For a period of some 10 years until about 1703, when he returned to the puppet theater, Chikamatsu Monzaemon (1653–1724) wrote a number of kabuki plays, many of them for Tojuro I, which gained public recognition for the craft of the playwright. The commanding stage presence and powerful acting of Ichikawa Danjuro I made him the premier kabuki performer in Edo, and as a playwright, under the name Mimasuya Hyogo, he was once considered the rival of the great Chikamatsu.

Kabuki and the Puppet Theater

The spectacular success of kabuki in the Kyoto-Osaka area during the late 17th century was followed by a period of diminished popularity due to the flourishing of the bunraku puppet theater. In the years following the departure of Chikamatsu, *maruhon-mono* (kabuki adaptations of puppet plays) were staged in an attempt to draw back the spectators who were now flocking to the puppet theater. The musical and narrative accompaniment of the puppet plays was transported to kabuki performances, and even stage techniques of bunraku, such as the distinctive movement of the manipulated dolls, were imitated by kabuki actors. Chikamatsu's *Kokusen'ya kassen* (1715), an early example of the maruhon-mono, enjoyed tremendous success in both the Kamigata area and in Edo when it was performed soon after its presentation as a puppet play. The works of later writers which are considered masterpieces in both theaters include: *Sugawara denju tenarai kagami* (1746), *Yoshitsune sembon-zakura* (1747), and *Kanadehon chushin-gura* (1748). In Edo, despite the growing popularity of the bunraku theater, kabuki remained in the ascendancy due to the undiminished power of the Ichikawa Danjuro family of actors and the regional preference for the *aragoto* style of performance, which was not suited for the puppet stage. Nevertheless the tight logical structure of the puppet plays and their realistic character portrayal eventually influenced the Edo kabuki theater. After enjoying immense success during the first half of the 18th century, the puppet theater rapidly declined in the Kamigata area, and kabuki recaptured the support of the townspeople. Today, half of the plays presented on the kabuki stage are adaptations of bunraku plays.

Kanadehon chushingura, Ichiriki at Gion (in Kyoto Prefecture.)

After the mid-17th century, the cultural center of Japan gradually shifted from the Kamigata region to Edo. During this transitional period, one of the more notable Kamigata playwrights was Namiki Shozo I (1730–1773), best known as the inventor of the revolving stage (*mawaributai*). It was a pupil of Shozo I, the dramatist Namiki Gohei I (1747–1808), along with Sakurada Jisuke I (1734–1806), who was instrumental in transmitting the social realism traditionally associated with the sewa-mono (domestic plays) of the Kyoto-Osaka area to Edo. Their plays laid the foundation for the development of the realistic *kizewa-mono* ("bare" domestic plays) written by Tsuruya Namboku IV, Segawa Joko III (1806–1881), and Kawatake Mokuami.

Late-Edo- and Meiji-Period Kabuki

After the death of Namboku IV in 1829, kabuki did not produce any prominent playwrights until the mid-1850s, when Joko III and Mokuami began to write for the theater. Their early successes, embellishments on the genre kizewa-mono—the masterpiece of which had been *Tokaido Yotsuya kaidan* (1825) by Namboku IV—intermingled brutality, eroticism, and macabre humor and introduced characters from the underworld. Mokuami created the *shiranami-mono* (thief plays), which had robbers, murderers, confidence men, and cunningly vicious women in the leading roles.

The Meiji Restoration of 1868 marked the collapse of the social order ruled by the *samurai*, whose loss of status was symbolized by a ban on the wearing of swords and by government discouragement of the continued wearing of topknots. During the early years of the Meiji period Mokuami developed the *zangiri-mono* ("cropped-hair" plays), which introduced soldiers dressed in Western-style uniforms and onnagata characters wearing Western dresses. These dramas were little more than caricatures of modern life and failed to draw audiences. Actors such as Ichikawa Danjuro IX (1838−1903) and Onoe Kikugoro V (1844−1903) urged the preservation of classical kabuki, and in the later years of their careers agitated for the continued staging of the great plays of the kabuki tradition and trained a younger generation of actors in the art that they would inherit.

Post-World War II Kabuki

In the postwar era the popularity of kabuki has been maintained and the great plays of the Edo period, as well as a number of modern classics, continue to be performed in Tokyo at the Kabukiza and the National Theater. However, offerings have become considerably shortened and, particularly at the Kabukiza, limited for the most part to favorite acts and scenes presented together with a dance piece. The National Theater continues to present full-length plays. The average length of a kabuki performance is about five hours, including intermissions. The roles once played by the great postwar actors Morita Kan'ya XIV (1907−1975), Ichikawa Danjuro XI (1909−1965), Nakamura Kanzaburo XVII (1910−1988), Onoe Shoroku II (1913−1989), Onoe Baiko VII (1915−), and Nakamura Utaemon VI (1917−) are now performed by younger actors, such as Ichikawa Ennosuke II (1939−), Matsumoto Koshiro IX (1942−), Nakamura Kichiemon II (1944−), Bando Tamasaburo V (1950−), Kataoka Takao (1944−), and Nakamura Kankuro (1955−). Dramas in which Tamasaburo V appears in the role of the onnagata and Takao that of the leading man, or tachiyaku, are always well attended.

Kabuki and Tokugawa Thought

The kabuki theater often incorporates the prevailing moral notions of Tokugawa society as the mechanism upon which plots turn. For example, *inga oho* (law of retributive justice), a Buddhist notion, may result in the destruction of an evildoer or the bestowal of prosperity and happiness upon a long-suffering woman. The notion of *mujo* (the impermanence of all things), also derived from Buddhism, may be illustrated by the fall of a powerful military leader or the demise of a proud family.

Certain ethical notions based on Confucian traditions, such as duty, obligation, and filial piety, may come into direct conflict with personal desires and passions, leading to a series of dramatic situations.

The Kabuki Stage

The kabuki theater uses a draw curtain. It has broad black, green, and orange vertical stripes and is normally drawn open from stage right to stage left accompanied by the striking of wooden clappers. The curtain may also serve as a backdrop for brief scenes given before or after the performance on the main part of the stage. *Kamite* (stage left) is regarded as the place of honor and is occupied by characters of high rank, guests, and important messengers or official representatives. *Shimote* (stage right) is occupied by characters of low rank and members of a household; most entrances and exits take place on this side, usually by way of the hanamichi. A unique feature of the kabuki stage is the *mawaributai*, a circular platform that can be rotated to permit a second scene to be performed simultaneously with the scene already in progress or to dramatize a flashback.

Roles in Kabuki Plays

Yakugara, or types of dramatic role, are determined on the basis of the personality, age, or social position of characters. Onnagata are assigned to such roles as housewife, samurai lady, heroic woman, and wicked woman. Within the rich repertory of kabuki plays, the roles of Agemaki in *Sukeroku yukari no Edo-zakura* and Masaoka, the loyal nanny in *Meiboku sendai hagi*, are regarded as among the most challenging. Standard male roles are virtuous hero, handsome lover, evil courtier, wicked samurai, and unscrupulous rake. Versatile performers sometimes play both male and female roles.

Kabuki Dialogue

The dialogue in kabuki plays ranges from the extremely stylized to the intensely realistic. Generally jidai-mono contain more formalized speech and the sewa-mono more colloquial speech. In general, lines tend to be marked by a seven-five syllabic pattern (similar to that of classical Japanese poetry) and are delivered with a distinctive rhythm and tempo that is closely identified with kabuki. The *tsurane*, a long declamatory speech occurring in jidai-mono, effectively employs this rhythmic pattern. Maruhon-mono, kabuki adaptations from bunraku puppet plays, are in particular noted for their mellifluous lines in the seven-five pattern.

Acting Forms

The powerful influence of a long theatrical tradition is graphically illustrated by *kata* (forms), the stylized gestures and movements of kabuki performers. Since kata are not subject to rejection at the whim of the actor, they have helped to maintain the artistic integrity of kabuki. *Tate* (stylized fighting), *roppo* (dramatic exit accompanied by exaggerated gestures), *mie* (striking an attitude), and *dammari* (silent scene) all belong to this category.

Costumes

Costume, wig, and makeup are carefully matched with the nature of a role. In general, the costumes in jidai-mono are more stlyized and elegant, befitting members of the nobility and the samurai class. By contrast, the prevailing fashions of society at large during the Edo period are portrayed quite realistically in sewa-mono plays. The costumes used in shosagoto dance pieces are especially noted for their color, design, and workmanship. Wigs are classified according to age of characters, historical period, social status, occupation, and other considerations. Makeup varies widely depending on the role. The most striking example is *kumadori*, an established set of masklike makeup styles numbering about 100 and used in jidai-mono.

Stage Assistants

In addition to the regular performers, the *koken* (stage assistant) serves a valuable function on the stage. He is especially important in dance pieces. During the demanding *hayagawari* (quick costume change), the koken must carefully follow the movements of the dancer, all the while remaining close behind him, and at the crucial moment assist in the *hikinuki* ("pulling out"), by which a layer of clothing is quickly removed revealing a costume of different pattern and color. The koken is also known as *kurogo* ("black costume") since he is often dressed all in black.

Acting Families

Each performer belongs to an acting family by whose name he is known. Professionally, he is part of a closely knit hierarchical organization, headed by one of the leading actors, and must spend many years as an apprentice. An actor may eventually receive a new name as a mark of his elevation to a higher position within the professional organization. It is awarded at a *shumei* (name-assuming) ceremony, and in the company of his colleagues he then delivers from the stage an address (*kojo*) in which he requests the continued patronage of the audience. The name Ichikawa Danjuro, which can be traced back to the formative years of kabuki, is regarded even today as the most illustrious of honors a kabuki actor can receive.

Rakugo

Popular form of comic monologue in which a storyteller (*rakugo-*

ka) creates an imaginary drama through episodic narration and skillful use of vocal and facial expressions to portray various characters. Typically, the storyteller uses no scenery; the only musical accompaniment is the *debayashi*, a brief flourish of drum, *shamisen*, and bamboo flute that marks his entrance and exit. The storyteller, dressed in a plain *kimono*, crosses to stage center and seats himself on a cushion before his audience, with a hand towel and a fan as his only props. There he remains until he has delivered his final line, usually a punning punch line (*ochi*; literally, "the drop"). This is the characteristic ending from which the term rakugo was coined, the word being written with two Chinese characters meaning "drop" (J: *raku*, also pronounced *ochi*) and "word" (*go*).

In a rakugo performance the interplay between performer and audience is extremely important. Since the repertory of classic rakugo is small, aficionados have heard the basic story many times. They delight in the storyteller's particular version, his arrangement of familiar episodes, and appreciate his timing and the verisimilitude of the details he adds, such as the sound of sake as he pours it into his imaginary cup. The introduction to the story proper must be completely original. The plots of the stories are never as important as the characterizations in them, for rakugo pokes fun at all manner of human foibles.

By the early 1670s professional performers called *hanashika* had emerged. Tsuyu no Gorobei (1643−1703) from Kyoto and Yonezawa Hikohachi (d 1714) from Osaka are regarded as the forefathers of Kamigata (Kyoto-Osaka) rakugo, while Shikano Buzaemon (1649−1699) is credited with founding the Edo rakugo tradition, later perfected by San'yutei Encho.

A regular entertainment feature at roadside shows, private banquets, and makeshift stages set up at restaurants during off-hours, this vagabond art found a home in 1791 when the first permanent Japanese-style vaudeville theater, or *yose*, was opened in Edo (now Tokyo). Soon afterward the popularity of yose spread to Kyoto and Osaka.

After surviving the challenge of cinema in the 1920s and 1930s, which significantly reduced yose attendance, rakugo performers met with increasing official disapproval during World War II, because they did not adapt their material to complement national ideology.

With the resumption of civilian broadcasting at the end of World War II, rakugo recovered its popularity. Although the proliferation of new entertainment media has greatly reduced the number of yose, the adaptability of rakugo to both radio and television has ensured its survival. There are still four traditional yose in Tokyo, along with rakugo halls, larger and more expensive, where all-rakugo programs are presented for devotees, often on a monthly basis. Many universities also sponsor raku-

go clubs whose members study and perform rakugo for their own entertainment.

Manzai

Performing art in which a comic dialogue is carried on by two comedians. Said to have had its beginnings in the Nara period (710 – 794), manzai spread throughout Japan in the Edo period (1600 – 1868).

Toward the close of the Edo period, manzai was performed in makeshift theaters, and by the first decade of the 20th century its popularity, especially in Osaka, increased rapidly. After World War II, passing from the age of radio to that of television, manzai has continued to flourish. Today the repartee of manzai performers—the wit is now called *tsukkomi* and the straight man *boke*—is distinguished by its fast pace, its use of current events, and its swift shifts, often by bizarre association, from topic to topic.

Music, traditional

(*hogaku*). Term applied to the varieties of music performed in Japan in premodern times and to forms of such music that are played today. Although archaeological materials and Chinese documents provide evidence of music in Japan as far back as the 3rd century BC, the traditional history of Japanese music normally starts with the Nara period (710 – 794). Japanese music had its roots in the music of Buddhism and the vibrant traditions of Tang dynasty (618 – 907) China.

History

Buddhism was established as an official court religion by the 6th century, and its sounds and music theories became influential in Japan. Chinese and Korean courts or monasteries were the sources and models of most of the music in courts and temples but, because of the international dynamism of continental Asia from the 7th through the 10th century, influences from South and Southeast Asia can be found as well. The fact that Japan seemed to be "at the end of the line" in this cultural diffusion is of particular interest, for many traditions remained in Japan long after they had disappeared in the lands of their origins. The instrumental and dance repertoires of the court, generically known as *gagaku*, reflect such origins in their classification into two categories: *togaku*, pieces derived from Chinese or Indian sources, and *komagaku*, music from Korea and Manchuria.

During the turbulent change from a court-dominated to a military-dominated culture at the end of the 12th century, more theatrical genres of music became popular. The *biwa* (lute) of the court became the accompaniment not only of itinerant priests and evangelists but also of chanters who recited long historical tales, particularly the *Heike monogatari*. Pantomime theatricals at Buddhist temples and Shinto shrines gradually combined in the 14th century with the rich heritage of folk theatricals to produce a new form known as No drama. The 13-stringed *koto* (zither) tradition is one of the few types of ancient courtly solo and chamber music that continued to develop in the 16th century, primarily in the mansions of the rich or in temples. At first there were remnants of older traditions, but by the 17th century quite different koto pieces appeared, particularly in the new Ikuta school. The founding of the Yamada school in the 18th century further enriched the repertoire. Both these schools have continued to the present day, and their solo and chamber music form the basis of what most Japanese would consider to be their "classical" music. The end-blown *shakuhachi* (bamboo flute) also developed new schools of performance and repertory during this period, but it is the three-stringed plucked lute (*shamisen*) that best represents the new musical styles and new audiences of the 16th through the 19th century. By the 18th century the narrative tradition of the puppet theater (known generically as *joruri*) had become a major source of literature, which was performed by skilled chanters (*tayu*) with shamisen accompaniment. The *kabuki* theater adopted some of this material for its own plays, but it also developed a combination of other genres of shamisen music plus the percussion and flute ensemble (*hayashi*) of the No, along with an eclectic assortment of folk and religious instruments. A logical outgrowth of an economically and socially supported theater music was the creation in the 19th century of compositions using theatrical genres and instruments but intended for dance recital or purely concert performances. The shamisen genre called *nagauta* was particularly active in this new field. Such concerts were originally held in private mansions but, by the end of the century, actual concert halls for such music were common.

Musical Characteristics

Although Japanese traditional music and the classical music of the West have equally long histories, the two musical traditions have very different theoretical bases. Most Japanese music shares with its East Asian counterparts a general tendency to be word-oriented. Except for the variation (*dammono*) pieces for the koto, Japanese traditional music has either a vocal part with text or a title that evokes some image. Instrumental genres differ widely in Japanese music, but the general concept of the Western chamber-music sound ideal seems to apply to almost all Japanese traditional ensembles over the past 1,200 years. No matter how large or small an ensemble may be, the tone color of the instruments combined is such that the sounds do not "melt" into a single experience as they do in some Western orchestral music.

G_agaku_

Traditional music of the Japanese imperial court. The term derived from the Chinese word _yayue_, which denotes ancient ritual music played by a large orchestra of stone chimes, bronze bells, flutes, drums, and numerous other instruments. Gagaku comprises three main bodies of music: _togaku_, music said to be in the style of Tang dynasty (618—907) China; _komagaku_, a music style said to have been introduced from ancient Korea; and, finally, all of the many forms of native Japanese music associated with rituals of the Shinto religion.

The oldest and most carefully preserved of the various forms of Shinto ritual music and dance used in the imperial court is the _kagura_, formally called _mikagura_ (court kagura) in order to distinguish it from the various folk forms of Shinto music that are also called kagura. Besides the mikagura, this group of Shinto ritual songs and dances includes the Yamato _uta_, Azuma _asobi_, and Kume _uta_. The mikagura is central to the Shinto ritual style, and the other three forms are in some way modeled on it. Also included in the gagaku repertoire are _saibara_ (regional Japanese folk songs reset in an elegant court style), though only a small number of saibara compositions continue to be performed by court musicians.

Gagaku stage at the Imperial Palace.

History

During the Nara period (710—794), a great number of styles of music existed, each with its own special musicians, dancers, and types of instruments. In the early Heian period (794—1185), the various styles of foreign music were combined into the togaku and komagaku categories and were performed both by the court nobles and by hereditary guilds of professional musicians. With the fall of the noble classes in the early part of the Kamakura period (1185—1333), the popularity of gagaku waned. It was maintained by guilds and the remaining nobles, each in relative isolation from the other. The guild musicians were divided into three groups and were in service in Kyoto, Nara, and Osaka.

After the Meiji Restoration of 1868 and the relocation of the Imperial Palace to Tokyo, the three groups were brought together as the official musicians of the newly established state. The musicians of the present-day Imperial Palace Music Department are still largely the direct descendants of the members of the first musicians' guilds that performed gagaku in Japan during the 8th century. They perform all the ritual music and dances required by the court and also give regular public gagaku concerts.

Instruments

The instruments used in performances of gagaku are Japanese modifications of those used in the Tang court ensembles. The instrumentation is determined by the type of music being performed. A small double-reed pipe similar to an oboe or shawm, called the *hichiriki*, is used in all the instrumental ensembles. Three different types of flute are used, the *kagurabue* generally for the Shinto rituals, the *komabue* for komagaku, and the *ryuteki* or dragon flute for togaku. In addition to these wind instruments, togaku uses a small mouth organ of 17 bamboo pipes called the *sho*, which plays tone clusters of 5 or 6 notes. Togaku and komagaku each use three percussion instruments, two of which are common to both types of music. These are a hanging *taiko*, or large drum, and the *shoko*, a small bronze gong. In komagaku there is also a small hourglass drum called *san no tsuzumi*, played with a single stick; the *kakko*, a small drum played with two sticks, is used in togaku. In Shinto vocal music, the only percussion instrument is a pair of wooden clappers (*shakubyoshi*). Stringed instruments are no longer used in the togaku dance repertoire or in komagaku, but two have been retained in the *kangen*, or chamber music setting of togaku: the *gakuso*, which is usually called by its common name, *koto*, and the biwa. Only one stringed instrument, the *wagon*, is used in Shinto music. The repertoire of gagaku music is played at tempos that, although varied, seem very slow when compared to Western music or even to other forms of Japanese music.

Film, Japanese

(Nihon *eiga*). The Japanese first imported motion pictures in 1896. By 1899 they were filming their own. Until the coming of talkies, movies in Japan were accompanied by a *benshi*, a live performer who sat by the side of the screen and orally interpreted the images of the film. Because *benshi* supplied expository connections and full dialogue, the first filmmakers replicated Japanese stage plays and generally ignored film techniques being developed in the West by such film directors as D. W. Griffith (1875–1948).

Early History

Makino Shozo (1878–1929), the father of the Japanese period film, gradually dropped *kabuki* elements from his costume dramas to concentrate on stories from juvenile literature and the traditional genre of oral storytelling known as *kodan*. Films with contemporary stories drew on the *shimpa* theatrical repertoire throughout the early 1900s. After World War

I, would-be filmmakers, influenced by the ideals of *shingeki* ("new theater") and by the flood of movies from abroad, cried for "modernization and realism." They sought naturalistic acting and the casting of actresses instead of traditional *onnagata* (female impersonators), subject matter that stretched beyond the narrow range of shimpa and kabuki plays, and the adoption of expressive techniques seen in foreign films.

The First *Jidaigeki* and *Gendaigeki*

The early 1920s marked the emergence of jidaigeki (period films), the genre that encompasses all films set before the Meiji period (1868−1912). In 1924 Makino Shozo collaborated with the Shinkokugeki drama troupe in a movie version of its swashbuckling hit *Kunisada Chuji*. The head of Shinkokugeki, Sawada Shojiro (1892−1929), had earlier developed *chambara* (spectacular sword-fighting scenes) as the basis for his popular theater. The plays staged by Sawada were derived, in part, from the *taishu bungaku* (popular literature) movement that had originated a decade earlier in the sword-fighter novels of Nakazato Kaizan (1885−1944). Jidaigeki subsequently evolved over 60 years through a symbiotic relationship among literary, theater, and film works focused on swords and solitary heroes.

Gendaigeki, the other genre of the post-1920 Japanese cinema, encompasses all stories with modern settings. Until 1926 the only gendaigeki that outdrew jidaigeki at the box office were either adventure stories patterned after foreign serials or sentimental love stories based on popular songs. Meanwhile, former Hollywood actor Abe Yutaka (1895−1977) led an "Americanism" school with his "smart, modern, speedy" comedies. Mizoguchi Kenji (1898−1956), the most eclectic of early gendaigeki directors, drew on sources ranging from the German film *The Cabinet of Dr. Caligari* to traditional shimpa drama.

The Late 1920s and Early 1930s

The economic depression that hit Japan before 1929 engendered left-wing tendencies in literature, shingeki, and films. Nihilistic, egocentric swordsmen became fighting protectors of the downtrodden in jidaigeki. After the invasion of Manchuria in 1931, more stringent government censorship ended these mildly radical efforts. The cutting edge of jidaigeki moved to satire and comedy after Itami Mansaku's (1900−1946) *Kokushi muso* (1932, Peerless Patriot). The most important new direction for jidaigeki was initiated by Yamanaka Sadao (1909−1938) and Inagaki Hiroshi (1905−1980), who brought the slice-of-life, lower-class urban milieu of many gendaigeki to the period film. In gendaigeki, Shimazu Yasujiro (1897−1945), with his *Tonari no Yae-chan* (1934, Our Neighbor Miss Yae), turned toward stories focused on the small joys and passive endurance of the world. The works of Ozu Yasujiro (1903−1963) best reflected the continuing development of the *shoshimin geki*, "dramas about the petite bourgeoisie." For three years in a row, critics chose his stories of imperfect fathers—*Umarete wa mita keredo* (1932, I Was Born, But ...), *Dekigokoro* (1933, Passing Fancy), and *Ukigusa monogatari* (1934, A Story of Floating Weeds)—as the best pictures of their respective years.

The Talkies

Gosho Heinosuke's (1902—1981) family comedy *Madamu to nyobo* (The Neighbor's Wife and Mine) was Japan's first technically successful talkie as well as the critical and popular success of 1931. Although talkies strained the capital resources of the industry (and drove the live benshi out of movie theaters), the innovation did not displace established film talent as it did abroad. Not until 1934—35 did talkies constitute more than half of all Japanese feature production.

The bulk of jidaigeki continued to be nihilistic chambara adventures. Several small studios survived throughout the 1930s by turning out cheap, silent jidaigeki for the surviving benshi market. Although feature production had risen to a steady average of 650 per year by the mid-1920s, the average annual output stabilized at 550 throughout the 1930s. Under wartime restraints this number suddenly decreased to 232 in 1941 and fell to 26 in 1945.

Censorship, the War, and the Postwar Era

Film censorship was consolidated under the control of the national Police Bureau (Keihokyoku) of the Home Ministry in 1925 and gradually tightened during the 1930s. In 1939 the Home Ministry ordered filmmakers to follow its list of essential "national policy" subjects, which accented patriotic home life and sacrifice for the nation. Despite strong official encouragement, fewer than one-fifth of all wartime features complied with government guidelines. Fewer than 2 percent of all films produced between the 1937 start of war in China and the 1945 surrender of Japan were stories about the military.

The American Occupation abolished Home Ministry censorship and set up its own office to supervise film content. In 1949 Occupation authorities eased their controls in return for the industry's establishment of a self-regulatory body, the Motion Picture Code Committee (Eirin), which administered a production code patterned after Hollywood's. Japanese cinema was without official, formal censorship and within a year sword fighting was back.

After disrupting production for two years, striking union militants occupied the Toho studios in 1948. Japanese police, aided by American tanks, quickly quashed the strike. Activists quit Toho and began to make a scattering of low-budget, independent features that had a defiant leftist sensibility long missing from the Japanese cinema.

In 1947, during the union turmoil, a large anticommunist faction left the parent Toho company to establish Shin Toho as the fourth major studio of the postwar period. (The two major studios in the late 1930s were Shochiku and the parent Toho company. In 1942, the government had engineered the amalgamation of the faltering Nikkatsu company with two lesser studios to create the third major studio, Daiei (Daiei Co, Ltd.) Two small postwar studios combined in 1951 to produce the fifth major studio, Toei (Toei Co, Ltd). A new Nikkatsu production company, with no connection to Daiei, became the sixth major studio in 1953. The six major studios controlled the industry through a cartel-like hold on film distribution and exhibition. The number of movie theaters reached an all-time high of 7,457 in 1960. This was 8.8 times as many as when the war ended. Two men whose directing careers had begun during the war came to the forefront during the early Occupation era: Kurosawa Akira (1910–) and Kinoshita Keisuke (1912–). Along with two other directors of their generation, Imai Tadashi (1912–1991) and Yoshimura Kozaburo (1911–), they dominated the 1947–1950 period with films about postwar life.

The 1950s

The decade of the 1950s, apart from being the most prosperous in the history of the Japanese cinema, is considered by many to be its creative Golden Age. Five times during this decade critics voted a film by Imai the best of the year, a streak that began with *Mata au hi made* (1950, Until the Day We Meet Again). When Kurosawa's innovative *jidaigeki Rashomon* (1950) won the top prize at the Venice Film Festival in 1951, it opened the Japanese cinema to international audiences. Kurosawa's cosmopolitan style alternated between such social issue–oriented gendaigeki as *Ikiru* (1952, To Live) and such seminal jidaigeki epics as *Shichinin no samurai* (1954, *Seven Samurai*).

Kurosawa's rival for international attention, Mizoguchi, abandoned his early postwar love stories to refashion the period film with such exquisite works as *Saikaku ichidai onna* (1952, The Life of a Woman by Saikaku; shown abroad as *The Life of Oharu*) and *Ugetsu monogatari* (1953, *Ugetsu*). Starting with *Banshun* (1949, Late Spring), Ozu Yasujiro and his scenarist Noda Kogo (1893–1968) concentrated on the emotional complexities of middle-class family life, while Naruse Mikio (1905–1969) and Gosho Heinosuke continued the prewar *shoshimin geki* tradition. Naruse later turned to a new major interest: portraits of women fighting the domination of men in such films as *Ukigumo* (1955, Floating Clouds). Gosho's major work was *Entotsu no mieru basho* (1953, Where Chimneys Are Seen).

Comedy grew in sophistication. Shibuya Minoru (1907–1980)

perfected the well-wrought farce in *Honjitsu kyushin* (1952, Clinic Closed Today), Kawashima Yuzo (1918–1963) created the definitive postwar jidaigeki comedy in *Bakumatsu taiyo den* (1957, A Tale of the Sun during the Last Days of the Shogunate), and Ichikawa pioneered black humor in *Kagi* (1959, The Key; shown abroad as *Odd Obsession*). The new Toei company captured a large new audience for jidaigeki by creating young chambara stars, and it also backed jidaigeki old masters: Ito Daisuke (1898–1981), Uchida Tomu (1898–1970), and Makino Masahiro (1908–1993). Toho and Daiei countered Toei with their own brands of jidaigeki program pictures, while they supported new directions for period films by Kurosawa, Mizoguchi, and Inagaki. To strengthen its principal market among urban, middle-class audiences, Toho made pop musicals and dozens of comedies about middle-aged white-collar workers. In 1954 Toho created Japan's first film monster in *Godzilla (Gojira)*. A horde of Toho and Daiei monsters followed for two decades. Kinoshita's *Karumen kokyo ni kaeru* (Carmen Comes Home) inaugurated a decade of technical innovation in 1951 with the first Japanese color feature. Three years later Kinugasa Teinosuke (1896–1982)'s *Jigokumon* (1953, Gate of Hell) won the highest international acclaim for innovative use of color. Anamorphic wide-screen features appeared in 1957, but it took more than seven years for the new frame dimensions to become standard in Japan. In the late 1950s, a new short-lived genre, *taiyozoku* (sun tribe) films, so called after a group of young people portrayed in the best-selling novel *Taiyo no kisetsu* (1955, Season of the Sun; tr *Season of Violence*, 1966) by Ishihara Shintaro (1932–), exploited the hedonism of affluent postwar youth. This accelerated interest in movie sex and violence.

Television and a New Wave

In 1958, five years after television broadcasting had begun, there were 1.6 million television sets throughout the country. By 1969 there were 21.9 million sets, a figure almost equal to the number of households. Attendance at the movies fell from the all-time high of 1.1 billion in 1958 to 300 million in 1968. The Shin Toho studios went bankrupt in 1961. Half of the movie theaters in the country closed during the 1960s.

In 1958 Masumura Yasuzo (1924–1986) called for the destruction of the established Japanese cinema and soon was joined by other young directors. Oshima Nagisa (1932–) demanded an end to lyricism, heaviness, naturalism, *mono no aware*, and the omnipotent conventions of the international cinema of realism. Oshima and two tradition-breaking fellow directors at Shochiku, Shinoda Masahiro (1931–) and Yoshida Yoshishige (1933–), were dubbed the "Shochiku Nuberu Bagu" (*nouvelle vague*, or new wave). Oshima's Brechtian *Koshikei* (1968,

Death by Hanging) and *Shinjuku dorobo nikki* (1969, Diary of a Shinjuku Thief) established him as the principal new talent of the cosmopolitan 1960s. Imamura Shohei (1926–) rivaled Oshima with a call to destroy the illusionistic pretensions of fiction and documentary films. Imamura searched for clues to Japanese national identity in the pseudobiography *Nippon konchuki* (1963, Story of a Japanese Insect; shown abroad as *The Insect Woman*) and the modern primitive myth *Kamigami no fukaki yokubo* (1968, The Profound Desire of the Gods; shown abroad as *Kuragejima: Tales from a Southern Island*).

In jidaigeki, major directors looked occasionally to the classical theater. Kurosawa adapted elements from the No theater to his syncretic version of Macbeth, *Kumonosujo* (1957, Throne of Blood). Uchida Tomu in *Naniwa no koi no monogatari* (1959, Naniwa Love Story) and Shinoda Masahiro in *Shinju Ten no Amijima* (1969, Love Suicide at Amijima; Double Suicide) used plays by Chikamatsu Monzaemon (1653–1724) and borrowed respectively from kabuki and *bunraku* drama. In 1963 Toei originated a new direction for ultraviolent chambara: the *yakuza* (gangster) genre. The plots of these films were invariably formalistic variations of intricate *giri-ninjo* sword-fighting dramas, portraying a righteous gangster amid low-life corruption in prewar Japan. The immediate popularity of Toei yakuza pictures soon wiped out jidaigeki as the main arena for chambara.

Since the Late 1970s

The dominant director of the 1970s was a major-studio man, Yamada Yoji (1931–) of Shochiku. Although his principal works were prize-winning portraits of lower-class family life, his overwhelmingly popular success was the *Tora san* series. Beginning in 1969 and continuing for more than two decades, Yamada has written and directed more than 40 films in this series, which fuses the two bedrock motifs of Japanese film: the everyday collective life of a family and the adventures of a lonely wanderer.

From the late 1960s most major directors as well as promising newcomers could not depend on the studios for employment. As independents, they had to raise money bit by bit themselves. After 1985, cash-heavy Japanese companies (including media conglomerates but not the poor movie studios) were backing Broadway shows and Hollywood movies. By the time Sony bought Columbia Pictures in 1989 as an investment in American, not Japanese, filmmaking, Oshima, Kurosawa, Shinoda, and Itami Juzo (1933–) were looking abroad for production funds.

Comedies dominated Japanese film production in the 1980s, especially Itami's satires *Tampopo* (1985, Dandelion) and *Marusa no onna*

Culture

(1988, A Taxing Woman). Exceptions are the serious films of Oguri Kohei (1945—), who won the jury prize at the 1990 Cannes Film Festival for *Shi no toge* (1990, The Sting of Death). By 1990 total annual movie admissions had declined to 143 million in a market now dominated by American blockbusters; the number of theaters decreased to about 1,900, and overall annual feature production dwindled to 239.

Nihongo

Japanese language

(*nihongo*). The native language of the overwhelming majority of the more than 100 million inhabitants of the Japanese archipelago, including the Ryukyu Islands, and significant numbers of Japanese immigrants in other countries, especially in North and South America.

Although the Japanese and Chinese languages are entirely unrelated genetically, the Japanese writing system derives from that of Chinese. Chinese characters were introduced sometime in the 6th century, if not before, and the modern writing system is a complex one in which Chinese characters are used in conjunction with two separate phonetic scripts developed from them in Japan. Japanese has also absorbed loanwords freely from other languages, especially Chinese and English, the former chiefly from the 8th to the 19th century and the latter in the 20th century.

Genetic Relationships

Some scholars have maintained that no genetic relationship of Japanese to any known language can be demonstrated. However, the syntactic similarity of Japanese to Korean is widely acknowledged, as is its resemblance in certain respects to the Altaic languages in general. The situation is complicated by similarities in vocabulary between Japanese and the Malayo-Polynesian languages. There seems to be a growing consensus among Japanese scholars that syntactically Japanese shows an Altaic affinity, but that at some time in its prehistory it received an influence in vocabulary and morphology from the Malayo-Polynesian languages to the south.

The Japanese Dialects and the Speech of Tokyo

Modern Japanese language has a large number of local dialects, existing alongside, but gradually being overwhelmed by, the officially recognized standard language (*hyojungo*), which is based on the speech of the capital, Tokyo. The Japanese dialects, however, show less variety in syntax and morphology than do the strong regional languages of Italy, for example, or Austria.

Two important urban dialects that flourish alongside the

standard language of Tokyo are those of the cities of Kyoto and Osaka. Kyoto was the imperial capital for more than 1,000 years, and, though it was not always the seat of real political or economic power, both it and its language continued to have the highest prestige. The language of its court nobility during the Heian period (794–1185) as preserved in the literary works of that period became the basis of Classical Japanese, which remained the standard for the written language until the beginning of the 20th century. During the Edo period (1600–1868), Edo (now Tokyo), which was the seat of the Tokugawa Shogunate, grew into an important commercial and administrative city. Both it and the older commercial city of Osaka became thriving centers of the culture and language of the merchant classes (*chonin*), and the language of Edo in particular—the locus of political power and the home of the *samurai* bureaucracy—gradually developed a prestige of its own.

The Phonology of the Standard Language

The short or unit vowels of standard Japanese, *a, i, u, e*, and *o*, are pronounced more or less as in Spanish or Italian. (In this description the phonemes of Japanese will be written in the standard Hepburn romanization used throughout this encyclopedia, phonetic symbols being added only when necessary for clarity.) The long vowels, *â, ii, û, ei*, and *ô*, are pronounced double the length of the short vowels (*a:, i:, u:, e:*, and *o:*), except that *ei* is often pronounced as a sequence of two separate vowels. (When transcribing the Japanese pronunciation of loanwords from Western languages, in this encyclopedia *ii* and *ei* are written *î* and *ê*, respectively.) The distinction between long and short vowels is essential for meaning. Aside from *ei*, sequences of vowels such as *ai, au, ae, oi, ue*, and so forth are so pronounced that the individual vowels retain their identity, although a glide often occurs; they are treated as separate syllables.

The consonants are *k, s, sh, t, ch, ts, n, h, f, m, y, r, w, g, j, z, d, b*, and *p*. The fricative *sh* (as in English "shoe") and the affricates *ch, ts*, and *j* (as in English "church," "patsy," and "judge," respectively) are treated as single consonants. *G* is always pronounced as in English "good" (never as in "genetics"). The rest are pronounced more or less as in English except that *f* is a bilabial rather than labiodental fricative, *r* is flapped, and *t, d*, and *n* are dental. When *n* is used at the end of a syllable as opposed to the beginning, it expresses a uvular syllabic nasal "N"; this changes to one of three different types of nasals when followed by certain consonants: *n* (dental) before *t, d*, or *n;* (velar, as in English "thank") before *k* or *g;* and *m* (bilabial) before *p, b*, or *m*. The older Hepburn spelling used in this encyclopedia reflects the last named of these pronunciations by changing *n* to *m* before *p, b*, or *m* as in *san* (three) versus *sammai* (three sheets); however, the modified Hepburn romanization used in many recent publications retains the *n* in all cases (*sanmai*). When followed by a vowel or *y*, this syllable-final *n* must be distinguished from syllable-initial *n*. In this encyclopedia an apostrophe is used after the former for this purpose (e.g., *jin'in* "personnel" as opposed to *jinin* "resignation"). In the double consonants, *-kk-, -pp-, -tt-,* and *-ss-,* and in the combinations *-ssh-* and *-tch-* (all of which are always medial) the consonants are pronounced—without release but with, in effect, a short interval of silence—much as in the English "bookcase," "shirttail," and "hatcheck."

Japanese has no stress accent like that of English. Each syllable is given equal stress, successions of syllables being pronounced with metronomic regularity. Standard Japanese and a number of the dialects do have, however, a high-low pitch accent system, accent in a word or sequence of words being marked by the syllable after which the pitch drops. The way in which the same word (or the same set of contrasting homophones) is accented can differ significantly among those dialects that have pitch accents.

Another characteristic of standard Japanese is the strong tendency to devoice the vowels *i* and *u* when they fall between two voiceless consonants, so that *shitakusa* (undergrowth) becomes *sh'tak'sa*. The vowels are not always dropped entirely, however: often they are sounded faintly, or at least their metronomic beat preserved. The vowel *u* at the end of a word after a voiceless consonant is also often devoiced or dropped, most notably in *desu*, the polite form of the copula, and in the polite verb ending *-masu*, which are often pronounced *des'* and *mas'*, respectively.

The Grammar of Modern Japanese

Nouns Japanese nouns are uninflected words that have neither number nor gender and do not influence the inflection of the adjectives modifying them.

In Japanese the grammatical function of nouns within a sentence is not indicated by word order as in English; neither are nouns inflected for grammatical case as in some languages. Instead grammatical function is indicated by grammatical particles (sometimes called postpositions), which follow the noun. Among the more important of these are *ga, o, ni,* and *no,* which function as case markers, *ga* indicating subject of verb, *o* direct object of verb, *ni* dative or indirect object, and *no* genitive. For example, in *kaze ga fuku* (the wind blows/will blow), *ga* marks *kaze* as the subject of the verb *fuku*; in *kodomo ga tomodachi no inu ni mizu o yaru* (the child gives/will give water to his/her friend's dog), *ga* marks *kodomo* (child) as the subject of the verb *yaru*, no marks *tomodachi* (friend) as possessor of *inu* (dog), *ni* marks *inu* as indirect object, and *o* marks *mizu* (water) as direct object of the verb. A particularly important particle is *wa*. This is not a case marker but rather marks the topic or theme of the sentence. In *zo wa hana ga nagai* (elephants have long noses; literally, "as for elephants, the nose is long"), *wa* marks *zo* (elephant/elephants) as the topic of the sentence and *ga* marks *hana* (nose/noses) as the subject of the adjective *nagai* (is long). All of these particles also have various other functions and meanings depending on grammatical structure and context. There are a number of other postpositions that function much as prepositions do in English.

Verbs Japanese verbal inflections do not indicate person or number. The dictionary forms of all verbs in the modern language end in the vowel -*u*. When citing the dictionary form of Japanese verbs in English, it is conventional to refer to them by the English infinitive; thus *kaku* is often cited as "to write," although this form is actually the present (more precisely the nonpast) tense, which means "write/writes" or "will write." Other inflectional forms include *kakanai* (negative: "does not/will not write"), *kako* (tentative or hortatory: "someone may write"; "let's write"), *kakitai* (often called "desiderative": "wants to write"), *kaita* (past: "wrote"), *kakeba* (provisional or conditional: "if someone writes"), and *kake* (nonpolite imperative: "write!"). Verbs can be used not only to form the predicate of a sentence or clause but also attributively to modify nouns (e.g., *kaku hito*, "the person who writes").

Verb conjugations are classified in two main types. One of these consists of the consonant-stem verbs (verbs whose stems end in consonants), including verbs such as *kaku* (write), *hanasu* (talk), and *utsu* (hit), whose stems are *kak-*, *hanas-*, and *uts-*, respectively (as mentioned above, ts is treated as a single consonant). The other type comprises the vowel-stem verbs, which are themselves of two types, with stems ending in either the vowel *i* or the vowel *e*; e.g., *miru* (see) and *taberu* (eat), whose stems are *mi-* and *tabe-*, respectively. (The dictionary forms of vowel-stem verbs all end in -*iru* or -*eru*; however, not all verbs so ending are vowel-stem verbs. Some are consonant-stem verbs with stems ending in *r*; e.g., *kiru* "cut"). In modern Japanese there are two fully conjugated irregular verbs, *kuru* (come) and *suru* (do), bringing the total number of standard verb conjugations to five.

The copula The Japanese copula or linking verb (plain form *da*; polite form *desu*) is used to link two nouns (or nominal phrases) in the pattern A *wa* B *da* or A *wa* B *desu* (A is B). The literal meaning of this pattern is "as for A, it is B" or "as for A, it is in the category of B," e.g., *neko wa dobutsu da* (cats are animals; literally, "as for cats, they are animals"). For this reason the Japanese copula cannot always be translated by the English "to be." For example, *watakushi wa biru desu* does not mean "I am beer" but "I am having beer" (literally, "as for me, it is beer").

Adjectives Japanese adjectives are inflected in some ways like verbs, and like verbs they can function either attributively, coming before the nouns they modify, or as the predicates of sentences or clauses, in the latter case appearing at the end of the sentence or clause. The dictionary forms of all adjectives end in one of four vowels (*a, i, u,* or *o*) followed by a final *i*. The stem of the adjective is obtained by dropping the final *i*; e.g., *takai* (high; stem *taka*), *utsukushii* (beautiful; stem *utsukushi*), *samui* (cold; stem *samu*), and *shiroi* (white; stem *shiro*).

Levels of speech Japanese expresses a consciousness of social relationships by various grammatical means. Plain versus polite verb forms distinguish between easy informality and abruptness on the one hand and a correct, neutral politeness on the other. In the system of levels known as honorific language (*keigo*), the speaker chooses among a number of alternative ways of saying the same thing, the choice being determined by such factors as relative age, sex, and social status. One uses respectful or exalting forms with reference to an addressee or third person of higher status and humble terms with reference to oneself or a third person who falls into the same category as oneself.

Some actions often referred to in social situations, such as "go," "come," "be," "say," "look," "eat," "give," and "receive," are represented by sets of three completely different verbs, one neutral, one humble, and one exalting. There are also sets of humble and exalting nouns for common kinship terms, and so forth. The passive forms of verbs are also often used as honorific verbs (with active meaning) when referring to actions of the exalted.

The sentence The typical Japanese sentence is built on the pattern of subject-object-verb (SOV), as in *neko ga nezumi o tsukamaeta* (the cat caught the mouse). However, since the particle *ga* marks *neko* (cat) as the subject, and the particle *o* marks *nezumi* (mouse) as the object of the verb *tsukamaeta*, a certain amount of inversion, as for stylistic purposes, is possible; *nezumi o neko ga tsukamaeta* (OSV) would have virtually the same meaning as the SOV sentence, whereas in English such inversion of subject and object would change the meaning entirely. To return to the basic SOV sentence, if an adverbial modifier, for instance *subayaku* (swiftly), is inserted, it may come before the subject, the object, or the verb, with slight differences of emphasis.

There are no relative pronouns in Japanese as in the English "the cat that caught the mouse died." In Japanese the entire subordinate clause is placed directly in front of the noun as a modifier: *nezumi o tsukamaeta neko ga shinda* (literally, "the caught-the-mouse cat died"). A sentence can also be made into a subordinate clause in another sentence by inserting either the nominalizing particle *no* (not to be confused with the genitive particle *no* mentioned earlier) or the function word *koto* (thing; matter) after the final verb of the sentence, which then modifies the particle, forming a noun clause.

Vocabulary Japanese has an extremely rich and varied vocabulary, not only its large stock of native words, which are felt to be particularly expressive and sonorous, but also a great quantity of words of Chinese origin. To these are added the many loanwords from English and other European languages that have come into Japanese, especially during the 20th century. Many of the loanwords from Chinese have been so thoroughly absorbed into the daily vocabulary that their foreign origin is no longer felt. Much of the intellectual and philosophical vocabulary is of Chinese origin, but not all of this is due entirely to Chinese cultural influence; an important part of the modern intellectual vocabulary consists of words coined in Japan in the late 19th and early 20th centuries by devising new combinations of Chinese characters as translations of concepts then being introduced from the West. This process of coinage still continues, but there is a growing tendency, particularly in the sciences, to use Western words intact. Aside from the sciences, words are often used with meanings quite different from those of their original languages, and new Japanese words are sometimes coined by combining parts of Western language words in startling ways. One particularly interesting feature of the native Japanese vocabulary is the large number of established onomatopoeic words it contains. These include not only words imitating sounds but also words expressing abstract qualities or subjective feelings.

Writing System

The Japanese writing system uses Chinese characters (*kanji*) in combination with two separate forms of the phonetic syllabic script known as *kana*: *hiragana* and *katakana*. Some words are written entirely in kana, others entirely in Chinese characters, and others in a combination of the two. In the latter case the stem of the word is written with a Chinese character, or characters, and inflectional endings or other suffixes with kana. Grammatical particles and function words (such as demonstratives and auxiliary verbs) are written in kana. The resulting text is sometimes sprinkled with Roman letters (e.g., acronyms such as PTA, model numbers, and occasionally entire foreign words), so that the number of scripts needed to write modern Japanese actually comes to four.

There are 1,945 Chinese characters in the *joyo kanji*, the list approved by the government for use in publications for the general public and for writing personal names. There are an additional 284 characters approved for writing names alone. The joyo kanji are learned (or at least taught) by the end of the ninth grade. Kanji in scholarly publications may exceed the government guidelines. Tens of thousands of kanji are contained in large dictionaries; however, the number of characters in actual use probably did not exceed 5,000 or 6,000 even before the post—World War II language reforms that led to adoption of the government-approved list.

Most Chinese characters have more than one pronunciation or "reading." There are two types: *on* readings and *kun* readings. The former are the pronunciations that result when characters are used to write Chinese loanwords. They reflect an original Chinese pronunciation of the character, but as pronounced in Japan. Some characters have two or three possible on readings, reflecting loanwords brought in from different parts of China or in different historical periods. *Kun* readings are native Japanese words that have the same meaning as the character (or more precisely, the Chinese morpheme the character represents); they are, in effect, the Japanese words that the character stands for.

Japanese is normally written or printed in vertical lines reading from top to bottom, with the lines starting at the right-hand side of the page and proceeding across from right to left.

K*anji*

(Chinese characters). Ideographs of ancient Chinese origin that are still used in China, Korea, and Japan and were formerly used in other areas influenced by Chinese culture such as Vietnam. Chinese characters are ideographs in that essentially each character or graph symbolizes a single idea and, by extension, the sound (i.e., spoken word or morpheme) associated with that idea. For example, the Chinese character 犬 is "dog" in English, quan in modern standard Chinese, and *ken* or *inu* in Japanese.

On and *Kun* Readings

Since in the Japanese writing system Chinese characters can be used to write either words of Chinese origin or native Japanese words, the pronunciations that can be assigned to them in reading fall naturally into two categories: (1) the Japanese imitations or approximations of the sound of the original Chinese syllable and (2) the native Japanese word that translates the meaning of the character. The former are called *on* readings (*on yomi*), on being written with a character that means "sound" (i.e., the original Chinese sound); these are often referred to as "Sino-

Japanese" readings in English. The latter are called kun readings (*kun yomi*), kun being written with a character that originally meant "to interpret the meaning" (i.e., the meaning of the character as expressed by the Japanese word).

Number of Characters in Use

The number of Chinese characters currently used in Japan is limited to a small percentage of the 40,000 to 50,000 contained in the larger dictionaries. A list of characters called *toyo kanji* (Chinese characters for daily use) was selected by the Ministry of Education in 1946, limiting the number of characters for official and general public use to 1,850. In 1981 this list was superseded by a similar but larger one (the *joyo kanji*) containing 1,945 characters.

Loanwords

(*gairaigo*). Foreign loanwords and phrases that are extensively used in Japanese and normally written in the *katakana* syllabary are called gairaigo. Loanwords from China are not normally treated as gairaigo, since they are not only numerous but written in Chinese characters and hence are not easily distinguishable from native words. The most important *gairaigo* are American and European loanwords.

Foreign words were introduced along with new things and new ideas from foreign cultures; many of these, such as the large number of technical terms, had no adequate Japanese equivalent. Even when Japanese had equivalent expressions, foreign words were in many cases employed for their novelty or the sense of prestige they gave the speaker. A foreign word is often substituted as a euphemism for a Japanese word, as in the case of "WC" and *toire* (from "toilet").

The earliest foreign loanwords, many from Sanskrit, Ainu, or Korean, are hardly recognized as such by present-day Japanese speakers. Most of them are written in Chinese characters rather than katakana. Many were introduced quite early in Japanese history and often refer to things closely associated with everyday Japanese life. After the arrival of the Portuguese in 1543, Christian and commercial terms were borrowed from Portuguese.

The Spanish also entered Japan about the same time as the Portuguese, but the number of Spanish words that remained in Japanese is limited. The Dutch arrived in 1600 and continued to have limited access to Japan even during National Seclusion, bringing a number of Dutch words into the language.

In the late Edo period (1600 – 1868), English, French, and Russian words began to arrive. At present English loanwords outnumber all others; among the countless examples are *sutoraiki* (labor strike), *depato* (department store), and *kare raisu* (curried rice). French words are especially numerous in fashion, cooking, foreign affairs, and politics. Russian has supplied words for foods and things Russian. After Japan reopened to foreign countries in the second half of the 19th century, a great number of German words also entered. They are most numerous in medicine and the humanities and among mountaineering and skiing terms. Italian words were also introduced beginning in the Meiji period (1868–1912), especially for music and food.

Feminine language

(*joseigo*). A variety of Japanese, called joseigo or *onnakotoba*, that is typically used by females as a reflection of their femininity. The existence of clearly marked, gender-differentiated language styles is a frequently mentioned characteristic of Japanese.

Feminine language can be described in terms of features that occur almost exclusively in the language of females and features that are, in a given context, more typical of the language of females. Aside from the high pitch, distinctive voice quality, and particular sentence-final intonations that are associated with the speech of Japanese females, and aside from the vocabulary associated with topics predominantly of interest to females, feminine features include lexical items, such as: (1) the self-reference terms *atashi* and *atakushi*, as less formal equivalents of *watakushi* (I); (2) the sentence particle *wa* in sentence-final position with rising intonation—or prefinal before *yo* or *ne*—indicating gentle assurance; (3) sentence-final *koto* occurring in exclamations, for example: *Kirei da koto* (How pretty it is!); (4) particular interjections, for example: *Ara, ma, uwa* (indicating surprise).

Most commonly, feminine language is characterized by certain features that occur in a particular context or with a marked frequency. The most striking example is the feature of politeness. Given the socialization process, which trains Japanese women to be polite and subservient to men, it follows that the honorific and formal varieties of Japanese language are used more frequently by women. This does not mean that the forms themselves are feminine, but rather that their frequent use and their occurrence in certain social situations are typical of female usage. Thus, a polite form that would be used by a man only when talking to a person of extremely high position might be used by a woman in talking to a casual acquaintance.

Names

(*namae*). Proper names in Japan present a problem since virtually all Chinese characters used in names have a multiplicity of readings—both *on* readings, based on Chinese pronunciation, and *kun* readings, based on native Japanese words. Moreover, since most names are written with two or more characters, it is often impossible to be sure of the combination of readings needed in any particular case without having personal knowledge. Conversely, the same name element usually can be found written with a number of different characters. In the case of personal names, for example, more than 130 characters have 10 or more possible name readings, and the common name elements *taka* and *nori* are found written with 168 and 225 different characters, respectively. Since some characters and readings are much more common in names than others, it usually is possible to arrive at the likely reading of a name, and the number of characters available for use when registering the personal names of children is now limited by law. However, since there is no restriction on the readings that can be given to these characters, many uncertainties remain in all types of names.

People's Names

In Japanese usage the family name comes before the personal name, but otherwise the treatment of names is much the same as in the West. A Japanese has a family name and an official personal name; artistic or professional names also are often used. Suffixes equivalent to titles such as Mr. or Mrs. (san) or Dr (sensei) are used after the family name in formal reference, and within the family or among intimates the familiar ending chan is used after personal names, often in abbreviated form, very much as -y is used in diminutives such as Willy or Lizzy.

Group (Clan and Family) Names

Up to the end of the 8th century, the two main types of group names within society were *uji*, to indicate lineage groups or clans, and *kabane*, hereditary titles of nobility granted to *uji* and individuals. In the case of an individual, the *kabane* was used between the name of the uji and the personal name; for example, Nakatomi no Muraji Kamako indicates one Kamako of the Nakatomi clan who had the rank of *muraji*.

During the Heian period (794–1185), clans such as the Ariwara, Minamoto, and Taira, which were related to the imperial line and had been granted their names by the court, increased in size so much that subdivisions became necessary. These smaller groups usually were distinguished by their locations.

From the 13th century on, military families in rural areas distinguished themselves from others of the same clan by using as their standard family name the name of their locality, and all types of group names had become wholly fixed by the early 17th century. With a few exceptions, the use of family names remained limited to the upper classes of society, with the lower orders generally being referred to only by their personal names or, where necessary, by prefixes indicative of their trade or location.

Two years after the Meiji Restoration of 1868, however, everyone was allowed to take a family name, and in 1875 family names were made compulsory. Certain names came to be adopted more generally in some areas than others, but the whole process led to the appearance of family names of every conceivable kind, and the frequent mistakes made in writing the characters for newly acquired names have in some cases survived to add to the present confusion of Japanese name readings.

At the present time, the names Sato and Suzuki each account for more than 1.5 percent of the population, and other common family names are Tanaka, Yamamoto, Watanabe, Kobayashi, Saito, Tamura, Ito, and Takahashi. In the case of family names, native Japanese readings are more frequent than *on* readings.

Personal Names

Various considerations may apply in the naming of children in modern Japan—seniority in the case of brothers, for example, or the advice of fortune-tellers in choosing characters deemed appropriate to the family name. In nearly all cases, though, names and characters are chosen primarily for their auspicious meanings and happy associations, that is, as talismans of good fortune.

The choice of characters permitted for use in personal names was first limited in 1948 and was restricted as of 1990 to the 1,945 *joyo kanji* and the 284 characters selected for use only in personal names.

Men's Names

In premodern Japan men of the upper ranks of society could have a variety of personal names. The main categories were as follows: (1) *Yomyo* or *domyo* (child name). Often ending in *-waka, -maru, -maro,* or *-o* (e.g., Ushiwaka), a name of this type was customarily given to a boy on or by the seventh day after birth (*shichiya*) and generally was used until superseded by other names at *gempuku* when he was about 15. Men of the lower classes normally used these child names throughout their lives. (2) *Tsusho* or *yobina, zokumyo, kemyo* (current name). This name was given to a male at gempuku together with his *jitsumyo* and was the one by which he generally was known (e.g., Taro). Some of these names could take prefixes to indicate a particular generation (Kotaro for Taro II) or lineage (Heitaro for a member of the Heike i.e., Taira clan). (3) Jitsumyo or *nanori* (true name). This was a formal adult name used in association with the clan name (Minamoto no Shitagau for Shitagau of the Minamoto clan) and so closely associated with the individual that other people would use it of him very rarely or never at all if he was their superior. Upon the death of a dignitary, his jitsumyo would be used as his *imina* (posthumous name).

Many other types of name were, and still are, used in special circumstances. Nicknames (*adana*) were not uncommon, used either alone or in conjunction with a *tsusho*—for example, Nossori Jubei ("Plodder" Jubei). More current are the *yago* (house names) traditionally associated with *kabuki* actors and families, which are shouted out by members of the audience during performances.

Women's Names

Before the 9th century most women's names seem to have ended in *-me, -iratsume,* or *-toji,* as in Shima-me. From then on, high-ranking court ladies had formal personal names consisting of one character followed by the suffix *-ko*—for example, Sadako—but the taboos against the general use of such jitsumyo led also to the wide use of yomyo, tsusho (e.g., Murasaki Shikibu), and, later, to the use of various elegant names, many of them derived from *The Tale of Genji.* Among humbler women the *-ko* suffix was never used, but the 16th century saw the introduction of the prefix *o-,* as in Oichi. This practice spread during the Edo period (1600–1868), when most women had two-syllable names, often written in *kana* (phonetic syllabic characters) and a woman's status was immediately evident from her name.

The changes brought about by the Meiji Restoration (1868), however, led to a vast increase in the use of Chinese characters. The employment of the formerly aristocratic suffix *-ko* grew steadily from about 3 percent in the mid-1880s to 80 percent in 1935. Today women follow the ancient court practice of having two-syllable names plus *-ko* or having elegant three-syllable names such as Harue with no suffix.

Place Names

Accounts of the origins of place names are a common feature of the earliest written works in Japan, especially those known as *fudoki* (regional chronicles), but many of their etymologies are still uncertain. In general, though, they can be said to derive from natural features or historical causes.

The names of geographical origin generally refer to such obvious features of the land as a river, mountain, valley, plain, moor, ford, or beach. These designations often are combined with prefixes describing such aspects as size, length, depth, or direction, such as Nagasaki (long cape), Yokohama (side beach), or Hiroshima (broad island).

History-based names include some derived from the Ainu, most typically those ending in -*betsu* or -*nai* in northern parts of Japan. Names such as Shinden (new rice fields) indicate the development of an area, while others show religious associations by the use of such components as *kami* (god), *miya* (shrine), and *tera* (temple). Also, Edo was renamed Tokyo (eastern capital) in 1868 in contrast to its predecessor Kyoto (capital metropolis).

Philosophy

F*uryu*

Refers to the refined taste of a cultivated, sophisticated person and to works of art and other things associated with such persons. The word was derived from the Chinese term *fengliu*, which literally meant "good deportment and manner. "After reaching Japan around the 8th century, it was employed in a more aesthetic sense, referring to the refined manners of an urbane person and later to all things regarded as elegant, tasteful, or artistic. The term *fuga* is sometimes employed in the same sense as furyu, but, in general, furyu is a more inclusive term, referring not just to poetry but to all the arts.

In the 12th century furyu began to follow two separate lines of semantic evolution. In one, furyu was applied to the more earthy, showy beauty manifest in popular arts. In the other, men attempted to discover furyu in the beauty of landscape gardens, flower arrangement, architecture, and Chinese nature poetry. This latter trend gave birth to the tea ceremony in the Muromachi period (1333–1568).

In the modern era Koda Rohan endeavored to achieve a union of love, art, and religion in the name of furyu in the short story "*Furyu-butsu*" (1889). In *Kusamakura* (1906; tr *The Three-Cornered World*, 1965) the novelist Natsume Soseki attempted to revitalize the concept by injecting it with compassion and humanism.

W*abi*

An aesthetic and moral principle advocating the enjoyment of a quiet, leisurely life free from worldly concerns. Originating in the medieval eremitic tradition, it emphasizes a simple, austere type of beauty and a serene, transcendental frame of mind. It is a central concept in the aesthetics of the tea ceremony and is also manifest in some works of *waka*, *renga*, and haiku. Its implications partly coincide with those of *sabi* and *furyu*.

The word wabi was derived from the verb *wabu* (to languish) and the adjective *wabishi* (lonely, comfortless), which initially denoted the pain of a person who fell into adverse circumstances. But ascetic literati of the Kamakura (1185—1333) and Muromachi (1333—1568) periods developed it into a more positive concept by making poverty and loneliness synonymous with liberation from material and emotional worries and by turning the absence of apparent beauty into a new and higher beauty. These new connotations of wabi were cultivated especially by masters of the tea ceremony, such as Sen no Rikyu (1522—1591), who sought to elevate their art by associating it with the spirit of Zen and stressed the importance of seeking richness in poverty and beauty in simplicity.

S*abi*

Poetic ideal fostered by Basho (1644—1694) and his followers in *haikai* (*haiku*), though the germ of the concept and the term existed long before them. Sabi points toward a medieval aesthetic combining elements of old age, loneliness, resignation, and tranquillity, yet the colorful and plebeian qualities of Edo-period (1600—1868) culture are also present. At times sabi is used synonymously or in conjunction with *wabi*, an aesthetic ideal of the tea ceremony.

Fujiwara no Toshinari (1114—1204), the first major poet to employ a *sabi*-related word (the verb *sabu*) in literary criticism, stressed its connotations of loneliness and desolation, pointing to such images as frost-withered reeds on the seashore. With later medieval artists such as Zeami (1363—1443), Zenchiku (1405—68), and Shinkei (1406—75), the implications of sabi focused so heavily on desolation that the emerging beauty seemed almost cold. Underlying this aesthetic was the cosmic view typical of medieval Buddhists, who recognized the existential loneliness of all men and tried to resign themselves to, or even find beauty in, that loneliness.

G*iri* and *ninjo*

(*giri to ninjo*). Social obligation (giri) and human feelings (ninjo). Giri refers to the obligation to act according to the dictates of society in relation to other persons. It applies, however, only to particular persons with whom one has certain social relations and is therefore a particular rather than a universal norm. Ninjo broadly refers to universal human feelings of love, affection, pity, sympathy, sorrow, and the like, which one "naturally" feels toward others, as in relations between parent and child or between lovers.

Giri is a norm that obliges the observance of reciprocal

relations—to help those who have helped one, to do favors for those from whom one has received favors, and so forth. The concept implies a moral force that compels members of society to engage in socially expected reciprocal activities even when their natural inclination (ninjo) may be to do otherwise. To feudal warriors, giri referred foremost to their obligation to serve their lord, even at the cost of their lives, and to repay *on* (favor) received from the lord. In Japan, to be observant of giri is an indication of high moral worth. To neglect the obligation to reciprocate is to lose the trust of others expecting reciprocation and eventually to lose their support.

Generally human feelings do not conflict with social norms, and observance of giri does not contradict ninjo. However, occasions sometimes arise where one is caught between social obligation and natural inclination. Though giri and ninjo as terms have outmoded connotations in modern Japan, the concepts are still important in guiding the conduct of the Japanese.

I*ki* and *sui*

(*iki to sui*). Aesthetic and moral ideals of urban commoners in the Edo period (1600—1868). The concept of sui was cultivated initially in the Osaka area during the late 17th century, while iki prevailed mostly in Edo (now Tokyo) during the early 19th century. Aesthetically both pointed toward an urbane, chic, bourgeois type of beauty with undertones of sensuality. Morally they envisioned the tasteful life of a person who was wealthy but not attached to money, who enjoyed sensual pleasure but was never carried away by carnal desires, and who knew all the intricacies of earthly life but was capable of disengaging himself from them. In their insistence on sympathetic understanding of human feelings, sui and iki resembled the Heian courtiers' ideal of *aware*, yet they differed from it in their inclusion of the more plebeian aspects of life.

Iki originally denoted "spirit" or "heart." Later it came to mean "high spirit" or "high heart" and referred also to the way in which a high-spirited person talked, behaved, or dressed. As it became expressive of the Edo commoners' ideal, its connotations were affected by the Osaka concept of sui and moved closer to the latter. Indeed, iki was sometimes used as an equivalent of sui. Yet usually it carried a slightly different shade of meaning. As an aesthetic concept iki leaned toward a beauty somewhat less colorful than sui. Also, iki seems to have had a slightly more sensual connotation than sui. It was often applied to the description of a woman, especially a professional entertainer who knew exactly how much display of eroticism was desirable by the highest standard of taste.

Mono no aware

A literary and aesthetic ideal cultivated during the Heian period (794–1185). At its core is a deep, empathetic appreciation of the ephemeral beauty manifest in nature and human life, and it is therefore usually tinged with a hint of sadness; under certain circumstances it can be accompanied by admiration, awe, or even joy. The word was revived as part of the vocabulary of Japanese literary criticism through the writings of Motoori Norinaga (1730–1801).

In Norinaga's view, then, mono no aware is a purified and exalted feeling, close to the innermost heart of man and nature. Theoretically the meaning of mono no aware is as comprehensive as the whole range of human emotions and can be viewed as a humanistic value, but in its actual usage it tends to focus on the beauty of impermanence and on the sensitive heart capable of appreciating that beauty.

Morality

(dotoku). In the West the concept of morality is based on custom and tradition, as can be seen in the derivation of the word morality from the Latin mores. This is not the case in China and Japan, where the corresponding word, pronounced dotoku in Japanese, is written with two Chinese characters, the first of which means "the Way." Confucius expounded the Way thus: "In the morning hear the Way; in the evening die without regrets" (Analects 4:8).

Morality in the East is thus not merely a system of ethics, that is, an act of human society, a model for living. It consists of the attitude of man toward absolute being (religion), other human beings (ethics), and other creatures and things (technology).

Japanese morality at present is going through a process of transition similar to what is taking place elsewhere as it seeks to come to terms with problems occasioned by the impact of technology on human life, e.g., problems of the environment, sexuality, and euthanasia.

Nature, concept of

(shizenkan). The basic, etymological meaning of the Japanese word shizen, which is used to translate the English word "nature," is the power of spontaneous self-development and what results from that power. The Chinese characters for the Japanese term shizen literally mean "from itself thus it is," expressing a mode of being rather than the existence of a natural order.

The term shizen as a general expression for nature is not found in ancient Japanese. The ancient Japanese people recognized every phenomenon as a manifestation of the *kami* (god or gods). Such terms as *ametsuchi* (heaven and earth) and *ikitoshi ikerumono* (living things) were the closest to a comprehensive word for nature in their literature.

In the mythology of the *Nihon shoki* (720) the first offspring of the primordial couple Izanagi and Izanami were neither kami nor human but islands and landmasses. Thus human beings were not considered to be superior or opposed to nature, as in Western thought, but related as if in one family.

Patriotism

(*aikokushin*). Prior to the rise of Meiji-period Japan (1868–1912) as a modern nation-state, there was no proper mental or emotional setting for patriotism to grow among the Japanese. The Japanese word *kuni* ("country") in phrases corresponding to "my beloved country" or "from the same country" referred to the speaker's domain (*han*) or home province within Japan, where the members of the province's upper class demanded *chugi* (loyalty) of those in the lower. In order to establish a centralized political structure the leaders of the new government after the Meiji Restoration (1868), skillfully making use of public education, transmuted the sense of feudalistic loyalty that had long been nurtured among the Japanese into the notion of loyalty to the emperor and the nation as a whole. Such ideas as "nation as family" and "society as organic entity" came into use, and the Japanese were required in the name of patriotism to submit unconditionally to the emperor, the nation, and the powers that be.

Etiquette

(*reigi saho*). "Etiquette" refers to conventional rules of behavior concerning interpersonal relationships. It differs from morality or ethics in that it concerns specific rules as applied to concrete situations rather than generalities and states requirements of outward conduct rather than inner beliefs or convictions. This distinction is important, because although at one level of consciousness Japanese recognize that etiquette and morality should go hand in hand, they also recognize that in reality the two may be discrepant.

Formalized Ideal and Real Behavior

Since Japanese society is based on the notion that one's existence is dependent upon those around one, it is essential to maintain smoothly operating human relations. Society thus demands the suppression of any antagonistic feelings one may have toward another and requires an outward behavior that reflects social harmony. This dichotomy is expressed in the Japanese concept of *tatemae*, or pro forma aspects of social relationships, versus *honne*, or one's inner feelings and intentions. The two are not expected to coincide in all cases, but socially proper conduct always takes precedence. Accordingly, Japanese strive to be aware of a possible discrepancy between outward conduct and true feeling and must be able to guess the latter, while interacting as if there were no discrepancy. This is often easier said than done—a reason why intermediaries are so often used in sensitive negotiations.

Although the discrepancy between expected conduct and inner feelings exists in all societies, in Japan it is openly condoned as natural. As a corollary to this, the rules of etiquette are more fully elaborated, and the social expectation to learn and conform to rules of etiquette is very strong.

Social Organization

By specifying rules of behavior appropriate for each status, etiquette helps to define social organization. Japanese etiquette specifies, for example, that the younger show deference to the older, and the female toward the male. The level of formality in speech is one of the more obvious ways in which status difference is manifested. The Japanese language is equipped with an elaborate set of expressions indicating different degrees of respect. Characteristically, Japanese wear clothes, such as uniforms, that readily manifest their social status, allowing others to interact with them in a socially appropriate manner. Seating arrangement is another way of defining status: those of higher social status are seated at a more honored place, closest to the *tokonoma* (decorative alcove) in a Japanese-style living room.

N*emawashi*

(prior consultation). A technique used in Japan to avoid conflicts and obtain a consensus in decision making. The literal meaning of nemawashi is to dig around the roots of a tree prior to transplanting, thus making the uprooting and movement much easier. But the term is used much more widely in a figurative sense to describe maneuvering behind the scenes to reach a consensus and obtain certain objectives, especially in politics and business. When various interests are potentially in conflict, reaching a consensus and attaining political objectives are very difficult through direct, public confrontation. Instead, in Japanese politics and business the practice is to discuss decisions in advance with various interested parties and to incorporate their views, wherever possible, into any final proposals. Much of the groundwork for decisions is therefore laid well in advance of meetings where final decisions are made, and, if the nemawashi is successful, conflicts can be avoided in public discussion.

Sempai-kohai

(senior-junior). An informal relationship ubiquitous in Japanese organizations, schools, and associations, in which older, experienced members offer friendship, assistance, and advice to inexperienced members, who reciprocate with gratitude, respect, and, often, personal loyalty.

The sempai-kohai tie is determined by the date of entrance into a particular organization. The sempai, perhaps a graduate of the same school or a senior in the work group, acts as a friend and patron, disciplining and teaching the neophyte appropriate conduct. Sempai-kohai ties permeate Japanese society.

Makuuchi (top division) Sumo Wrestler waiting for the *dohyo-iri* (ring-entrance ceremonies) prior to the start of the day's bouts.

Life cycle

(*raifu saikuru*). Society's schedule of stages for an individual's life. The cycle is generally thought to extend from birth to death, although an individual is considered a social entity before birth, and many religions posit continuing life for the soul after death. Stages of the cycle mark a person's readiness to participate in social roles and institutions. The schedule has evolved over time and has been altered radically by the institutions of 20th-century mass society and by the greater longevity of modern populations.

Age Reckoning

For social purposes age is reckoned in both relative and absolute terms. Relative age is set by order of birth: one is senior, peer, or junior to someone else. Japanese often claim that theirs is a uniquely "vertical" society, pervaded by rules of seniority. Seniority rules, however, are common to modern institutions such as schools, corporations, and bureaucracies in all societies.

Certain ages traditionally have been considered favorable, others dangerous. The most favorable years—60, 70, 77, and 88—mark successful aging. The danger years (*yakudoshi*) occur earlier: 19 and 33 for women, 25 and 42 for men. Although most Japanese scorn the danger years as superstition, many continue to observe them. To ward off danger, people obtain protective amulets and purifications at Shinto shrines and avoid new ventures during the year.

The following outline depicts life stages as a typical individual might pass through them.

Infancy

In Japan it is common for an expectant mother to don an abdominal sash in the fifth month of pregnancy: this is society's first overt recognition of a new individual. One month after birth the infant is taken to a local Shinto shrine to be introduced to the guardian gods and symbolically to all of society. Annual celebrations for children occur on 3 March for girls (Doll Festival), 5 May for boys (Children's Day), and on 15 November for girls aged seven and three and boys aged five (Shichigosan).

Childhood (about 7-13 years)

In the past, when children reached the age of seven they were expected to help their parents with household tasks and to assume community duties as members of the children's group (*kodomo-gumi*). Today, however, a child's first duty is to study. Under the modern school system in Japan the most important rites of passage are matriculation and graduation. During this stage of life one's "age" is reckoned more by years-in-school than by years-since-birth.

Youth (about 13-25 years)

Although only nine years of schooling are required, more than 90 percent of Japanese young people complete high school, and 40 percent enter college. In middle school and high school many students also attend special tutoring academies (*juku*) to prepare for entrance examinations for the next level of schooling. The demands of this "examination hell" have had a great impact on the daily lives not only of students but of their families and friends as well.

Today one attains legal maturity at age 20, and municipal governments celebrate Coming-of-Age Day (Seijin no Hi) for 20-year-olds on 15 January.

Maturity (about 26-60 years)

A man's pace of life and focus of ambition are caught up in promotions, raises, and occupational skills, and less in the family dynamics. Most women find paid work after leaving school, but few are able to sustain long-term occupational careers because social expectation dictates that they attend to housekeeping and child-rearing duties. In contrast to a century ago, however, today the typical woman gives birth to only two or three children, spaced closely together, so that she has completed the period of intensive child care within about a decade after marriage. Many women later take up paid employment, though they are at a disadvantage in the labor market.

Old Age (about 61 and over)

The 60th birthday, when the zodiac signs complete a full cycle, was the traditional beginning of old age; today many Japanese celebrate this birthday with family and friends. In some organizations, retirement (*teinen*) occurs before age 60, and long-term employees receive pension benefits. Most men and many women, however, take other jobs and remain in the labor force for another 10 years. Often this is because retirement incomes are thought to be inadequate.

After Death

In Buddhist tradition, at death an individual is given a posthumous name by the priest of the family temple. This is inscribed on the tombstone and on a personal memorial tablet (*ihai*) kept in the home. In the early weeks and months after death, frequent rites are held to comfort the soul. Thereafter, deathday anniversaries are honored for up to 50 years. After that, one's individuality dissolves into the collective body of the household ancestors, and, except for the famous or notorious, social recognition ceases.

Change and Conflict

Under the impact of modernization different parts of the life-cycle schedule have changed in ways that may often be contradictory.

Legal maturity is granted at age 20, but popular opinion regards anyone as immature until married or embarked on a working career. Family versus work is a serious issue for many men and women. Retirement before 60 seems unduly early when life expectancy is now 80 years.

Family

(*kazoku*). The most common Japanese terms for family are *ie*, kazoku, and *setai*; although these words are often used interchangeably today, in the past they had different meanings. Ie (often translated as "household") has come to be used by scholars for Japan's traditional type of family, especially as it existed during the Edo period (1600—1868); it means a united or corporate group of people who share residence and economic and social life and who regard themselves as a continuing unit of kin. The term kazoku appears to be more recent than ie. When used distinctively, it means a corporate domestic group consisting only of genetic and affinal kin or in-laws. *Setai* denotes a residential group or household, regardless of the relationships of its members, although these are most commonly kin. Neither kazoku nor setai carries the connotation of continuity of the term ie.

The Traditional Family

The family was organized as a hierarchy with the male household head at the apex, theoretically in a position of absolute authority over others. Until after World War II, this authority was supported by law. The authority of the wife of the family head related to domestic matters. Seniority in age conferred prestige, but sex and specific position of authority strongly affected status. A retired household head was respected but had little or no authority. Generally, when the head retired, his eldest son succeeded him, remaining with his parents after marriage and maintaining the continuity of the family line. The future household head held a status much superior to that of his younger siblings; however, an eldest son who showed no promise of becoming an effective family head might be replaced by a younger son or an outsider. Likewise, a bride, who traditionally held the lowest status in the family, might also be divorced if she failed to please her in-laws or produce a child.

Authority meant responsibility as well as privilege. The family head was responsible for the economic welfare and also the deportment of other members. He exercised control over family property and the conduct of farming or other occupations, and he was also responsible for the welfare of deceased ancestors, seeing that proper ceremonies were conducted in their honor.

The Contemporary Family

The typical Japanese family today is a nuclear family, with a mother, father, and two children, in a two- or three-bedroom apartment or house in an urban area. Most typically, the father commutes by train to his job in the city, while the wife cares for the children and the house, creating a nurturing environment for the whole family.

Western culture and values have had a large influence, inspiring postwar legal reforms and general social change. The ancient distinctions between eldest and younger sons, and between sons and daughters, have decreased, although they have not disappeared. Eldest sons are no longer universally expected to live with and take care of their parents, and daughters-in-law have been freed from the absolute authority of their mothers-in-law. Women, less restricted to the home, are freer to pursue education, jobs, and hobbies, and to initiate divorce.

As a result of Japan's postwar prosperity, almost all families consider themselves middle class and, in fact, the urban middle-class family is the dominant type and model for all Japan. Middle-class ideals and standards of living have penetrated rural areas as well. Notable variations on this model exist among families where husbands and wives work together in a family business, or in farm families where the husband is employed in an outside job while his wife and possibly his parents maintain the farm.

Marriage planning Decision about marriage are largely cooperative decisions shared by parents and children. The Japanese distinguish between the more traditional arranged marriage (*miai*) and the more Western-style love marriage (*ren'ai kekkon*). In a miai, the young couple are introduced after both families tentatively approve the match. In a ren'ai kekkon, the young couple meet each other on their own, for instance, at school or work. But even in the latter case, the families' approval is important. If the family strongly disapproves, the couple may well decide against marriage, recognizing the interdependence of family members.

Both men and women often live with their parents until they marry, because of strong family ties as well as the high cost of housing. Since young Japanese marry primarily to start a family, they do not marry until they are economically and socially prepared to do so. In 1991 the average age at marriage was 25.9 years for women, 28.4 for men. The first baby often arrives about a year after the wedding. In 1990 households with children had an average of 1.81 children.

Husband-wife relationships In contrast to the past, today a woman's relationship with her husband is much more important than her relationship with any of his relatives. Most young people, influenced by the West, want to have a more companionable and romantic marriage than their parents had. Nevertheless, after a year or two of marriage, most couples settle into a pattern of separate social worlds and a clear-cut division of labor. The husband's life is absorbed in his company; he works long hours and socializes with his work group. The wife becomes absorbed in her mothering role as soon as she becomes pregnant. Her social life revolves around her children but may include female relatives and friends.

Though some couples are quite close and companionable, emotional intimacy is less important than in the West. Fulfillment of one's duties as a parent takes precedence over affective needs. The continuity of the family is thought to be more important than marital gratification. Accordingly the divorce rate in Japan has remained rather low (around 1.3 per 1,000 persons in 1990), although the number fluctuates slightly.

Child rearing and education Motherhood and the careful nurturing of children are valued as supremely important in Japan. In order to assure a child's success in the Japan of today, whether the child is a boy or a girl, the mother must spend much time and thought on education. Often from the time her children enter the fourth grade in elementary school, she arranges for tutors or after-school study in *juku* to prepare the child for middle-school, high-school, and the all-important college entrance examinations. Though Japanese complain about the examination system and often make fun of the so-called education mother (*kyoiku mama*) who single-mindedly drives her children toward educational achievement, most middle-class mothers feel they have no choice but to be one.

Attitudes toward working women Economic growth has produced an increase in the number of women in the work force, especially the number of older married women. In 1990, 50.1 percent of women of working age were in the labor force, and 64.9 percent of all women working were married. Women want to work for a variety of reasons such as to increase the family's ability to pay for better housing, children's education, or personal luxuries. Some better-educated women want to work in order to pursue careers of their own.

Grandparents Filial piety is no longer the cornerstone of Japanese morality. Still, most Japanese consider it "natural" to take care of their parents in their old age. There are a few nursing homes, but most middle-class adults would consider it shameful to allow their parents to live in one. Elderly parents ideally live with or near one grown child, and while there remains some tendency to choose an elder son, many parents now prefer to live with a daughter, since mother-in-law problems are avoided. After a man's retirement, his world and his wife's world come together. Some wives, however, complain that they can never really retire, for they always have to take care of their husbands. Men who have been devoted to their companies all their lives may feel lost when separated from the company. Mothers may experience the loneliness of the "empty nest" after their children grow up and leave home. However, for some elderly couples the later years are often a pleasant time for enjoying hobbies and grandchildren without the responsibilities of the working years.

Family planning

(*kazoku keikaku*). The concept of limiting births for economic reasons has existed in Japan at least since the Edo period (1600−1868).

The Family Planning Movement

With the economic depression after World War I, efforts to advocate birth control developed. These efforts were initially led by the physician Majima Kan (1893−1969). In the late 1920s the cause was taken up by the women's movement, whose leaders appealed for protection of women's health and a more liberal sexual morality. In 1922 the general-interest magazine *Kaizo* invited family planning advocate Margaret Sanger to visit Japan. Although the government confiscated pamphlets encouraging sympathy for her cause and prohibited her from lecturing in public, she succeeded in heightening interest in birth control. Under the slogan *umeyo fuyaseyo* (Bear Children, Swell the Population), prewar militarist governments made population growth an official policy. Following the outbreak of the Sino-Japanese War of 1937-1945, laws against birth control were rigidly enforced, and the movement remained suppressed until the end of World War II.

After the war 5 million people were repatriated from occupied areas and former overseas territories. The population was also swelled by a postwar baby boom. The population increase, the diminished size of Japan's territory, the devastation of industries, and underproduction in rural areas led to an acute lack of food and housing. In response there was a much greater interest in birth control. Japan's birthrate began to fall, mainly because of abortions, which were legalized in 1948.

Contraceptive Methods

Gradually, contraceptive practices became widespread as the government began to encourage family planning through legislation and numerous programs. Public health nurses (*hokenfu*) and midwives (*josampu*) were given instruction and then licensed to sell condoms and spermicides. As of 1990, the most commonly reported contraceptive method was the condom (73.9 percent), followed by the rhythm method (15.3 percent); there were a small number of diaphragm users (0.3 percent). The rhythm method is based largely on research by the physician Ogino Kyusaku (1882−1975), so it is popularly known in Japan as the Ogino method. Oral contraceptives ("the pill") remain controversial in Japan, as conservatives see a danger of moral coruption. Reported side effects have strengthened the government's refusal to approve the sale of the pill for contraceptive purposes, and it is sold only as a treatment for menstrual problems. Use of the Ogino method, even in combination with the condom, entails a high number of unwanted pregnancies, leading to a large number of abortions. The annual number of reported abortions, which were legalized in 1948, reached a peak of 1,170,143 in 1955 and declined to the present figure of about 500,000 per year, although, as this number represents only those abortions that are reported, the actual number may be much higher. There seems to be very little tendency to use female sterilization to prevent pregnancy.

Work away from family

(*tanshin funin*; literally, "proceeding to a new post alone"). In the 1970s and 1980s increasing numbers of Japanese business and government employees who were transferred to distant cities within Japan or abroad left their families behind indefinitely and proceeded to their new posts alone. Despite the hardships involved (there were increasing reports of husbands whose health was affected and of wives and children suffering psychological disorders), most Japanese employees accepted such transfers as a matter of course. Acceptance was commonly seen as a passport to advancement.

According to Ministry of Labor estimates, in the mid-1980s as many as 134,000 employees a year from firms employing 1,000 or more people were accepting transfers that made it necessary to leave their families behind. Of these employees, 30 percent were men in their forties and 40 percent men in their fifties. Three out of four companies provided special expense allowances to help with the cost of maintaining separate households.

Holidays and vacations

(*kyujitsu*). In fiscal year 1989, Japanese working people had an average of 114 days off. This included weekends, 13 national holidays, paid vacation, 3-7 days (average 4.2) at New Year's, and 3-7 days (average

3.5) of summer vacation. Overall, Japanese have relatively few days off compared with citizens of other countries; for example, the French have 138 days off; the British, 136; and Americans, 132. The two main reasons for this gap are that the five-day workweek is still not widespread in Japan, and only a small percentage of paid vacation days are actually taken. Some 40.3 percent of all companies (16.4% of all employees) have a six-day workweek, while 58.3 percent (82.7% of employees) use some form of a five-day workweek. However, many companies in this second group have a two-day weekend only every other week or once a month, and a true five-day workweek exists for only 9.6 percent of all companies (36.9% of all employees).

Consumption and saving behavior

(*chochiku to shohi*). The ratio of saving to income among Japanese households has declined in recent years but remains high. Average household savings in 1990 stood at ¥11,810,000 (US $81,600), or 1.9 times average annual income. The average household savings portfolio for 1990 shows the Japanese preference for low-risk saving methods over speculative investments: 46.5 percent of savings (¥5,490,000; US $37,900) was in bank and other savings deposits, and 21.2 percent (¥2,500,000; US $17,300) was in life and nonlife insurance policies. Stocks and bonds accounted for 16.2 percent (¥1,910,000; US $13,200) of savings, and other speculative investments made up the remaining 16.1 percent. The main saving objectives of the Japanese—providing for illness and accident (74.3 percent) and for old age (52.4 percent)—point to a lack of adequate social welfare programs in Japan as a significant factor behind the high rate of saving.

In 1990 the percentage of income remaining after expenditures (the "propensity to save") reached 24.7 percent (16.9 percent if only savings and insurance premiums are considered). In the same year the average amount saved monthly by the household of a male office worker (*sarariman*) was ¥108,900 (US $750), 70.6 percent of which represented a net increase in such financial assets as savings deposits, insurance, stocks, and bonds; 22.4 percent, a net decrease in liabilities through housing loan or other credit repayments; and the remaining 7.0 percent, a net increase in nonfinancial assets.

According to Management and Coordination Agency statistics, the monthly expenditures of a male office worker's household in 1990 were ¥331,600 (US $2,290). Of the 10 major expenditure categories listed by the agency, "other expenses" at ¥90,600 (US $630), or 27.3 percent, was the largest. This category includes entertainment and other miscellaneous expenses that have increased significantly with improvements in the standard of living. Food, the next largest category at ¥79,000 (US $550), or 24.1 percent, continued its post-World War II decline as a percentage of total expenditures. The relative weight of Japanese expenditures on consumer durables—5.1 percent for educational and recreational products, such as televisions and videocassette recorders, and 4.0 percent for furniture and household appliances, including refrigerators and air conditioners—remains fairly low.

Clothing

(*ifuku*). Clothing in Japan is broadly categorized as either *wafuku* (Japanese style) or *yofuku* (Western style). *Kimono* is the modern designation for the traditional Japanese robelike garment that is worn belted at the waist, but this garment was historically called a *kosode* ("kimono" can also mean traditional dress in general). The history of Japanese clothing is in large part the history of the evolution of the kosode and the Japanization of imported styles and textiles.

Ancient Clothing (to AD 794)

The type of clothing worn during the Jomon period (ca 10,000 BC—ca 300 BC) is unknown, although jewelry from that period has been found. People probably used fur and bark to cover themselves. With the Yayoi period (ca 300 BC—ca AD 300) came the rise of sericulture (silkworm breeding) and weaving techniques.

Influenced by the importation of Buddhism and the Chinese government system, Prince Shotoku (574—622) followed the practice of the Sui court (589—618), establishing rules of dress for aristocrats and court officials. Figures depicted in paintings and embroideries wear long, loose clothing that shows the influence of Han-dynasty (25—220) fashion. The Taiho Code (701) and Yoro Code (718; effective 757) reformed clothing styles, following the system used in Tang China (618—907). Garments were divided into three categories: ceremonial dress, court dress, and working clothes.

Heian Period (794—1185)

As Japan drew away from continental influence, clothing became simpler in cut but more elaborate in layers. For formal occasions the male aristocrat's layered outfit (*sokutai*) included loose trousers stiffened by divided skirts (*oguchi*), worn underneath, and many layers of long, loose upper garments (*ho*).

The formal costume of the Heian lady-in-waiting was the *karaginumo*, often referred to after the 16th century as the 12-layered garment (*junihitoe*). Its most important element was the *uchiki*, the layers of lined robes (5, 10, or more) also called *kasane-uchiki* or *kasane* (layers). Great consideration was given to the combination of colors in the layers of uchiki. Each layer was longer than the one over it, so that the edge of each color showed, creating a striking effect.

Kamakura (1185 – 1333) and Muromachi (1333 – 1568) Periods

With the establishment of the Kamakura shogunate and the decline of the prestige of the imperial court, stiffened military garments replaced luxurious silk. The highest officials wore the formal *sokutai* of the Heian period, but the informal hunting jacket (*kariginu*) became the standard uniform of the *samurai*, along with a stiffened cloak (*suikan*).

At the beginning of the Kamakura period, women wore a combination of uchiki robes and *hakama* skirt-trousers as the formal outfit. Later these were replaced by the small-sleeved undergarment, the kosode, worn with hakama. In the Muromachi period an extra jacket (*uchikake* or *kaidori*) was worn over the kosode to complete the formal dress; today it is part of the bridal outfit.

Azuchi-Momoyama Period (1568 – 1600)

In the late 16th century the powerful generals Oda Nobunaga and Toyotomi Hideyoshi, great patrons of the arts, encouraged a wave of bold, decorative brilliance. The samurai continued to wear matched upper and lower garments (*kamishimo*). The upper garment was sleeveless. Gradually the material was made stiffer and the shoulders more flared; together with trailing pleated trousers (*nagabakama*), this continued as formal wear for samurai throughout the Edo period.

Edo Period (1600 – 1868)

During the 250 peaceful years of Tokugawa government, the wealthy merchant community (*chonin*) supported new forms of artistic expression. The *kabuki* theater and the entertainment quarters led fashion. The kosode, the basic garment for both men and women, was more brilliantly decorated after the development of *yuzen* dyeing and tie-dyeing patterns.

Over the kosode the Edo man often wore a *haori* jacket, a loose garment with a straight collar. The Tokugawa shogunate reformed clothing regulations for the military class toward the close of the period. The standard uniform became a kosode, ankle-length hakama, and haori. A number of early-Edo-period fashions reflected Portuguese influence. From the Portuguese large cape came the *kappa* raincoat. The *juban* kimono, worn under the kosode, derived its name from the Portuguese word for underwear: *gibao*.

Modern Developments

After the Meiji Restoration of 1868 the Japanese slowly changed over to Western clothing. The process began with a government decree that civil servants, such as soldiers, police, and postmen, should wear Western dress. Soon students were also wearing Western uniforms. By World War I, almost all men dressed in trousers, shirts, and jackets.

Women were generally slower in adopting Western styles. The aristocracy, however, sported imported Western gowns and accessories at the European-style balls held at the Rokumeikan from 1883 to 1889, and after World War I professional and educated women began to adopt Western clothing as their daily wear. It was not until after World War II that the habit of wearing Western clothing became the norm for all classes. Today most Japanese women wear their traditional kimono only on special occasions, such as festivals and weddings. Men wear traditional clothing even more rarely. The cotton summer kimono or *yukata* is worn by both men and women at resorts and summer festivals.

Housing, modern

(*gendai no sumai*). In 1988 there were 42,007,300 housing units in Japan, of which 37,413,400 were permanently occupied units, with an average of 3.2 persons per unit, and the remainder were second houses, resort condominiums, and so forth. Of the total, 62.3 percent were single-family units and 37.7 percent multiple-unit dwellings. Of the single-family units, 80.8 percent were owned and 10.2 percent rented; of the multiple-unit dwellings, 15.1 percent were owned and 79.4 percent rented.

The Modern Japanese House

There has been a progressive shrinking of the living space available to the middle-class household, from an average total floor space of 165 square meters (1,776 sq ft) at the turn of the century to 100 square meters (1,076 sq ft) by the beginning of the Showa period (1926-89), and by 1988 average total floor space had shrunk to 89 square meters (958 sq ft). In the 1980s this trend was exacerbated by the rapid rise in the cost of land, which forced would-be homeowners into the suburbs and into the market for small *tateuri jutaku* (developer-built houses). Large tracts of tateuri jutaku housing have become a common sight within a two-hour commuting distance of major urban centers such as Tokyo, Osaka, and Nagoya.

Whether built by the owner on his or her own property or by a developer, the two-story detached house with a tiled roof, a small (sometimes tiny) ornamental garden enclosed by a high stone wall or hedge, and garage space for the family automobile remains the ideal for the majority of Japanese. Such houses are basically wooden structures with overlaid plaster walls. The average total floor area in a house built by a salaried worker about 40 years of age is about 115.48 square meters

(1,242 sq ft). There is a dining room-kitchen, two or three Japanese-style rooms with *tatami* mats, and one or two Western-style rooms with carpeted, tiled, or wooden floors.

Multiunit Dwellings

Overall, multiunit dwellings increased to 52.8 percent of total housing constructed from 1986 to 1988. Wood-construction rental apartments (*mokuzo chintai apato*) continue to be a widespread form of multiunit housing. The earlier small units had shared kitchens and toilets, but in recent years the majority of apartments of this type have private kitchen and toilet facilities.

In 1955 the Japan Housing Corporation (JHC) was established, and apartment buildings and housing projects (*danchi*) became a familiar sight in Japan. The JHC standardized apartment layouts, introducing the concept of the dining room-kitchen ("dining-kitchen"; DK), a space of about 8 square meters (86 sq ft) used for both cooking and dining. This soon became a popular feature.

The most common unit in early JHC housing was the 2DK, or two rooms and the dining-kitchen area; in such apartments one of the rooms would serve as a living room during the day. An enlarged DK is called an LDK, or living room-dining-kitchen area. The emphasis in recent JHC housing has been on 3DK and 3LDK units.

In addition to the publicly subsidized danchi apartments, there are a great number of mid- to high-rise buildings constructed by private developers since the 1960s; these have individual units for sale or rent and are known as *manshon* (the English word "mansion" was borrowed to distinguish them from the more spartan 1960s public danchi apartment buildings). Townhouses—basically, connected rows of single-unit, rather more expensive dwellings—are an increasingly popular alternative to apartment dwelling.

Bath

(*furo*). The typical Japanese bath consists of a tub deep enough for the bather to immerse the body up to the neck when sitting. Water is piped to the tub from a water heater or heated in the tub by a gas burner at one end. There is a drain in the floor of the bathroom, and the bather washes and rinses the body completely before entering the tub to soak, thus keeping the bathwater as clean as possible for other bathers, who usually use the same water throughout the day.

Modern public baths (*sento*) now have separate entrances, dressing rooms, and bathing rooms for men and women. Plastic stools and basins are provided for the use of customers, who sit in rows before sets of hot- and cold-water faucets where they wash before entering one of the large tubs to soak. However, because people increasingly have baths in their own homes, many sento are going out of business. In 1964 there were 23,016 public baths in Japan, but in 1991 there were only 9,704.

Modern-day baths in the home are in small rooms, usually separate from the toilet. The room is usually tiled. Although traditionally made of wood, tile, or, more rarely, metal, tubs are now often made of polypropylene reinforced with fiberglass. On Children's Day (5 May) many people still put the fragrant leaves of the *shobu* plant in the bathwater. Several customs of the furo have entered other aspects of Japanese life. For example, the square cloth known as *furoshiki* ("bath spread"), used since the Edo period (1600−1868) to carry toilet articles into the sento and to stand on while dressing, is now a common article used to wrap gifts or to carry many other items.

Sports

Martial arts

(*bujutsu*). Also called *bugei*; now usually called *budo* or "the martial Way." The Japanese terms encompass such martial arts as *kendo* (fencing), *judo*, and *kyudo* (archery). The old expression *bugei juhappan* (the 18 martial arts) refers to the arts of archery, horsemanship, spearmanship (*sojutsu*), fencing, swimming, *iai* (sword drawing), the short sword, the truncheon (*jitte*), dagger throwing (*shuriken*), needle spitting, the halberd (*naginata*), gunnery, roping, *yawara* (present-day judo), *ninjutsu* (spying), the staff, *mojiri* (a staff with numerous barbs on one end), and the chained sickle (*kusarigama*). *Karate* is not considered one of the traditional Japanese martial arts, although it is sometimes referred to as such outside of Japan. In the Edo period (1600−1868), in addition to academic subjects, warriors were required to learn six martial arts: fencing, spearmanship, archery, horseback riding, *jujutsu* (now known as judo), and firearms. These six, together with military strategy, were called the seven martial arts. These were taught under the name *bushido* (the Way of the warrior).

After the Meiji Restoration (1868) the content of martial arts changed greatly, reflecting the fact that they were no longer meant to be used in combat and were no longer exclusive attainments of the warrior class. Reflecting this new circumstance, bujutsu was replaced by the term budo, implying that one would be trained in spiritual principles rather than for combat.

Modern budo seeks the development of skills through physical exercise and, by establishing objective standards of skills, provides opportunities for competition. In this sense it can be considered a form of sport. Yet behind the martial arts lie the philosophies of Confucianism, Buddhism, and Taoism. Japanese martial arts started with *waza* (skills) for killing and fighting and, through searches for *kokoro* (or *shin*, heart), the heart that transcends victory and defeat, were led to the Buddhist view of life and death and the Confucian way of natural harmony, yawara (pliancy).

The martial arts entail danger. As soon as one has dodged the enemy's attack through proper posture and body movement, one counters by attacking when the enemy is off guard. The means and methods for this are the basis for classification of the various martial arts. They can be roughly divided into those that use weapons and those that use the hands. Skills employing weapons aim to "strike and kill." Even when attacking the enemy empty-handed, the purpose of blows, thrusts, and kicks is to "strike and kill." On the other hand, unarmed skills such as throwing, restraining, squeezing, and immobilizing do not necessarily aim to kill and injure, but to "control violence yet not hurt life." However, these too, depending upon how they are employed, can be dangerous.

After World War II, there was a need to modify certain views of the martial arts, and the emphasis shifted from practical arts intended for national defense to sports that stress harmony and universality.

Judo

(literally, "the Way of softness"). One of the martial arts; a form of unarmed combat that stresses agile motions, astute mental judgment, and rigorous form rather than sheer physical strength. The Chinese character for *ju* derives from a passage in the ancient Chinese military treatise Sanlue, which states, "softness (*ju*; Ch: rou) controls hardness well." Judo techniques (*waza*) include throwing (*nagewaza*), grappling (*katamewaza*), and attacking vital points (*atemiwaza*). The first two techniques are used in competition, but the *atemiwaza* is used only in practice. Developed as a sport by Kano Jigoro (1860—1938) from *jujutsu*, judo has been valued as a method of exercise, moral training, and self-defense.

Jujutsu began with *sechie-zumo* (court banquet wrestling), a court event popular in the Nara (710—794) and Heian (794—1185) periods. During the sustained peace of the Edo period (1600—1868) jujutsu developed as a self-defense martial art and was used in making arrests. Jujutsu schools proliferated during this period but declined with the collapse of the samurai class after the Meiji Restoration of 1868. In 1882 Kano Jigoro organized the Kodokan judo school at Eishoji, a temple in Tokyo.

Kano Jigoro set up a system of ranks (*dan*) and classes (*kyu*) as an encouragement for his disciples. These designations have been recognized internationally. There are ranks from 1 to 10, with 10 the highest. Those in ranks 1 to 5 wear a black belt, ranks 6 to 8 have a scarlet and white striped belt, and those in ranks 9 to 10 have a scarlet belt. The classes are below the ranks and range from the fifth class to the first and highest class. Adults in the first to third class wear a brown belt; children in the first to third class wear a purple belt. Those in the fourth and fifth class wear a white belt.

Kendo

(the Way of the sword). Japanese fencing based on the techniques of the two-handed sword of the *samurai*. Before the Showa period (1926–1989) it was customarily referred to as *kenjutsu* or *gekken*. Kendo is a relatively recent term that implies spiritual discipline as well as fencing technique.

Fencing with the single-edged, straight-blade sword was probably introduced from Sui (589–618) or early Tang (618–907) China. The cultivation of sword skills flourished during the Kamakura shogunate (1192–1333). With the establishment of nationwide peace by the Tokugawa shogunate in the early 17th century, kenjutsu went into a decline. The moral and spiritual element became prominent, drawing on Confucianism, Shinto, and Buddhism, especially Zen. Kenjutsu became an element for training the mind and body. In the late 18th century protective equipment and bamboo training swords (*shinai*) were introduced.

The weapon is a hollow cylinder made of four shafts of split bamboo. It is bound with a leather grip and cap connected by a silk or nylon cord and a leather thong wound three times around the bamboo cylinder and knotted. The length varies for different age groups. Fencers are protected by the *men* (face mask); the trunk of the body is protected by the *do* (chest protector). The thighs are protected with five overlapping quilted panels (*tare*), and the hands with padded mittens (*kote*). Training is based on a variety of movements of attack and defense known as *waza*. Most fundamental are stance, footwork, cuts, thrusts, feints, and parries.

Kyudo

Japanese archery; literally, "the Way of the bow." *Kyujutsu*, the technique of the bow, was the term more commonly used until well into the 19th century. Under the influence of Chinese culture from the 6th century, Japanese archery was divided into military and civil archery. Military archery was primarily mounted archery, while civil archery was shooting in the standing position, with emphasis on form and etiquette. Over the centuries the rules of archery became systematized, and schools began to proliferate. Those of the Ogasawara school, the Heki school, and the Honda school dominate modern kyudo.

The bow is usually 2 meters 21 centimeters (7 ft 3 in) in length. It is an eccentric bow; that is, two-thirds of its length is above the grip and one-third below. Two target distances are used in modern kyudo competition. Usually the archer stands 28 meters (92 ft) from a circular target 36 centimeters (14 in) in diameter. In contrast to Western archery, in *kyudo* the emphasis is on form rather than accuracy. Certain schools are strongly influenced by Zen. The Amateur Archery Federation of Japan was formed in 1949; membership in 1990 was about 300,000.

Sumo

A 2,000-year-old form of wrestling that is considered by many to be the national sport of Japan. Sumo became a professional sport in the early Edo period (1600 – 1868), and although it is practiced today by clubs in high schools, colleges, and amateur associations, it has its greatest appeal as a professional spectator sport.

The object of this compelling sport is for a wrestler to force his opponent out of the center circle of the elevated cement-hard clay ring (*dohyo*) or cause him to touch the surface of the dohyo with any part of his body other than the soles of his feet. The wrestlers may spend as much as the first four minutes in the ring in a ritual of stamping, squatting, puffing, glowering, and tossing salt in the air, but the actual conflict is only a matter of seconds. To decide who has stepped out or touched down first is often extremely difficult and requires the closest attention of a referee (*gyoji*), dressed in the court costume of a 14th-century nobleman, on the dohyo and judges (*shimpan*) sitting around the dohyo at floor level.

Dohyo-iri (ring-entrance ceremonies) by *Makuruchi* wresters.

The Japan Sumo Association (Nihon Sumo Kyokai), the governing body of professional sumo, officially lists 70 winning techniques consisting of assorted throws, trips, lifts, thrusts, shoves, and pulls. Of these, 48 are considered the "classic" techniques but the number in actual daily use is probably half that. Of primary concern in sumo are ring decorum and sportsmanship.

Unique to sumo is the use of a belly band or belt called a *mawashi*, which is folded, looped over the groin, wrapped tightly around the waist, and knotted in the rear. Most sumo matches center on the wrestlers' attempts to get a firm, two-handed grip on their opponent's mawashi while blocking him from getting a similar grip on theirs. With the right grip they then have the leverage to execute a throw, trip, or lift. During tournaments, but not in practice, a string apron (*sagari*) is also worn tucked into the front folds of the mawashi, whence it falls frequently in the heat of the match.

The Wrestlers

Traditionally sumo has drawn the majority of its recruits from rural communities. Most wrestlers start in their mid-teens and retire from this rigorous sport in their early thirties. Top-ranking wrestlers have an average height of 185 centimeters (6 ft) and an average weight of 148 kilograms (326 lb), with successful exceptions running from as light as 102 kilograms (225 lb) to as heavy as 239 kilograms (527 lb).

The wrestlers in professional sumo are organized into a pyramid. Progress from the ranks of beginners at the bottom to the grand champion's pinnacle at the top depends entirely on ability. The speed with which a wrestler rises or falls depends entirely on his win-loss record at the end of each tournament. Based on this, his ranking is calculated for the next tournament and then written with his name and those of other wrestlers in Chinese characters on a graded list called the *banzuke*. The only permanent rank is that of *yokozuna*, "grand champion," but a yokozuna who cannot maintain a certain level of championship performance is expected to retire.

Only wrestlers in the top two divisions, *juryo* and *makuuchi*, receive regular salaries. They also enjoy the title *sekitori*, "top-ranking wrestler," and the right to have their long, oiled hair combed into the elegant *oichomage* (ginkgo-leaf knot) during tournaments.

Annual Tournaments

Traditionally only two tournaments were held each year, but by 1958 this number had grown to six, where it stood in the early 1990s. The big six are held every other month in four different cities.

In 1949 the length of a tournament increased from the traditional 10 days to 15 days. A tournament day starts with the apprentices of *maezumo* (pre-*sumo*) fighting in the qualifying rounds, then the long march of the four lower divisions across the dohyo begins. The boy-men in these divisions—*jonokuchi*, *jonidan*, *sandamme*, and *makushita*—wrestle on 7 of the 15 days of the tournament. For them a winning record (*kachikoshi*) begins with 4 wins against 3 losses, which ensures promo-

A Sumo match of
makuuchi wresters.

tion. Anything less is a losing record (*makekoshi*) and demotion. A *zensho* record (all wins, no losses) of course boosts a wrestler way up the ladder, usually into a higher division.

Sekitori in the juryo and makuuchi divisions wrestle once a day for 15 days. Sekitori must win 8 of their 15 bouts for a kachikoshi record. Makekoshi starts with 8 losses. The entire tournament is won by the makuuchi wrestler with the most wins.

The Stable System

The sumo stable system has as its purpose the training of young wrestlers into senior champions while inculcating them with the strict etiquette, discipline, and special values of sumo.

Physically, a stable (*heya*; literally, "room") is a self-contained unit complete with all living-training facilities. Every professional sumo wrestler belongs to one, making it his home throughout his ring career and often even into retirement. The only exceptions to the live-in rule are the married sekitori, who may live outside with their wives and commute to daily practice at the *heya*. As of June 1992 there were 44 active heya.

A stable is managed under the absolute control of a single boss (*oyakata*). All oyakata are former senior wrestlers and members of the Japan Sumo Association. The stable they run is usually the stable where they wrestled. Oyakata are generally married and live in special quarters with their wives, known by the title of *okamisan*, the only women to live in heya. Okamisan play an important behind-the-scenes role in the smooth operation of a stable, but their duties never include cooking or cleaning for the wrestlers. These and all other housekeeping chores outside the oyakata's quarters are performed by apprentices and low-ranked wrestlers. Heya expenses are paid for by regular allowances from the Japan Sumo Association and gifts from the heya fan club.

Sumo Practice

Keiko, "practice," is a sacred word in sumo, and a brief description of the morning practice that takes place every day in every heya will give an idea of the sumo way of life.

The day begins at 4:00 or 5:00 AM for the youngest, lowest-ranked wrestlers, who ready the ring and begin their exercises. The higher a wrestler's rank, the longer he may sleep. Makushita are up at 6:30 and in the ring at 7:00. Juryo wrestlers enter the ring around 8:00 and makuuchi shortly after.

At 11:00 AM the wrestlers head for the baths, seniors first, followed by the lower ranks. Next is brunch, the first and largest sumo meal of the day. This consists of *chankonabe*, a high-calorie stew made with a seaweed-base stock and containing chicken, pork, fish, *tofu*, bean sprouts, cabbage, carrots, onions, and other vegetables. The senior wrestlers eat bowl upon bowl of this stew together with bowl upon bowl of rice washed down with quarts of beer; the younger wrestlers get what is left.

The Japan Sumo Association

Every aspect of professional sumo is controlled by the Japan Sumo Association, composed of 105 retired wrestlers known as elders (*toshiyori*) and including representation from sumo's "working ranks," i.e., active wrestlers, referees, and ring stewards (*yobidashi*). The Japan Sumo Association is organized in several divisions such as Business, Judging, Off-Season Tours (Jungyo), Out-of-Tokyo Tournaments (Chiho Basho), Training, and Guidance, supervised by an elected 10-man board of directors under the leadership of a president or managing director (*rijicho*).

Baseball, professional

(*puro yakyu*). The first professional baseball team was organized in Japan in 1934, when the mass media entrepreneur and politician Shoriki Matsutaro formed the core of the team that is known today as the Yomiuri Giants. Six additional teams had been established by 1936, when the first professional baseball league was organized. Since 1950 there have been two professional leagues: the Central League and the Pacific League. In 1993 the following teams constituted the Central League: the Yomiuri Giants, the Chunichi Dragons, the Hanshin Tigers, the Hiroshima Toyo Carp, the Yakult Swallows, and the Yokohama BayStars. In the same year, the Pacific League comprised the following teams: the Kintetsu Buffaloes, the Seibu Lions, the Fukuoka Daiei Hawks, the Nippon-Ham Fighters, the Orix BlueWave, and the Chiba Lotte Marines. Each team plays the five other teams in its league 26 times each season for a total of 130 games. The teams with the highest winning percentage in each league face each other in the Japan Series to decide that year's championship team. Approximately 20 million fans attend baseball games annually in Japan, and millions more watch it on television, making baseball one of the nation's most popular professional sports.

Japan Professional Football League

(*Nihon puro sakka rigu*). The first professional soccer league in Japan. Commonly referred to as the "J. League," the Japan Professional Football League was founded in February 1991. It held its first professional tournament, the Cup Matches, in the fall of 1992. Games for the regular season, known as the League Matches, began on May 1993. The ten original member teams are: the Kashima Antlers, JEF United Ichihara, Urawa Red Diamonds, Verdy Kawasaki, Yokohana Flügels, Yokohama Marinos, Shimizu S-Pulse, Nagoya Grampus Eight, Gamba Osaka, and Sanfrecce Hiroshima. Two new teams, Júbilo Iwata and Bellmare Hiratsuka joined The League in 1994, bringing the total current membership to twelve teams. To gain membership to the League, teams are required to meet four conditions. Each team must: 1) be a legally incorporated body; 2) have the official local support of a designated "hometown"; 3) have access to a home stadium with a seating capacity of over 15,000; 4) foster the development of future soccer players by maintaining its own youth division.

Ekiden kyoso

Long-distance relay race in which the distance to be run is divided into sections and a cloth sash is passed among the runners on a team and worn by each member as they run their section. The word ekiden derives from the names of two ancient Japanese relay systems of transportation using horses. The average number of team members ranges from 5 to 10. The distance run per section by men ranges from 5 to 20 kilometers (3−12 mi); women runners run from 2 to 10 kilometers (1−6 mi) per section. The first ekiden kyoso was run in 1917 between Kyoto and Tokyo. Today a wide variety of ekiden kyoso are held in Japan, one of the oldest of which is the Tokyo-Hakone Ofuku Daigaku Ekiden, a competition for male college students. There are also international competitions to which foreign teams are invited.

Leisure

Tea ceremony

(chanoyu; literally, "tea's hot water"; also called chado or sado; the Way of tea). A highly structured method of preparing powdered green tea in the company of guests. The tea ceremony incorporates the preparation and service of food as well as the study and utilization of architecture, gardening, ceramics, calligraphy, history, and religion. It is the culmination of a union of artistic creativity, sensitivity to nature, religious thought, and social interchange.

History of Tea in Japan

According to tradition, Bodhidharma, who left India and introduced Zen (Ch: Chan) Buddhism to China in 520, encouraged the custom of tea drinking for alertness during meditation. In Buddhist temples during the Tang dynasty (618−907), a ritual was performed using tea in brick form. This was ground to a powder, mixed in a kettle with hot water, and ladled into ceramic bowls.

Buddhism was brought to Japan sometime in the first half of the 6th century. During the Nara period (710−794), the influence of Chinese culture included the introduction of tea in conjunction with Buddhist meditation. Early in the Kamakura period (1185−1333), the Japanese priest Eisai (1141−1215) returned from Buddhist studies in China, bringing the tea ritual practiced in Chinese Buddhist temples during the Song dynasty (960−1279). In this ritual, called *yotsugashira* ("four heads"), powdered green tea (*matcha*) is whisked in individual conical bowls called *temmoku* ("heaven eye"), after the Chinese mountain where they were used in Buddhist temples. The bowl is supported on a lacquered stand (*dai*). Eisai also brought tea seeds from the plant that was to become the source of much of the tea grown in Japan today. Although wild tea grew in Japan, it was considered inferior, and the tea grown from Eisai's seeds became known as "true tea" (*honcha*).

In Sakai, south of Osaka, there was a group of wealthy merchants called the *nayashu* ("warehouse school"), which espoused a modest manner of tea drinking. Out of this tradition came Takeno Joo (1502−1555), who taught the use of the *daisu* (the stand for the tea utensils), as it had been handed down from Murata Shuko (1422−1502, tea master to shogun Ashikaga Yoshimasa), as well as a sensitive connoisseurship and the aesthetic sensibility known as *wabi*, the contrast of refinement and rusticity. His influence was widely felt but was most important in his instruction of his student Sen no Rikyu (1522−91).

Rikyu transformed the tea ceremony, perfected the use of the daisu, and substituted common Japanese objects for the rare and expensive Chinese tea utensils used previously. Tea was no longer made in one room and served to guests in another, but rather was made in their midst. Many people began to practice the tea ceremony following the precepts and example of Rikyu.

Rikyu's successor, Furuta Oribe (1544−1615), introduced a decorative style that some considered superficial. Oribe's pupil Kobori Enshu (1579−1647) continued the grand style and was teacher to the Tokugawa shoguns, moving freely among the nobility, while also designing gardens and teahouses.

There were many masters of tea, with heirs and followers who eventually gathered into schools such as Ura Senke and Omote Senke. Both are the leading schools in Japan today.

Practice of the Tea Ceremony

The manner of preparing powdered green tea may be influenced by many styles and techniques, depending on the practices of the various schools. The following procedure is adapted from the Ura Senke way of preparation. A full tea presentation with a meal is called a *chaji*, while the actual making of the tea is called *temae*. A simple gathering for the service of tea may be called a *chakai*. The selection of utensils (*dogu*) is determined by time of year, season, and time of day or night, as well as special occasions such as welcoming someone, bidding farewell, a memorial, a wedding, flower viewing, and so on.

The tea is prepared in a specially designated and designed room, the *chashitsu*. It is devoid of decoration with the exceptions of a hanging scroll (*kakemono*) and flowers in a vase (*hanaire*). The scroll, inspired by Buddhist thought, provides the appropriate spiritual atmosphere for serving tea. The Buddhist writing, usually by a recognized master, is called *bokuseki* ("ink traces"). Flowers for tea (*chabana*) are simple, seasonal, and seemingly "unarranged," unlike those in *ikebana* (flower arrangement).

The following are some of the highlights of a chaji: The guests, ideally four, assemble in a *machiai* (waiting room) and are served *sayu* ("white" hot water) by the host's assistant, the *hanto*, in order to sample the water used in making tea. The guests enter the *roji* ("dew ground"), a water-sprinkled garden path devoid of flowers, in which the guests rid themselves of the "dust" of the world. They take seats at the *koshikake machiai* (waiting bench), anticipating the approach of the host, who is called *teishu* (house master).

The host replenishes the water in the stone basin set in a low arrangement of stones called *tsukubai* (literally, "to crouch"). The host purifies his hands and mouth and proceeds through the *chumon* (middle gate) to welcome the guests with a silent bow. This gate separates the mundane world from the spiritual world of tea. The guests purify their hands and mouths and enter the tearoom by crawling through the small door, or *nijiriguchi*, which the last guest latches. Individually they look at the scroll in the *tokonoma* (alcove), the kettle, and the hearth and take their seats.

Prior to the guests' entry, the kettle of water (*kama*) is placed in the room on a portable hearth (*furo*) with a charcoal fire. In winter a ro, a hearth set into the floor, replaces the furo to provide warmth. The host greets the guests. A charcoal fire to heat the water is built in the presence of the guests; this presentation (*sumi-demae*) is performed after the meal in the *furo* season and before the meal in the *ro* season. Incense, held in a *kogo* (incense container), is put into the fire; sandalwood (*byakudan*) is used in the furo, kneaded incense (*neriko*) in the ro.

The Tea Meal

The host serves the tea meal, which is called *kaiseki* or *chakaiseki*. The foods are fresh, seasonal, and carefully prepared without decoration.

The meal concludes with the sweet. In order to make preparations for serving the tea, the host then asks the guests to leave the room.

Preparing and Serving Tea

Alone, the host removes the scroll and replaces it with flowers, sweeps the room, and sets out utensils for preparing *koicha* (thick tea), which is the focal point of the gathering. The *mizusashi*, a jar filled with fresh water, is displayed; the water represents the *yin* to complement the fire in the hearth, which is *yang*. The *chaire*, a small ceramic jar containing the powdered tea, covered by a fine silk bag (*shifuku*), is set in front of the water jar. An appropriate *tana*, or stand, on which to display the tea utensils is chosen for the occasion. A gong (*dora*) is struck to summon the guests during the day; at night a small bell (*kansho*) is rung. The guests once again purify their hands and mouth at the *tsukubai* and reenter, look at the flowers and displayed utensils, and latch the door.

The host enters with the *chawan* (teabowl), which holds the *chakin* (tea cloth), a bleached white linen cloth used to dry the bowl; *chasen* (tea whisk); and *chashaku* (tea scoop), a slender bamboo scoop used to dispense the tea powder. The chashaku often bears a poetic name. These are set next to the tea jar, which represents the sun (symbolic of *yang*); the bowl represents the moon (symbolic of *yin*). The host brings in the *kensui*, a waste-water bowl; the *hishaku*, a bamboo water ladle; and the *futaoki*, a rest for the kettle lid made of green bamboo, and closes the *sadoguchi* (tea way entrance). The host uses a *fukusa*, a silk cloth representing the host's spirit, to purify the tea container and scoop; examining, folding, and handling the fukusa deepen the host's concentration and meditation. Hot water is ladled into the bowl to warm it; the whisk is examined and rinsed. The emptied bowl is dried with the linen cloth. Three scoops of tea in increasing amounts are put into the bowl; then the tea jar is emptied into the bowl. Hot water is ladled into the bowl, sufficient to form a thin paste when kneaded with the whisk. A little more water is added to bring it to a drinkable consistency. The bowl is offered to the guests.

The first guest takes the bowl, drinks, and passes it to the others. The bowl is returned and rinsed. The whisk is rinsed, the chashaku wiped, and the kettle replenished. The tea jar is cleaned and, with the tea scoop, is offered to the guests to examine more closely. The utensils are taken from the room. During the presentation, the utensils and related subjects are discussed.

The fire may be rebuilt in anticipation of serving *usucha* (thin tea), which helps to rinse the palate and to prepare the guests psychologically for their return to the mundane world. Smoking articles—a *hiire* (fire receptacle), a ceramic cup with a lighted piece of charcoal set in a bed of ash; a *haifuki* (ash blow), a length of green bamboo containing water to extinguish the ash; and a *kiseru* (pipe)—are offered on a *tabakobon* (tobacco tray). Since one rarely smokes in the tearoom, the tray is presented as a sign for relaxation. *Zabuton* (cushions) and *teaburi* (hand warmers) may be offered. *Higashi* (dry sweets) are served on a wooden tray to complement the bitterness of the thin tea. Thin tea is prepared in a way similar to that of thick tea, except that less tea powder, of a lesser quality, is used, and it is dispensed from a *natsume*, a date-shaped lacquered wooden container; the bowl has a more casual or decorative character; and the guests are served individually prepared bowls of frothy, light tea. At the conclusion, the guests thank the host and leave; the host watches their departure from the open door of the tearoom.

The Japanese tea ceremony, a social act founded on reverence for all life and all things, is enacted in an idealized environment to create a perfect life. Its quiet atmosphere of harmony and respect for people and objects, with attention to cleanliness and order, strives to bring peace to body and spirit.

Flower arrangement

(*ikebana*; literally, "flowers kept alive"). Also called *kado*, or the Way of flowers. Japanese flower arrangement had its origin in early Buddhist flower offerings and developed into a distinctive art form from the 15th century, with many styles and schools. The attention given to the choice of plant material and container, the placement of the branches, and the relationship of the branches to the container and surrounding space distinguished this art from purely decorative uses of flowers.

Traditional *Ikebana*

Buddhist ritual flower offerings (*kuge*) were introduced to Japan from China early in the 7th century by Ono no Imoko, from whom the Ikenobo school of arranging claims descent. The important "three-element" (*mitsugusoku*) offering placed in front of a Buddhist image consisted of an incense burner flanked by a candlestick and a vase of flowers. These flower offerings were arranged with the main stem approximately one and a half times the height of the container and set vertically at its center; two additional stems were placed symmetrically to the left and right.

Aside from religious offerings, there is no record of any systematized form of flower arrangement in Japan prior to the late 15th century. From the *mitsugusoku* tradition developed the style known as *rikka* ("standing flowers"), a more sophisticated arrangement that sought to reflect the majesty of nature and from which all later schools of Japanese flower arrangement derive.

During the 16th and 17th centuries, although the Ikenobo school predominated, various schools of rikka rose and flourished under the patronage of the aristocracy.

In the late 16th century, a new form of flower arrangement called *nageire* ("to throw or fling into") emerged for use in the tea ceremony. An austere and simple form was required for *chabana*, a general term for flower arrangements used in the tea ceremony, rather than the increasingly elaborate rikka styles. Sen no Rikyu (1522—1591) is regarded as the founder of both the ritualistic tea ceremony and the accompanying nageire style of flower arrangement, in which a single vase might hold only one flower disposed with deceptively simple elegance.

The late 17th century saw the emergence of a thriving merchant class and a shift away from aristocratic and priestly forms of flower arrangement. A growing demand for simplification of the increasingly contrived rikka styles gave rise to a new form of arrangement called *shoka* or *seika* (living flowers), basically consisting of three main branches arranged in an asymmetrical triangle. Whereas rikka expressed the majesty of nature by symbolic representation of a landscape, the ideal in shoka was to convey the plant's essence. Shoka combined the dignity of rikka with the simplicity of nageire, and by the end of the 18th century it had become the most popular style. Diverse angles of placement and varying lengths of branches define the styles of the various schools of shoka. Early in the 19th century, the three main branches used in shoka became commonly known as *ten* (heaven), *chi* (earth), and *jin* (man). The height of the jin varies, but the ten is two-thirds as high as the jin, while the chi is one-third as high.

Modern Ikebana

After the Meiji Restoration of 1868, traditional Japanese arts, including ikebana, were temporarily overwhelmed by enthusiasm for Western culture. In the late 19th century, however, there was a revival of ikebana when Ohara Unshin (1861—1914), founder of the Ohara school, introduced his *moribana* (piled-up flowers) style. Based on the classic principles of the three-branch design, moribana stressed color and natural plant growth, utilizing low arrangements that sometimes nearly touched the sides of shallow, wide-mouthed containers. It was probably designed to employ newly introduced Western flowering plants.

In the late Taisho (1912—1926) and early Showa (1926—1989) periods, the foundations of modern ikebana were laid in the work of

Ohara Koun (1880–1938) and Adachi Choka (1887–1969), among others. Up until about 1930, ikebana was taught exclusively by private instructors in upper-class homes, but now masters began to concentrate on developing ikebana schools that could attract large numbers of students from all social classes. They emphasized three-dimensional arrangements that were loosely derived from the traditional triangle pattern of the ten-chi-jin (heaven-earth-man) form of shoka.

In the postwar era, avant-garde ikebana (*zen'eibana*), spearheaded by Sogetsu school founder Teshigahara Sofu (1900–1979), Ohara Houn (1908–   ), and Nakayama Bumpo (1899–1986), revolutionized the materials considered acceptable. These artists used not only live flowers and grasses but also plastic, plaster, and steel to express surrealistic and abstract concepts in their arrangements.

Today, there are approximately 3,000 ikebana schools in Japan, with 15 million to 20 million students, mostly women between the ages of 18 and 26. The most popular styles are the Ikenobo, Ohara, and Sogetsu, each of which attracts some 3 million students. Still practiced are rikka and shoka, as well as more modern styles.

Before World War II, foreign interest in, and knowledge of, ikebana was scant. After the war, however, ikebana became popular with the wives of Allied military officers stationed in Japan, and many returned home as certified teachers, bringing the influence of ikebana to untold numbers of students abroad. Ikebana International, founded in Tokyo in 1956 by Ellen Gordon Allen (1898–1972), encourages the teaching of ikebana as an art form throughout the world. Overseas expansion of ikebana schools, which began seriously in the 1960s, continues today.

Calligraphy

(*shodo*; the Way of writing). In Japan, as in other countries in the Chinese cultural sphere, calligraphy is considered one of the fine arts. In China, the birthplace of the East Asian tradition of calligraphy, the three disciplines—poetry, calligraphy, and painting—were considered the proper attainments of every cultured person, and excellence in writing thought to be a manifestation of the practitioner's character. The respect accorded to calligraphy in Japan is essentially an extension of its status in China.

The history of Japanese calligraphy begins with the introduction into Japan of the Chinese writing system in about the 5th century AD. Initially the Japanese wrote in Chinese, but they soon began using Chinese characters, or *kanji*, in new ways to suit the requirements of their native language. The poetry anthology *Man'yoshu* (mid-8th century), for example, was written using Chinese characters to convey either Japanese words or syllables. The latter phonetic method of writing is now known as *man'yogana*. This practice ultimately led to the creation in the early 9th century of Japanese syllabaries, or *kana*, that were used either alone or in combination with Chinese characters. The Japanese kana script was in wide use in the 10th century and emerged as a major calligraphic form after the 11th century. Nevertheless, for a long time the Chinese language retained its status as the literary language of the elite, and to varying degrees it was favored in later periods as well.

Scripts

Various types of Chinese-character scripts, or *shotai*, representing the historical development of writing in China, are practiced. *Tensho*, or archaic script, is traditionally used for carving official seals. *Reisho*, or clerical script, was once used for official documents. These are very ancient Chinese scripts and did not come into extensive use in Japan until the Edo period (1600−1868), when Chinese historical studies received much attention. More common is *kaisho*, or block-style script, perhaps the most popular style since the characters are easily recognizable. *Gyosho*, or "running-style" script, is created by a faster movement of the brush and some consequent abbreviation of the character. This script is frequently used for informal writing. *Sosho*, or "grass-writing," is a true cursive style that abbreviates and links parts of a character, resulting in fluid and curvilinear writing. In sosho writing, variations in the size of different characters may occur in the flow of a column, and some characters may be joined to the next, creating rhythmic and artistic forms.

Implements

Compared to writing styles, calligraphy implements have changed very little since the early days of the art. There are two basic kinds of brush: *futofude* (thick brush) and *hosofude* (slender brush); the former is generally used for the main body of a text, and the latter for inscriptions and signature at the end of a work, or for small-character calligraphy or fine cursive writing. *Sumi*, or Chinese ink, is usually made of soot from burned wood or oil mixed with fishbone or hide glue and dried into a stick. To make liquid ink the stick is rubbed on an inkstone, or *suzuri*, that has an indentation at one end to hold water that gradually darkens as the stick is rubbed. The *suiteki*, or small water dropper, which is either ceramic or metal, completes the basic paraphernalia. When not in use, writing equipment is kept in a box called a *suzuribako*, which is usually lacquer ware and often elaborately decorated.

Early History

With the introduction of Buddhism and Confucianism to Japan around the 6th century, numerous examples of Chinese writing entered Japan, mostly sutras and Buddhist commentaries written in brush and ink on paper in varied script styles. The earliest extant handwritten text by a Japanese is thought to be the *Commentary on the Lotus Sutra*, which is purported to have been written by Prince Shotoku (574−622). It is written in a typical clerical-cursive style that was current in China from the late 4th century to the late 6th century.

From the late 7th century through the 8th century, early Tang (618−907) dynasty calligraphic styles were rapidly mastered in Japan, notably through increased sutra-copying activities that began in earnest with the establishment of the Shakyojo, or Sutra-Copying Bureau, in the capital city of Nara.

An early influence upon the development of Japanese calligraphy was the monk Kukai (774−835), who introduced the calligraphic style of Yan Zhenqing (709−785), then popular in metropolitan Tang China, and promoted an awareness of calligraphy as an aesthetic form. Kukai and his contemporaries, Emperor Saga (786−842) and the courtier Tachibana no Hayanari (d 842), were known to later generations as the Sampitsu (the "Three Brushes").

A major transformation in calligraphy from a rigid emulation of Chinese styles to creative assimilation occurred in the 10th and 11th centuries. This was the time of the Sanseki (Three Brush Traces): Ono no Tofu (894−966), Fujiwara no Sukemasa (944−998), and Fujiwara no Yukinari (or Fujiwara no Kozei; 972−1028).

Kamakura and Muromachi (1333 − 1568) Periods

Chinese Song (960−1279) calligraphy had a great impact on Japanese practitioners, especially through Zen monks. Eisai (1141−1215) and Dogen (1200−1253) returned from pilgrimages to China in the late 12th and early 13th centuries, respectively, and their surviving calligraphic works reflect the influence of the Southern Song revival of Northern Song calligraphy, a trend embodied in the works of Su Shi (Su Shih; 1036−1101) and Huang Tingjian (1045−1105). Huang Tingjian, in particular, was eagerly emulated by the monks of the Gozan Zen temples, such as Kokan Shiren (1278−1346), who mastered both the semicursive gyosho and cursive sosho modes. No calligrapher, however, was so artistically aware of the expressive potential of Song calligraphy as Soho Myocho (1282−1337). His powerful style follows in the Song tradition, particularly that of Huang Tingjian, without being overly imitative. Lanqi Daolong (J: Rankei Doryu; 1213−1278), one of a number of Chinese monks who came to Japan, wrote in the style of the

Song calligrapher Zhang Jizhi (1186–1266), best known for his regular script.

Works of calligraphy by Zen monks came to be known as *bokuseki* ("ink traces") and were prized by monastic communities, which treated them as icons symbolizing spiritual transmission from master to master.

Edo (1600–1868) Periods

The establishment in 1661, largely by Chinese monks, of the Obaku sect of Zen in Uji, south of Kyoto, contributed to an influx of Ming-dynasty (1368–1644) styles of calligraphy. They were enthusiastically received by Japanese men of letters, who created a new orthodoxy called *karayo* (Chinese mode), which eventually overshadowed the *wayo* tradition. Hosoi Kotaku (1658–1735), Rai San'yo (1781–1832), and Sakuma Shozan (1811–1864) are among the more famous calligraphers who wrote in this mode, which was greatly favored by literati scholars and artists throughout the Edo period.

Contemporary Calligraphy

In the modern era, calligraphy has continued to thrive, and it is represented, along with painting and sculpture, at the government-sponsored annual Nitten exhibitions. In post–World War II Japan, avant-garde calligraphy (*zen'ei shodo*) was born—a genre in itself. This recent trend in calligraphy asserts new artistic forms of pure abstraction, coming close to some aspects of 20th-century Western pictorial art and deviating sharply from the traditional script styles and emulative aspects of the age-old art of calligraphy.

Bonsai

(literally, "tray planting"). The art of dwarfing trees or plants by growing and training them in containers according to prescribed techniques. The word bonsai also refers to the miniature potted trees themselves. Bonsai, which first appeared in China more than 1,000 years ago, was introduced to Japan in the Kamakura period (1185–1333) on the wave of cultural borrowings that included Zen Buddhism. In Japan the art was refined to an extent unapproached in China.

Bonsai can be developed from seeds or cuttings, from young trees, or from naturally occurring stunted trees transplanted into containers. Most bonsai range in height from 5 centimeters (2 in) to 1 meter (approximately 3 ft). Bonsai are kept small and trained by pruning branches and roots, by periodic repotting, by pinching off new growth, and by wiring the branches and trunk so that they grow into the desired shape.

Grown in special containers, bonsai are usually kept outdoors, although they are often displayed on special occasions in the *tokonoma*, the alcove in traditional Japanese rooms designed for the display of artistic objects. An unglazed, dark-colored container is usually chosen for a classic bonsai or to impart a look of age, but glazed containers are often used for flowering trees. As a rule, oval containers complement deciduous trees; rectangular ones, evergreens.

Growing Bonsai

Given proper care, bonsai can live for hundreds of years, with prized specimens being passed from generation to generation, admired for their age, and revered as a reminder of those who have cared for them over the centuries. Venerable bonsai are generally more respected than young ones, but age is not essential. It is more important that the tree produce the artistic effect desired, that it be in proper proportion to the appropriate container, and that it be in good health. The two basic styles of bonsai are the classic (*koten*) and the informal or comic (*bunjin*). In the former, the trunk of the tree is wider at the base and tapers off toward the top; it is just the opposite in the bunjin, a style more difficult to master.

Bonsai are ordinary trees or plants, not special hybrid dwarfs. Small-leaved varieties are most suitable. In Japan varieties of pine, bamboo, and plum are most often used. The artist never merely duplicates nature but rather expresses a personal aesthetic or sensibility by manipulating it. The miniaturized tree may suggest a scene from nature, a family grouping, a scene from a play, or a foolish or even grotesque character. But in all cases the bonsai must look natural and never show the intervention of human hands.

Aesthetics and Philosophy

The bonsai with its container and soil, physically independent of the earth since its roots are not planted in it, is a separate entity, complete in itself, yet part of nature. This is what is meant by the expression "heaven and earth in one container." A bonsai tree should always be positioned off-center in its container, for not only is asymmetry vital to the visual effect, but the center point is symbolically where heaven and earth meet, and nothing should occupy this place. Another aesthetic principle is the triangular pattern necessary for visual balance and for expression of the relationship shared by a universal principle (life-giving energy or deity), the artist, and the tree itself. Tradition holds that three basic virtues are necessary to create a bonsai: *shin-zen-bi* (truth, goodness, and beauty).

Karaoke

(literally, "empty orchestra"). Prerecorded musical accompaniment, usually on compact or laser disc. An essential part of one of the most popular leisure-time activities in Japan: the singing of songs backed by karaoke musical accompaniment at bars and pubs, at parties, or at home. Recording studios and radio stations started using music-only karaoke tapes in the mid-1960s, and in the 1970s bar owners hit upon the idea of outfitting their establishments with karaoke sound systems so that patrons could sing along (today's systems display the song lyrics on a separate video monitor, and smaller systems are available for home use). Most karaoke establishments have a large and eclectic catalog of songs; the sentimental songs known as *enka* and contemporary music are among the most popular selections.

Comic magazines

(*manga zasshi*). The flourishing of a "comic culture" is one of the significant features of mass culture in present-day Japan. Comic magazines fall into four categories: boys' comics (*shonen manga*), girls' comics (*shojo manga*), youth comics (*seinen manga*), and adult comics (*seijin manga*). Comic magazines are published weekly, biweekly, and monthly.

Boys' and girls' comics average around 400 pages, and a given issue usually contains some 15 serialized stories. Especially popular serials may continue for 10 years. Total combined circulation of the major weekly boys' comic magazines is about 10 million, and it is estimated that two-thirds of all boys aged 5 to 18 read these magazines on a regular basis. More than one-sixth of Japanese girls in the same age group are regular readers of girls' comics. Youth and adult comics average about 250 pages and contain about 10 serialized "story cartoons" and 5 "nonsense cartoons" in each issue. Including the so-called vulgar (*zoku-aku*) comics, 40 to 50 different youth and adult comic magazines are published.

Hot springs

(*onsen*). Hot springs are numerous in Japan, and for centuries the Japanese people have enjoyed hot spring bathing. Visits to hot spring resorts were hailed not only as a means of relaxation but also for the beneficial medicinal properties attributed to thermal spring water. Hot springs are still major attractions for vacationing Japanese, and many have been modernized and developed into large-scale resort complexes. Under the 1948 Hot Spring Law (Onsen Ho), the Japanese government recognizes as *onsen* only those hot springs that reach certain standards regarding temperature and mineral composition; the number of these as of 1990 was about 2,300. Since 1954 the Ministry of Health and Welfare has accorded special recognition to 64 hot spring resorts capable of providing medical treatment.

History of Utilization

Dogo Hot Spring in Iyo Province (now Ehime Prefecture) is reputedly the oldest hot spring in Japan. It was the site, according to tradition, of therapeutic bathing by several legendary or early historical emperors. Buddhist monks developed hot springs for medicinal purposes and used hot springs for the bathing that is part of the Buddhist purification ritual. Farmers and fishermen engaged in ritualistic baths at various times of the year.

Goto Konzan, a doctor in Edo (now Tokyo), noticed the effectiveness of hot spring bathing as a cure for certain disorders and in 1709 initiated the first medical study of hot springs, advocating the use of baths as therapy for various ailments. In 1874 the Japanese government undertook the chemical analysis of mineral springs. After the founding of the Balneotherapy Institute (now called the Medical Institute of Bioregulation) at Beppu Hot Spring in Oita Prefecture by Kyushu University in 1931, the medical study of hot springs began to be systematized, with many universities establishing research facilities at various hot springs. After World War II, national hot spring hospitals were created, making hot springs for medical treatment available around the country. Hot springs are utilized in the treatment of chronic rheumatism; neuralgia; chronic diseases of the stomach, intestines, liver, and gallbladder; hypertension; hemiplegia; glucosuria; and gout. They are also used for treating external injuries and for postoperative treatment and rehabilitation.

Foods

Cooking, Japanese

(Nihon *ryori*). There are three fundamental types of traditional full-course Japanese cuisine: *honzen ryori*, an assembly of dishes served on legged trays at formal banquets; *chakaiseki ryori*, a series of dishes sometimes served before the tea ceremony; and *kaiseki ryori*, a series of dishes for parties, often served at restaurants specializing in Japanese cuisine (*ryotei*). Other types are *osechi ryori*, dishes traditionally served on important holidays such as New Year's, and *shojin ryori*, Buddhist vegetarian dishes.

The main ingredients in Japanese cooking are seafood, vegetables, and rice. The consumption of raw seafood has long been a distinguishing feature of native cuisine, and its preparation requires that fish be very fresh and that it be skillfully cut with a very sharp knife (*hocho*). Because of the abundance of foods supplied by the seas surrounding Japan and the influence of Buddhism, which militated against the killing of animals, Japanese cooking formerly made little use of the flesh of animals and fowl, dairy products, and oils and fat. Principal seasonings are fermented products of soybeans, such as soy sauce (*shoyu*) and *miso* (soybean paste), or of rice, such as *sake*, vinegar, and *mirin* (sweet *sake*). Mirin has a smoother sweetness than sugar and is used in small amounts to enhance the taste of soy sauce and miso, as well as to mitigate the acidity of vinegar. To preserve the natural flavors of ingredients, strong spices are avoided in favor of milder herbs and spices, such as *kinome* (aromatic sprigs of the tree known as *sansho*), *yuzu* (citron), *wasabi* (Japanese horseradish), ginger, *myoga* (a plant of the same genus as ginger), and dried and ground sansho seeds.

In preparing foods for serving one arranges them in a manner that harmonizes colors and textures, on plates or in bowls that accord with the season of the year; for example, glass and bamboo are considered appropriate for summer. Dishes of contrasting shapes, sizes, and patterns are used during the course of a meal to achieve an aesthetic balance between food and receptacle that pleases the eye and stimulates the appetite.

Traditional Japanese cuisine.

The basis of all Japanese cooking is stock (*dashi*), the standard form of which is made with the type of seaweed known as sea tangle (*kombu*) and dried bonito-fillet (*katsuobushi*) shavings.

The categories into which all Japanese cooking falls are described below. Each Japanese term that appears in subheadings not only expresses the method of cooking but also denotes the dish itself.

Shirumono

Shirumono (soups) can be roughly divided into two types, *sumashijiru* and *misoshiru*. Ingredients may include white-fleshed fish, prawns, shellfish, *tofu*, fowl, seaweed, and seasonal vegetables; one or two ingredients that accord with the remainder of the menu are selected from among these. To add more zest and aroma, yuzu, kinome, sansho, ginger, or *mitsuba* (a trifoliolate herb of the same genus as honewort) may be added.

For sumashijiru, or clear soup, *dashi*, to which salt and soy sauce have been added, is customarily used.

Yakimono

The principal ingredients of yakimono (grilled foods) are fish, shellfish, meat, and vegetables. Foods are pierced with a skewer or placed on a wire net and grilled over an open fire. One may also make yakimono using an iron skillet or oven broiler. The basic type of yaki-mono is *shioyaki*, in which salt is sprinkled over the food before grilling. The distinctive flavor of fish is best enjoyed in this way. For *tsukeyaki* the food is first marinated for about an hour in *awase-joyu*, a mixture of soy sauce and sake or mirin. *Teriyaki* is a yakimono prepared with a stronger-flavored awase-joyu. For *misozukeyaki*, the food is marinated in miso flavored with sake or mirin. In arranging a grilled whole fish on a plate, the head of the fish is positioned to the left with the belly facing the diner.

Nimono

Nimono are stewed dishes seasoned with salt, soy sauce, sake, mirin, sugar, vinegar, or other condiments. The most common nimono is *nitsuke*—fish or shellfish cooked briefly in a relatively thick mixture of sake, soy sauce, mirin, and sugar. In the case of the white-fleshed fish *tai* and *buri* (yellowtail), the fillets are removed and used for *sashimi* or yakimono and the head and backbone chopped in pieces, washed in hot water, and cooked with a relatively light mixture of water, sake, mirin, and soy sauce until the juice is almost entirely absorbed. Bluefish, such as mackerel, sardines, and saurel, are first cooked in a mixture of water, sake, and mirin. Miso that has been diluted with a ladleful of the broth (*nijiru*) is then added to mask the strong flavor of the fish. This is called *misoni*. *Mizoreni* is a method of preparation in which bluefish is cooked in seasoned dashi with a generous amount of grated white radish. In making nimono it is important to use heavy covered pots so that the heat and the nijiru spread evenly.

Agemono

Agemono, or deep-fried foods, are of three basic types. *Suage*, in which foods are fried without a coating of flour or batter, is appropriate for freshwater fish, eggplant, green peppers, and other vegetables whose color and shape can be utilized to good effect. *Karaage* frying, in which food is first dredged in flour or arrowroot starch, preserves the natural water content of the food and crispens the outer surface. In *tatsutaage*, a variant of karaage, pieces of chicken are marinated in a mixture of sake, soy sauce, and sugar, lightly covered with arrowroot starch, and deep-fried. *Tempura* belongs to a third type of agemono, in which foods are coated with batter.

Mushimono

Mushimono are steamed foods. With this method, natural flavors do not escape and the taste is very light. Foods may be sprinkled with salt and steamed (*shiomushi*) or sprinkled with salt and sake (*sakamushi*). The latter method is particularly appropriate for clams or abalone. Mushi-mono are served with seasoned dashi thickened with arrowroot starch and sprinkled with grated ginger, yuzu rind, or chopped scallion. The foundation of *chawan mushi* is a mixture of beaten eggs and lukewarm dashi (about three times the volume of the eggs). Ingredients such as shrimp, mushrooms, and chicken are placed in individual bowls. The egg mixture is poured in and the bowls covered and steamed over medium heat.

Sunomono and *Aemono*

Sunomono are vinegared fish or vegetables; aemono are fish or vegetables with a dressing, the basic ingredient of which is ground sesame seed, miso, or mashed tofu. Fish and shellfish are sometimes broiled or steamed, or they may be sliced, sprinkled with salt, and marinated in vinegar or sea-tangle stock. Vegetables are either blanched, rubbed with salt, boiled, or steamed. Excess water should be eliminated.

Yosemono and *Nerimono*

Yosemono are molded dishes made with agar-agar or gelatin. Foods such as rock trout, flounder, and chicken that have a relatively high gelatin content are used. Nerimono are foods that have been mashed into a paste. For one such dish, fish or shellfish is chopped into small pieces and mashed in a mortar with a pinch of salt. The paste is mixed with beaten eggs, grated *yamanoimo* (a type of yam), and dashi and divided into portions for boiling, deep-frying, or steaming. It is eaten with soy sauce and grated ginger. Both yosemono and nerimono should be served in small portions.

Gohammono

Gohammono are dishes consisting of rice combined with other ingredients. *Takikomigohan* is made by cooking rice and another ingredient—in spring, green peas or pieces of bamboo shoot; in autumn, *matsutake* mushrooms or chestnuts—in seasoned water or dashi. *Gomokumeshi* (also known as *kayakugohan*) is prepared by adding finely diced chicken, carrot, fried tofu, *shiitake* mushroom, and burdock to rice and cooking it in dashi seasoned with soy sauce, sake, and sugar. *Domburimono* are dishes in which cooked rice is placed in a bowl (*domburi*) that is larger than the usual rice bowl and then topped with various prepared ingredients.

Menrui

Menrui is a category of dishes, served hot or cold, whose chief ingredient is noodles. The most common types of noodles are *udon*, *somen*, and *soba*. The first two are made with wheat flour, and soba with buckwheat flour. Somen is always dried; soba and udon may be either fresh or dried.

Nabemono

Nabemono are dishes cooked in a pot of simmering broth at the table. Ingredients are arranged on platters so that each person may cook what he or she likes. The chief types of nabemono are *mizutaki, yudofu, udonsuki, kanisuki, dotenabe, shabushabu,* and *sukiyaki*. Mizutaki is prepared by cooking fillets of white-fleshed fish with vegetables, tofu, and *harusame* (thin potato-starch noodles) in a pot of *kombu* stock, or chicken and vegetables in chicken broth. Grated white radish, red pepper, and chopped onion are used as condiments, and the food is dipped in *ponzu,* a sauce made from citron and soy sauce.

Chopsticks

(*hashi*). All Japanese dishes are eaten with hashi; in the case of soups, the solid ingredients are eaten with hashi and the stock sipped directly from the soup bowl. Hashi are commonly made of light but strong wood, such as cypress or willow, and then lacquered; they are also made of bamboo or, increasingly, of plastic. It is customary in the Japanese household for each person to have a pair of hashi reserved for his or her exclusive use. Disposable plain-wood chopsticks (*waribashi*), which the diner splits apart before using, are common in restaurants. Long chopsticks made of bamboo and used for cooking are called *saibashi*. Long metal chopsticks with wooden handles are used for deep-frying. When not in use during a meal, hashi are rested upon small ceramic, wooden, or glass stands called *hashioki*.

Kaiseki ryori

One of the three basic styles of traditional Japanese cooking. Kaiseki ryori is a type of cuisine served at sake parties and developed in its present form as restaurants became popular in Japan in the early 19th century. Although the basic features of kaiseki ryori can be traced to the more formal styles of Japanese cooking—*honzen ryori* and *chakaiseki ryori*—in kaiseki ryori diners are able to enjoy their meal in a relaxed mood, unrestricted by elaborate rules of etiquette. Today this type of cooking can be found in its most complex form at first-class Japanese-style restaurants (*ryotei*). *Sake* is drunk during the meal, and, because the Japanese customarily do not eat rice while drinking sake, rice is served at the end. Appetizers (*sakizuke* or *otoshi*), *sashimi* (sliced raw fish; also called *tsukuri*), *suimono* (clear soup), *yakimono* (grilled foods), *mushimono* (steamed foods), *nimono* (simmered foods), and *aemono* (dressed saladlike foods) are served first, followed by *miso* soup, *tsukemono* (pickles), rice, Japanese sweets, and fruit. Tea concludes the meal. The types and order of foods served in kaiseki ryori are the basis for the contemporary full-course Japanese meal.

Rice

(*kome*). Principal Japanese staple crop; an annual marshland plant of tropical origin; introduced into Japan in the Yayoi period (ca 300 BC — ca AD 300), either from China or the Korean peninsula. Rice cultivation was traditionally regarded as a religious act—an invoking of the *inadama* or spirit of the rice plant. Supplications to the deity survive today in various forms of folk performing arts. Many festivals in honor of tutelary deities are also harvest festivals. It is generally agreed that the Japanese extended family (*ie*) system evolved within the context of the rice culture, which required intensive farming, a sophisticated system of water control, and communal cooperation. In this sense rice may be said to have determined the very contours of Japanese society.

More than 100,000 varieties of rice are grown in more than 100 countries, with several thousand in Japan alone. In Japan, improvement of rice plants on an institutionalized and modern scientific basis was started in 1904 with hybridization experiments; pure line selection and, later, radiation breeding have also been utilized. These experiments have resulted in improved productivity, early maturity, and resistance to disease, cold weather, and lodging (stalk collapse). Koshihikari and Sasanishiki, both grown in the northeast, are among the most popular types of Japanese rice and command a high price. Since World War II, with land improvement, breeding of varieties responsive to fertilizers, improvement of fertilizing techniques, and the development of chemical fertilizers, herbicides, and insecticides, average yields have increased to more than 4.0 metric tons per hectare (1.8 short tons per acre). Since the beginning of the 1960s agricultural machinery has largely replaced human and animal labor, and threshing and hulling as well as transplanting of seedlings are now done by machines. At the same time, because of herbicides, there has been a reduction in the work load.

Rice consumption has decreased dramatically in Japan since the early 1960s. This phenomenon may be explained by the increased consumption of bread and animal food products. Rice contains somewhat less protein than wheat, but the quality of the protein is superior. Although customarily boiled and eaten plain, rice can be processed in many ways. Cooked glutinous rice is pounded into a kind of dough called *mochi*, which is then prepared in various ways. It may also be thinly sliced and then dried, roasted, and flavored with soy sauce to be made into a variety of rice crackers called *arare*. Rice confections, such as *dango*, are made from rice flour, as are the type of rice crackers known as *sembei*. Rice is also brewed as rice wine (*sake*), rice vinegar, and cooking wine (*mirin*), and by adding *koji*, a fermenting agent, is made into a sweet, fermented rice drink (*amazake*) or used as a pickling base.

Despite the decrease in rice consumption, rice is still considered a staple, and rice production and supply is a key element in agricultural policy. The present policy regarding rice production is based on the 1942 Foodstuff Control Law, which put the pricing and distribution of rice under government control. The import of rice, which has also been strictly controlled by the government, was permitted early in the postwar era when Japanese domestic production was unable to meet demand. As domestic production increased, imports were curtailed, and since 1983 the import of rice for table use has been prohibited. Japan was under strong pressure from the United States and other countries to open its rice market to imports.

In December, 1993 Japan officially announced that it accepted a partial opening of its rice market. Japan opens 4 percent of its domestic rice market to imports in the first year (1995) with the rate increasing each year until it reaches 8 percent in 2000.

Sake

A brewed alcoholic beverage made from fermented rice. Sake is also used as a generic term for all alcoholic drinks. The formal name for refined sake, the kind most commonly drunk in Japan, is *seishu*; it is often referred to as *nihonshu* to distinguish it from Western liquors (*yoshu*). The other traditional Japanese alcoholic beverage is a distilled spirit called *shochu*. Malted rice (*koji*) is the fermenting agent in both refined sake and shochu.

Today there are about 3,000 manufacturers of refined sake in Japan. The chief producing districts are Kyoto and Hyogo prefectures. A few national brands are also produced in places such as Akita and Hiroshima prefectures. *Jizake* (local brands) are numerous and are produced all over Japan.

Sake is made with a yeast of rice, malted rice, and water. This is placed in a vat, additional amounts of the three yeast ingredients are added, and the mixture is left to ferment for 20 days (the drained solids of the mixture, called *sakekasu* or dregs, are used in cooking and in the preparation of *tsukemono* or pickles). After fermentation the mixture is ready for pressing, filtration, and blending. The sake is then pasteurized, bottled, and stored. The alcohol content of crude sake is about 40 proof; sake on the market is about 32 proof. A good-quality sake has a subtle blend of the so-called five flavors (sweetness, sourness, pungency,

Barrels of sake in Fukushima Prefecture.

bitterness, and astringency) and a mellow fragrance. Older sake has a soft, mellow taste, but sake is rarely stored for more than a year. There are also carbonated, sweet, dry, hard, and aged types. Unrefined sake is called *nigorizake*. A sweet sake called *mirin* is made especially for cooking.

Bento

(box lunch). In premodern Japan box lunches, usually consisting of dried rice, rice balls (*nigirimeshi*), or sweet potatoes, wrapped in a leaf or in the sheath of a bamboo shoot, were eaten chiefly by travelers and people who worked outdoors. In the Edo period (1600—1868) elaborate meals were prepared and carried in tiered lacquer boxes (*jubako*) on outings. Bento sold at theaters to be eaten during intermission were called *makunouchi bento* ("entr'acte box lunches"), the prototype of today's *shidashi bento*, which are usually ordered in quantity and delivered by the restaurant that prepares them. Since the middle of the Meiji period (1868—1912) bento known as *ekiben* ("station box lunches") have been sold at railway stations. In recent years there has been a proliferation of shops that specialize in take-out bento.

Confections, traditional

(*wagashi*). The development of what are now considered "traditional" Japanese confections was affected by a series of stimuli from abroad, beginning in the Nara period (710—794) with the introduction of Chinese confections by Japanese scholars studying in China, then the spread of Zen Buddhism (also from the continent, where wagashi were an integral part of the priests' vegetarian diet) during the Kamakura period (1185—1333), and later by such *namban-gashi* ("southern barbarian" confections) as *kasutera*, brought to Japan by Portuguese missionaries during the Muromachi period (1333—1568).

Traditional confections.

The popularization of the tea ceremony during the Edo period (1600—1868), especially in the Genroku era (1688-1704), saw a dramatic increase in wagashi varieties, many of which have remained unchanged into the present. Around this time the first stores specializing in confections (*kashiya*) began to appear in Edo (now Tokyo), in Osaka, and particularly in Kyoto, where confections called *kyogashi* were developed as religious offerings and to be presented to the imperial household.

Among the defining characteristics of wagashi are their distinctive ingredients. The principal ingredient is *an*, a sweet paste made of red *azuki* beans or white bush beans, sugar, and water, which was first developed in the Kamakura period. Wheat and rice flours are also used, but dairy products and vegetable oils are not. Instead, sparing use is made of such ingredients as walnuts, peanuts, or sesame seeds, which have their own natural oils. Artificial flavoring is not added, and even natural flavorings with strong aromas are avoided. Another characteristic is the way seasonal change is incorporated in the shapes and colors of wagashi, as well as in the names chosen for each variety. For instance, *sakuramochi* ("cherry" confections) are the color of cherry blossoms (white or light pink) and are wrapped in pickled cherry leaves. Until recently, many varieties were available only during specific seasons.

Restaurants

(*inshokuten*). Today among the more than 1 million restaurants in Japan there are many that offer foreign cuisines. Chief among these are restaurants that specialize in Chinese, Korean, French, or Italian cooking, and recently Southeast Asian cuisines, such as Thailand's, have enjoyed particular popularity.

Restaurants serving Japanese cooking range from elegant *ryotei*, which provide elaborate multicourse meals, to simple eating houses. Many restaurants specialize in one type of Japanese food, such as *sushi*, *tempura*, *sukiyaki*, broiled eel (*unagi*), deep-fried pork cutlets (*tonkatsu*), grilled chicken (*yakitori*), simmered foods (*oden*), pancakes containing vegetables (*okonomiyaki*), or *tofu*. There are also restaurants that serve regional cuisine, such as that of Okinawa Prefecture or Akita Prefecture, as well as locally brewed brands of *sake*.

One of the more popular noon meals consists of Japanese noodles (*soba*; *udon*), which are served at restaurants known as *sobaya*. Many such restaurants also serve *domburimono*, a bowl of rice topped with any of a variety of ingredients. *Ramen*, a Japanese version of Chinese-style noodles, is also a common lunchtime repast. *Ramen'ya*, the Chinese restaurants that specialize in it, serve other simple Chinese dishes as well, such as fried rice (*chahan*) and fried or steamed pork dumplings (*gyoza*). *Yoshokuya*, which specialize in Japanese variations of Western dishes, offer such foods as sauteed pork cutlets, spaghetti, and beef stew.

On their way home office workers often stop at drinking houses (*nomiya* or *izakaya*) that serve a variety of foods such as yakitori, grilled fish (*yakizakana*), raw fish (*sashimi*), chilled *tofu*, and pickles (*tsukemono*) to go along with beer, *sake*, or the distilled liquor known as *shochu*. Young people in particular have acquired a taste for Western-style fast foods, and a number of franchise chains have established restaurants throughout the country. There is also a type of large restaurant known as a *famiri resutoran* (family restaurant) that serves a wide range of Western foods from club sandwiches to steak and to which parents often take their children.

Coffeehouses

(*kissaten*). Establishments that serve coffee, tea, and other beverages and snacks. Japan's first modern coffeehouse, the Kahii Sakan, opened its doors in 1888 in the Ueno district of Tokyo. In addition to serving coffee, it provided magazines and board games for customer use. Soon after, similar establishments began springing up around the Ginza area. After World War II "specialty" coffeehouses, establishments that play a particular type of music (such as jazz or classical) or are designed with some special theme in mind, became popular. Today coffeehouses can be found all over Japan, especially in urban areas. Certain coffeehouses have breakfast and lunch menus and are more like American-style coffee shops. Although a cup of coffee can be expensive, ranging from ¥300 to ¥500 (US $2.35-$3.90), customers are permitted to stay as long as they like and are not required to order anything else. Coffeehouses are popular places for meeting with business associates or, informally, with friends.

INDEX

■K

■L

■T

■|U

■|V

■|W

■Y

■|Z